Clinical Sociology: Research and Practice

Series Editor

Jan Marie Fritz, University of Cincinnati, Cincinnati, Ohio, USA, University of Johannesburg, Johannesburg, South Africa

The series explores key research and practice in this rapidly expanding field. Topics include ethical and legal aspects of intervention; the nature of client relationships; methods of intervention and evaluation; and the role of clinical sociology in specific settings. This open-ended series appeals to practitioners, policymakers, students and professors in sociology, social work, community psychology, public health, health education, social policy and counseling.

Kammila Naidoo • Oluwafemi Adeagbo •
Xiaoming Li
Editors

Young People, Violence and Strategic Interventions in Sub-Saharan Africa

Springer

Editors
Kammila Naidoo
Department of Sociology
University of Johannesburg
Johannesburg, South Africa

Oluwafemi Adeagbo
Department of Community and Behavioral Health, College of Public Health
University of Iowa
Iowa, IA, USA

Xiaoming Li
Arnold School of Public Health
University of South Carolina
Columbia, IN, USA

ISSN 1566-7847
Clinical Sociology: Research and Practice
ISBN 978-3-031-20678-8 ISBN 978-3-031-20679-5 (eBook)
https://doi.org/10.1007/978-3-031-20679-5

This Springer imprint is published by the registered company Springer Nature Switzerland AG
The registered company address is: Gewerbestrasse 11, 6330 Cham, Switzerland

Foreword

Abigail M. Hatcher and Chuka N. Emezue

Cause for Celebration: And Call to Action

At no other time in our history has it been more critical to bring together the voices of African scholars, youth, community workers, and advocates drawing our attention to various forms of violence impacting young people. From local gender hegemonies to case studies of community (in)action, innovative and disruptive thinking, to legal and policy successes and failures, this book presents several novel threads that have, to date, been understudied in the literature. Chapters in this book break new ground in Sub-Saharan African settings and represent significant advances for adolescent health and violence prevention globally, sometimes contextualized within the current pandemic era—a time when forms of violence have morphed and escalated. There are three ways that this collection addresses important gaps in what is known about violence prevention among young people: its expansion of populations of interest, its addition to the types of violence considered in the African context, and its intentional focus on submissions from authors who are from Sub-Saharan Africa and focus their research on the continent.

Several topical and critical chapters have emerged to make this collection robust. The authors highlight the lived experiences of sub-groups of adolescents and young adults, from immigrant youth to lesbian, gay, bisexual, transgender, queer, and others (LGBTQ+) youth, from pregnant adolescent women to young boys as victims of violence in the hands of men, women, and girls. These and other youth cohorts discussed here remain severely under-examined and deserve our scholarly and policy attention. In response, Mkhize and Maharaj focus on lesbian, gay, bisexual, and transgender (LGBT) youth in South Africa and highlight how health systems are complicit in their persistent discrimination. In their systematic review, Gumede et al. similarly highlight an understudied group in South Africa—young men exposed to intimate partner violence, so that the age-old erasure of the experiences of young male victims of violence is brought into the spotlight, even as we remain vigilant in supporting female survivors, and moving the field beyond this scholastic dichotomy.

The types of multiform violence and youth at various stations of vulnerabilities identified in this book extend far beyond a traditional definition of gender-based violence. These forms of abuse remain intricately linked to other forms of persistent violence. Makanishe and Umubyeyi, as well as Akanle and Uzieyi, draw our attention to xenophobic violence against immigrant youth and a televised government-endorsed political violence in Nigeria, respectively. From a policy and legal perspective, Brand and Fawole dive deeper into technology-enhanced and online violence, including stalking, online harassment, and Internet fraud, while centering this experience within the coronavirus disease (COVID-19) pandemic. It is important to note that even as these types expand our definition of violence, they retain a gendered and socio-ecological framing.

Certainly, just as global masculinity and femininity take on diverse life forms and interpretations in the African context, we find some of these gender domains revived as emergent identities that initiate, sustain, and occasionally resist forms of violence. In reading about how local hegemonies impact "feminine boys" or how young women in the Eastern Cape, South Africa, attempt to resist patriarchal violence by finding economic agency through "sugar daddies," we are reminded of the intersection of socio-economic disadvantage, discrimination, fragile policies, and strict gender norms. These factors reliably sustain violence perpetration while determining who is at risk of surviving and resisting it. The violence prevention field has a long way to travel before it adequately reflects the lived realities of young people. Still, these authors transcend the "forever discussions" we have grown accustomed to and the African way of "constantly returning to the drawing board" to highlight and centralize some actionable solutions. In short, they help push new and emerging frontiers.

Methodologically, the next version of this book might draw upon longitudinal qualitative and ethnographic work. This could be deepened through non-traditional research methods and methodologies, such as photovoice, arts-based approaches, or community-based participatory methods. It would be remarkable if the rich qualitative data from many chapters were one day complemented by more extensive population-based quantitative studies or intervention trials. As highlighted in the introduction by Naidoo et al., very little is known about how we might prevent violence against young people. Several countries and corners of the continent remain outside the majority scholarship. These are critical omissions in the literature and practice. The theoretical underpinnings of the adolescent stage in the life course deserve more attention in future observational and intervention studies. Likewise, we must become comfortable with including youths in this work's planning, design, implementation, and dissemination. The uniqueness of adolescence, physiologically, behaviorally, and socially, will require tailored approaches. Some theoretical frameworks that might offer fertile ground include queer feminist theory, positive youth development, de-coloniality, post-coloniality, as well as strength-based and other critical practices, particularly from African scholars or researchers of color.

Yet, even where the will exists, adolescent research is growing increasingly arduous to fund—outside the narrow biomedical framing of the human immunodeficiency virus (HIV) and sexually transmitted infections (STIs), substance use, or pregnancy prevention. The intersection of these comorbidities with violence is often an afterthought. The lion's share of research funding for adolescent health or violence prevention goes to white researchers from high-income countries, who face lesser gatekeeping in institutional support and indeed in accessing education and employment required to secure research grants.

Ethical stipulations continue to exclude young people from safely participating in research without parental permission. Rather than protecting young people, this often means that researchers are unable to focus on this population or develop the science around preventing violence in younger participants. Adolescent research also succumbs to complexities of community backlash and paternalism that assume young people cannot have a say in how they stay well, have sex, or conduct their peer relationships. These complexities are not by accident. They reflect the colonial, paternalistic, and often racist undertones of global research funding and, in turn, research implementation. The same structures that place Sub-Saharan African adolescents at greater risk of violence than peers in other settings or older counterparts equally guide how resources are put in place to solve (or be complicit towards) violence exposure.

However, this book highlights how overcoming such barriers to research can push the violence prevention and adolescent health fields forward. It is a cause for celebration and a reinforcement that African-led research efforts will ultimately improve the well-being of citizens across the continent. We have high hopes that the authors included in this book—and the facts, arguments, solutions, and visions for our youth they cogently raise—will indeed frame the continent's next generation.

Contents

Chapter 1
Setting the Scene

Kammila Naidoo, Oluwafemi Adeagbo, and Xiaoming Li

1.1 Introduction

Sub-Saharan Africa (SSA) currently exhibits the highest proportion of young people in the world, with more than one-third of all people living there aged 10–24 years (United Nations Population Fund, 2012). It is projected that by 2050, the number of people in this age group will be more than 600 million. The broadly defined "youth" category, that is, those below 35 years, makes up 65% of the population. This is a stark reminder that SSA's present and future developmental prospects are linked to the ways in which this youthful population is catered for, inspired, and afforded economic, social, and educational opportunities. While acknowledging the immense potential of a burgeoning youthful population, the multiple susceptibilities, historical struggles, and social disruptions impacting young lives evident across this broad expanse are often not fully explored or engaged with nor sufficiently taken into account when new policies and programs are being devised (Blum, 2007; Kabiru et al., 2013).

The motivation for an edited book on "*Young People, Violence and Strategic Interventions in Sub-Saharan Africa*" follows the publishing of a guest-edited

K. Naidoo (✉)
University of Johannesburg, Johannesburg, South Africa
e-mail: kammilan@uj.ac.za

O. Adeagbo
Department of Community and Behavioral Health, College of Public Health, University of Iowa, Iowa, IA, USA
e-mail: oluwafemi-adeagbo@uiowa.edu

X. Li
University of South Carolina, Columbia, SC, USA
e-mail: xiaoming@mailbox.sc.edu

K. Naidoo et al. (eds.), *Young People, Violence and Strategic Interventions in Sub-Saharan Africa*, Clinical Sociology: Research and Practice,
https://doi.org/10.1007/978-3-031-20679-5_1

journal issue on the topic of "Sexual and Reproductive Health Needs of Adolescent Girls and Young Women (AGYW) in Sub-Saharan Africa: Research, Policy, and Practice" (Naidoo et al., 2019). One of the strongest themes emerging from the above-mentioned peer-reviewed articles was young African women's engagement with violence, which not only marked their life stories but also forged specific resistances and defensive responses. The theme of violence has arguably become much more compelling in the coronavirus disease (COVID-19) era, where lockdowns and security measures intended to protect people against death and debilitation have constrained mobility and autonomy, heightened adversity, and increased encounters with violence. In March 2020, shortly after the World Health Organization (WHO) announced the global pandemic, lockdowns in SSA became the norm. For the greater part, the concept of "lockdown" was unfamiliar, linked with environments subjected to authoritarian governments and suppression of human rights.

Attempts to control the spread of the virus through restricting movements and congregations of people have disrupted the rhythm of life and the fragility of political economies leading to loss of jobs, schooling in crises, and families under pressure. COVID-19 increased death rates of older people, and harsh lockdowns have impacted young people's health, mental well-being, and sense of security. Media reports suggest that SSA countries have also experienced a surge in sexual and gender-based violence (SGBV) (including femicide). In 2021, it was reported that fewer than expected schoolgirls have returned to school due to factors such as pregnancy, deepening household poverty, and disillusionment (Bhengu, 2021). Thus, the needs and resilience of young women and men in a broader SSA context of violence, institutional difficulties, and shifting political economies require continuing analysis. As the world begins to recover from the devastating losses exacted by the COVID-19 pandemic, the COVID-19 lens offers researchers an instrument to consider the extent to which young African lives have been setback (Ezeh et al., 2021) and in what ways possibilities exist for reimagining transformed futures.

1.2 Focusing on Violence

One of the central problems we aimed to draw out in the different chapters is how violence is understood, experienced, and challenged in the life courses of young women and men. The key question that the chapters sought to speak to was: "How do young African women and men experience and resist violence, and what mediations and interventions have been evident and/or successful in the different societal contexts?" In Johan Galtung's (1971, 1990) frameworks of violence, three forms are predominant: direct or personal violence, structural or institutional violence, and cultural violence. Direct violence is evident in assaults of various kinds, such as acts of physical violence, verbal attacks, or psychological abuse. Structural violence emphasizes how societal structures and institutions cause harm, as in the case of exploitative and discriminatory systems that shorten life spans or create chronic illnesses. Cultural violence draws attention to ideologies, practices, and ways of life that legitimate and condone direct or structural violence, such as the "cultural defense" of non-consensual sex in marriage (marital rape) as culturally "normal." These frameworks are acknowledged and drawn upon in different ways by the authors of the various chapters.

Violence has become a global phenomenon and human rights issue for researchers, practitioners, and policymakers across the world. Violence claims over 1.3 million lives yearly and has enormous health impacts through generating mental disorders, poor sexual health, increased substance abuse, and mortality (Devries et al., 2013, 2014; Ndungu et al., 2022; Stöckl et al., 2013). Globally, research has shown that an estimated 30% of women aged 15 years and above have experienced physical or sexual intimate partner violence (IPV) (Devries et al., 2013). Other studies (including literature reviews) have shown similar findings that one in three women has experienced various forms of violence (e.g., sexual, psychological, or physical) in her lifetime (Breiding et al., 2014; Emezue & Bloom, 2021; Jewkes et al., 2014; Parkes et al., 2016). While violence affects everyone irrespective of their gender, race/ethnicity, sex, or sexual orientation, it disproportionally impacts women, especially those living in resource-limited settings, such as SSA. For example, the prevalence of violence against women (VAW) is 24% in Serbia and Montenegro but 71% in rural Ethiopia (García-Moreno et al., 2013; Keynejad et al., 2020). Similarly, in 2002 and 2007, 18% of women aged 16–60 experienced IPV in the past twelve months in eight (Botswana, Lesotho, Malawi, Mozambique, Namibia, Swaziland, Zambia, and Zimbabwe) Southern African countries (Andersson et al., 2008). Studies including meta-analysis have shown several adverse sequelae such as mental health disorders associated with violent experiences, especially among women (Breiding et al., 2014; Emezue & Bloom, 2021; Lagdon et al., 2014). Evidence also reveals that survivors of gender-based violence (GBV) are more likely to become involved in higher-risk behaviors and accept high-risk practices (Andersson et al., 2008).

In 2002, the WHO published a comprehensive report—*World Report on Violence and Health*—on the impact of violence (e.g., self-directed, interpersonal, and collective violence) on individuals, families, and societies (Krug et al., 2002). The report pays special attention to child maltreatment, youth violence, IPV, sexual violence, and elder abuse (Krug et al., 2002). In the USA, one in four high school students has experienced physical or sexual abuse, while two-thirds reported psychological abuse (De La Rue et al., 2017; Foshee et al., 2014; Vagi et al., 2013). Also, American young people who had experienced IPV were more likely to be suicidal, depressed, perform poorly academically, and have unintended pregnancies (Adhia et al., 2019; Miller-Perrin et al., 2020). Evidence from Africa and other continents has shown the link between experiences of violence among young people to future violence perpetration in adulthood (Pensak, 2014; Swedo et al., 2019). For example, a multi-country study conducted among young people aged 13–24 years in four African countries showed that perpetration of physical or sexual violence was high among males (29.5% in Nigeria and 51.5% in Malawi) and females (15.3% in Zambia and 28.4% in Uganda) (Swedo et al., 2019). The study further revealed a significant association between childhood experience of physical, emotional, or sexual violence and violence perpetration (Swedo et al., 2019).

IPV is one of the most common forms of interpersonal violence (Jewkes et al., 2014; Krug et al., 2002; Ndungu et al., 2022). It could be emotional, physical, sexual, verbal, and economic abuse, and it is mostly perpetrated by men against their intimate partners, especially female partners (Emezue & Bloom, 2021; Jewkes et al., 2014; Peterson et al., 2018). An estimated ten million adults are physically abused annually by their intimate partners in the USA (Breiding et al., 2014). Similarly, in South Africa, one in five women (18 years and older) has ever experienced IPV, 6% of ever-partnered women have ever experienced sexual violence by any partner, 16% of divorced or separated women had experienced sexual violence by a partner, while 10% of women in partnerships had experienced sexual violence by a partner (SADHS, 2019). According to the United Nations Office on Drug and Crime report on Global Homicide (UNODC, 2019), 87,000 women were killed globally in 2017 by their intimate partners or other family members, including 20,000 in Asia, 19,000 in Africa, 8000 in America, and 3000 in Europe (UNODC, 2019). Reducing the menace of violence, particularly GBV, is at the top of the agenda of resolutions such as the Convention on the Elimination of All Forms of Discrimination Against Women (CEDAW) and the Convention on the Rights of the Child. Initiatives such as the Millennium Development Goals (MDGs) and Sustainable Development Goals (SDGs) reiterated the need to reduce violence in communities and schools and promote healthy gender norms and equality (Ndungu et al., 2022; Parkes et al., 2016).

1.3 Research on Violence Affecting Young People: Knowledge and Gaps

Globally, young people are confronted with various forms of psychological, physical, verbal, and sexual violence within their social settings (Emezue & Bloom, 2021; Gibbs et al., 2022; Kovalenko et al., 2020; Parkes et al., 2016), for example, a teacher seeking sex for higher grades from a student, older boys bullying and beating younger boys, youth physically and verbally abusing their intimate partners to assert power, etc. As cultural violence, the hidden realities of sexual coercion, bullying, and emotional abuse are often tolerated within schools and families, and the strands of this intersect to negatively shape the lives of young people across the world (Crooks et al., 2019; Gibbs et al., 2022; Parkes et al., 2013, 2016). A review of existing literature by Parkes and colleagues shows that school-related gender-based violence (SRGBV) is one of the most appalling forms of GBV affecting young boys and girls and requires coordinated multilevel approaches to be eradicated (Parkes et al., 2016). Although various interventions have been developed to reduce young people's experiences of violence, recent studies (including systematic reviews) have shown that many of the interventions have little or no effect, and few are effective in reducing various forms of violence (Crooks et al., 2019; Emezue & Bloom, 2021; Leach et al., 2014; Parkes et al., 2016).

Increasingly, research on violence is confronted with conceptual, methodological, and ethical challenges (Kovalenko et al., 2020; Leach, 2015; Parkes et al., 2013; Ridde et al., 2019). For example, since knowledge and attitudes are not always excellent predictors of behaviors, quantitative tools are often used to assess people's self-reported experiences of violence (Parkes et al., 2016). However, the varying terminologies used in other research may be insufficient to capture young people's descriptions of violence (Leach, 2015; Parkes et al., 2016; Ridde et al., 2019). In addition, it is difficult to apply standard international tools to measure violence in different social contexts since violence is imbricated in the social and gender norms of individual societies.

Various methodological limitations of violence prevention programs constitute major barriers to ascertaining what works to prevent different kinds of violence, for whom, and its level of impact. Multiple reviews (including systematic reviews and meta-analysis) on violence prevention programs targeting antisocial behavior, bullying, and IPV have shown that most of the interventions were developed, implemented, and evaluated in the USA despite the prevalence of violence, particularly sexual violence, in Africa, the Eastern Mediterranean, and Southeast Asia (Emezue & Bloom, 2021; Kovalenko et al., 2020; Lester et al., 2017; Parkes et al., 2016). Another review of violence prevention programs targeting bullying (including cyberbullying) found that most interventions had little or no impact on behavioral change (Zych et al., 2015). There is a lack of evidence-based programs to prevent interpersonal violence, particularly IPV, among sexual and gender minorities youth and young women with disabilities despite their higher risk of experiencing violence (Crooks et al., 2019). There are significant gaps in knowledge on effective violence prevention interventions among adolescents and young adults.

Apart from conceptual and methodological challenges in research on violence, the most disturbing concerns are societal taboos and the culture of silence, especially sexual violence, which is very common in Africa. There are ethical issues relating to how violence data are obtained from young people, especially younger adolescents and children. Young people may be afraid to share their experiences of violence with an adult or peer researcher (Parkes et al., 2016). However, some qualitative studies have attempted to address some ethical issues with young people, especially children, using various research techniques such as participatory research methods (e.g., drama and art) (Gibbs et al., 2022; Ndungu et al., 2022). For example, a study conducted in Mozambique found that girls' reporting of violence was lower at baseline but increased after 5 years of active campaigning, collaborating, and working with girls, communities, and schools (Parkes et al., 2013).

1.4 Violence Prevention Interventions Among Young People: What Works?

Numerous prevention programs have been established, and their effectiveness has been assessed. Most violence prevention interventions have sought to influence attitudinal change, awareness, and responses to the negative impact of interpersonal violence across societies. However, many violence prevention programs developed and evaluated over the past two decades have shown limited geographic coverage and mixed results (Crooks et al., 2019; Kovalenko et al., 2020; Ndungu et al., 2022). A review of violence prevention interventions reveals that 80% of the intervention evaluations were conducted in high-income countries (HICs) (Ellsberg et al., 2015). Comprehensive interventions, guidelines on program design, implementation, and evidence on what works in violence prevention among young people, especially in SSA, are limited.

School-Based Programs A systematic review (including meta-analyses) of youth violence prevention programs revealed that most of the interventions were school-based, targeting substance abuse, bullying, and antisocial behavior, and some showed positive impacts (Matjasko et al., 2012). Many of the existing violence prevention interventions that have shown positive effects have been school-based, and most were conducted in North America (Crooks et al., 2019; Ellsberg et al., 2015; Emezue & Bloom, 2021). For example, due to the prevalence of violence in schools across the USA, the 2013 Campus Sexual Violence Elimination Act compelled schools to report any forms of violence, particularly sexual and intimate partner violence, develop and implement violence prevention programs, as well as report on post-violence experiences of survivors (Taylor et al., 2013). Similarly, the United Nations Children's Fund (UNICEF) and the Global Partnership for Education (GPE) launched the "End Gender Violence in Schools Initiative" to reduce violence at schools, promoting gender equality and inclusion, especially in SSA countries (e.g., Côte d'Ivoire, Ethiopia, Togo, and Zambia) through rigorous "research, capacity building and knowledge exchange" (Parkes et al., 2016). It was found that the most promising interventions to reduce GBV targeted various concepts (e.g., identities and social and cultural norms). However, there is a dearth of data on their sustainability in communities and schools (Parkes et al., 2016). Evaluation of these interventions has shown mixed results. A meta-analysis found moderate effects of violence prevention interventions implemented with young people up to the age of 15 years (Lee et al., 2015). Generally, there were moderate effects of violence prevention interventions, especially bullying perpetration and victimization (Kärnä et al., 2013; Kovalenko et al., 2020; Palladino et al., 2016). Most school-based programs on antisocial behavior often focus on conflict management skills and have been found to reduce violent behaviors (Kovalenko et al., 2020). While some interventions showed positive effects on knowledge and awareness, few showed little or no effects on behavioral change (Kovalenko et al., 2020; Newton et al., 2010; Stephens & George, 2009; Taylor et al., 2013). Three interventions targeting bullying among students aged 15 years and older had few effects on the perpetration and victimization of violence (Baldry & Farrington, 2004; Olweus, 1994; Ortega & Lera, 2000).

Multilevel Intervention Some interventions have been implemented at numerous levels (e.g., individual, classroom, and school) using various participatory research techniques such as role-playing and peer support groups. Perez and colleagues (2013) report a significant reduction in young people's (15 years and older) experience of bullying. They adopted multilevel strategies such as a bullying complaint box, skills development, and one-on-one meetings with students, teachers, and parents (Pérez et al., 2013). Similarly, another study that used activities such as skills development and individual counseling with students and parents found a reduction in violence perpetration (Varela, 2011). It is evident that the few studies that have shown some effects adopted socioecological approaches. This, therefore, signals the potential of multi-leveled interventions to reduce or eradicate issues such as youth violence. Overall, there appears to be some consensus among authors that violence prevention interventions that adopt multi-leveled strategies across various forms of violence are most useful but remain scarce (Cassidy et al., 2016; Cox et al., 2016; Fagan & Catalano, 2013; Jiménez-Barbero et al., 2016; Kovalenko et al., 2020).

Participatory Approach One major approach that has worked in violence prevention research in South Africa is group-based participatory interventions such as the "Microfinance for AIDS and Gender Equity and Stepping Stones" program that focuses mainly on change of problematic gender norms (Gibbs et al., 2017, 2022; Jewkes et al., 2021). Participatory approaches can address issues of power imbalances and can provide an in-depth understanding of individuals' meanings of violence within a specific cultural or community context (Gibbs et al., 2022; Ndungu et al., 2022). Participatory approaches (e.g., through drama and art) were also adopted to address some of the methodological and ethical challenges in violence prevention among young people, especially children (Gibbs et al., 2022; Ndungu et al., 2022). Likewise, participatory approaches using role-playing and peer support groups were also adopted in some multilevel violence intervention programs that have shown positive effects on reducing bullying (Pérez et al., 2013).

1.5 Embracing Clinical Sociology: Chapter Summaries

All the chapters selected in this edited book refer to relevant interventions that have been tried, tested, and developed for use in particular African settings. As such, the chapters are solidly framed in terms of a clinical sociology paradigm and seek to capture core themes focusing on the ways in which young people engage vulnerabilities and contend with and counteract violence (sexual and gender-based—but also structural, political, socio-economic, intimate, and familial). As a project on Clinical Sociology, we draw on Fritz and Rhéaume (2014, p. 3), who suggest that

"Clinical Sociology needs to be *creative* in order to be innovative/inventive/novel as well as useful... While individuals can hold on to paradoxical ideas that lead to unique outcomes, creativity is perhaps more likely to be found in the interplay that comes through networks or groups, particularly ones that include contributors with different disciplinary and practical backgrounds." Clinical sociologists might focus on strategic solo interventions but find opportunities to recommend change at other levels (Fritz & Rhéaume, 2014, p. 6). Thus, a keen interest of all the authors is in "strategic interventions" such as health, politics, education, and community-based domains. Currently, many of the "best practice" interventions targeting young people are educational and delivered using different platforms such as peers, the media, youth centers, and schools.

The chapters that follow refer to data and case studies from a range of SSA countries, notably Botswana, Eswatini, Ghana, Kenya, Malawi, Mozambique, Namibia, Nigeria, Senegal, South Africa, Tanzania, Uganda, and Zambia. While the findings and insights are diverse, a core set of themes predominate: they reveal that violence, embedded in everyday and mundane lived realities, is a complex issue and should be probed using intersectional tools of analysis (Buiten & Naidoo, 2020). While moments of political and xenophobic violence are reflected upon, critical attention is firmly on young women and their grappling with SGBV. With brisk growth in Internet access, social media, and online engagements in recent years, cyberviolence has emerged as a new threat to young women and men. The COVID lens has magnified micro-struggles and long-standing structural problems showing how inequities and social and political disadvantages have created an infrastructure through which violence has been exacerbated. Simultaneously, there is a critical focus on masculinities constructed by colonial and apartheid histories, social and economic crises, racism, and state disregard, but with the message that marginality should not be reified nor the gendered practices of young men oversimplified. Generally, in all the chapters, contextual specificities and insightful case studies offer thoughts and arguments about the ways in which violence manifests, what interventionist strategies are compelling, and how young people's proactive involvement in interventions could begin to address the problem of violence.

The authors of the various chapters conducted their research primarily during the harshest period of the COVID-19 pandemic when schooling was disrupted, hospital systems were at breaking point, and death rates rose. Health systems, the state, media, communities, families, and law enforcement all feature in the research. As active researchers on the continent—based in academic institutions and research centers—our authors have been passionate about exploring African realities and thinking through solutions to tackle the various evident problems. This is reflected in the different narratives and arguments emerging from the contributions.

In Chap. 2, *Yvonne Gamuchirai Tagwireyi* and *Lorenza Fluks* discuss "Effective linkages of young people to Sexual and Reproductive Health and Rights (SRHR) services as protective measures against adolescent sexual and gender-based violence (SGBV) in Africa." The chapter highlights the severity of the SGBV problem, which has been exacerbated during COVID-19, thus placing structural problems and inequalities under the spotlight. Young people face numerous hindrances in attempting to access SRHR. Devising strategies to improve access to services can effectively protect young people against SGBV. The study's findings were drawn from research on SRHR services in Botswana, Eswatini, Malawi, Mozambique, Namibia, South Africa, Uganda, and Zambia. The study reveals the need to strengthen and make more relevant policy or government directives on SRHR to prevent and respond to SGBV. In order to ensure the success of programs, there should be greater involvement of young people in guiding both the design and implementation of SRHR programs. Interventions that link young people to SRHR services will need to be sufficiently nuanced to maximize their efficacy, especially during global pandemics such as COVID-19.

Chapter 3, written by *Anke Brand* and *Adebola Fawole*, focuses on the Internet as a trigger of VAW. Violations can be experienced in various ways: receiving offensive and sexually explicit messages or inappropriate advances on social networking sites. While Internet use is comparatively low in SSA, an increasing number of women have been exposed to cyberviolence, particularly during the lockdown period. The chapter investigates the phenomenon of cyberviolence against women during a critical phase of the pandemic and assesses the root causes and impact of online violence. As with Chap. 2, recommendations for action on how to curb cybercrime against women in SSA are made, and policies, legislation, and implementation are probed. The government and other stakeholders have not succeeded in informing, supporting, and protecting victims of cyberviolence or apprehending perpetrators. There is often victim blaming, with victims suffering both offline and online. The authors refer to the lack of data on this vital area and recommend that researchers replicate, share, and collaborate more across the globe to create a safe cyberspace for women and girls.

In Chap. 4, *Madeline Gerber, Sofi Le Berre*, and *Denise Buiten* turn the focus toward literature representations of young masculinities in South Africa. They argue that gaps in the research surveyed appear to unintentionally reinscribe notions of marginal masculinities as unambiguously violent. Boys and male youth tend to be positioned as objects of harm and as future risks to women and girls. However, a growing number of publications adopt more critical stances and identify sites for the disruption of violent practices of masculinity in a way that challenges patriarchal relations while acknowledging variations and nuances in boys' experiences. Building on more progressive or feminist work can productively complicate our understanding of the relationship between marginality, power, and violence—and how boys from different backgrounds engage with this. Further work on a wider range of boys and young men—such as sexual or gender minorities as well as economically and racially privileged boys and violence—will also be of value to address some of the concerns about collective representations of young masculinities in South Africa and their relationship to violence.

Chapter 5 addresses xenophobic violence in South Africa. Here, *Bisimwa Makanishe* and *Beatrice Umubyeyi* refer specifically to Afrophobia because the bouts of xenophobic violence have emerged as black South Africans engaging in violence against black African immigrants (while non-African immigrants are treated differently). The South African government contests descriptions of the violence as xenophobic. This study explores young traders' experiences during the COVID-19 pandemic. The study participants offer insight into the way in which xenophobic violence and the hard lockdown impacted their lives, including economic impacts, business disruptions, and loss of income. From a sustainable livelihood perspective, the sudden loss of income and disrupted livelihoods have led to a loss of savings and investments—the savings of the migrants acquired over time had to be consumed when their ability to earn an income ended due to business disruptions from xenophobic attacks. The study offers insight into the views of foreign nationals and asylum seekers in KwaZulu-Natal on what gave rise to the outbreak of xenophobic violence. Here, state discourses, the role of liberation struggle veterans (M.K.), and the fomenting of the tabloid press are seen as complicit.

Chapter 6 addresses lesbian, gay, bisexual and transgender (LGBT) youth's access to healthcare in South Africa. *Sthembiso Pollen Mkhize* and *Pranitha Maharaj* refer to hegemonic and societal power hierarchies that health systems might embrace and perpetuate, leading to differential health outcomes. They illuminate that violence can often be indirect or structural, impacting those most vulnerable and marginal, including non-binary or LGBT individuals. The chapter presents data that offers insight into the barriers that LGBT individuals face in attempting to access effective and reliable healthcare. The prejudice and disregard that LGBT youth endure contradict the declaration of rights and emphasis on equality enshrined in the South African Constitution. It is suggested that structural interventions are needed to address the structural problems; there should be an integrated approach toward building inclusion and diversity in healthcare provision. Interventions need to be part of an intersectional effort that considers vulnerabilities due to non-normative identities. Applying an intersectional lens to the health system can offer a way to address health inequities created by persistent cisgenderism and heteronormative culture.

In Chap. 7, *Sinethemba Sidloyi* explores young women's pursuit of blesser–blessee relationships and how this strategy was reworked during the COVID-19 pandemic when lockdown measures restricted movement. It is argued that young urban women form relationships with financially stable men to attain particular economic and social benefits, but that this strategy has been set back by COVID-19. Young women became more dependent on men during this time, as they could not adopt diverse economic strategies to enable them to get money to meet their lifestyle goals. The process of gaining funds from men for things like data, airtime, and alcohol frequently led to episodes of emotional and other kinds of abuse. Men asserted more control over women, perpetuating patriarchal power imbalances. Thus, although transactional sexual relationships reflect young women's sexual agency, they are framed by vulnerabilities and unequal power imbalances that aggravate exploitation and GBV. Thus, sexual agency is compromised within a patriarchal context, as evident by efforts to suppress young women's sexual assertiveness. "Securing the bag" refers to agentic economic action, but also simultaneously, a way in which young women become locked in a cycle of financial dependence on men.

Chapter 8 entails a focus on the well-being of Namibian youth. In this chapter, *Immaculate Mogotsi, Maria Kaundjua,* and *Nelago Indongo* reflect on how COVID-19 regulations have impacted youth-related activities and youth lives. Young people are bearing the brunt of financial pressure due to a constrained economy. As such, their economic agency is restricted, which generates distress, loneliness, and ill-health. While socio-economic conditions have been experienced as violent for young people, young people's stress at the current juncture is causing some of them to act out violently as well.

In most cases, violent behavior among the youth is triggered by multiple factors emerging in their environment. As a result, youth violence harms all people—perpetrators, victims, their respective families, friends, and communities. The chapter offers thoughts about interventions that provide anti-violence initiatives, services, and mediation. The chapter further elaborates on the impact of COVID-19 in Namibia in relation to what is happening in the region and beyond; it also looks at legislation and rights and cultural beliefs (or cultural violence) reducing women's control over their lives. Finally, the chapter proposes interventions to alleviate the impacts of COVID-19 on the lives of young Namibians.

In Chap. 9, *Eugene Krupa, Albert Manasyan, Kate Woodman, Nobutu Muttau,* and *Anitha Menon* discuss "Catalyzing Action on Intimate Partner Violence Against Pregnant Adolescent Girls and Young Women in Zambia." They identify IPV as a serious, ongoing problem affecting the lives of AGYW in Zambia, across Africa, and worldwide but acknowledge that effective strategies are emerging. In many SSA countries, Zambia included, men have considerable community endorsement to discipline and assert themselves powerfully in intimate unions. To present their strategies, the authors of this chapter draw on their action research project in Lusaka as a case study. The conditions making girls and women vulnerable to IPV and three key WHO frameworks (ecological, social determinants of health, and INSPIRE) are brought together to offer an intersectional view of the forces that shape social identities, power relations, and dynamics contributing to violence. Interventions for pregnant AGYW who experience IPV, including an evidence-based psychotherapy intervention during pandemic times, are discussed. Finally, the authors introduce lessons learned using the INSPIRE framework and propose strategies and approaches to consider in attempts to address IPV in Zambia and globally.

Chapter 10, written by *Dumsani Gumede, Manono Luthuli, Sphesihle Hlongwane, Kingsley Orievulu, Ntombizonke Gumede,* and *Oluwafemi Adeagbo,* takes the position that while general discourses of GBV emphasize women and children as victims, men also bear the brunt of violence. GBV against men is underreported due to misconceptions about men's experiences of GBV, perceptions of power and control in gendered relations, cultural grooming, and other factors. There have been limited studies to date probing GBV in varying forms affecting men in SSA countries. The COVID-19 scenario and lockdown measures have opened opportunities to look more closely at gender relations and IPV against the background of men enduring increased unemployment, higher levels of substance abuse, and reduced economic status during the pandemic. The academic literature does not sufficiently explore males' experiences of violence in SSA but instead discusses males as perpetrators and females as victims. More critical work will inform law and policy change, thus offering male victims some protection in SSA. The authors argue that further research into males' perceptions and experiences of violence is needed if effective strategies to combat GBV are to be devised.

In Chap. 11, *Olayinka Akanle* and *Goodluck Uzieyi* discuss the EndSARS protest in Nigeria as a metaphor for youth exclusion and make a case for greater recognition of the various struggles young people face and for improved inclusion at various levels. The initial protests against the Special Anti-Robbery Squad (SARS) began peacefully but turned violent. Initiated during the height of COVID in 2020, the protest remains a historic showcase in Africa and globally. Going forward, it will serve as a reminder of the youth's challenge against systemic exclusion and neglect—and the need for young people's interests to be incorporated in planning for development, governance, human security, and policing, among other areas. There are many important lessons to be drawn from the EndSARS experience, and these lessons are relevant for Nigeria, Africa, and the world at large. This broad reflection is the main purpose of this chapter. The chapter is based on an extensive review of secondary data and literature and brings in autoethnography. Living through the SARS moment, the authors draw in their own primary insights on the issues of youthhood, human security, societal developments, and the inclusion of youth in the Nigerian polity and economics.

1.6 Digital Interventions to Address Violence in Africa

During COVID, much interest was recently expressed in digital interventions for violence prevention due to increased global Internet connectivity, mobile phone use, and telehealth medications that limit face-to-face interactions, including physical intervention delivery (Emezue & Bloom, 2021; Ndungu et al., 2022). Digital and technology-based interventions consist of different telehealth platforms, mobile health (mHealth), and electronic health (eHealth) (Adeagbo et al., 2019; Emezue & Bloom, 2021). The proliferation of technology and mobile phones in Africa signals the potential for such interventions to reduce violence and improve survivors' health outcomes (Adeagbo et al., 2019; Gibbs et al., 2022; Ndungu et al., 2022). The recent COVID-19 pandemic exacerbated the use of digital interventions across different sectors, especially healthcare (Emezue & Bloom, 2021; Qiao et al., 2020). Existing and new digital interventions are being developed and adapted to meet the needs of violence survivors (Emezue & Bloom, 2021). Prior to COVID-19, violence prevention digital interventions such as MyPLAN, IMPACT, and I-DECIDE were developed, implemented, and produced important data that showed the need to explore and develop more virtual interventions to prevent violence (Drabkin et al., 2021; Glass et al., 2015; Hegarty et al., 2019). For example, MyPlan is a decision aid digital intervention with personalized safety options to help domestic violence survivors identify danger in their relationships (using a danger assessment tool) and provide sufficient information to help them make informed decisions about their safety (Decker et al., 2020; Glass et al., 2021). MyPlan has been evaluated in clinical trials in Kenya, New Zealand, and the USA among heterosexuals (particularly women) and sexual and gender minority populations. Digital interventions have also been developed to target mental disorders such as suicidal ideation, depression, anxiety, and posttraumatic stress disorders (PTSD) (Braithwaite & Fincham, 2011; Constantino et al., 2015). Digital interventions that target violence could improve awareness about various forms of violence, safety planning and quality of life, and social and emotional support (Constantino et al., 2015; Ndungu et al., 2022).

Growing evidence has shown the potential of digital and technology-based interventions to complement existing traditional interventions to support survivors (Emezue & Bloom, 2021). Digital interventions are also expected to facilitate linkages between providers and violence survivors and improve survivors' health outcomes (Emezue & Bloom, 2021; Glass et al., 2010, 2017). Compared to provider-initiated interventions at health centers, digital interventions such as telehealth is private, confidential, safe, and reliable while offering real-time care to improve the mental health outcomes as well as the overall well-being of violence survivors (Adeagbo et al., 2021; Gibbs et al., 2022; Glass et al., 2017; Young et al., 2018). Digital interventions have been demonstrated to assist hard-to-reach violence survivors in resource-constrained settings (Akinsulure-Smith et al., 2013; García-Moreno et al., 2013; Gonçalves & Matos, 2016). Various forms of digital interventions have shown promising results in chronic disease management (e.g., diabetes and human immunodeficiency virus (HIV) care), bullying, and tobacco use (Adeagbo et al., 2021; Anderson-Lewis et al., 2018; Firth et al., 2017; Li et al., 2014; Luk et al., 2019; Ybarra et al., 2016). Similarly, trauma-informed digital interventions have been shown to be acceptable among violence survivors, particularly those who have experienced IPV (Glass et al., 2017; Koziol-McLain et al., 2015; Littleton et al., 2016). This could be because of its perceived safety, convenience, and confidentiality.

Notwithstanding its potential, some studies have highlighted challenges linked to safety, privacy, Internet connectivity, and cultural suitability that could hinder digital violence prevention interventions (Adeagbo et al., 2019; Choi et al., 2017; El Morr & Layal, 2020; Gibbs et al., 2022; LeFevre et al., 2020; Ndungu et al., 2022). Other studies, however, have shown general acceptability and willingness of young people to use digital interventions because they are private, confidential, within their control (autonomy), and in non-judgmental spaces (Adeagbo et al., 2019; Ford-Gilboe et al., 2020; Hegarty et al., 2019; Ndungu et al., 2022; Tarzia et al., 2017). Therefore, future studies must develop, explore, and evaluate digital interventions' effectiveness in reducing violence and/or improving the health outcomes of survivors in SSA.

1.7 Conclusion

Young people, especially those in SSA, are disproportionately affected by violence, which poses significant challenges to their health and well-being, development, and future lives and livelihoods. Despite significant evidence that violence prevention programs for heterosexual, cisgender, and better-off youth work reasonably well, several knowledge gaps persist in violence prevention efforts among SSA youth, particularly with regard to addressing the needs of sexual and gender minorities. Future interventions or programs must be culturally-affirming, identity-affirming, and unambiguous in targeting root causes of violence at different socioecological levels among young people, irrespective of their race, ethnic group, religion, gender, sex, and sexual orientation. Future violence prevention intervention efforts need to consider adopting the approaches that have been proven effective and feasible in the global literature, including the research reported in this book. These approaches may include multilevel approaches, participatory approaches, and digital approaches. Future efforts also need to pay attention to the methodological rigor in program design and the sustainability of the school- and community-based prevention intervention programs.

Finally, we are keen to see that this interdisciplinary contribution serves as a resource for analysis and critical engagement of scholars working in the fields of gender, violence, global health, development and population studies, youth studies, African studies, intersectionality, sociology, and psychology, amongst others, to examine the range of conceptual, empirical, legal, policy, practice, as well as institutional and operational issues these challenges present. It is thus expected that, amongst other things, this book will stimulate further debate on what is driving violence in different SSA contexts and why an African, intersectional, COVID lens is valuable.

References

Adeagbo, O., Herbst, C., Blandford, A., McKendry, R., Estcourt, C., Seeley, J., & Shahmanesh, M. (2019). Exploring people's candidacy for mobile health-supported HIV testing and care services in rural KwaZulu-Natal, South Africa: Qualitative study. *Journal of Medical Internet Research, 21*(11), 15681.

Adeagbo, O., Kim, H.-Y., Tanser, F., Xulu, S., Dlamini, N., Gumede, V., Mathenjwa, T., & Blandford, A. (2021). Acceptability of a tablet-based application to support early HIV testing among men in rural KwaZulu-Natal, South Africa: A mixed method study. *AIDS Care, 33*(4), 494–501.

Adhia, A., Kernic, M. A., Hemenway, D., Vavilala, M. S., & Rivara, F. P. (2019). Intimate partner homicide of adolescents. *JAMA Pediatrics, 173*(6), 571–577.

Akinsulure-Smith, A. M., Chu, T., Keatley, E., & Rasmussen, A. (2013). Intimate partner violence among West African immigrants. *Journal of Aggression, Maltreatment & Trauma, 22*(2), 109–126.

Anderson-Lewis, C., Darville, G., Mercado, R. E., Howell, S., & Di Maggio, S. (2018). mHealth technology use and implications in historically underserved and minority populations in the United States: Systematic literature review. *JMIR mHealth and uHealth, 6*(6), e8383.

Andersson, N., Cockcroft, A., & Shea, B. (2008). Gender-based violence and HIV: Relevance for HIV prevention in hyperendemic countries of Southern Africa. *AIDS, 22*, S73–S86.

Baldry, A. C., & Farrington, D. P. (2004). Evaluation of an intervention program for the reduction of bullying and victimization in schools. *Aggressive Behavior: Official Journal of the International Society for Research on Aggression, 30*(1), 1–15.

Bhengu, L. (2021). Gauteng records more than 23,000 teen pregnancies in one year, some moms as young as 10. Available via News 24. Retrieved August 17, 2021 from https://www.news24.com/news24/southafrica/news/gauteng-records-more-than-23-000-teen-pregnancies-in-oneyear-some-moms-as-young-as-10-20210817

Blum, R. W. (2007). Youth in sub-Saharan Africa. *Journal of Adolescent Health, 41*, 230–238.

Braithwaite, S. R., & Fincham, F. D. (2011). Computer-based dissemination: A randomized clinical trial of ePREP using the actor partner interdependence model. *Behaviour Research and Therapy, 49*(2), 126–131.

Breiding, M. J., Chen, J., & Black, M. C. (2014). Intimate partner violence in the United States–2010. Retrieved from Atlanta GA: file:///C:/Users/Oluwafemi.Adeagbo/Downloads/cdc_21961_DS1.pdf

Buiten, D., & Naidoo, K. (2020). Laying claim to a name: Towards a sociology of "Gender-Based Violence". *South African Review of Sociology, 51*(2), 61–68.

Cassidy, T., Bowman, B., McGrath, C., & Matzopoulos, R. (2016). Brief report on a systematic review of youth violence prevention through media campaigns: Does the limited yield of strong evidence imply methodological challenges or absence of effect? *Journal of Adolescence, 52*, 22–26.

Choi, Y. J., Phua, J., Armstrong, K. J., & An, S. (2017). Negotiating the cultural steps in developing an online intervention for Korean American intimate partner violence. *Journal of Aggression, Maltreatment & Trauma, 26*(8), 920–936.

Constantino, R. E., Braxter, B., Ren, D., Burroughs, J. D., Doswell, W. M., Wu, L., Hwang, J. G., & Greene, W. B. (2015). Comparing online with face-to-face HELPP intervention in women experiencing intimate partner violence. *Issues in Mental Health Nursing, 36*(6), 430–438.

Cox, E., Leung, R., Baksheev, G., Day, A., Toumbourou, J. W., Miller, P., Kremer, P., & Walker, A. (2016). Violence prevention and intervention programmes for adolescents in Australia: A systematic review. *Australian Psychologist, 51*(3), 206–222.

Crooks, C. V., Jaffe, P., Dunlop, C., Kerry, A., & Exner-Cortens, D. (2019). Preventing gender-based violence among adolescents and young adults: Lessons from 25 years of program development and evaluation. *Violence Against Women, 25*(1), 29–55.

De La Rue, L., Polanin, J. R., Espelage, D. L., & Pigott, T. D. (2017). A meta-analysis of school-based interventions aimed to prevent or reduce violence in teen dating relationships. *Review of Educational Research, 87*(1), 7–34.

Decker, M. R., Wood, S. N., Hameeduddin, Z., Kennedy, S. R., Perrin, N., Tallam, C., Akumu, I., & Frankel, A. (2020). Safety decision-making and planning mobile app for intimate partner violence prevention and response: Randomised controlled trial in Kenya. *BMJ Global Health, 5*(7), e002091.

Devries, K. M., Child, J. C., Bacchus, L. J., Mak, J., Falder, G., Graham, K., Watts, C., & Heise, L. (2014). Intimate partner violence victimization and alcohol consumption in women: A systematic review and meta-analysis. *Addiction, 109*(3), 379–391.

Devries, K. M., Mak, J. Y., Bacchus, L. J., Child, J. C., Falder, G., Petzold, M., Astbury, J., & Watts, C. H. (2013). Intimate partner violence and incident depressive symptoms and suicide attempts: A systematic review of longitudinal studies. *PLoS Medicine, 10*(5), e1001439.

Drabkin, A. S., Baden, L., Solomon, J., & Card, J. J. (2021). IMPACT: Effects of an online capacity-building intervention for IPV prevention professionals. *Journal of Interpersonal Violence, 36*(15–16), NP7899-NP7919.

El Morr, C., & Layal, M. (2020). Effectiveness of ICT-based intimate partner violence interventions: A systematic review. *BMC Public Health, 20*(1), 1–25.

Ellsberg, M., Arango, D. J., Morton, M., Gennari, F., Kiplesund, S., Contreras, M., & Watts, C. (2015). Prevention of violence against women and girls: What does the evidence say? *The Lancet, 385*(9977), 1555–1566.

Emezue, C., & Bloom, T. L. (2021). PROTOCOL: Technology-based and digital interventions for intimate partner violence: A meta-analysis and systematic review. *Campbell Systematic Reviews, 17*(1), e1132.

Ezeh, A., Silverman, M., & Stranges, S. (2021). The impact of COVID-19 has been lower in Africa. We explore the reasons. The conversation. Retrieved August 17, 2021 from https://theconversation.com/the-impact-of-covid-19-has-been-lower-in-africa-we-explore-the-reasons-164955

Fagan, A. A., & Catalano, R. F. (2013). What works in youth violence prevention: A review of the literature. *Research on Social Work Practice, 23*(2), 141–156.

Firth, J., Torous, J., Nicholas, J., Carney, R., Rosenbaum, S., & Sarris, J. (2017). Can smartphone mental health interventions reduce symptoms of anxiety? A meta-analysis of randomized controlled trials. *Journal of Affective Disorders, 218*, 15–22.

Ford-Gilboe, M., Varcoe, C., Scott-Storey, K., Perrin, N., Wuest, J., Wathen, C. N., Case, J., & Glass, N. (2020). Longitudinal impacts of an online safety and health intervention for women experiencing intimate partner violence: Randomized controlled trial. *BMC Public Health, 20*(1), 1–17.

Foshee, V. A., Reyes, L. M., Agnew-Brune, C. B., Simon, T. R., Vagi, K. J., Lee, R. D., & Suchindran, C. (2014). The effects of the evidence-based safe dates dating abuse prevention program on other youth violence outcomes. *Prevention Science, 15*(6), 907–916.

Fritz, J. M., & Rhéaume, J. (Eds.). (2014). *Community intervention. Clinical sociology perspectives*. Springer.

Galtung, J. (1990). Cultural violence. *Journal of Peace Research, 27*(3), 291–305.

Galtung, J., & Höivik, T. (1971). Structural and direct violence: A note on operationalization. *Journal of Peace Research, 8*(1), 73–76.

García-Moreno, C., Pallitto, C., Devries, K., Stöckl, H., Watts, C., & Abrahams, N. (2013). *Global and regional estimates of violence against women: Prevalence and health effects of intimate partner violence and non-partner sexual violence.*

Gibbs, A., Gumede, D., Luthuli, M., Xulu, Z., Washington, L., Sikweyiya, Y., Adeagbo, O., & Shahmanesh, M. (2022). Opportunities for technologically driven dialogical health communication for participatory interventions: Perspectives from male peer navigators in rural South Africa. *Social Science & Medicine, 292*, 114539.

Gibbs, A., Washington, L., Willan, S., Ntini, N., Khumalo, T., Mbatha, N., Sikweyiya, Y., Shai, N., Chirwa, E., & Strauss, M. (2017). The stepping stones and creating futures intervention to prevent intimate partner violence and HIV-risk behaviours in Durban, South Africa: Study protocol for a cluster randomized control trial, and baseline characteristics. *BMC Public Health, 17*(1), 1–15.

Glass, N., Clough, A., Case, J., Hanson, G., Barnes-Hoyt, J., Waterbury, A., Alhusen, J., Ehrensaft, M., Grace, K. T., & Perrin, N. (2015). A safety app to respond to dating violence for college women and their friends: The MyPlan study randomized controlled trial protocol. *BMC Public Health, 15*(1), 1–13.

Glass, N., Eden, K. B., Bloom, T., & Perrin, N. (2010). Computerized aid improves safety decision process for survivors of intimate partner violence. *Journal of Interpersonal Violence, 25*(11), 1947–1964.

Glass, N. E., Clough, A., Messing, J. T., Bloom, T., Brown, M. L., Eden, K. B., Campbell, J. C., Gielen, A., Laughton, K., & Grace, K. T. (2021). Longitudinal impact of the myPlan app on health and safety among college women experiencing partner violence. *Journal of Interpersonal Violence*, 0886260521991880.

Glass, N. E., Perrin, N. A., Hanson, G. C., Bloom, T. L., Messing, J. T., Clough, A. S., Campbell, J. C., Gielen, A. C., Case, J., & Eden, K. B. (2017). The longitudinal impact of an internet safety decision aid for abused women. *American Journal of Preventive Medicine, 52*(5), 606–615.

Gonçalves, M., & Matos, M. (2016). Prevalence of violence against immigrant women: A systematic review of the literature. *Journal of Family Violence, 31*(6), 697–710.

Hegarty, K., Tarzia, L., Valpied, J., Murray, E., Humphreys, C., Taft, A., Novy, K., Gold, L., & Glass, N. (2019). An online healthy relationship tool and safety decision aid for women experiencing intimate partner violence (I-DECIDE): A randomised controlled trial. *The Lancet Public Health, 4*(6), e301–e310.

Jewkes, R., Gibbs, A., Jama-Shai, N., Willan, S., Misselhorn, A., Mushinga, M., Washington, L., Mbatha, N., & Skiweyiya, Y. (2014). Steppingstones and creating futures intervention: Shortened interrupted time series evaluation of a behavioural and structural health promotion and violence prevention intervention for young people in informal settlements in Durban, South Africa. *BMC Public Health, 14*(1), 1–10.

Jewkes, R., Willan, S., Heise, L., Washington, L., Shai, N., Kerr-Wilson, A., & Christofides, N. (2021). Elements of the design and implementation of interventions to prevent violence against women and girls associated with success: Reflections from what works to prevent violence against women and girls? Global programme. *International Journal of Environmental Research and Public Health, 18*(22), 12129.

Jiménez-Barbero, J. A., Ruiz-Hernández, J. A., Llor-Zaragoza, L., Pérez-García, M., & Llor-Esteban, B. (2016). Effectiveness of anti-bullying school programs: A meta-analysis. *Children and Youth Services Review, 61*, 165–175.

Kabiru, C. W., Izugbara, C. O., & Beguy, D. (2013). The health and well-being of young people in sub-Saharan Africa: An under-researched area? *BMC Int Health Hum Rights, 13*, 11. Retrieved from https://doi.org/10.1186/1472-698X-13-11

Kärnä, A., Voeten, M., Little, T. D., Alanen, E., Poskiparta, E., & Salmivalli, C. (2013). Effectiveness of the KiVa antibullying program: Grades 1–3 and 7–9. *Journal of Educational Psychology, 105*(2), 535.

Keynejad, R. C., Hanlon, C., & Howard, L. M. (2020). Psychological interventions for common mental disorders in women experiencing intimate partner violence in low-income and middle-income countries: A systematic review and meta-analysis. *The Lancet Psychiatry, 7*(2), 173–190.

Kovalenko, A. G., Abraham, C., Graham-Rowe, E., Levine, M., & O'Dwyer, S. (2020). What works in violence prevention among young people: A systematic review of reviews. *Trauma, Violence & Abuse*, 1524838020939130.

Koziol-McLain, J., Vandal, A. C., Nada-Raja, S., Wilson, D., Glass, N. E., Eden, K. B., & Case, J. (2015). A web-based intervention for abused women: The New Zealand isafe randomised controlled trial protocol. *BMC Public Health, 15*(1), 1–8.

Krug, E. G., Mercy, J. A., Dahlberg, L. L., & Zwi, A. B. (2002). The world report on violence and health. *The Lancet, 360*(9339), 1083–1088.

Lagdon, S., Armour, C., & Stringer, M. (2014). Adult experience of mental health outcomes as a result of intimate partner violence victimisation: A systematic review. *European Journal of Psychotraumatology, 5*(1), 24794.

Leach, F. (2015). *Researching gender violence in schools in poverty contexts: Conceptual and methodological challenges. Gender violence in poverty contexts* (pp. 46–64). Routledge.

Leach, F., Dunne, M., & Salvi, F. (2014). *A global review of current issues and approaches in policy, programming and implementation responses to school-related gender-based violence (SRGBV) for the education sector*. Retrieved from https://www.eccnetwork.net/sites/default/files/media/file/SRGBV%20UNESCO%20Global%20Review%20Jan%202014.pdf

Lee, S., Kim, C.-J., & Kim, D. H. (2015). A meta-analysis of the effect of school-based anti-bullying programs. *Journal of Child Health Care, 19*(2), 136–153.

LeFevre, A. E., Shah, N., Bashingwa, J. J. H., George, A. S., & Mohan, D. (2020). Does women's mobile phone ownership matter for health? Evidence from 15 countries. *BMJ Global Health, 5*(5), e002524.

Lester, S., Lawrence, C., & Ward, C. L. (2017). What do we know about preventing school violence? A systematic review of systematic reviews. *Psychology, Health & Medicine, 22*(1), 187–223.

Li, J., Theng, Y.-L., & Foo, S. (2014). Game-based digital interventions for depression therapy: A systematic review and meta-analysis. *Cyberpsychology, Behavior and Social Networking, 17*(8), 519–527.

Littleton, H., Grills, A. E., Kline, K. D., Schoemann, A. M., & Dodd, J. C. (2016). The from survivor to thriver program: RCT of an online therapist-facilitated program for rape-related PTSD. *Journal of Anxiety Disorders, 43*, 41–51.

Luk, T. T., Wong, S. W., Lee, J. J., Chan, S. S.-C., Lam, T. H., & Wang, M. P. (2019). Exploring community smokers' perspectives for developing a chat-based smoking cessation intervention delivered through mobile instant messaging: Qualitative study. *JMIR mHealth and uHealth, 7*(1), e11954.

Matjasko, J. L., Vivolo-Kantor, A. M., Massetti, G. M., Holland, K. M., Holt, M. K., & Cruz, J. D. (2012). A systematic meta-review of evaluations of youth violence prevention programs: Common and divergent findings from 25 years of meta-analyses and systematic reviews. *Aggression and Violent Behavior, 17*(6), 540–552.

Miller-Perrin, C. L., Perrin, R. D., & Renzetti, C. M. (2020). *Violence and maltreatment in intimate relationships*. Sage Publications.

Naidoo, K., Adeagbo, O. A., & Pleaner, M. (2019). *Editorial*. SAGE Open Special issue on 'Adolescence, Sexuality and Reproductive Health in Sub-Saharan Africa'. July–September 1–3.

Ndungu, J., Ngcobo-Sithole, M., & Gibbs, A. (2022). Researchers or practitioners' opinion of the possibilities for creating virtual safe social spaces for violence prevention interventions for young people. *Health Education Research, 37*(3), 155–166.

Newton, N. C., Teesson, M., Vogl, L. E., & Andrews, G. (2010). Internet-based prevention for alcohol and cannabis use: Final results of the climate school's course. *Addiction, 105*(4), 749–759.

Olweus, D. (1994). Bullying at school: Basic facts and effects of a school-based intervention program. *Journal of Child Psychology and Psychiatry, 35*(7), 1171–1190.

Ortega, R., & Lera, M. J. (2000). The Seville anti-bullying in school project. *Aggressive Behavior: Official Journal of the International Society for Research on Aggression, 26*(1), 113–123.

Palladino, B. E., Nocentini, A., & Menesini, E. (2016). Evidence-based intervention against bullying and cyberbullying: Evaluation of the NoTrap! Program in two independent trials. *Aggressive Behavior, 42*(2), 194–206.

Parkes, J., Heslop, J., Oando, S., Sabaa, S., Januario, F., & Figue, A. (2013). Conceptualising gender and violence in research: Insights from studies in schools and communities in Kenya, Ghana and Mozambique. *International Journal of Educational Development, 33*(6), 546–556.

Parkes, J., Heslop, J., Ross, F. J., Westerveld, R., & Unterhalter, E. (2016). *A rigorous review of global research evidence on policy and practice on school-related gender-based violence*. UNICEF.

Pensak, R. (2014). Must be 18 or older: How current domestic violence policies dismiss teen dating violence. *Wm. & Mary J. Women & L., 21*, 499.

Pérez, J. C., Astudillo, J., Varela, J., & Lecannelier, F. (2013). Evaluación de la efectividad del Programa Vínculos para la prevención e intervención del Bullying en Santiago de Chile. *Psicologia Escolar e Educacional, 17*(1), 163–172.

Peterson, C., Kearns, M. C., McIntosh, W. L., Estefan, L. F., Nicolaidis, C., McCollister, K. E., & Florence, C. (2018). Lifetime economic burden of intimate partner violence among U.S. adults. *American Journal of Preventive Medicine, 55*(4), 433–444.

Qiao, S., Li, Z., Weissman, S., Li, X., Olatosi, B., Davis, C., & Mansaray, A. B. (2020). Disparity in HIV service interruption in the outbreak of covid-19 in South Carolina. *AIDS and Behavior*, 1–9.

Ridde, V., Dagenais, C., & Daigneault, I. (2019). It's time to address sexual violence in academic global health. *BMJ Specialist Journals, 4*, e001616.

SADHS. (2019). *South Africa demographic and health survey 2016*. Pretoria. Retrieved from https://dhsprogram.com/pubs/pdf/FR337/FR337.pdf

Stephens, K. A., & George, W. H. (2009). Rape prevention with college men: Evaluating risk status. *Journal of Interpersonal Violence, 24*(6), 996–1013.

Stöckl, H., Devries, K., Rotstein, A., Abrahams, N., Campbell, J., Watts, C., & Moreno, C. G. (2013). The global prevalence of intimate partner homicide: A systematic review. *The Lancet, 382*(9895), 859–865.

Swedo, E. A., Sumner, S. A., Hillis, S. D., Aluzimbi, G., Apondi, R., Atuchukwu, V. O., Auld, A. F., Chipimo, P. J., Conkling, M., & Egbe, O. E. (2019). Prevalence of violence victimization and perpetration among persons aged 13–24 years—Four sub-Saharan African countries, 2013–2015. *Morbidity and Mortality Weekly Report, 68*(15), 350.

Tarzia, L., Iyer, D., Thrower, E., & Hegarty, K. (2017). Technology doesn't judge you: Young Australian women's views on using the Internet and smartphones to address intimate partner violence. *Journal of Technology in Human Services, 35*(3), 199–218.

Taylor, B. G., Stein, N. D., Mumford, E. A., & Woods, D. (2013). Shifting boundaries: An experimental evaluation of a dating violence prevention program in middle schools. *Prevention Science, 14*(1), 64–76.

United Nations Population Fund. (2012). *Adolescents and young people in sub-Saharan Africa: Opportunities and challenges*. Retrieved from https://www.k4health.org/toolkits/youthpolicy/adolescents-and-young-people-sub-saharan-africa-opportunities-and-challenges

UNODC. (2019). *Global Study on Homicide 2019: Executive Summary*. Retrieved from Vienna: United Nations Office on Drugs and Crime.

Vagi, K. J., Rothman, E. F., Latzman, N. E., Tharp, A. T., Hall, D. M., & Breiding, M. J. (2013). Beyond correlates: A review of risk and protective factors for adolescent dating violence perpetration. *Journal of Youth and Adolescence, 42*(4), 633–649.

Varela, J. (2011). Efectividad de estrategias de prevención de violencia escolar: la experiencia del programa Recoleta en Buena. *Psykhe (Santiago), 20*(2), 65–78.

Ybarra, M. L., Prescott, T. L., & Espelage, D. L. (2016). Stepwise development of a text messaging-based bullying prevention program for middle school students (BullyDown). *JMIR mHealth and uHealth, 4*(2), e4936.

Young, S. M., Pruett, J. A., & Colvin, M. L. (2018). Comparing help-seeking behavior of male and female survivors of sexual assault: A content analysis of a hotline. *Sexual Abuse, 30*(4), 454–474.

Zych, I., Ortega-Ruiz, R., & Del Rey, R. (2015). Systematic review of theoretical studies on bullying and cyberbullying: Facts, knowledge, prevention, and intervention. *Aggression and Violent Behavior, 23*, 1–21.

Kammila Naidoo , Ph.D. is the Executive Dean of the Faculty of Humanities, University of Johannesburg. She is also a Professor of Sociology publishing in the areas of gender relations, family, violence against women, poverty, and inequality. She completed her Ph.D. (2001) at the University of Manchester, United Kingdom. She taught at four other South African institutions before joining the University of Johannesburg in 2010. She is currently involved in an international project, The GendV Project, building comparative and substantive insights on the drivers of gender-based violence. She has served as a journal editor of the *South African Review of Sociology* and guest editor for *Development Southern Africa* and *Sage Open*. She has served on several review panels for universities, institutional bodies, and science councils.

Oluwafemi Adeagbo, Ph.D. is an Assistant Professor in the Department of Community and Behavioral Health at the University of Iowa College of Public Health in the USA. He is an applied socio-behavioral scientist with academic training in multiple social science disciplines (B.A. [Hons] Philosophy, M.A. in Migration Studies, and Ph.D. in Sociology). He is a Visiting Professor in the Department of Sociology at the University of Johannesburg (UJ), South Africa, and an Honorary Senior Research Fellow at the University College London. He has extensive research experience working collaboratively with local and international institutions on HIV-related research in South Africa, Nigeria, Zambia, and the USA. He is interested in global health, stigma reduction interventions, human immunodeficiency virus/acquired immunodeficiency syndrome (HIV/AIDS), social aspects of health, social justice, gender and sexualities, implementation science, and the evaluation of complex interventions. He was recently recognized by the African Academy of Sciences (2021) and the South African National Research Foundation (NRF) (2019) for his scientific contributions.

Xiaoming Li, Ph.D. is a Professor and Endowed Chair of clinical translational research and the Director of the SmartState Center for Healthcare Quality at the Arnold School of Public Health at the University of South Carolina. He received his Ph.D. in Educational Psychology at the University of Minnesota, Minneapolis, USA. His research interests include developing, delivering, and evaluating culturally appropriate best practices in mental health and human immunodeficiency virus/acquired immunodeficiency syndrome (HIV/AIDS) behavioral prevention interventions among vulnerable populations across various cultural settings. His research areas include resilience-based psychosocial interventions, HIV disclosure, stigma reduction, mental health, and HIV treatment and care. He has conducted or participated in HIV-related research in the USA, China, Namibia, Vietnam, India, Mexico, Zambia, Nigeria, and the Bahamas. Since 2019, he has distinguished himself as one of the world's most active authors in AIDS-related stigma and discrimination and has been elected a fellow of the Association of Psychological Science. He is a Distinguished Visiting Professor in the Department of Psychology, University of Johannesburg, South Africa.

Chapter 2
Protecting Young People in Sub-Saharan Africa Against Sexual and Gender-Based Violence via Sexual and Reproductive Health and Rights

Yvonne Gamuchirai Tagwireyi and Lorenza Fluks

2.1 Introduction and Background

Levels of violence against children (VAC)[1] and young people in Africa are alarmingly high and continue to rise (African Platform to End Violence Against Child End Violence, 2021). It is estimated that every 5 s, a child in Africa accesses a helpline service for children to report abuse and violence (ACPF & APEVAC, 2021a, p. 9). Over the last decades, many achievements have been made across the continent to protect children from harm. However, much remains to be done, especially with regard to ending adolescent sexual and gender-based violence (SGBV).

There has been progress in developing new legal and policy frameworks and improving existing ones to address gender-based violence (GBV) experienced by children. In particular, program investments in strengthening child protection systems are increasing, and linkages made to sexual and reproductive health and rights (SRHR) and various forms of support and services are provided regarding the latter. These all serve as critical entry points for violence prevention in child populations.

This chapter is dedicated in honour of the late Prof Finn Reygan who was the Principal Investigator of the School's Out project, which supported rolling out sexual and reproductive health and rights for young people in Eastern and Southern Africa, funded by Amplify Change.

[1] In this chapter, we adopt the United Nations Convention on the Rights of the Child's (UNCRC) definition of children as "every human being below the age of 18 years unless under the law applicable to the child, majority is attained earlier" (Part 1, Article 1).

Y. G. Tagwireyi (✉)
Article21 Consulting, Harare, Zimbabwe

L. Fluks
Human Sciences Research Council (HSRC), Pretoria, South Africa
e-mail: lfluks@hsrc.ac.za

K. Naidoo et al. (eds.), *Young People, Violence and Strategic Interventions in Sub-Saharan Africa*, Clinical Sociology: Research and Practice,
https://doi.org/10.1007/978-3-031-20679-5_2

Nevertheless, Africa continues to record some of the highest rates of SGBV in the world (ACPF & APEVAC, 2021b, p. 7).

Recent statistics also show that one in four African children experiences sexual violence. For example, three million girls on the continent are annually at risk of female genital mutilation and cutting (FGM/C) (WHO, 2021). Globally, an estimated five million more girls have married annually before turning 18, with 40% of such child marriages occurring in Sub-Saharan Africa (SSA) (Girls Not Brides, 2019). In addition, four out of ten boys in residential care institutions suffer physical violence, while two in ten experience some form of sexual violence (Global Initiative to End All Corporal Punishment of Children & Save the Children (Sweden), 2010, p. 4). Violent and degrading punishment of children has been documented in care settings and penal reform institutions in many African countries (Ibid.).

Furthermore, reports on SSA reveal the highest rates of child trafficking in the world, with girls and boys more or less equally affected (ACPF, 2019a). The coronavirus disease (COVID-19) pandemic has seen an escalation in SGBV globally, particularly violence against women and girls (VAWG). It has also magnified pre-existing structural problems that perpetuate SGBV, including poverty, inequality, high unemployment, harmful cultural norms, mental ill-health, and systemic failures in criminal justice, education, and healthcare systems to address SGBV in several countries effectively (MIET AFRICA, 2021a, p. 88).

SRHR services and support for young people are essential in enabling them to enjoy a healthy and productive life. These services and support initiatives include a broad spectrum of healthcare, such as access to age-appropriate information about their developing bodies, access to contraceptives, maternal and newborn care, and prevention and treatment of the human immunodeficiency virus (HIV), and other sexually transmitted infections, amongst others. However, despite its importance, SRHR provisioning and access for young people, particularly comprehensive sexuality education, are contested globally in many countries, including Africa (Starrs et al., 2018; Tirado et al., 2020; Wekesah et al., 2019). This leads to the unfulfilled potential to implement child rights and diminished capacity of adolescent girls and boys to claim their SRHR, including in SSA countries and other African regions (Buller & Schulte, 2018; Tirado et al., 2020).

Key hindrances that often impede effectively linking young people to SRHR education, services, and other forms of support include local cultures with biased gender norms in which restrictive and binary gender roles apply (Wekesah et al., 2019). This facilitates discrimination among boys and girls, negative attitudes to healthcare workers in relation to adolescent SRHR, and limited education and information reaching youth to assist them in making informed decisions about their reproductive health, including their safety and protection, amongst other things. These hindrances restrict young people from accessing vital SRHR services and support and contribute to their vulnerability to various forms of violence. Young women and girls, young people with disabilities, and sexual- and gender minorities are most adversely affected in this regard (Freedman et al., 2020; Hanass-Hancock et al., 2018; Lynch & Reygan, 2021).

In this chapter, we argue that effectively linking young people in Africa to essential SRHR support and services can provide them with protective measures against SGBV. First, we consider some of the available legal and policy instruments on SRHR and VAC in selected African countries, arguing these as key tools that create an enabling environment for adolescents accessing SRHR and healthcare. We then discuss key drivers of VAC and young people in Africa, followed by some approaches or SRHR models used by various organizations addressing the issue of VAC.

Thereafter, we discuss effective links to SRHR as crucial in the context of young people faced with crises involving VAC. Finally, we present empirical study findings to demonstrate the barriers that civil society organizations' children activists identified in considering supportive factors for SRHR regarding young people in Eastern and Southern Africa (ESA).[2]

SRHR support and services for young people in Africa are necessary and act as critical enabling measures for achieving healthy and productive lives and contributing to their protection from SGBV. However, we acknowledge that many of the programs implemented on the continent have been developed in the Global North, a differently resourced environment with different socio-cultural contexts vis-à-vis the African context. It is thus necessary to contextualize a nuanced understanding of effective strategies to link young people to SRHR services in Africa.

Our empirical study in selected African contexts gave rise to a qualitative study undertaken online from July to September 2020 as researchers who conducted this study for the Human Sciences Research Council (HSRC) in South Africa. This component formed part of a broader project funded by Amplify Change, which investigated how best to engage civil society organizations in effectively rolling out SRHR education and support in selected ESA countries. The findings presented in this chapter were derived from a narrative assessment. This qualitative methodology generates narrative accounts of advocacy workers regarding their thinking and reasons for adopting the particular approaches they do, including how they determine if such approaches work or not in the contexts in which they undertake their support work. As a qualitative evaluation tool, narrative assessment emerged from critiques about the results-focused approach of many traditional monitoring and evaluation methods (Van Wessel, 2018; Van Wessel & Ho, 2018).

Thirteen semi-structured, in-depth interviews were conducted via the Zoom online platform with 17 purposefully selected Civil Society Organization (CSO) representatives from eight ESA countries. The study countries included Botswana, Eswatini, Malawi, Mozambique, Namibia, South Africa, Uganda, and Zambia. The interviews were recorded after permission was sought and obtained from participants and afterward transcribed into transcripts for analysis. A grounded approach for thematic analysis was performed on the data collected using the ATLAS.ti

[2]In this chapter, while we use the UNRC definition of the "child," the term distinguishes between younger children below the pre-adolescent range and older children who are pre-adolescents, adolescents, and teenagers below the age of 18 years.

qualitative data analysis software. This process involved several steps for coding and organizing the data to create themes. The analysis surfaced several supportive factors and barriers that hinder the effective linking of young people to SRHR support and services in the ESA region. This also notably included the impact of COVID-19 on the operations of CSOs that work with young people in ESA.

2.2 Legal and Policy Landscape of SRHR and VAC in Selected African Countries

Legislation can be a key tool for changing behavior, cultural and social norms, and perceptions that support violence, GBV, and SGBV. National governments are thus primarily responsible for establishing, implementing, and enforcing international, national, and regional legal and policy frameworks to address violence, including VAC, GBV, and SGBV. The eight SSA countries in the study (Botswana, Eswatini, Malawi, Mozambique, Namibia, South Africa, Uganda, and Zambia) have strong national legal and policy frameworks that broadly meet international and regional human rights standards regarding the above forms of violence.

They are all, respectively, state parties to the United Nations Convention on the Rights of the Child (UNCRC), the African Charter on the Rights and Welfare of the Child (ACRWC), and the Convention on the Elimination of Discrimination Against Women (CEDAW). They are also committed to the East and Southern Africa SRHR commitments, entailing health and education ministers to scale up comprehensive sexuality education (CSE) and SRHR services for young people, including adolescents. Botswana and Uganda have set the minimum age of marriage at 18 years, without exception. Eswatini, Malawi, Mozambique, Namibia, South Africa, and Zambia, while setting the age of marriage at 18 years, have exceptions in place for parental consent.

Three countries (Malawi, South Africa, and Uganda) have made legislative provisions for the age of consent for HIV testing and counseling by setting the minimum age at 12 years (ACPF, 2019b). On the other hand, Botswana, Mozambique, Eswatini, and Zambia have set their age at 16 years (Ibid.). The minimum age of sexual consent is 18 years in Uganda, 17 years in South Africa, and 16 years in Botswana, Eswatini, Namibia, and Zambia (UNFPA, 2017, p. 11). In addition, Malawi sets a gender-discriminatory minimum age of sexual consent at 14 years for girls and 12 years for boys (Ibid.).

Tallarico et al. (2021, p. 95) argue that "setting an appropriate age of consent to sexual activity requires a balance of rights to protection and the recognition of the evolving capacity and autonomy of adolescents and young people as they mature." This means that when promulgating laws, states are required to put in place legislative provisions that promote and protect the child while providing an enabling environment for children and young people to claim their rights in accordance with their age and abilities. All eight countries each have a Child Act or Child Protection

Act to protect children and young people from various forms of abuse, violence, maltreatment, and exploitation.

Programs and services to address adolescent SGBV are provided by state and non-state institutions and vary widely in scope and quality among the different countries. These include awareness-raising, child protection case management, economic and social rehabilitation and reintegration, economic strengthening of households, positive parenting training, access to sexual reproductive health (SRH), education and skills training, and life skills development. Some countries (Botswana, Namibia, South Africa, and Uganda) also have state-sponsored cash transfer programs to provide social support for poverty-stricken and/or low-income children and families. However, our assessment found that SGBV prevention programs tend to be a lower priority for governments and funders compared to VAC response services (Botswana Ministry of Local Government and Rural Development, 2019).

Significant gaps also remain regarding the effective implementation and enforcement of laws. Governments lack the capacity to enforce laws that prevent and protect children against violence. Poor coordination and overlaps between the relevant sectors within different government departments and institutions hinder governments' efforts to address SGBV. Geographic coverage, the scope of services, and the quality of VAC prevention and response services suffer from inconsistency, understaffing, and extreme underfunding. Most VAC services rely on donors to finance them and are generally not geared for impact because of underfunding. These persistent challenges suggest the range and depth of work that still needs to be done to attain visible and impactful progress in addressing violence against young people.

The paucity of comprehensive data on VAC in Botswana, Malawi, and Zambia impedes effective planning, implementation monitoring, and evaluation of child protection programs in these countries. This lack of sufficient and reliable data on VAC contributes to African countries' inability to make informed programmatic decisions for the prevention of and response to violence suffered by children (Government of Botswana Report on Violence Against Children Survey 2019). In addition, inadequate multi-sectoral coordination and national child protection services financing continue to hamper implementation in countries like Zambia and Uganda. A child-friendly government is defined by the African Child Policy Forum (ACPF) as "one which is making the maximum effort to meet its obligations to respect, protect and fulfill girls' rights and ensure gender equality among children" (ACPF, 2020, p. 8). Therefore, a government is considered child-friendly if it is making concerted efforts to put the necessary laws and policies in line with international standards, allocates the necessary budgets and spends efficiently (according to its economic growth), and establishes robust well-coordinated institutional mechanisms to facilitate effective implementation. The eight countries are making efforts to improve the lives of children, albeit with varying levels of success.

African governments' efforts to protect children are ultimately reflected in the laws and policies each country adopts, its allocation of financial and human resources, the effectiveness of government spending, and the visible achievement of positive outcomes for children. While this might seem common sense, progress in addressing gender inequality among children in many African countries is lacking. The ACPF uses a composite child-friendly index (CFI) to determine how African governments are performing regarding the implementation of normative frameworks for child safety and protection. In 2020, South Africa and Namibia ranked at the top for being among the most girl child-friendly African states. They were found to have exerted maximum effort to respect, protect, and fulfill girl children's rights, as stipulated in regional and international child rights treaties (ACPF, 2020).

Eswatini and Botswana ranked 10th and 14th, respectively, were classified as friendly. Mozambique was considered fairly friendly due to its efforts to address child marriages. Malawi, Uganda, and Zambia were ranked childless friendly in their general child and specifically girl child protection. They were characterized by a lack of policy harmonization, weak coordination structures, funding gaps, and unclear institutional arrangements and accountability mechanisms, particularly weak child justice systems. As a result, they failed to protect their children from violence, particularly girl children (Ibid.).

Gaps in law enforcement and policy implementation have resulted in a high prevalence of abuses and violations against children and young people in less child-friendly countries like Malawi, Uganda, and Zambia (ACPF, 2020, p. 71). The weak implementation also explains children and families' uneven access to social services and protection, which results in the high incidence among children and young people of sexual exploitation and deprivations that are detrimental to their development, health, and well-being. This is particularly true for girl children and young women.

2.3 Key Drivers of Violence Against Children and Young People in Africa

A literature review of the key drivers of VAC and young people in Africa shows that negative social and cultural norms and a lack of knowledge about SGBV predominate in most African societies. Gender norms that propagate unequal power structures between boys/men and girls/women perpetuate constant violence against women and children, particularly girls and young women. Furthermore, unsafe environments such as migration routes, spaces experiencing emergencies, and those in conflict situations have minimal access to SRHR services. In addition, household poverty ranks with the above as a key structural driver of violence in Africa (ACPF & APEVAC, 2021b; UNICEF & ICRC, 2017). Institutional drivers of violence, such as poor legal structures, weak accountability, child-friendly justice systems, ineffective and/or uncoordinated child protection systems, and weak school governance structures, often reinforce children's vulnerabilities to violence (Ibid.).

Cultural tolerance of violence is a major barrier to VAC prevention and response (UNICEF, 2017, pp. 10–12). There is abundant evidence that cultural norms and values determine what constitutes violence and what is considered acceptable.

SGBV restricts the choices available to and decision-making in children and young people, especially girl children who experience it, impacting their rights across their life cycle, including to access critical SRHR information and services. SGBV is also a significant risk factor for sexually transmitted infections (STIs), including HIV and unwanted pregnancy in girls and young women (Ibid.). In addition, SGBV is a direct cause of physical and mental ill-health among children and young people (Ibid.). Therefore, it is critical to identify and address unequal power dynamics in the home, at school, in workplaces employing children and young people, and in the community as a key strategy for preventing violence, particularly SGBV, against children and young people.

2.4 Effective Linking to SRHR as an Approach to Prevent and Effectively Respond to Violence and SGBV

Holistic approaches for preventing and addressing violence and SGBV are a key priority that African governments must urgently take on board. The role of the health sector as part of a multi-sectoral initiative to address violence and SGBV against children and young people cannot be emphasized enough. The healthcare system is a strategic entry point to initiate a continuum of care for survivors or young people at risk of violence and SGBV. The potential role of SRHR services in GBV prevention should not be limited to secondary and tertiary prevention for victim identification, care, and support (UNFPA, 2018, p. 23). SRHR is also an essential primary prevention strategy.

Therefore, SRHR services are ideal channels to detect women and girls at high risk of violence and provide counseling or referral to related services to prevent a possible first experience of violence. In addition, SRH providers may also be able to detect instances of emotional abuse not fully escalated to physical abuse. Implementation of quality GBV screening and counseling in SRH services with referrals to appropriate community services for follow-up must thus form key components in the interventions needed for the primary prevention of violence and SGBV, specifically.

Many countries across the globe make use of a combination of models and approaches to addressing violence and SGBV against children and young people. To provide integrated services, the establishment of dedicated spaces, such as the one-stop crisis center or women and girls' only spaces, must be undertaken. Such services must include medical counseling and access to legal help. These have been undertaken in many countries in the ESA region to varying degrees. For example, in Botswana, the Botswana Gender-Based Violence Prevention and Support Center (BGBVC) runs a Girls and Women Center that supports women and girls with economic empowerment interventions, psychosocial counseling, and SRHR services (Fair Planet, 2020). Similar centers have been established in Malawi, Namibia, and Zambia as a less stigmatizing and easier entry point for survivors to access coordinated services physically (UNDP Zambia, 2020). However, the sustainability of these centers is guaranteed only when they are fully institutionalized, as in South Africa. Nevertheless, many countries face challenges in running such centers, including insufficient rollout to cover all areas, lack of financial and human resources, limited committed leadership, and a dearth of case managers.

Other models and approaches currently being utilized in the ESA region include integrating GBV into primary healthcare or SRH support and services. The SRHR-HIV Knows No Borders, the implementation of which is coordinated by the International Organization for Migration (IOM), is aimed at improving the sexual and reproductive health of migrants, adolescents, young people, and sex workers in six countries in the Southern African Development Community (SADC) region (IOM, Save the Children, & University of Witwatersrand, 2019, pp. 14–15). These countries include Lesotho, Malawi, Mozambique, South Africa, Eswatini, and Zambia.

SRHR-HIV Knows No Borders focuses on enhancing the knowledge of young migrants regarding access to SRHR, reporting against violence within migratory routes, and providing health and HIV services (Ibid.). It also works with local, national, and regional authorities to create awareness about the importance of SRHR for migrant and mobile populations. It is essential for health systems to facilitate and simulate such links between SRHR and young people.

The FutureLife-Now! program implemented by MIET AFRICA in Lesotho, Malawi, Zambia, and Zimbabwe provides a combination of activities for young people in an effort to enable them to protect themselves against VAC and SGBV (MIET AFRICA, 2021b). Activities include strengthened HIV education policies, enhanced comprehensive sexuality education, access to youth-friendly HIV/SRHR services facilitated through schools, peer-support groups on health and protection from violence, and targeted programming for boys (Ibid.). These approaches also contribute to the program's overall objective of reducing new HIV infections and increasing adherence to antiretroviral therapy (ART) amongst children and youth in the SADC region. Effective links between schools to SRHR services provide young people with access to trained healthcare workers who can support them in accessing services and referrals in cases of violence and SGBV (Ibid.).

The Hands Off! Sex Workers program, coordinated by Aidsfonds (Netherlands), is aimed at addressing violence against sex workers in Botswana, Mozambique, Namibia, South Africa, and Zimbabwe (Aidsfonds, 2021). The program focuses on linking sex workers with SRHR support services and supporting them in undertaking and contributing to research on effective strategies in responding to violence against them (Ibid.). In Malawi, Eswatini, Zambia, Zimbabwe, and Botswana, victim-friendly units have been set up at police stations and local healthcare facilities as service points for young people at which they can access SRH services relating to GBV, such as prophylaxis for STI and HIV, and emergency contraception for survivors (MIET AFRICA, 2021b).

The Spotlight Initiative is a multi-annual European Union-United Nations (EU-UN) collaboration launched in 2017 and aimed at combatting VAWG (Spotlight Initiative, 2020). The Spotlight Initiative's regional program in Africa has been implemented in Malawi, Mozambique, Uganda, and Zimbabwe. It provides a regional response to addressing SGBV, harmful practices, and SRHR in general.

The program focuses on access to SRH services for young people as a protective mechanism against GBV and SGBV (Ibid.).

School-based initiatives are well placed to prevent violence against young people. School-based programs can address discriminatory gender norms and attitudes prevalent in society to prevent these from becoming deeply ingrained in children and young people (UNESCO, 2015). Such initiatives, where they occur, address gender norms and violence and sexual abuse among adolescents, teenagers, and young adults, as well as the link between the two. Comprehensive Sexuality Education (CSE) programs in SSA are predominantly school-based in primary and secondary schools (Wekesah et al., 2019). Teachers teach CSE as part of the school curriculum and classroom settings. In some cases, CSE is taught as a stand-alone subject or alongside other life skills-based subjects. However, CSE is usually integrated into relevant "carrier subjects" such as Biology, General Science, and Home Economics (Ibid.).

A specially trained teacher is required to teach CSE as a stand-alone subject. Stand-alone CSE classes are taught in South Africa, Namibia, Uganda, and Eswatini (Ibid.). CSE integrated into carrier subjects is preferred by most implementers as it reduces pressure to create space in the school timetable for a new subject, find trained staff, and provide new training needs for teachers. CSE is integrated into one or more carrier subjects in Malawi, Mozambique, Rwanda, and Zambia (Ibid.).

Program evaluations regarding the effectiveness of the various programs above are yet to be fully conducted (Wekesah et al., 2019). However, from our review, it is nonetheless abundantly clear that political will needs to be strengthened and sustained to institutionalize a systemic SGBV response into routine SRHR care for young people. Integration of SGBV prevention and services in the health and education systems needs to be achieved sustainably to reach all adolescents and young people, including sexual and gender minority youth (Lynch & Reygan, 2021). Effective program/project-based interventions must be sustained, and coordination mechanisms with government institutions and CSOs supporting these should be prioritized.

Most importantly, models for SRH that are effectively being linked to adolescents and young people as a response to SGBV and VAC violence must be included in child protection approaches. Programs/projects must emphasize the need to apply rights-based and gender-sensitive approaches to address GBV and SGBV. This will enable children to protect themselves and access the necessary information and support they need to make informed sexual and reproductive health decisions to protect themselves from VAC and recover from different types of violence should they be survivors of these. Monitoring and formal evaluations also need to be regularly conducted to assess if interventions work by achieving their aims and impact on VAC, GBV, and SGBV amongst children and young people.

Earlier, we cautioned to view and use approaches regarding linking SRHR to VAC, GBV, and SGBV to better protect children that predominantly emanate from contexts in the North. Again, we stress the need to formulate and implement these approaches in a context-based way, including the evaluation of entry points and programs to understand how and why some work and others do not in an SSA context or that of a specific African country or region such as the ESA. These might take time to develop properly but will yield best practices as evaluations and nuanced interventions occur. However, there must be political will and carry through of not just effective but also flexible and sustainable implementation as dynamism is a feature of most societies. Changes regarding VAC, GBV, and SGBV relating to children and young people will inevitably occur, and interventions must accommodate social/community flux.

2.5 SRHR Services and Support for Young People During the COVID-19 Pandemic

The COVID-19 pandemic has more starkly exposed underlying inequalities in our socio-economic, education, and health systems. During emergencies, particularly ones that involve quarantines, GBV often increases, as evidenced during the COVID-19 pandemic globally, so much so that the UN has termed the considerable rise in GBV occurrence as the "shadow pandemic" (UN Women, 2020). What has also been exposed is the limited access to SRH support and services available to survivors, including children and young people who face restrictions in their home environments more than they otherwise would. A rise in GBV and SGBV has been reported in many countries, with women and children, particularly girl children, identified as bearing the brunt of the "shadow pandemic" and COVID-19 pandemic (Ibid.). Many low-income households experience difficulty accessing food, water, access to healthcare, and other basic needs and services due to unemployment and restrictions to remain at home when these are in place.[3]

Africa, and SSA, on which we focus in this chapter, have not escaped the above impacts. If anything, the sharply worsened GBV and SGBV rates and lack of support for survivors and measures for prevention became overwhelmingly exposed in African countries. While the full impacts and experiences of these still require careful study, our own study has provided an opportunity to home in on VAC,

[3] A similar case of quarantine occurred 7 years earlier in SSA with the Ebola Virus Disease (EVD) outbreak and is worth noting for comparative reasons with the current COVID-19 pandemic. The EVD outbreak adversely impacted service provision relating to education and health, particulary SRH and the protection of children, adolescents, and young people in affected countries (Nidhi, 2020, p. 18; UNFPA, 2015). Schools were closed in Guinea, Liberia, and Sierra Leone between July 2014 and April 2015 (Ibid.). The lack of access to formal schooling and adolescent SRH services amidst persistent VAC, GBV, and SGBV situations resulted in increased teenage pregnancies, especially among adolescent girls. The Ebola crisis demonstrated how health emergencies expose fragile health systems and disproportionately affect the rights of women and girl children in SSA. In Sierra Leone and Liberia, radio programs and mobile clinics were used as entry points to provide SRH services and raise awareness against these forms of violence afflicting girl children. In addition, protection desks were established to respond to the increase in GBV cases in these countries, including for children/girls (Hallgarten, 2020, pp. 7–8).

GBV, and SGBV experienced by children and look at the work of Community-based Organizations (CBOs) attempting to address child protection issues in this regard.

Our assessment shows that all the study countries report an increase in VAC linked to the effects of COVID-19 and associated containment measures (MIET AFRICA, 2021b). The closure of child and youth-friendly spaces and adolescent corners has led to the loss of vital social support and related networks. These social support spaces and networks are essential for coping with violence, particularly when young people experience violence from their caregivers in the domestic environment. Countries previously showing lower levels of SGBV are seeing a worrying upsurge in numbers during the current COVID-19 pandemic.

The closure of schools has made the most available space in communities for reporting child abuse inaccessible—the classroom. As a result, it has become difficult to identify learners who may be experiencing violence in the home and support them with seeking appropriate interventions. CSOs that provide preventive and response protection and preventive interventions at a community level have experienced interrupted and uneven operational capacity. In many instances, programs have experienced scaling down or have been brought to an abrupt halt as SRHR services and GBV referral mechanisms were deemed non-essential under lockdown restriction measures. Included among CSO programs affected have been sensitization programs on GBV and awareness-raising focusing on sexual/gender diversity and the rights of lesbian, gay, bisexual, transgender, queer, and intersex (LGBTQI) persons, including adolescents and young people developing sexually and exploring their sexuality as part of their life cycle.

As case management and home visits for adolescents and women at risk of abuse became disrupted, child and crisis helplines stepped up efforts to provide psychosocial support, referral to legal aid services, and access to needed SRHR services for sexual abuse survivors. Childline services in Lesotho, South Africa, Zambia, Malawi, and Zimbabwe report that their toll-free emergency lines for children have become inundated with calls from young people reporting domestic violence by caregivers, cyberbullying, and sexting. Many also called for counseling to cope with mental stress related to lockdowns (MIET AFRICA, 2021b). This highlights the need to intensify media and digital CSE access for children and young people, including support for them as students undertaking their education online because of quarantine requirements.

Many countries have introduced measures on VAC prevention and response to mitigate the impact of the COVID-19 pandemic. Social welfare and healthcare service providers are part of government COVID-19 task forces. For example, Namibia's government COVID-19 task force includes a psychosocial support unit and government SRH focal points (ACPF and APEVAC, 2021a). In Uganda, the Ministry of Gender collaborates with the Ministry of Local Government to include district probation and social welfare officers in district task forces. VAC services and programs were revised and realigned as the pandemic progressed in Botswana, Eswatini, South Africa, Malawi, and Zambia (UNICEF, 2021). For instance, social ministries and state institutions developed COVID-19 response plans and adapted service delivery guidelines. Standard operating procedures were developed by government and CSO service providers in response to SGBV (MIET AFRICA, 2021b). Information on access to SRHR and protection from SGBV was communicated online via radio, public address systems, and community volunteers. MIET AFRICA's FutureLife-Now! radio programs provide information on SRHR as part of GBV responses in Lesotho, Malawi, Zambia, and Zimbabwe (MIET AFRICA, 2021c).

SGBV prevention and SRHR services are lifesaving interventions in emergencies. Crises must not disrupt or divert these essential services, increasing vulnerabilities among those already suffering. If anything, these essential services should be stepped up and included in government crises task forces, not gradually or as an afterthought, as was reported in all the countries discussed above. Policymakers must utilize community and civil society expertise, information communication and technology (ICT), and gold standard existing global guidelines to ensure a continuum of care for children and young people. In emergencies, governments must respond rapidly to VAC, GBV, and SGBV to protect and support children and young people, many of whom experience and struggle to recover from these forms of violence.

The government must set up mobile and/or remote SGBV services and leverage the available ICT (e.g., communication companies) to support adolescents and young people accessing SRHR and protection. For example, free data or airtime should be provided, even if only for a limited number of hours daily. The same with electricity, so poor people, children, and young people who generally do not have access to money can use digital equipment to communicate with others and seek help for VAC, GBV, or SGBV. SGBV and SRHR services should be provided as essential services during any emergency. As essential services, the provision of these services should be prioritized and included in the earliest stage of responding to crises. Timely, efficient, and accessible services will greatly minimize risk to children and young people, particularly those at increased risk, such as girl children, young people with disabilities, and young people in the LGBTQI community.

2.6 Barriers and Supportive Factors for Linking Young People to SRHR Services and Support: Findings of Qualitative Study

As mentioned at the beginning of this chapter, this study was conducted online. It involved 13 semi-structured in-depth interviews with CSO representatives in Botswana, Eswatini, Malawi, Mozambique, Namibia, South Africa, Uganda, and Zambia. The broader study focused on participants' perspectives regarding contextual factors that support or impede the effective linking of SRHR and SGBV for young people in the ESA region. Below we first discuss some of the key barriers as a brief background. Then, we focus more closely on what CSO representatives think supportive and protective environments might look like in relation to linking young people to SRHR services and support in the ESA region.

2.6.1 Key Barriers to Accessing SRHR Services and Support

There is ample literature about the barriers young people face to accessing SRHR services and support, globally and in Africa specifically (Starrs et al., 2018; Wekesah et al., 2019). Keys among these cited in the literature and discussed by our study participants are negative attitudes of health workers in clinics, distance to health facilities, limited knowledge about content in SRHR programs among teachers and parents, and lack of political will and budgets allocated to SRHR. In addition, there are also persistent cultural barriers and resistance by caregivers and those in authority (teachers, healthcare workers, social workers, etc.) to address sexuality and discuss it comprehensively. Regarding the latter, cultural perceptions of young people position them as passive or invisible in decision-making about their health and inequitable gender norms (Buller & Schulte, 2018; Starrs et al., 2018).

In many African cultures, young people who do not have a voice about or hold an opinion, especially regarding sex and sexuality, are regarded as showing respectful behavior. Young people are generally expected to abstain from sex until they marry. Many African societies also display disparate gender norms that accord more leniency to boys than girls. Discussing sex and diverse sexual orientations is also taboo (Ibid.). These views limit conversations between young people and the adults in their lives, including parents, guardians, teachers, religious leaders, and others. This also prevents many young people from disclosing VAC, GBV, or SGBV they might experience to the adults in their lives or seeking these adults' support to protect themselves and heal.

Thus, intervention programs must engage the broader community on SRHR in relation to children and young people. Such SRHR outreach should not just address providing knowledge and information but must also engage attitudes, values, and fundamental cultural beliefs. The interview extracts below speak to some of these barriers.

> The culture is still an issue prohibiting youth health services because sometimes they take it as family planning only for adults. That's why it's difficult to convince a young person, an adolescent, to go for longer anti-methods. So they go for the shorter ones, which then normally take frequently for that matter for those that have good access. Gender roles are also a big issue because it's perceived that family planning is for women and girls and not for boys... (Male participant, Malawi)

> So, in the communities, the one major complaint that always comes up or has been coming up for years despite all the effort that has been put into building capacity is the attitude of health workers...Negative attitudes... (Female participant, Zambia)

In schools and health facilities, persistent stigma and discrimination toward sexual and gender minorities are a severe barrier to young people. It impedes their access to services, leaving them more vulnerable to violence. In many instances, young people in these marginalized groups fail to access services because of discriminatory treatment at health facilities or because they hide their sexual identity. Providing youth-friendly services and cultivating safe spaces are thus critical in SRHR services as a protective measure for children and young people.

> The other thing is in the schools; unfortunately, our schools are not friendly spaces for LGBT young people, even with the work we are doing with teachers and other people who work at the school. It's not easy to be LGBT people in schools. There is extreme discrimination from other students, teachers, and healthcare workers. They don't accept and recognize LGBT people as humans who need respect, love, and patience. (Male participant, Mozambique)

2.6.2 Supportive Factors in Relation to Linking Young People to SRHR Services and Support

Below we discuss some of the supportive factors CSO representatives identified as significant in effectively linking children and young people experiencing SGBV with SRHR.

2.6.2.1 Creating Supportive Environments: Youth-Friendly Services and Safe Spaces

Youth-friendly healthcare services, especially SRHR services, need to be *available* and *accessible* to young people as opposed to where services exist. However, young people are unable to obtain these services for various reasons, e.g., cost and distance. Such services must also be *acceptable* to young people, meaning services must, for example, respect their privacy and ensure confidentiality. SRHR services need to be *equitable*, that is, friendly for young people from diverse socio-economic backgrounds and sexual orientations and young people with disabilities (WHO, 2012). Ninsiima et al. (2021, p. 2) describe youth-friendly services as an "amalgamation of health facility characteristics, health service provision techniques, and health services offered which are key strategies for improving the health of adolescents in Africa." In many countries, globally and in SSA specifically, CSOs work alongside governments to provide services to young people, which creates an enabling environment for youth-friendly SRHR services.

Participants in our study described youth-friendly services similar to that in the literature (Mazur et al., 2018). They emphasized several important aspects that make SRHR services youth-friendly. Firstly, offering wide-ranging services at one location addresses one of the persistent barriers to youth accessing SRHR services, namely, the stigma attached to visiting a clinic for SRHR services. These services are often offered at youth centers in a safe and enabling environment where young people can access the Internet, engage with other young people, read, study, and play games. Additionally, the services are affordable or offered at no cost to young people. Programs or organizations employ innovative techniques to attract young people, for example, not assuming young people will show up but actively strategizing with them about and involving them in reaching their peers. Programs are tailored for different age- and interest groups, understanding that the needs among young people differ. Staff at these facilities and programs are trained in operationalizing youth-friendly approaches. Below are some interview extracts illustrating the strategies CSO representatives identified as supportive to young people accessing SRHR services.

> What else makes it youth-friendly? It's free of charge, no cost, no administration cost involved, and we have implemented a youth-centered approach where young people are part of a Clinic Board where they decide what types of services they will be offering. Furthermore, it's open; it has a space for young people to access free Wi-Fi and accommodates young people who want to use the facility when studying mathematics. So, it's a free space for young people. (Male participant, Namibia)

> We're a very youth-friendly team. We are trained adequately to provide non-discriminatory services to ensure that young people feel safe, comfortable, and free within the center. The center operates as a drop-in center. We have different activities for young people, such as games, and provide Internet access for those who want to summarize their assignments. (Male participant, Botswana)

The benefits and value of a well-trained, knowledgeable, respectful, sensitized, and non-judgmental team should not be underestimated (Mazur et al., 2018). Providing SRHR services and support to young people must take substantial cognizance of the fact that young people are in many respects at a vulnerable and susceptible stage in their development. CSOs can have the best programs and interventions at their disposal, but ultimately implementation depends on their employees. Participants in our study noted that being passionate about seeing young people thrive and having compassion for their circumstances are critical in effectively running SRHR services and programs. Staff can often empathize with young people because they themselves share challenges similar to their young clients, which is valuable in reaching them. The latter is especially important in organizations that work with key populations or groups made vulnerable by societal norms that marginalize them. The emphasis is thus on creating welcoming and safe spaces for young people to access services and support.

> All of our staff, from technical staff to non-technical staff, go through the training on non-discriminatory services. These are very basic things on non-discriminatory basic services, on providing services to key population communities, particularly people living with HIV, LGBTI, and sex workers. We train them on gender violence, othering, and the dynamics within the broader community. (Male participant, Botswana)

> We make sure that whomever we employ within this organization gets briefed adequately in terms of how we go about dealing with young people. So, it's not just a matter of naming it youth-friendly services. Our services are indeed youth-friendly. (Female participant, South Africa)

The term "safe space" means different things to different people, including distinguishing between physical and psychological safety. It may vary in how it is expressed (Lewis et al., 2015). Even so, a safe space in relation to SRHR services for youth refers to places where young people can engage with each other in non-discriminatory ways and express their views and experiences without fear of being judged or ridiculed, importantly, within a context that is motivated to cultivate their healthy development. Participants in our study shared their understandings and provisioning of safe spaces for young people in their organizations and SRHR programs.

> We have safe spaces where we just discuss issues to do with assertiveness, sexual and reproductive health, and access to information and services. . .In these safe spaces, there is a lot of freedom to ask questions and share as much information as possible. It's very easy for young people, after being through such experiences, to make informed decisions to go to a facility. (Female participant, Zambia)

> Well, when we talk about being youth-friendly, we are talking of a space or service without any discrimination. For example, our principal focus is LGBT people, but if other youths want to access our safe space and programs, they are free to do so. (Male participant, Mozambique)

2.6.2.2 Being Supportive of Young People's Evolving Capacities: Providing Comprehensive Information and Meaningful Youth Participation

The concept of evolving capacities in young people was first introduced by the UNCRC and specified the right of the child to be heard (Lansdown, 2005, p. ix; UNCRC, 2009, para 28–30 & para 84) and maintains that "direction and guidance, provided by parents or others with responsibility for the child, must take into account the capacities of the child to exercise rights on his or her own behalf." This means that as children develop and gain more competencies, there is less need for direction from parents and guardians, and children have increased abilities to take responsibility for making decisions concerning their lives. However, these capacities are developed in different environments and cultural contexts at different ages. As a result, according to Lansdown (Ibid.), "children, therefore, require varying degrees of protection, participation and opportunity for autonomous decision-making in different contexts and across different areas of decision-making."

However, applying the principle of evolving capacities faces some challenges when it comes to SRHR relating to adolescents and young people. In many African contexts and elsewhere, adults, as guardians of children, act "in the moral interest of children" by not providing them with comprehensive information about sex, sexuality, and related concerns. This is, however, a persistent cultural barrier to young people accessing SRHR information from a trusted source that is appropriate for their age and accurate. Participants in our study contend that effectively linking young people to SRHR services and support should prioritize their evolving capacities. Such an approach considers their agency and active role in making decisions affecting their lives. Participants thus maintain that giving young people information means empowering them with the knowledge to make healthy and productive choices about their bodies and lives.

> We will not give the information in a piecemeal manner; we are giving the information in a manner that is easy to understand. We want to give as much information as these young people can take so that, if they have an unplanned pregnancy, they can go to a facility to access pregnancy termination services if required. It will be part of a comprehensive package

> that will provide them with all the required information. . .They will also know what services to enquire for—if they are going to get contraceptives or protective measures like condoms or any other commodities. . . (Female participant, Zambia)

Thus, increasingly, young people are included in program development and implementation. However, the active role they are allowed to play as decision-makers in their lives is debatable, as their socialization often acts as a barrier to their full participation as decision-makers regarding their bodies and lives. For example, young people, especially in African contexts, might participate with the belief that they are not allowed to speak on such issues in the presence of adults; they need to be re-socialized to believe their opinions matter and that their voices are valuable and will be heard. Meaningful youth participation is thus a critical approach to providing effective SRHR services and support to young people. This approach includes young people at different stages of program development and implementation, and meaningfully centering programs on their needs and opinions, especially regarding what they think can work for themselves and their peers. Participants in our study alluded to this approach and emphasized the importance of young people actively participating in their organizations and programs.

> So, I can say that what has worked for us so far is just pulling back a little bit as an organization and allowing the young people to run everything themselves, and trust me, these young people are so innovative. They've got great ideas, but most of the time, you find out they do not have somebody who can listen to them. So, we've tried as much as possible to be a listening organization and more than a talking organization. We have learned that you need to let young people be at the forefront of projects and activities. (Male participant, Eswatini)

2.6.2.3 Building Supportive SRHR Communities: Collaboration Between Organizations and Adopting Community Approaches

Mulubwa et al. (2020) highlight the value of adopting a community-based health system (CBHS) approach, especially in low- and middle-income countries, in relation to SRHR services and support for adolescents' needs. This approach includes "all individuals, places, relationships and processes involved in 'speaking for' and supporting SRHR of adolescents in the communities and are at the same time linked to the local health facility" (Ibid., p. 2). Youth-friendly healthcare services are different from the traditional adult-centered approach and have generally not gained traction; where available, such services are still limited to clinics or other primary health facilities. As earlier pointed out, this is not conducive for youth access as many avoid them for fear of being stigmatized.

Furthermore, other barriers to access persist, such as negative attitudes of healthcare workers toward young people, resulting from ingrained cultural norms. Therefore, a community-wide approach responds to some of the challenges with clinic-based programs and attempts to focus on youth-friendly health facility-based services by including other role players in young people's lives, such as schoolteachers and the broader community (Wekesah et al., 2019). In many African contexts, the broader community includes cultural and religious leaders who are key influencers in communities.

> We bring the traditional leaders, train them to become champions, and give them platforms to speak on the radio. Our services, for example, when we are doing outreach, it's given to the headman of that community to announce that [name of organization] is going to be here for the whole week to provide services to young people. (Male participant, Namibia)

We view SRHR service providers as a community that needs to support each other and work together collectively to support young people accessing SRH services. Participants highlighted the importance of collaboration between CSOs providing SRH services and youth programs. The benefits of CSO collaboration include, amongst others, pooling resources, sharing costs, and combining different strengths, skills, knowledge, and expertise of various organizations. This approach is likely to tackle a shared problem more effectively. Moreover, it provides solidarity and support for working on challenging redress issues, such as the marginalization of sexual and gender youth minorities. A greater impact can potentially be achieved than working in silos.

> We cannot do these things on our own; it is impossible. We try to bring other people with skills to the forefront so that we can actually complement each other's work, get a better service, or get a better product, at the end of the day, to our young people. So, we partner with quite a lot of different people across South Africa and abroad. It's all about offering collective experiences and expertise to give a proper outreach to young people. (Female participant, South Africa)

2.6.2.4 Creating Supportive SRHR Legal Environments

A key component of supportive and protective SRHR access for young people is prioritizing relevant government legislation and policies. As discussed earlier, numerous international, continental, and regional agreements on adolescent SRHR for young people's healthy development and protection exist. However, persistent opposition to providing comprehensive SRHR information and services to adolescents impacts governments prioritizing SRHR provision in their budgets and implementation via structural support. Several participants alluded to gaps in different pieces of domestic legislation and policy regarding SRHR services for adolescents, which denies them critical access.

> Ultimately what the government is trying to achieve is that as much as we have laws, there are always different ages. The government has shown commitment through the Adolescent Health Strategy. However, adolescents are still getting pregnant. . .so what are we going to do about it? So, now it's about advocating, for policies that are more flexible than it is now, or for behavior change, through behavior change communication programs. Sometimes policies are more flexible than the actual laws. So, it's a matter of advocating that if the laws are amended, they should be amended to the extent that they have flexible information, like policy documents. (Female participant, Zambia)

2.6.2.5 Impact of COVID-19 on Civil Society Organizations

As discussed in this chapter, COVID-19 and the ensuing lockdown regulations have brought countless challenges to civil society organizations already struggling before the pandemic in many respects. Eghtessadi et al. (2020) warn, "as efforts intensify to tackle the pandemic, it is prudent to prevent COVID-19 from potentially becoming 'the crisis that crumbled CSOs [civil society organizations]'" (p. 288). Despite challenges like looming stock-outs of essential SRH commodities in the ESA region due to closed borders, limited access to the people they usually serve, and unintended impacts on already limited budgets, CSOs adapted swiftly to ensure effective delivery of programs and ensuring the safety of their staff and clients.

In line with current literature on CSOs in Africa, the participants in this study also mentioned that they are currently navigating multiple impacts of COVID-19 regulations on their staff and programs. Restrictions on personal movement, school closures, and limitations on the number of people allowed at gatherings appear to be factors causing the most adverse impact. Most notably, organizations that work with young people in schools suddenly have no access to their target populations. Furthermore, the focus has shifted primarily to managing COVID-19-related issues at health facilities. In many instances, CSO operational models have had to be revised.

> ... the numbers had gone down because we haven't been able to meet with our customers in the same way we used to meet them before COVID-19 came in. (Male participant, Malawi)

> It has really impacted our programs. . .like the number of young people we need to reach. We are not even reaching as many as we thought we would. (Male participant, Namibia)

CSO activities usually conducted in person have been adapted for online implementation where possible, which is challenging in countries with poor Internet connectivity and substantial data costs. Where people are able to access online services, limited technological know-how presents challenges too.

> Uganda as a country, you know, telecommunication is one of the places that are really, really expensive, uhm. . .and then they have smartphones, but they don't know how to use it. So, there was no way, you know, of helping them to let them know how to use the phone, you know, they were hearing Zoom calls and stuff like that; what is that?... How can I participate in this workshop when I cannot connect to Zoom? You know, to connect, stuff like that, that part became such a barrier. (Male participant, Uganda)

In some instances, programs have been scaled down or halted altogether; the latter deemed non-essential. Among these are sensitization programs about GBV and orientation and awareness programs focusing on diversity and the inclusion of LGBTQI persons. Participants viewed such stalling of programming as potentially threatening the advances they had made pre-COVID-19. There is hardly any opportunity currently to provide refresher courses or to reach the target number in programs due to movement restrictions and the additional cost of repeating activities with smaller numbers of participants, including via online platforms.

Several CSO participants working from home reported mental fatigue resulting from pandemic isolation. Moreover, for LGBTQI people in harsh legislative contexts, isolation has meant coping with an additional layer of fear and anxiety as they face being isolated from people in domestic settings. They would normally avoid it by spending long periods outside the home. This has placed an added burden on CSOs to provide ongoing psychosocial support to staff, with many organizations using wellbeing-focused check-in meetings via Zoom platforms.

> I think initially, the fact that we must start working from home, we weren't able to go and implement as staff and interns the way we were working. I think uhm...there was a lot of mental fatigue because we couldn't interact with people, we couldn't work, we couldn't do anything, and it was a very gloomy period. So, what we did is... we would have check-ins, check-ins on Zoom just to know "how you are doing", "how is your mental state" and all those things... So, on that aspect, I think we were able to manage. (Female participant, Zambia)

2.7 Conclusion

This chapter has highlighted SSA's robust legal and policy frameworks for protecting young people from SGBV. Persisting challenges, however, continue to impede the full protection of young people from SGBV and critical access to SRHR services as part of a continuum of services for youth, especially during emergencies like COVID-19. The findings reveal a clear need to strengthen domestic policies and government directives on SRHR to prevent and respond effectively to SGBV among young people, including young people with disabilities and sexual and gender minority youth. It is critical that even during the COVID-19 pandemic, young people are given access to and linked to SRHR services and support.

This must be achieved by establishing supportive environments with safe spaces in which young people have access to youth-friendly and accurate information according to their evolving capacities. The involvement of adolescents and young people in SRHR program design and implementation cannot be emphasized enough. Despite the impact of COVID-19 on CSO operations, particularly in regard to SGBV response and SRHR service provision, collaboration and information sharing amongst CSOs on best practices to link adolescents and young people with such services should be prioritized.

For SRHR services and support to be effective, preventive and response mechanisms against SGBV need to be adapted for the needs of adolescents and young people. At the same time, the local contexts in which they live must be carefully considered to enhance accessibility and uptake of such services and support. Thus, interventions that link young people to SRHR services must robustly consider societal, cultural, and other barriers to access to maximize their efficacy. This is even more critical during global pandemics such as COVID-19 when the underlying inequalities in our socio-economic-, education-, and health systems come starkly to the fore as more children and young people fall victim to or face increasing risk from SGBV.

References

ACPF. (2019a). *Sexual exploitation of children in Africa: A silent emergency*. Retrieved August 8, 2021 from https://violenceagainstchildren.un.org/content/sexual-exploitation-children-africa-silent-emergency-report-african-child-policy-forum

ACPF. (2019b). *The child law resources. Harmonisation of laws–minimum age of sexual consent summary*. Retrieved August 9, 2021 from https://www.africanchildforum.org/clr/

ACPF. (2020). *The African report on child well-being – How are African government friendly towards girls*. Retrieved February 7, 2022 from https://www.africanchild.report/

ACPF & APEVAC. (2021a). *National capacity to address violence against children: assessment in ten African countries*. Retrieved August 12, 2021 from https://violenceagainstchildren.un.org/

ACPF & APEVAC. (2021b). *Here to stay. Home-grown solutions to end violence against children*. Retrieved August 8, 2021 from https://violenceagainstchildren.un.org/sites/violenceagainstchildren.un.org/files/2021/here_to_stay_home-grown_solutions_to_violence_against_children.pdf

African Platform to End Violence Against Child End Violence. (2021). www.endviolenceinafrica.org

Aidsfonds. (2021). *What works to reduce violence against sex workers*? Retrieved August 8, 2021 from https://aidsfonds.org/what-works-to-reduce-violence-against-sex-workers

Botswana Ministry of Local Government and Rural Development. (2019). Report on Violence Against Children Survey (VACS)/National Survey on Life Experiences and Risk of HIV infection among 13–24 years old males and females in Botswana (2019). Retrieved February 6, 2022 from https://www.togetherforgirls.org/wp-content/uploads/Botswana-VACS-Report_Final_Dec-2019.pdf

Buller, A. M., & Schulte, M. C. (2018). Aligning human rights and social norms for adolescent sexual and reproductive health and rights. *Reproductive Health Matters, 26*(52), 38–45.

Eghtessadi, R., Mukandavire, Z., Mutenherwa, F., Cuadros, D., & Musuka, G. (2020). Safeguarding gains in the sexual and reproductive health and AIDS response amidst COVID-19: The role of African civil society. *International Journal of Infectious Diseases, 100*, 286–291.

Fair Planet. (2020). *End the abuse of women in Botswana*. Retrieved August 8, 2021 from https://www.fairplanet.org/support/end-the-abuse-of-women-in-botswana/

Freedman, J., Crankshaw, T. L., Aantjes, C., Armstrong, R., & Poku, N. K. (2020). Young key populations in Southern Africa: An analysis of the social determinants of HIV risk and barriers to sexual and reproductive health services. In K. Govender & N. K. Poku (Eds.), *Preventing HIV among young people in southern and Eastern Africa* (pp. 174–187). Routledge.

Girls not Brides. (2019). *Child marriage: A form of violence against children*. Retrieved August 17, 2021 from https://www.girlsnotbrides.org/learning-resources/resource-centre/child-marriage-a-form-of-violence-against-children/

Global Initiative to End All Corporal Punishment of Children & Save the Children (Sweden). (2010). *Ending corporal punishment and other cruel and degrading punishment of children through law reform and social change*. Retrieved August 12, 2021 from https://resourcecentre.savethechildren.net/document/ending-corporal-punishment-and-other-cruel-and-degrading-punishment-children-through-law/

Hallgarten, J. (2020). *Evidence on efforts to mitigate the negative educational impact of past disease outbreaks. Knowledge, evidence, learning for development (K4D)*. Retrieved August 16, 2021, from https://opendocs.ids.ac.uk/opendocs/bitstream/handle/20.500.12413/15202/793_mitigating_education_effects_of_disease_outbreaks.pdf?sequence=6

Hanass-Hancock, J., Nene, S., Johns, R., & Chappell, P. (2018). The impact of contextual factors on comprehensive sexuality education for learners with intellectual disabilities in South Africa. *Sexuality and Disability, 36*(2), 123–140.

IOM, Save the Children, & University of Witwatersrand. (2019). *Sexual and Reproductive Health and Rights (SRHR)-HIV knows no borders- Stories of change and best practices*. Retrieved August 8, 2021 from https://migrationhealthresearch.iom.int/sexual-and-reproductive-health-and-rights-srhr-hiv-knows-no-borders-stories-change-and-best

Lansdown, G. (2005). *The evolving capacities of the child, innocenti insights*. No. 11. United Nations Children's Fund (UNICEF). Retrieved February 12, 2022, from https://www.unicef-irc.org/publications/pdf/evolving-eng.pdf

Lewis, R., Sharp, E., Remnant, J., & Redpath, R. (2015). Safe spaces: Experiences of feminist women-only space. *Sociological Research Online, 20*(4), 105–118.

Lynch, I., & Reygan, F. (2021). Sexual and reproductive justice for LGBTQI youth in policy responses across Eastern and Southern Africa. In *Oxford Research Encyclopedia of Education*. Retrieved from https://doi.org/10.1093/acrefore/9780190264093.013.1363

Mazur, A., Brindis, C. D., & Decker, M. J. (2018). Assessing youth-friendly sexual and reproductive health services: A systematic review. *BMC Health Services Research, 18*(1), 1–12.

MIET AFRICA. (2021a). *Impact of COVID-19 on adolescents and young people in SADC region*. Retrieved October 19, 2021 from https://mietafrica.org/

MIET AFRICA. (2021b). *Programme overview*. Retrieved October 19, 2021 from https://mietafrica.org/

MIET AFRICA. (2021c). *Our time to act*! Radio carries FutureLife-Now! Messages throughout SADC. Retrieved October, 19, 2021 from https://mietafrica.org/our-time-to-act-radio-carries-futurelife-now-messages-through out-sadc/

Mulubwa, C., Hurtig, A. K., Zulu, J. M., Michelo, C., Sandøy, I. F., & Goicolea, I. (2020). Can sexual health interventions make community-based health systems more responsive to adolescents? A realist informed study in rural Zambia. *Reproductive Health, 17*(1), 1–15.

Nidhi, K. (2020). *Care international gender analysis: Prevention and response to ebola virus disease in the Democratic Republic of Congo*. Retrieved August 25, 2021 from https://www.careinternational.org/files/files/Ebola_Gender_Analysis_English_v2.pdf

Ninsiima, L. R., Chiumia, I. K., & Ndejjo, R. (2021). Factors influencing access to and utilisation of youth-friendly sexual and reproductive health services in sub-Saharan Africa: A systematic review. *Reproductive Health, 18*(1), 1–17.

Spotlight Initiative. (2020). *Spotlight initiative grantees in Africa and Latin America*. Retrieved August 24, 2021 from https://spotlightinitiative.org/press/spotlight-initiative-grantees-africa-and-latin-america

Starrs, A. M., Ezeh, A. C., Barker, G., Basu, A., Bertrand, J. T., Blum, R., Sathar, Z. A., Say, L., Serour, G. I., Singh, S., Stenberg, K., Temmerman, M., Biddlecom, A., Popinchalk, A., Summers, C., & Ashford, L. S. (2018). Accelerate progress—Sexual and reproductive health and rights for all: Report of the Guttmacher–Lancet Commission. *The Lancet, 391*(10140), 2642–2692. https://doi.org/10.1016/S0140-6736(18)30293-9

Tallarico, R., Ozah, K., & Orievulu, K. S. (2021). Age of consent: A case for harmonizing laws and policies to advance, promote and protect adolescents' sexual and reproductive health rights. *African Journal of Reproductive Health, 25*(2), 94–102.

Tirado, V., Chu, J., Hanson, C., Ekström, A. M., & Kågesten, A. (2020). Barriers and facilitators for the sexual and reproductive health and rights of young people in refugee contexts globally: A scoping review. *PLoS One, 15*(7), e0236316. https://doi.org/10.1371/journal.pone.0236316

UUNDP Zambia. (2020). *Launched one-stop centre is a key node in protecting GBV victims in resettlement schemes*. Retrieved November 25, 2021 from https://www.zm.undp.org/content/zambia/en/home/stories/launched-one-stop-centre-is-a-key-node-in-protecting-gbv-victims.html

UNESCO. (2015). *Comprehensive sexuality education in teacher training in Eastern and Southern Africa*. Retrieved August 21, 2021 from https://healtheducationresources.unesco.org/sites/default/files/resources/cse_in_teacher_training_in_esa.pdf

UNFPA. (2015). *Response to sexual and reproductive health in the context of Ebola*. Retrieved August 24, 2021 from https://reliefweb.int/sites/reliefweb.int/files/resources/unfpa_srh_response_in_evd_context_220715_final.pdf

UNFPA. (2017). *Harmonising the legal environment for adolescents sexual and reproductive health and rights*: *A review of 23 countries in East and Southern Africa*. Retrieved September 19, 2021 from https://esaro.unfpa.org/sites/default/files/pub-pdf/2017-08-Laws%20and%20Policies-Digital_0.pdf

UNFPA. (2018). *Addressing violence against women and girls in sexual and reproductive health services: A review of knowledge assets*. Retrieved August 23, 2021 from https://www.unfpa.org/sites/default/files/pub-pdf/addressing_violence.pdf

United Nations International Children's Emergency Fund (UNICEF). (2017). *Preventing and responding to violence against children and adolescents–theory of change*. Retrieved August 10, 2021 from https://www.unicef.org/media/83206/file/Violence-Against-Children-ToC.pdf

UNICEF. (2021). Eastern and Southern Africa highlights 2021-HAC-ESA.pdf (unicef.org).

UNICEF & ICRC. (2017). *The multi-country study on the drivers of violence against children*. Retrieved August 25, 2021 from https://www.unicef-irc.org/publications/pdf/MCSDVAC_revised12072017.pdf

UN Women. (2020). *The Shadow Pandemic: Violence against women during COVID-19*. Retrieved February 12, 2022 from https://www.unwomen.org/en/news/in-focus/in-focus-gender-equality-in-covid-19-response/violence-against-women-during-covid-19

UUNCRC. General Comment No. 12. (2009). The right of the child to be heard para 28–30 & para 84. Retrieved September 13, 2021 from https://www2.ohchr.org/english/bodies/crc/docs/AdvanceVersions/CRC-C-GC-12.pdf

Van Wessel, M. (2018). Narrative assessment: A new approach to evaluation of advocacy for development. *Evaluation, 24*(4), 400–418.

Van Wessel, M. G. J., & Ho, W. W. S. (2018). *Narrative assessment: A new approach to advocacy monitoring, evaluation, learning and communication*. Hivos.

Wekesah, F. M., Nyakangi, V., Onguss, M., Njagi, J., & Bangha, M. (2019). *Comprehensive sexuality education in Sub-Saharan Africa*. African Population and Health Research Center (APHRC).

WHO. (2012). *Making health services adolescent friendly: Developing national quality standards for adolescent friendly health services*. Retrieved February 12, 2022 from https://apps.who.int/iris/bitstream/handle/10665/75217/9789241503594_eng.pdf

WHO. (2021). Newsroom. *Female genital mutilation*. Key facts. Retrieved August 23, 2021 from https://www.who.int/news-room/fact-sheets/detail/female-genital-mutilation

Yvonne Gamuchirai Tagwireyi , LLM is a Legal Researcher and Social Policy Specialist with over 14 years' experience in the child rights sector. She holds an LLB and LLM degree from the Nelson Mandela Metropolitan University (NMMU), Port Elizabeth, South Africa. Her areas of expertise include child law reform, child protection systems strengthening, child-sensitive social protection, public investment in children, and child participation. She has sound knowledge of international and regional human instruments on access to sexual and reproductive rights of young people in Sub-Saharan Africa and gender equality. She has worked previously with Save the Children International East and the Southern African Regional Office, Terre des hommes Netherlands, and the African Child Policy Forum, supporting organizations to create strategic engagements to influence mainstreaming of child and youth rights within regional mechanisms, including the African Union and the Regional Economic Communities (EAC, SADC, ECOWAS). Her current work focuses on research on the impact of COVID-19, youth agency in the South African Development Community (SADC) region, and child participation in implementing the sustainable development goals and African Union Agendas 2063 and 2040. As an independent consultant, she supports the African Union Commission (AUC) in developing an African Union strategy for education, health, and well-being. She was recently appointed as an External Expert on Children Rights and Business for the African Committee of Experts on the Rights and Welfare of the Child (ACERWC).

Lorenza Fluks, Ph.D. is a Research Specialist in the Human and Social Capabilities Division at the Human Sciences Research Council in South Africa. She holds a Ph.D., Master's degree, and BPsych degree in Psychology from Stellenbosch University. Her background in community psychology and community engagement informed her interest in studying social issues via qualitative, participatory, and action-oriented methodologies. Her latest work focuses on sexual and reproductive health, the rights of young people in Africa, gender and intersectionality in research, grant-making, and human capital development. In her current role, she coordinates the Human Sciences Research Council (HSRC)-led consortium involving implementation partners Gender at Work, Jive Media Africa, and the Council for the Development of Social Science Research in Africa (CODESRIA) in the multi-year Science Granting Councils Initiative's gender and inclusivity project, which aims to strengthen the capacities of 16 Sub-Saharan African science granting councils in gender and inclusivity.

Chapter 3
A Study of Internet-Facilitated Violence Against Women During the COVID-19 Pandemic Lockdown in Sub-Saharan Africa

Anke Brand and Adebola Fawole

3.1 Introduction

Before the influx of Information Communication Technologies (ICTs) in Sub-Saharan Africa (SSA), Africa was seen as a dark continent (Agwe-Mbarika et al., 2011). In 2016, the United Nations General Assembly passed a non-binding resolution declaring Internet access a human right and the intentional Internet disruption a human rights violation. This is contained in resolution A/HRC/32/L.20 of 2016. Recent reports also declare that Internet access falls under the freedom of expression (La Rue, 2011).

According to the Spring 2017 Global Attitudes Survey Q70 and Q72 Pew Research Center, while Internet access is growing globally, its use remains higher in advanced economies. The percentage of people who use the Internet in each country is highly correlated with the country's gross domestic product per capita (PPP). Regionally, Internet use is lowest in SSA, with a median of 41% across six countries. These six countries are Ghana, Kenya, Nigeria, Senegal, South Africa, and Tanzania. With 59%, South Africa is the only country in the region where at least half the population has Internet access. According to the global attitudes survey, many Internet users in SSA go online for social communication purposes.

However, access to the Internet is fast becoming a necessity for day-to-day living in SSA. Internet use cuts across socio-economic groups, education, health, agriculture, and communication (Silver & Cortney, 2018). In Tanzania, for example, cell phones were used as surveillance equipment to manage data from a rabies outbreak (Mtema et al., 2016). Comparably, in Malawi, people living with human immunodeficiency virus (HIV) and acquired immunodeficiency syndrome (AIDS) receive

A. Brand (✉) · A. Fawole
Southern African Higher Christian Education Trust (SAHCET), Pretoria, South Africa
e-mail: anke@thekingsinstitute.org; debola@thekingsinstitute.org

K. Naidoo et al. (eds.), *Young People, Violence and Strategic Interventions in Sub-Saharan Africa*, Clinical Sociology: Research and Practice,
https://doi.org/10.1007/978-3-031-20679-5_3

daily text messages on their cell phones reminding them to take their medicines on schedule. In Ghana, farmers in rural areas check the price of tomatoes in Accra, the capital city several kilometers away, via a text message and decide whether it is worth the effort to transport their items there for sale or not (Aker, 2010). In Nigeria, citizens can report domestic and sexual violence via phone calls or emails to law enforcement agencies (UN Broadband Commission, 2015).

These developments in frontier technologies in SSA have led to accessibility, efficiency, wealth creation, and connection with the rest of the world to establish it as a part of the global community and have shown tremendous potential for sustainable development. Yet, these developments also increase inequalities by exacerbating and creating new digital divides between the technology haves and have-nots. The novel coronavirus, SARS-CoV2, commonly called the coronavirus disease (COVID-19) pandemic has further exposed this dichotomy. This pandemic lockdown "triggered an unpreceded reliance on ICTs among large segments of the world population" (Yang et al., 2020, p. 2). Due to this, more and more people consider information technology an indispensable dimension for work and connectivity. They use the Internet for, among other things, e-learning, remote working, wellness, instant messaging, video streaming, social media, and video calls.

A publication from the United Nations (UN) in 2020 shows that this is true even for low- and middle-income countries where mobile technology accounts for 87% of all broadband connections. The leap of African countries into the world of connectivity with its attendant problem of the rapid rate of diffusion of cybercrime in Africa is a cause for concern. This concern increases when one considers the statistics that of the top ten countries in the world with a high level of cybercrime, SSA is host to four. These countries are Nigeria, Cameroon, Ghana, and South Africa, according to the Global System for Mobile Communication Association (GSMA). On the positive side, the pandemic has led to significant innovations in ICT (WHO, 2020). A new World Health Organization (WHO) study finds that 13% of all new or modified technology developed in response to COVID-19 is in Africa. They have been specifically developed or adapted to suit the situation in Africa.

Despite vast technological contributions aimed at alleviating the impacts of the COVID-19 pandemic, the crisis is threatening to erase years of progress in advocacy for women and girls. While men have been most affected in terms of fatalities, COVID-19 has intensified economic crises, care deficits, and the "shadow pandemic" of gender-based violence (GBV), with disproportionate impacts on women (UN Women Headquarters, 2020). The gains of increased availability of ICTs in terms of connectivity, visibility and access, and opportunities are eroded by the violence experienced by women and girls, especially during the lockdown period. This technological advancement, coupled with the existing pandemic of violence against women and girls (VAWG), has led to its emergence as a growing global problem with potentially momentous societal and economic consequences (UN Broadband Commission, 2015).

According to a UN News article (November 2020), certain types of cybercrimes like online sexual abuse, revenge pornography, and sexist hate speech are not gender-neutral and are targeted primarily at women and girls. Cyberviolence has exposed women to cyber defamation, sexual harassment and abuse, pornography, email misrepresentation, cyberstalking, psychological torture, and sexual abuse. Women are often harassed through sexual and disturbing messages from unknown emails and phone numbers. These often strip them of their self-confidence and dignity and may, in some cases, lead to suicide. Moreover, the 2020 Global Initiative Against Transnational Organized Crime confirmed that the coronavirus has exacerbated trafficking globally and hindered efforts to tackle the crime, provide safety, security, and justice, and help survivors. Although the UN, the Council of Europe, and the European Union institutions partly recognize the phenomenon of cyberviolence and online hate speech against women, cyber VAWG has not been fully conceptualized, defined, or legislated.

It is estimated that one in ten women has experienced a form of cyberviolence from age 15 (UN Broadband Commission, 2015). This includes receiving unwanted, offensive, sexually explicit emails or SMS messages or offensive, inappropriate advances on social networking sites. This relatively new phenomenon of cyber VAWG will significantly increase the figure. Research from the final report of the Broadband Commission Working Group on Gender (September 2015) suggests that 73% of women have already been exposed to or have experienced some form of online violence. With social networks still in their relative infancy and connectivity in SSA on the rise, VAWG is a problem that urgently needs to be addressed if the worldwide web remains relatively open and safe for all. Against this background, the chapter investigates the phenomenon of cyberviolence against women during the COVID-19 lockdown period between March 2020 and March 2021 in SSA. Furthermore, the study assesses the root causes and impact of online violence on women in SSA as seen in consulted reports and briefs from different organizations. Finally, the chapter concludes with recommendations for action on how to curb cybercrime against women.

3.2 Cyberviolence as a Form of Gender-Based Violence

In practice, acts of cyberviolence may involve different forms of harassment, violation of privacy, sexual abuse, sexual exploitation, and prejudice offenses against communities or social groups. Cyberviolence may not be just online but also physical in nature (Council of Europe, n.d.). Unfortunately, there is no stable lexicon or typology of offenses considered cyberviolence. Many examples of cyberviolence are interconnected or overlapping or consist of a combination of acts.

The Cybercrime Convention Committee (T-CY), a working group on cyberbullying and other forms of violence (Council of Europe, 2018), defines cyberviolence as:

> ...the use of computer systems to cause, facilitate, or threaten violence against individuals that results in, or is likely to result in, physical, sexual, psychological, or economic harm or suffering and may include the exploitation of the individual's circumstance, characteristics, or vulnerabilities.

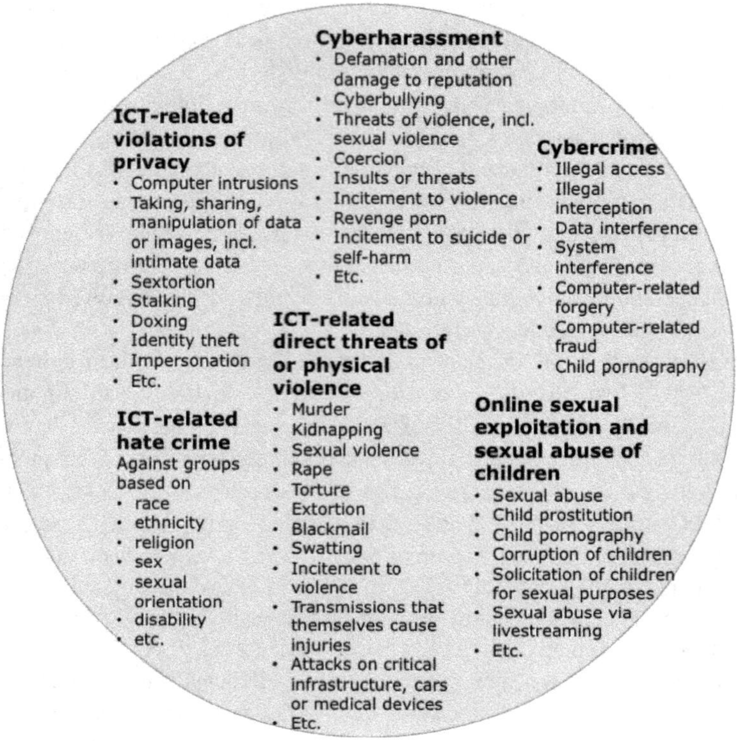

Fig. 3.1 Cyberviolence framework (Council of Europe, 2018)

The Council of Europe's (COE) Cybercrime Convention Committee has proposed a framework to categorize forms of cyberviolence. All six categorizations in the framework relate to sexual abuse in one way or another. These categorizations highlight online crimes relating to sexual abuse as a major crime committed using the Internet and technology. These are listed in Fig. 3.1.

Online platforms where these various forms of abuse and violence occur comprise search engines like Google; social media sites like Twitter, Facebook, LinkedIn, and Instagram; web content and discussion sites like Reddit; blogging platforms like Tumblr and WordPress; forums; dating websites and apps like Hitwe Hookups and Twoo; messaging services like WhatsApp, TikTok, Snapchat, WeChat, Facebook Messenger; Skype or Zoom; comment sections of media, newspapers, and book reviews, and chat rooms of online video games, etc. The list increases with the innovation of novel and different online communication methods. Social media companies are aware of the misuse of the cyberspace they create, and so to keep the space safe, they have defined what will constitute misuse. Facebook defines "hate speech" as:

> ...anything that directly attacks people based on what is known as their "protected characteristics"—race, ethnicity, national origin, religious affiliation, sexual orientation, sex, gender, gender identity, or serious disability or disease. (Facebook Newsroom, 2017)

In addition, Twitter defines "abusive behavior" in its section for rules and policies as "an attempt to harass, intimidate, or silence someone else's voice" and further defines "non-consensual nudity sharing" as "sharing explicit sexual images or videos of someone online without their consent." (Twitter, n.d.)

Before the COVID-19 pandemic, around the world, one in three women had experienced physical violence, most often by an intimate partner (Black et al., 2010). Africa was no exception. Since the beginning of lockdowns in March 2020, emerging and subjective data suggest that VAWG in Africa has increased significantly. This is seen in the increase in sexual assault in Nigeria and South Africa and child molestations and sex trafficking in Kenya (US Department of State, 2020). Additionally, the lockdown has led to social isolation, restriction of movement, crowded homes, financial pressure, food insecurity, inability to avoid abuse, and reduced support networks. Emerging data from Harvard Medical School's Center for Primary Care (May 1, 2020) showed increased calls to domestic violence helplines in many countries since the pandemic outbreak.

Morgane Nicot, team leader of the Human Trafficking and Migrant Smuggling Section of the United Nations Office on Drugs and Crime, stated that

> Traffickers have also expanded their reach through the misuse of Internet and communication technology to advertise, recruit and exploit persons, and especially lure children they groom for sexual online exploitation. (Johnson, 2020)

VAWG has become a major concern due to increased interactions online and other forms of cybercrimes. Jurgita Peciuriene,[1] the program coordinator of the European Institute for Gender Equality (EIGE, 2017), opines that "women are more likely than men to be victims of severe forms of cyberviolence and the impact on their lives is far more traumatic" ("Cyber violence is a growing threat" June 2017). Cyber VAWG should not be considered a separate phenomenon from "real-world" violence when it is more appropriately seen as a continuum of offline violence. For example, cyberstalking by a partner or ex-partner follows the same patterns as offline stalking and is, therefore, intimate partner violence[2] simply facilitated by technology (Burney, 2009). Cyberstalking found that over half (54%) of the cases reported involved a first encounter in a real-world situation (Pathe & Mullen, 1997). Furthermore, data from the 2014 FRA survey (FRA, 2014) and EIGE (2017) show that 77% of men

---

[1] Jurgita Peciuriene.
Email: jurgita.peciuriene@eige.europa.eu

[2] "Intimate Partner Violence" is defined as a pattern of assaultive and coercive behaviors, including physical, sexual, and psychological acts, as well as economic coercion, which adults or adolescents may use against their intimate partners without their consent. The resulting feelings of shame, fear, and helplessness lead to low levels of reporting and, subsequently, relatively few convictions. The largest burden of intimate partner violence is inflicted by men against their women partners (http://eige.europa.eu/rdc/thesaurus/terms/1265).

and 70% of women have experienced cyber-harassment and at least one form of sexual or/and physical violence from an intimate partner.

3.3 Defining Forms of Cyberviolence Against Women and Girls in SSA

Historically and traditionally, women in SSA are housewives, family caregivers, and farmers. A synthesis report of the Africa Region states that women make up the largest share of the agricultural labor force in Africa (FAO, 1995). This fact, coupled with various barriers to education for the girl child, means that females have had limited opportunities to access and learn modern ICTs. However, gradual positive changes and the exponential development of ICT give many SSA women and children access to digital devices, the Internet, and other related technologies. Approximately half a billion people subscribe to mobile services in SSA, but the figure is still only a 45% penetration rate for the region (Gilbert, 2020). The author predicts that the region will continue growing at a compound annual growth rate of 4.3% until 2025, hit the half-a-billion mark in 2021 for unique mobile subscribers, and have a 50% subscriber penetration rate by 2025 (Gilbert, 2020). SSA will have more than 130 million new subscribers by 2025, half of whom will come from just five markets: Nigeria, Ethiopia, the Democratic Republic of the Congo, Tanzania, and Kenya. Despite these gains, there is increasing documentation on how new ICTs open different avenues of control for abusers.

The non-consensual distribution of images occurs when sexual pictures and videos are taken with or without consent and shared online. Statistics from the United States Cyber Civil Rights Initiative found that 90% of the victim-survivors of "revenge porn" were women and that the number is escalating (Lenhart et al., 2016). The term is used to describe a situation when people (usually men) post naked and/or sexually explicit pictures of their ex-partners (usually women) on designated revenge porn websites with their exes' contact information, including phone number, email address, social media profile, and home address, for humiliating and getting revenge on their ex-partner (McGlynn & Rackley, 2015, 2016a, 2016b, 2017; McGlynn & Downes, 2015). The action often results in women being bombarded with threatening, harassing, and humiliating messages from strangers.

Another disconcerting act of violence is when non-consensual sexual acts (like rape) are recorded digitally and then shared online, or when children are groomed, coerced, and blackmailed into live-streaming their sexual abuse over webcams, tablets, and mobile phones (Internet Watch Foundation May, 2018). The foundation reported that 98% of images found on the Internet in Southeast Asia were children aged 13, 28% were aged ten or under, and the youngest victim was just three years old. Exploitation, coercion, and threats (also referred to as sextortion) are emerging forms of online abuse. Sextortion refers to the broad category of sexual exploitation in which a person is coerced to participate in sexual acts online. Sexualized bullying occurs when a person is targeted by and methodically excluded from a group or community using sexual content that humiliates, offends, intimidates, or discriminates against them.

Cyberbullying has been widely reported across several countries in SSA, including, among others, Botswana, Ethiopia, Ghana, South Africa, Senegal, Nigeria, and Uganda (Madanda et al., 2009). In Nigeria, about 40% of young people have experienced some form of cyberbullying, though many were also perpetrators (Olumide et al., 2015). This includes, but is not limited to, gossip, jokes, comments, or lies about sexual behavior posted online, either naming someone directly or indirectly; offensive or discriminatory sexual language, insults, and name-calling online; and being bullied because of actual or perceived gender and/or sexual orientation. Others include impersonating someone and damaging their reputation by sharing sexual content such as pornography or sexually harassing others; personal information shared non-consensually online to encourage sexual harassment ("doxing"); body shaming, and "outing" someone where the individual's sexuality or gender identity is publicly announced online without their consent. Unwanted sexualization is when a person receives unwelcome sexual requests, comments, and content. This is linked to the sexual objectification of pictures, images, emojis, or messages.[3]

3.4 The Scope of the Cyber VAWG Problem During the COVID-19 Pandemic

As mentioned earlier, the COVID-19 pandemic underscored why the Internet is now considered a fundamental human right and why ICT is an essential tool to communicate with others and engage in business and education. A resolution of the 32nd International Conference on Sexual and Gender-Based Violence (2015) elucidates that all emergencies lead to increased levels of GBV. Research by the International Federation of Red Cross (IFRC) has further demonstrated how the increases transpire. For example, during the 2014 Ebola outbreak, parts of Sierra Leone saw an increase of 65% in teenage pregnancies due to increased rapes during the epidemic. The recent COVID-19 pandemic is no exception. A report prepared by World Vision International, "COVID-19 Aftershocks" (World Vision, 2020), estimates that as many as one million girls across SSA may be barred from returning to school due to pregnancies during COVID-19-related school closures.

Project DeShame (2017) findings showed that online sexual harassment emerges from a complex combination of societal, peer, relational, and developmental factors mediated and facilitated by digital technology. One can also include individual risk factors and others pertaining to the COVID-19 pandemic. Societal factors are

[3]There are no agreed definitions at European Union level. An explanation of each form of cyber VAWG can be found here: http://wmcspeechproject.com/online-abuse-101/

societal and gender norms that create a climate where sexual violence is normalized. An imbalance of power and control supports male supremacy and sexual entitlement, leading to a pervasive culture of misogyny and sexual submissiveness of women. It also means that there is weak governance and policies related to sexual violence and gender equity and that crime and other forms of violence against women go unpunished. Peer group factors refer to intense peer pressure on a person to engage in sexual activities online to gain peer approval and acceptance. Relational factors include childhood history of physical, sexual, or emotional abuse from emotionally unstable or unavailable parents or guardians. Poor parent–child relationships, particularly lack of emotional bonding with fathers, have also been identified as a causative factor.

In addition to other factors, developmental factors refer to the emotional, psychological, cultural, and ideological drivers behind the perpetrator's behavior. Individual risk factors include harmful Internet use, exposure and/or addiction to pornography, and coercive sexual fantasies. Factors pertaining specifically to the COVID-19 pandemic include living conditions during the pandemic, unemployment, economic instability, psychological distress over the lockdown period, history of abuse and assault post lockdown, and access to digital devices and the Internet. Women of African descent, rural women, and those living in informal settlements are at higher risk.

3.5 Methodology

We reviewed reports from international organizations to gain insight into Internet-facilitated violence during the first 12 months of the pandemic lockdown. Publications from the UN, the International Criminal Police Organization (INTERPOL), and the United Nations International Children's Emergency Fund (UNICEF) were chosen for review because the organizations are immensely involved in issues pertaining to the welfare of women and children as well as crime globally. We have concentrated on reports from organizations for information rather than academic articles because organizational reports are considered primary sources of information. Research articles often refer to these reports, and we believe that using the reports will provide a more authentic view and holistic approach to answering our research question. Our study design included reports from international organizations in which contributors were surveyed, and longitudinal data were collected from women and girls over time, focusing on a smaller group of individuals connected by the common trait of being victims of some form of cyberviolence.

In addition to the reports from organizations, we also interviewed the founder of a non-governmental organization (NGO) involved in educating people about cyber safety and rescuing victims of Internet-facilitated violence. Her work in educating and rescuing victims of online violence gives her unique insight that she shared with us. A semi-structured interview format was used, and we employed a thematic analysis of both the review of the reports and the interview. The following questions were posed to the interviewee:

(a) definition of cyberviolence,
(b) types and forms of online sexual violence that women encounter,
(c) methods used to recruit victims,
(d) statistics of cyberviolence before/after and during COVID,
(e) insight into the factors responsible for the violence and the targeting of women,
(f) the effect of the acts of violence on the victims,
(g) categorization of the women/girls who are targeted,
(h) reasons why women are afraid to come out,
(i) what has been done to help abused women,
(j) how women are protected from cyberviolence.

3.6 Analysis of Reports from International Organizations

Publications from selected organizations were searched for in their digital libraries. The reviewed publications spanned 12 months (April 2020 to March 2021). The aim was to provide a descriptive overview of the reports on online sexual abuse during the first 12 months of the COVID-19 lockdown. The study reviewed the content of publications with titles generally related to cyberviolence and specifically to online sexual abuse during the specified period. The following words and phrases were used in searching the organizations' websites: online sexual abuse, technology-facilitated crime, COVID-19, cyberviolence, and SSA. An overview of the search is presented in Table 3.1.

The UN, with 26 reports, has the highest number of reports focusing on topics relating to violence against women—18 of them were on COVID-19 and its effect on women, while two focused on women trafficking and only one on online Internet-facilitated violence. The only brief that focused on Internet-facilitated violence did not present any data from Africa. The brief highlighted the different types of abuse reported.

Data from Africa were included in the 13 publications from UNICEF, which were related to gender violence, but only two of them mentioned Internet-facilitated sexual abuse. The reports highlighted an increase in the types of violence during the lockdown. The list includes abuse like grooming children for sexual exploitation, commercial sexual exploitation of children, live-streaming of sexual abuse by family members, sexting, and self-generated sexualized content. It is noteworthy that although the last type is self-generated, it is still classified as abuse because no one voluntarily engages in self-demeaning acts under normal circumstances.

Interpol had four reports, but none related to online sexual abuse for the period researched. The report on cybercrime was limited to fraud.

Table 3.1 Overview of reports on online violence

Organization	Number of publications related to gender violence/ cyberviolence/COVID-19	Mention of Internet-facilitated violence	Form/type of violence highlighted
United Nations	26	1	Physical threats Sexual harassment Stalking Zoom bombing Sex trolling
UNICEF	13	2	Groom children for sexual exploitation Commercial sexual exploitation of children Livestreaming of sexual abuse by family members Sexting Self-generated sexualized content
Interpol	4	0	Focuses on cybercrime generally and not Internet-facilitated violence

3.7 Identified Themes

Both the reports and interviews were analyzed for themes and answers to the research question. The identified themes are discussed below.

3.7.1 Lack of Data

A gross lack of data on online sexual abuse is apparent in the different publications, giving a wrong view that online sexual abuse is not rampant in SSA. The fear is that with Africa being visibly absent from the list of reported continents, efforts to combat this type of violence against women and children may also elude the continent as a whole, with the severely underdeveloped ones at the highest disadvantage. The paucity of data on Africa raises the question of why this is so. The increased online accessibility and usage coupled with Africa's identity as a trafficking hotspot should have necessitated scrutiny, study, and subsequent report.

In general, there is relatively little research on cyber VAWG in SSA, especially during the COVID-19 pandemic. Only one identified study attempted to quantify the level of technology-facilitated violence in the region. As a result, little is known about the nature and dimensions of cyber VAWG, specifically in SSA, providing enough reason for additional investigations of these issues. Gaining a better understanding of these issues will be important for developing strategic advocacy, policy, draft legislation, and preventive action to respond to cyberviolence in SSA.

3.7.2 Increased Assault During COVID-19

Although there are scant data on Africa, data from other countries show an increase in violence against women during the COVID-19 lockdown. A report from UNICEF in April 2020 indicated increased Internet use and subsequent online sexual exploitation during the lockdown. Being in proximity to their abusers increases abuse offline and online, as those who abuse online are likely to abuse offline. It was, however, noted that while reports of violence increased in some places during the lockdown, it decreased in some others. This was not necessarily because the abuse decreased but because women could not leave their homes to call relevant offices for help. Hence, the cases did not get reported.

3.7.3 Shame and Fear

The feelings of shame and fear kept victims from reporting abuses in any form they might come. They were ashamed because they sometimes blamed themselves for the abuse. Victims feared further or worse attacks if reported and often concluded that it was better to suffer in silence. They were unaware that silence further empowered the perpetrators of the abuse. They also feared pornographic materials might reappear (Joleby et al., 2020).

3.7.4 Hidden Identity

The identity of online sexual abusers is often hidden, with the perpetrators hiding under cover of the Internet. Being anonymous or having their identities hidden in cyberspace makes identifying or prosecuting them difficult. Being online also means it is not confined to a specific geographical location, and someone in South Africa may abuse a person in Mali. Some websites like revenge porn are notoriously difficult to work with and can employ various techniques to hide their contact information. They often request exorbitant fees in exchange for removing an individual's content. An inappropriate photo can destroy future job interviews or ruin careers and reputations.

The founder of the NGO added that another profound reason why data, case studies, and in-depth information on the victims of cyberviolence and the adverse consequences are not readily available is that these victims go to great lengths to remove themselves from the Internet search results and hide their identities. In effect, they want to disappear. Moreover, victims of cyberviolence do not want to become public figures or want their stories in the news because it can lead to more searches of the person's name, generating more digital traffic.

3.7.5 *Victim Blaming*

Due to cultural and religious undertones, victims are often blamed for being victimized in the first place (Aborisade, 2021). References are made to their dressing, the people they associate with, and the forms of recreation they engage in as the reasons for being targeted by abusers (Rentschler, 2015; Zauner, 2021). Victim blaming keeps many from reporting the crime against them. Many victims are revictimized in their school, workplace, or community, and some have attempted or committed suicide as a result. Unfortunately, a significant number of victim blaming exists in some of these cases, suggesting that the victim should not have shared the images in the first place. Even if the images were obtained without consent or permission (secretly recording someone or recording a sexual assault), the victim's actions are often questioned.

The above themes form a cycle where the perpetrators are enabled to continue the abuse and harassment because they are not reported due to shame, denial, and fear. Lack of reporting also leads to a lack of data used in research and creates a pseudo situation of no abuse. Victim blaming and shaming due to cultural and religious beliefs may be responsible for SSA's lack of available data.

3.7.6 *Poverty and Ignorance*

Poverty is noted as a contributory factor to sexual abuse (Muridzo & Chikadzi, 2020). The interviewee noted that poverty and ignorance are responsible for some girls being targets of online sexual abuse. Girls in rural areas are often paid paltry sums of money to have photographs of their breasts taken to be displayed in erotic magazines or pornography websites. These pictures or recordings may have future negative impacts, and the girls have no control over the distribution of these pictures once they are released online. Victims hardly report perpetrators to relevant authorities for fear of being stigmatized and often prefer financial settlement rather than allowing justice to take its course (Sossou & Yogtiba, 2009).

3.7.7 *Emotional Scarring*

Just as physical childhood sexual abuse leaves scars on victims, so does online sexual abuse (Lassri et al., 2018). While online sexual abuse may not leave physical scars, it leaves massive emotional ones. Victims of dating scams and cyber dating abuse are left with the emotional trauma that affects their psychological health due to emotional and financial losses. Incidents of cyberviolence may cause the victim to experience depression, low self-esteem, social anxiety, and suicidal tendencies. There is evidence of severe physical and sexual violence arising from Internet-facilitated dating and intimate relationships in Africa (Edwards et al., 2018). Five cases of women who met their abusers on Facebook or were reunited with them through this channel after not being in contact for a while have been recorded in Nigeria (Makinde et al., 2016). Two of the victims were raped, while the other three were victims of attempted rape. One of the victims was murdered, while two others suffered severe physical violence. This is just one of several instances of severe abuse, sexual violence, or death.

3.7.8 Unresponsive Law Enforcement

The founder of the NGO that we interviewed highlighted the impact of the unresponsive attitude of law enforcement officers. A recent study on violence and abuse among young adults in SSA (Makinde et al., 2021) stated that none of the victims who had experienced instances of technology-facilitated violence and abuse indicated that they had reported to the police or other security agencies for assistance. The attitude of law enforcement agencies reflects the gap in regulation of digital media in SSA and the limited action that Internet users can take to seek redress when they have been violated online. It highlights the possibility that the growth in ICT use in SSA has outpaced its regulatory framework. This is evident in the strategies victims use to cope with online abuse. Similar challenges with policing cyberviolence have been reported in developed countries. Thus, survivors may be left with few options to seek recompense when violated. The two primary stakeholders committed to the fight against cybercrime are the police (local and international) and the anticrime commissions in most world regions, including SSA.

Most governments struggle to establish safeguards to combat cybercrime and VAWG in society. The prevalence of cybercrime has triggered a renaissance in the fight against cybercrime in SSA. This fight involves not only law enforcement agencies but also all stakeholders. Stakeholders in the fight against cybercrime in SSA countries range from the average person that knows and fraternizes with cybercriminals to the presidents of the various countries who enact decrees and sign laws passed by the legislature. This fact highlights the wide scope of whom and what is involved in combating this malaise.

In many countries in SSA, there are no clear laws about the distribution of sexually related images. In South Africa, the distribution of images without consent is criminal if the sexually explicit content is of a minor or noticeable criminal activity, such as a sexual assault. In cases where the victim is not a minor or when the images were originally taken with the victim's consent, the law is often not as protective when those images are shared by someone else with the intent to harm.

Many survivors are left without recourse and without adequate laws to address this type of intentional abuse and violation of privacy. Concerns over the distribution of images must also be addressed in legislation. Fortunately, laws and policies that will capture effective cybercrime laws are slowly changing where legislation has been passed specifically to address the distribution of explicit images without the individual's consent in South Africa, and other countries have pending legislation. According to statistics from the United Nations Conference on Trade and Development (UNCTAD, n.d.), out of 53 African countries, 39 (72%) have legislation, two (4%) have draft legislation, and 12 (22%) countries have no legislation. Weighing the high number of countries with legislation and few prosecutions of perpetrators, the legislation seems ineffective.

3.7.9 Example of the Effort of South African Government

Internet crime legislation is at various stages of implementing computer crime laws in SSA. However, the nature and extent of this legislation are not specifically on the protection of VAWG. South Africa is an example of a nation taking steps to combat cybercrime through adequate legislation. On 26 May 2021, President Cyril Ramaphosa signed the Cybercrimes Act (Cybercrimes Act 19 of 2020) into an Act of Parliament and a law of the Republic of South Africa. The Act defines three types of harmful messages that have been criminalized in South Africa. They are messages which incite damage to property or violence, threaten people with damage to property or violence, and unlawfully contain an intimate image. The Act also includes other offenses, such as cyber fraud, forgery, extortion, and theft of incorporeal property. The unlawful and intentional access of a computer system or computer data storage medium is also considered an offense, along with the unlawful interception of or interference with data. South Africa also has a national strategic plan on GBV and femicide. Cyberviolence is mentioned 18 times in the document.

These new laws criminalize this abusive behavior regardless of the victim's age or the context in which the images were originally taken. In addition to the new laws, any existing laws may be used to hold the abuser accountable. Harassment, stalking, illegal surveillance, illegal access to electronic information, unauthorized recording/taping, impersonation, identity theft, and privacy or confidentiality violations are some of the offenses that the laws can and have been used depending on the details of the case. Victims can rely on other criminal and/or civil law remedies to obtain some form of legal recourse, such as a protection order. They can also report crimes incidental to cyberbullying, like crimen injuria, sexual exploitation and grooming, and criminal defamation.

3.8 Suggestions to Prevent and Counter Online Violence

Efforts to prevent and counter online violence and bring perpetrators to book fall under the general umbrella of measures to combat general VAWG. The UN Women Annual Report 2019–2020 (2020) recommended allocating additional resources, including evidence-based measures to address VAWG and strengthen services for women who experienced violence during COVID-19. Other recommendations are building the capacity of key services to improve the quality of response; putting women at the center of policy change, solutions, and recovery, and ensuring that sex-disaggregated data are collected to understand the impact of COVID-19 on VAWG to inform the response and integrating GBV prevention into women's socio-economic empowerment initiatives.

Empowerment initiatives can only be effective if safety protocols are put in place by relevant stakeholders who are significant digital gatekeepers. The stakeholders include mobile phone companies, Internet service providers, online dating and gaming sites, social networking sites, website operators, and software developers. Technology-based enterprises need to identify cyber VAWG as a crime and demonstrate increased and expedited cooperation in providing relief to victims/survivors within the capacities that companies have. Social media platforms should be transparent about the effectiveness of their algorithms, conduct regular reviews, and work to ensure that they are sensitive to diverse cultural contexts. There should be better systems for cooperating with law enforcement. People need more control over their settings, especially privacy settings, and there should be more effective takedown procedures for abusive and harmful content. The possibility of account suspension and other actions for misconduct should be used as a deterrent.

All the suggestions above require funding. Gender budgeting is an initiative by the International Monetary Fund (IMF) that uses fiscal policy and administration to address gender inequality and women's advancement (Stotsky, 2016). SSA countries were among the earliest countries to adopt gender budgeting with mixed success. Some successes have been achieved in South Africa, Rwanda, and Uganda. Leadership by the finance ministry and input from other stakeholders, namely NGOs and donors, are some of the key success factors. UNCTAD's (n.d.) "Cybercrime legislation" maintains that the importance of leadership was demonstrated with the waning of gender budgeting efforts in South Africa due to changes in parliamentarians. It is important to continue contributing funds for conducting research. In early 2019, the End Violence Partnership[4] invested $6.6 million to develop *Disrupting Harm*, a holistic and innovative method and approach to conducting comprehensive assessments of online child sexual exploitation and abuse at national and regional

[4]The Global Partnership and Fund to End Violence Against Children were launched in July 2016 by the UN Secretary-General. The Partnership is the only global entity focused solely on Sustainable Development Goal 16.2: ending all forms of violence against children by 2030. The End Violence Partnership is a platform for collective, evidence-based advocacy and action (https://www.end-violence.org/who-we-are).

levels. *End Violence* brought together and funded three organizations, namely End Child Prostitution and Trafficking (ECPAT International), Interpol, and UNICEF, to research and assess the nature of online violence in 14 countries across Eastern and Southern Africa and Southeast Asia. Efforts like this should be continued.

Lastly, law enforcement agencies should be made to produce transparent reports of records specific to cyber VAWG, detailing how and when they have responded. Technology companies should form global and cross-platform collaboration and best practices to fight cyber VAWG. Furthermore, there should be educative preventative measures through public sensitization. People need to be taught to protect themselves online and report abuse. There should be a change in social attitudes and norms in shifting the way online abuse is understood and the seriousness with which it should be treated. It is also important to put in place and enforce sanctions through courts and legal systems to define and enforce compliance and effective punitive consequences for perpetrators. We recommend that the various stakeholders, i.e., law enforcement, legislators, anticrime commissions, and researchers, liaise to share data and knowledge to promulgate laws and policies on protecting women and girls online in line with the current technological development and use.

3.9 Conclusion

Incidents of violence perpetrated through digital technology platforms or facilitated by these means have been reported, often in high-income countries. Very little scholarly attention has been given to the nature of cyber VAWG across SSA despite an explosion in the use of various technologies. The paucity of data from SSA needs to be corrected to ensure that the region also benefits from research findings and international aids. This study focused on violence against women, specifically on Internet VAWG, and concluded that many of these atrocities go unreported for various reasons. The influence on the victim's emotional, financial, and overall well-being varies from person to person, and victims use numerous methods to cope with cyberviolence, including blocking the abuser or deleting the abused profile on social media.

The overwhelming importance of the Internet to the development and the economy of any country in the current information age cannot be overemphasized. However, despite the many advantages of technology on a country's economy and populace, there are emerging negative consequences of using technology that require additional investigation on their dimensions and consequences and possible action to mitigate their effect. Cyberviolence in SSA has emerged as one of these consequences. It has been increasingly studied in developed countries that birthed and embraced the widespread use of ICT long before SSA countries.

This chapter was concerned with the incidence of VAWG in SSA and stakeholders involved in the fight against cyber VAWG. It also aimed at discussing the present situation in SSA regarding laws, policies, legislation, and how they are implemented. Thus far, the steps taken by the government and stakeholders have not been successful in informing, supporting, and protecting the victims of cyberviolence and holding perpetrators accountable. Since cyber VAWG is a cross-border crime, we recommend that other researchers replicate, share, and provide their findings in all corners of the globe to create a safe cyberspace for women and girls.

References

Aborisade, R. A. (2021). Image-based sexual abuse in a culturally conservative Nigerian society: Female victims' narratives of psychosocial costs. *Sexuality Research and Social Policy, 19*(1), 1–13.

Agwe-Mbarika, E., Akuta, E., Ong'oa, I., & Jones, C. (2011). Combating cyber crime in sub-Sahara Africa; a discourse on law, policy and practice. *Journal of Peace, Gender and Development Studies*. Retrieved from https://www.researchgate.net/publication/267994503_Combating_Cyber_Crime_in_Sub-Sahara_Africa_A_Discourse_on_Law_Policy_and_Practice

Aker, J. C. (2010). Information from markets near and far: Mobile phones and agricultural markets in Niger. *American Economic Journal: Applied Economics, 2*(3), 46–59.

Black, M. C., Basile, K. C., & Breiding, M. J. (2010). *The National Intimate Partner and sexual violence survey (NISVS): Summary report* (p. 2011). Center for Disease Control and Prevention.

Burney, E. (2009). Making people behave: Anti-social behaviour. Politics and policy. In N. Chakraborti & J. Garland (Eds.), *Hate crime: Impact, causes and responses* (2nd ed.). Sage.

Council of Europe. (2018). Cybercrime convention committee (T-CY) working group on cyberbullying and other forms of online violence, especially against women and children. *Mapping study on cyberviolence*. Retrieved August 21, 2021 from https://rm.coe.int/t-cy-mapping-study-on-cyberviolence-final/1680a1307c

Council of Europe. (n.d.). *Types of cyberviolence*. Retrieved August 21, 2021 from https://www.coe.int/en/web/cyberviolence/types-ofcyberviolence#:~:text=Cyberviolence%20may%20also%20involve%20direct,of%20a%20combination%20of%20acts

Edwards, M., Suarez-Tangil, G., Peersman, C., Stringhini, G., Rashid, A., & Whitty, M. (2018). The geography of online dating fraud. *In Workshop on technology and consumer protection (ConPro)* (Vol. 7). IEEE.

European Institute for Gender Equality. (2017). *Cyber violence is a growing threat, especially for women and girls*. Publication date 19 June 2017. Retrieved from https://eige.europa.eu/news/cyber-violence-growing-threat-especially-women-and-girls

Facebook Newsroom. (2017). *Hard questions: Who should decide what is hate speech in an online global community?* Retrieved August 21, 2021 from https://newsroom.fb.com/news/2017/06/hard-questions-hate-speech/

FAO. (1995). *A synthesis report of the Africa Region - Women, agriculture and rural development*. Retrieved August 21, 2021 from https://www.fao.org/3/x0250e/x0250e00.htm#TopOfPage

FRA. (2014). *Violence against women: An EU-wide survey*. Main results report, 29, 95. Retrieved from http://fra.europa.eu/en/publication/2014/violence-against-women-eu-widesurvey-main-results-report.

Gilbert, P. Connecting Africa. Strong mobile growth predicted for sub-Saharan Africa – GSMA. Publication date 30 September 2020. Retrieved August 21, 2021 from http://www.connectingafrica.com/author.asp?section_id=761&doc_id=764310

Harvard Medical School. Centre for Primary Care. (2020, May 1). *A second, silent pandemic: Sexual violence in the time of COVID-19*. Retrieved June 16, 2021 from http://info.primarycare.hms.harvard.edu/blog/sexual-violence-and-covid

Internet Watch Foundation (IWF). (May 2018). *Trends in online child sexual exploitation: Examining the distribution of captures of live-streamed child sexual abuse.* Retrieved August 21, 2021 from https://www.iwf.org.uk/sites/default/files/inline-files/Distribution%20of%20Captures%20of%20Live-streamed%20Child%20Sexual%20Abuse%20FINAL.pdf

Johnson, C. (2020) *How are human traffickers taking advantage of the pandemic?* Retrieved on August 10, 2022 from https://www.reuters.com/article/us-global-trafficking-expertview-idUSKBN27300T

Joleby, M., Lunde, C., Landström, S., & Jonsson, L. S. (2020). All of me is completely different: Experiences and consequences among victims of technology-assisted child sexual abuse. *Frontiers in Psychology, 11*, 3432.

La Rue, F. (2011). *Report of the special rapporteur on the promotion and protection of the right to freedom of opinion and expression.* Retrieved February 12, 2021 from https://www.scribd.com/document/56634085/Report-of-the-Special-Rapporteur-on-the-promotion-and-protection-of-the-right-to-freedom-of-opinion-and-expression-Frank-La-Rue

Lassri, D., Luyten, P., Fonagy, P., & Shahar, G. (2018). Undetected scars? Self-criticism, attachment, and romantic relationships among otherwise well-functioning childhood sexual abuse survivors. *Psychological Trauma: Theory, Research, Practice, and Policy, 10*(1), 121–129. https://doi.org/10.1037/tra0000271

Lenhart, A., Ybarra, M., Zickuhr, K., & Price-Feeney, M. (2016). *Online harassment, digital abuse, and cyberstalking in America.* Retrieved from http://datasociety.net/pubs/oh/Online_Harassment_2016.pdf

Madanda, A., Berna, N., & Amuriat, G. Z. (2009). *Uganda: Violence against women and information and communication technologies*. Association for Progressive Communications (APC).

Makinde, O. A., Odimegwu, C. O., Abdulmalik, J. O., Babalola, S. O., & Fawole, O. I. (2016). Gender-based violence following social media acquaintance in Nigeria. *African Journal of Reproductive Health, 20*(4), 67–76.

Makinde, O. A., Olamijuwon, E., Ichegbo, N. K., Onyemelukwe, C., & Ilesanmi, M. G. (2021). The nature of technology-facilitated violence and abuse among young adults in sub-Saharan Africa. *The Emerald International Handbook of Technology-Facilitated Violence and Abuse*, 83–101.

McGlynn, C., & Downes, K. (2015, April 15). We need a new law to combat "upskirting" and "downblousing". *Inherently Human.* https://inherentlyhuman.wordpress.com/2015/04/15/we-need-a-new-law-to-combat-upskirting-and-downblousing/

McGlynn, C., & Rackley, E. (2015, November 18). New law on 'revenge pornography' is unlikely to tackle hackers distributing intimate images. *Holyrood.* https://www.holyrood.com/articles/comment/new-law-revenge-porn-unlikely-tackle-hackers-distributing-intimate-images

McGlynn, C., & Rackley, E. (2016a). *Not revenge porn but abuse: Let's call it image-based sexual abuse.* Everyday Victim Blaming, 9 March. http://everydayvictimblaming.com/news/notrevenge-porn-but-abuse-lets-call-it-image-based-sexual-abuse-by-%E2%80%8Fmcglynnclareerikarackley

McGlynn, C., & Rackley, E. (2016b). *Research briefing: Image-based sexual abuse: More than just revenge porn.* https://claremcglynn.com/revenge-pornography/revenge-pornography-quick-reads/

McGlynn, C., & Rackley, E. (2017). Image-based sexual abuse. *Oxford Journal of Legal Studies, 37*, 1–17. https://doi.org/10.1093/ojls/gqw033

Mtema, Z., Changalucha, J., Cleaveland, S., Elias, M., Ferguson, H. M., Jo, E., & Hampson, K. (2016). Mobile phones as surveillance tools: Implementing and evaluating a large-scale intersectoral surveillance system for rabies in Tanzania. *PLoS Medicine, 13*(4), e1002002.

Muridzo, N. G., & Chikadzi, V. (2020). Zimbabwe's poverty and child sexual abuse. *Children Australia, 45*(4), 222–228.

Olumide, A. O., Adams, P., & Amodu, O. K. (2015). International note: Awareness and context of cyber-harassment among secondary school students in Oyo state, Nigeria. *Journal of Adolescence, 39*, 10–14.

Pathe, M., & Mullen, P. E. (1997). The impact of stalkers on their victims. *The British Journal of Psychiatry, 170*(1), 12–17.

Project DeShame. (2017). *Young people's experiences of online sexual harassment.* Retrieved June 23, 2021 from https://www.childnet.com/wp-content/uploads/2021/11/Project_deSHAME_Dec_2017_Report.pdf

Rentschler, C. (2015). # Safetytipsforladies: Feminist twitter takedowns of victim blaming. *Feminist Media Studies, 15*(2), 353–356.

Silver, L., & Cortney, J. (2018). *Internet connectivity seen as having a positive impact on life in sub-Saharan Africa.* But digital divides persist. Pew Research Centre. Retrieved August 12, 2021 from https://www.pewresearch.org/global/2018/10/09/internet-connectivity-seen-as-having-positive-impact-on-life-in-sub-saharan-africa/

Sossou, M. A., & Yogtiba, J. A. (2009). Abuse of children in West Africa: Implications for social work education and practice. *British Journal of Social Work, 39*(7), 1218–1234.

Stotsky, J. G. (2016). *Gender budgeting: Fiscal context and current outcomes.* Paper by the International Monetary Fund. Retrieved on June 22, 2021 from https://www.imf.org/en/Publications/WP/Issues/2016/12/31/Gender-Budgeting-Fiscal-Context-and-Current-Outcomes-44132

Twitter Help Center. (n.d.). *Abusive behavior.* Retrieved on August 22, 2021 from https://help.twitter.com/en/rules-and-policies/abusive-behavior

UN Broadband Commission. (2015). *Cyber violence against women and girls: A worldwide wake-up call.* Retrieved June 15, 2021 from http://www.unwomen.org/-/media/headquarters /attachments/sections/library/publications/2015/cyber_violence_gender%20report.pdf?vs=4259

UN News. (2020). *Social media-based trafficking on the rise during coronavirus pandemic.* Retrieved August 15, 2021 from https://news.un.org/en/story/2020/11/1077402

UN Woman Annual Report (2019–2020). UN Women headquarters. (2020) *The world for women and girls.* Retrieved July 08, 2022 from https://www.unwomen.org/en/digital-library/publications/2020/06/annual-report-2019-2020

UN Women Headquarters. (2020). *From insights to action: Gender equality in the wake of Covid-19.* United Nations entity for gender equality and the empowerment of women (UN Women). Retrieved June 15, 2021 from https://www.unwomen.org/en/digital-library/publications/2020/09/gender-equality-in-the-wake-of-covid-19

UNCTAD. (n.d.). *United Nations conference on trade and development.* Cybercrime legislation worldwide. Retrieved August 14, 2021 from https://unctad.org/page/cybercrime-legislation-worldwide

US Department of State. (2020). *Trafficking in persons report: Kenya.* Retrieved June 16, 2021 from https://www.state.gov/reports/2020-trafficking-in-persons-report/kenya/

World Health Organization. (2020). *Covid-19 spurts health innovation in Africa.* (2020, October 29). Retrieved June 15, 2021 from https://www.afro.who.int/news/covid-19-spurs-health-innovation-africa

World Vision. (2020). *Adolescent pregnancy threatens to block a million girls across sub-Saharan Africa from returning to school.* Retrieved June 15, 2021 from https://www.wvi.org/sites/default /files/2020-08/Covid19%20Aftershocks_Access%20Denied_small.pdf

Yang, S., Fichman, P., Zhu, X., Sanfilippo, M., Li, S., & Fleischmann, K. R. (2020). The use of ICT during *COVID-19. Proceedings of the Association for Information Science and Technology, 57*(1), e297. Retrieved from. https://doi.org/10.1002/pra2.297

Zauner, J. (2021). The continuum of symbolic violence: How sexting education neglects image-based sexual abuse, dismisses perpetrators' responsibility, and violates rights to sexual autonomy. *Journal of Gender-Based Violence, 5*(3), 483–498.

Anke Brand , Ph.D. is a respected Speaker, Researcher, Consultant, and author on the pressing issues of technology and its devastating effects on people. She obtained her Bachelor's degree in Commerce from the University of Pretoria (UP) and a second Bachelor's degree in Ministry from Christian Life Training, a Master's degree (Cum Laude) in Christian Counselling from Calvary University, and a Ph.D. in Theology (Cum Laude) with specialization in digital addiction from St. Clements Private Swiss University. She is currently enrolled at Calvary University for a Ph.D. in Interdisciplinary Studies. She has extensive academic and professional knowledge of problematic computer use and Internet addiction. Based on years of experience with clients suffering from Internet addiction, she equips people of all ages with strategies and techniques for the prevention, reduction, and interventions against addictive digital behaviors. She works with school organizations, churches, and law enforcement agencies through a private counseling practice alongside her research and writing. She is currently the Research and Development Director at the Southern African Higher Christian Education Trust (SAHCET). She is passionate about digital addiction, research, and ministry.

Adebola Fawole , Ph.D. is a Teacher, Researcher, Educational Consultant, Administrator, and Writer. She obtained her Bachelor's degree in English from the University of Ilorin, her Master's degree in Language and Communications Arts from the University of Ibadan, Postgraduate Certificate in Education (PGCE) from the University of Pretoria (UP), and her Ph.D. in Translation Studies and Linguistics from the University of Limpopo. She is currently the Academic Director at the Southern African Higher Christian Education Trust (SAHCET). She is also involved in editing, tutoring, and teaching English and Yoruba languages online. She has published several articles in Department of Higher Education and Training (DHET) accredited journals. Her research interests include identity in language use, teaching, learning, and use of language in diverse cultural, linguistic, and professional environments and communication in gendered spaces. She is an avid reader, poet, and advocate for women and children-related issues.

Chapter 4
Young Masculinities and Violence in South Africa: Reflections on the Literature

Madeline Gerber, Sofi Le Berre, and Denise Buiten

4.1 Introduction

Much recent work on violence in South Africa, particularly violence against women and girls, has stressed the importance of constructions and practices of masculinity in producing and sustaining violence (see, for example, Bantjes & Nieuwoudt, 2014; Bhana & Chen, 2020; Edelstein, 2018; Gqola, 2007; Jewkes et al., 2010; Wood et al., 2008). When a widely publicized study revealed that over a quarter of South African men surveyed had admitted to committing rape and that the majority of these had first committed it in their teens (Jewkes et al., 2010), the question of young masculinities and violence garnered international attention as a social problem. Since then, a substantial body of work has continued to examine the role of young masculinities in the perpetration of violence (see, for example, Bhana & Mayeza, 2019; Gqola, 2015; Graaff & Heinecken, 2017; Jewkes & Morrell, 2018).

Within this matrix of work, reflecting on how young masculinities have been constructed within scholarship is important and timely. This chapter presents a literature review of recent work on violence in relation to boys and male youth[1] in South Africa, identifying key themes in the construction of young masculinity within a corpus of literature. While our focal interest is on the construction of boys in research, we also include work pertaining to male youth (up to 24 years old), given

[1] This paper focuses on the literature related to boys and young men aged 3 years to 24 years. This is detailed in the research methodology.

M. Gerber · S. Le Berre
School of Arts and Sciences, The University of Notre Dame Australia, Sydney, Australia
e-mail: madeline.gerber@my.nd.edu.au; sofi.le.berre@my.nd.edu.au

D. Buiten (✉)
Department of Sociology, University of Johannesburg, Johannesburg, South Africa
e-mail: denise.buiten@nd.edu.au

K. Naidoo et al. (eds.), *Young People, Violence and Strategic Interventions in Sub-Saharan Africa*, Clinical Sociology: Research and Practice,
https://doi.org/10.1007/978-3-031-20679-5_4

that much work in this area overlaps. Our question is: how does recent literature on boys' and male youth's experiences and/or use of violence in South Africa construct young masculinities and their relationship to violence? Further, what implications do they have in terms of how young South African masculinities are understood (Bacchi, 2009)?

We highlight the rich intersectional, empirical, and critical studies on young masculinities that have been undertaken in South Africa—works that strongly contextualize the production of violence as a normative feature of hegemonic masculinity at three interrelated levels—the micro, meso, and macro. Much work on young masculinities and violence in South Africa pays sharp attention to context and temporality, locating young South African masculinities within histories of colonial and apartheid violence and the marginalizing structures these processes produced (for example, Bantjes et al., 2017; Bhana & Mayeza, 2016; Gibbs et al., 2015; Sedite et al., 2010; Wood, 2005). We argue that the literature examined in the current review offers a robustly contextualized account of young masculinities and their relationship to violence. We found, however, that there was a relative scarcity of work investigating various boys' and male youth's resistance to hegemonic masculinity, examining the place of more varied and subordinated masculine subjects and expressions of masculinity, and researching violence (in its myriad forms) among racially and economically privileged boys and youth. Violence among economically and racially marginalized boys and youth was largely represented as a feature of hegemonic masculinity and a means to attain it when social structures threatened their power. Simultaneously, economically and racially privileged masculinities and their relationship to violence remained largely uninterrogated. The consequences of this pattern in the literature are, we argue, to inadvertently reify constructions of poor, black South African boys, and youth as invariably (and obdurately) violent, implicitly constructing marginality as violence-prone and privilege as violence-resistant (Roberts & Elliott, 2020). Frequently situating the violence perpetrated by marginalized boys and youth as an expression of hegemonic masculinity while also leaving the violent practices of powerful groups on the fringes of research can collectively operate to represent marginal boys as hegemonic (Ratele, 2014) mistakenly. Further, focusing primarily on practices that align with hegemonic constructions of masculinity can silence opportunities for (and contemporary practices of) caring masculinities and social change, especially from within the margin.

That said, we point to an expanding body of work that contributes to addressing these concerns, work that considers boys' and young men's experiences along other vectors of marginality and that examines the diversity of boys' relationships to gendered norms and practices, including resistance strategies against heteronormative gender norms, and the social reflexivity and caring practices that some boys and young men engage in. Further such work can contribute to identifying sites for discursive intervention (and disruption) of violent masculinities, locate practices of solidarity and caring from which interventions against gendered violence can build, and strengthen feminist research in the study of boys that is at once critical of patriarchy and affirming of the diversity and complexity of boys' experiences (Laurie et al., 2021). Along with this important work, we consider how further intersectional work on young masculinities and violence beyond the margin can contribute to interrogating the relationship between power and violence, testing implicit assumptions that violence in marginality means that greater economic, racialized, or social power for boys and young men will ameliorate violence against women and girls (Roberts & Elliott, 2020).

4.2 Methodology

The literature review involved gathering recent publications (published between January 2005 and August 2021)[2] on South African boys and male youth (defined as ages 3–24) that referenced violence issues. We chose this period to capture a sample that would reflect more recent scholarly conversations about young masculinities and violence in South Africa. The age group, while broad, captured the work being done in the field, which often traverses across categories such as "children" and "young people" and reflects a range of spheres of influence throughout the lives of boys in South Africa up to when they become young men. Focusing on "boys" as children and "male youth" enabled us to gain a wider perspective on how scholarship treats gendered socialization processes. We searched for the terms "boys," "male youth," "youth," and "masculinity" in conjunction with "violence" and "South Africa." Initially, we aimed to focus on literature pertaining to "boys" as research subjects. However, we noted that much literature referencing boys did not directly examine them as subjects; boyhood was most often mentioned in relation to studies on men. Adding the term "school" to our search achieved a more relevant set of results that focused on younger masculinities. This was likely for reasons relevant to other international contexts, namely that research involving children is often conducted through schools for a range of ethical and practical reasons. Often, such studies attending to boys as subjects included male youth (18–24 years), for example, where male youth formed part of school populations under study. As such, we note that the literature examined here references both boys and male youth. While the addition of "schools" enabled a greater focus on younger masculinities, we also acknowledge the potential to exclude some studies on boys that may not reference boys' experience with schools and were, therefore, potentially not included (Table 4.1).

We gathered literature across four databases: Scopus, JSTOR, EBSCOhost, and Sage Publications. These databases were selected for their accessibility, user-friendliness, and overall relevance to the search results yielded. Each database had a unique interface and different refinement tools. Therefore, while the criteria for inclusion remained the same across databases, we found we had to adjust aspects of the search protocol across databases to yield the most relevant and manageable

[2]The search was conducted between 23 June 2001 and 6 August 2021.

Table 4.1 Searches conducted as part of the review by keyword

Database	Scopus	EBSCOhost	Sage	JSTOR
Search terms	i. "Boys + School + Violence + South Africa" ii. "Masculinity + School + Violence + South Africa" iii. "Boys + Masculinity + Violence + School + South Africa"	i. "Boys + Violence + School + Masculinity + South Africa" ii. "Boys + Violence + Masculinity + Youth + South Africa + School"	i. "Boys + School + Violence + South Africa" ii. "Boys + Masculinity + Youth + School + Violence + South Africa" iii. "Male Youth + Southern Africa + Violence"	i. "Youth + Boys + Masculinity + School + Violence + South Africa" ii. "Boys + School + Violence + South Africa"
Refinement by year	2005–2021 (July)	2005–2021 (July)	2005–2021 (July)	2005–2021 (July)
Further refinements	n/a	i. Arts Databases + Academic Search Ultimate; Geography (South Africa) ii. Academic Search Ultimate + Sociology Source Ultimate; Geography (South Africa)	i. Source type (research article); Subject (Social Sciences and Humanities) ii. Source type (research article); Subject (Social Sciences and Humanities) iii. Top results (pages 1–5)	i. Sociology + Cultural Studies + Feminist and women's studies + Gender studies + top results (pages 1–8) ii. Top results (pages 1–5)

dataset for qualitative analysis. Databases that produced large volumes of search results or captured a high number of results that did not fit within the parameters of the research question required additional refinements. While Scopus, for example, produced a smaller number of results, most of which were relevant to the question, other databases produced over 10,000 results for the same search terms, many of which did not meet inclusion criteria, and further refinements were required. We were most interested in how the *social* problem of boys' experiences and/or use of violence was constructed. Therefore, refinements were generally applied by area or subject (social sciences such as sociology, for instance) to distill search results down. We acknowledge that results from subject areas outside of these (such as medical journals) may have been disadvantaged within the review. Results were triangulated to delete any duplicates and subjected to a rating process[3] with respect to their relevance in terms of (a) focusing on the South African context, (b) focusing on boys

[3]The rating system was based on EndNote X9's zero (0)–five (5) stars rating function, including only articles rated as four or five stars. Articles with four or five stars were focused on the South African context, had as either key subjects (four stars) or sole subjects (five stars) boys and male youth, and focused on their use and/or experiences of violence.

or younger masculinities as subjects, and (c) discussing their relationship to issues of violence. The final sample of literature was 160 articles.

Discourse analysis was applied to the literature, using Bacchi's (2009) What's the Problem Represented (WPR) framework. This framework was developed to analyze policy representations of social problems critically but has also been applied in research on representations in news media (for example, Buiten, 2020; Zufferey, 2014) and academic scholarship (for example, Buiten & Naidoo, 2016). For Bacchi (2009), all representations—whether in policy, media, or academic texts—involve interpretations and choices that actively construct social "problems" in particular ways. Further, the discursive production of social problems that are engendered by these representations affects our ability to understand social problems in particular ways, on how the subjects of social problems are viewed (by others and themselves), and on lived experience where discourse shapes policy and practice. Bacchi's (2009) framework for discourse analysis offers several interrelated questions adapted to the research topic and applied to representations to identify ways of framing the issue. In this case, the following questions were asked regarding the dataset:

- What is the "problem" of violence as experienced and/or perpetrated by young masculinities in South Africa represented to be?
- What assumptions or presuppositions about young masculinity and violence are embedded within these representations?
- What is silenced or left unemblematic in these accounts?
- How do these representations come about, and how might they be questioned, disrupted, or replaced?

4.3 Overview of the Literature

The study of violence and young masculinities in South Africa spanned a range of disciplines, most commonly disciplines within the social sciences, and appeared in local and international publications. However, the majority appeared in the latter.[4] While work within sociology, cultural studies, and studies in sexuality and gender were prominent, a range of work was also captured from the fields of health, psychology, and education. The relative scale of engagement on this topic within health and medical journals strongly emphasized gendered violence as a public health issue, particularly in relation to HIV. Most studies examined boys and girls side-by-side in particular contexts, with comparatively few studies pertaining solely to boys or girls. In this way, relational analyses of gender prevailed. It is worth observing that compared to work on adult men and masculinities, where men as subjects are often the focus of research, less work has been explicitly dedicated to boys as the primary subjects of the research.

[4]Thirty-two of the articles reviewed came from African journals, of which 16 were published in South African journals.

Empirical studies involving fieldwork dominated the literature, with comparatively few theoretical studies (Morrell et al., 2012; Pasura & Christou, 2018; Ratele, 2014). Within the fields of sociology, gender, and educational studies, ethnographic studies were common, directly observing boys and youth in their interactions with others. Publications from the fields of health and psychology more frequently deployed quantitative survey studies. However, gender theory was widely applied in empirical research across a range of disciplines, including Connell's (1983, 1995) concept of hegemonic masculinity (Morrell et al., 2013) and other frameworks from within critical men and masculinities studies. Overall, there was a deep appreciation across a range of disciplines regarding the importance of gender, in sociological terms, in constructing boys' identities, experiences, and practices. Indeed, Connell's framework of hegemonic masculinity appears to have become a core basis for much scholarly discourse on male youth and gendered violence in South Africa (Buiten & Naidoo, 2016; Morrell et al., 2013; Ratele, 2014) across a range of disciplines ranging from psychology and sociology to education and health. Connell (1995, p. 77) defines hegemonic masculinity as "the configuration of gender practice which embodies the currently accepted answer to the problem of the legitimacy of patriarchy which guarantees (or is taken to guarantee) the dominant position of men and the subordination of women." Connell's concept of hegemonic masculinity, while attending to gender and relations of power and patriarchy (and notably the role of violence in hegemonic gender practice), also stresses the hierarchies constructed between men and the way some masculinities are subordinated to others across a range of social vectors. As such, as a concept, it has been popularly applied not only within sociological and feminist research and its cognate fields but also extensively in the fields of public health and psychology, offering a tool through which to examine both the problem of male violence and the varied and intersecting vectors of privilege and marginality that characterize South African boys' and men's experiences (Morrell et al., 2013).

Intersectional analyses were widely applied, considering young masculinities at the nexus of race, class, and to some extent, age. There was a temporal dimension to much of the research, which frequently situated the experiences and identities of boys and male youth within a post-apartheid context and its attendant political, social, and economic legacies. The combined depth and breadth of empirical work and the application of an intersectional and historically attuned gender lens produced a literature that was, overall, deeply grounded in context, examining masculinity in a way that placed it in geographic, historical, and political perspective. Reflected here, as noted elsewhere, was the tendency within scholarship from within the global South to be "more consistently attuned to these intersecting dimensions" toward understanding gendered violence (Buiten & Naidoo, 2020, p. 6).

While various forms of violence were examined in the literature, including work on the perpetration and experience of bullying, harassment, and corporal punishment, boys' and young men's perpetration of sexual violence against women and girls was the most common analysis point. Few studies examined boys as victims of sexual violence, though some acknowledged that boys could be victims, for instance, at the hands of teachers (Chabaya et al., 2009). A small number of more recent studies attended to boys as victims of sexual violence and coercion at the hands of women and (often older) girls (Kramer & Bowman, 2021; Miller et al., 2021). While this issue is relatively rare compared to male sexual violence against women and children, as Kramer and Bowman (2021) point out, it is a subject that needs further research. More broadly, boys' experiences of violence of various forms and girls' perpetration of violence were identified as needing more research (Bhana, 2008; Dziewanski, 2020). Boys as subjects were implicitly represented as both the primary perpetrators of violence and victims of the violent contexts in which they are situated. While not always identified as direct victims of "violence" themselves, research on the prevalence of "bullying" and "corporal punishment" as well as verbal abuse, suggests that boys are subject to violence in a range of ways (Chitsamatanga & Rembe, 2020; Mayeza & Bhana, 2021). Overall, the corpus of literature positioned boys and male youth simultaneously as objects of harm and as current and future risks to women and girls.

4.4 Multi-level Analyses of Gender and Violence

The breadth and depth of contextually situated work in this area were reflected in the way studies spanned multiple levels of analysis. Scholarship confirms the experiences of violence and harm and the etiology of young male violence at three interrelated levels. At the micro-level, much research examined boys' experience of trauma, abuse, and exposure to violence within the household and extended family, as well as the household as a site in which gender norms and divisions of labor are formed and practiced (Bojuwoye & Sylvester, 2012; Edelstein, 2018). Much work in this vein suggested "absent fathers" or damaged relationships with fathers as central to understanding the origins of harmful and risky masculinities (Anderson, 2010).

At the meso level, a prolific body of work examined schools as a "social-political terrain" (Bhana & Mayeza, 2016, p. 41) for the (re)production of gender and violence (Bantjes & Nieuwoudt, 2014; Bhana, 2015; Chitsamatanga & Rembe, 2020). The school's institutional culture was often identified as having a significant influence on the learning and performance of gender, particularly hegemonic masculinity and the reproduction of gender inequalities. Research into violent practices within schools, from "bullying" and "corporal punishment" to sexual abuse and harassment, suggested that young masculinities are cultivated within a range of violent contexts, including school spaces (Chitsamatanga & Rembe, 2020).

However, much research on young masculinities also contextualized violence and gender norms at the micro- and meso levels within a broader macro-level context of gender, power, and violence. In particular, the interlocking roles of class, race, and gender were deeply embedded within analyses, whether intersectionality (Crenshaw, 1991) as a framework was explicitly or implicitly applied (Colpitts, 2019; Helman & Ratele, 2016). A key theme in the literature, as observed elsewhere, was the way South African masculinities are shaped by histories of colonialism and apartheid, entrenched racism, poverty, economic disempowerment and unemployment, gender inequality, and state failure (Buiten & Naidoo, 2016). Within these social conditions, high rates of violence were understood to have become an endemic element of South African society and culture. This broader context was understood to translate to the interpersonal level, where violence was suggested as a key tool for marginalized boys and male youth, particularly poor black boys and youth, to reckon with the structural violence they experience (Jewkes et al., 2016; Walker, 2005; Wood, 2005).

In much work, the notion of a "crisis" of masculinity was invoked to explain boys and youth violence. This was at times referenced more explicitly[5] or through references to the "reworking" of masculinities in a context described as a state of "limbo" (Bantjes et al., 2017, p. 238)—a context at once *post-* (post-colonial, post-apartheid) while characterized by tremendous racialized inequalities. Violence among young men and boys was, in this context, often represented as a means of seeking or acquiring power, social mobility and normative masculinity, and navigating socialization into manhood within a fractured social, economic, and political context (Gibbs et al., 2015; Jewkes et al., 2016; Walker, 2005).[6] Violence among racially and economically disadvantaged boys was therefore represented as a way of "doing" hegemonic masculinity in a context in which other normative performances of masculinity (for example, in providing for the family) are threatened by structural disadvantage and social flux.

As noted elsewhere, violent masculinities, including those of boys, were therefore largely linked in research "to socio-economic and political contexts, and tied to an economically and racially oppressive apartheid system that undermined gender norms and left the private sphere as the main space in which men can enact masculine dominance and power" (Buiten & Naidoo, 2016, p. 539). The literature examined broadly concluded that although poor black boys and male youth are not *inherently* violent, they are victims of social structures that inhibit their agency from resisting violent, hegemonic constructions of masculinity (Bhana & Chen, 2020; Govender et al., 2019).

4.5 Reflections on the Literature

The themes outlined above reflect richness in work on boys, male youth, and violence in South Africa, which has largely produced strongly contextualized empirical work that simultaneously takes gender seriously in understanding violence

[5] See, for example, Govender et al. (2019) for a critique of this discourse.

[6] It is worth noting that some work looks at similar issues with respect to white masculinities, particularly work that examines how white boys and men may seek out new tools for the maintenance of their social advantage in a changing context in which some other vectors of privilege are diminished (Rubin, 2013).

while being alert to the intersectional complexities of gender at multiple interacting levels. At the same time, we wish to draw attention to some collective patterns in the research that can, if they continue to be reproduced, operate to inadvertently reify particular constructions of marginalized boys and youth in the South. Here, we apply Bacchi's (2009) framework to consider some of the silences and implicit assumptions in this area's broader configuration of scholarly work. As Bacchi argues, all representations of social problems involve choices and interpretations—choices as to what to include and exclude, what to foreground and render to the periphery, and interpretations of the meanings and significance of the information available. These choices and interpretations lead to social problems being constructed in particular ways (Bacchi, 2009). Here, our aim is not to critique individual studies but to point to some of the ways collective patterns in the research on young masculinities and violence in South Africa produce a form of representation in themselves; that is, we examine some of the collective effects of a patterned set of choices and interpretations in the body of research in discursively constituting South African boy subjects. We reflect on the subjectification effects (Bacchi, 2009) of the given corpus of research—the way representation makes available a particular set of subject positions with implications for how social groups are perceived by themselves and others.

Overall, there was a general dearth of work examining the dynamics of more economically and racially privileged masculinities and violence in South Africa (Bhana, 2009; Buiten & Naidoo, 2016; Rubin, 2013). While the etiology of violence among economically disadvantaged boys was contextualized within this disadvantage, the production of violence among middle-class boys was, first, under-researched and, second, connected primarily to gender, assuming class to be less relevant to violence perpetration among those with class advantages. Regarding race, where scholarship did feature white boys, it was typically in multi-racial studies rather than centered on white masculinities, and discourses of violence and violent practices were largely absent from literature centering on the white boy subject. In contrast, an overwhelming focus of current scholarship was on young, poor, black boys and youth in rural areas and urban townships related to their practices of violence. There may be some important reasons for this. For example, suppose research suggested that gender-based violence (GBV) was more prevalent in such communities than in others (Jewkes et al., 2010), or the need to understand better various dynamics that shape marginalized boys and youth experiences. In that case, this may inform a focus on marginalized boys. Still, this pattern in the research is neither inevitable nor consequentially neutral.

For instance, while Jewkes et al.'s (2010) landmark study on rape revealed higher levels of self-reported rape among marginalized racial groups in South Africa, it also revealed notably high rates of self-reported rape-perpetration among racially and economically privileged men. Further, their study showed that higher levels of rape-perpetration were not neatly correlated with marginality, with greater perpetration among men who completed secondary school and entered tertiary education, for instance, than those who never completed high school (Ibid.). This reveals a more complex relationship between racial and economic marginality and gendered violence than is often assumed (Roberts et al., 2021; Roberts & Elliott, 2020). The relative overall scarcity of work on white and middle-class young South African masculinities and violence mistakenly reinforces presuppositions that gendered violence and other harmful practices of masculinity are entrenched within marginalized groups (Ratele, 2014) and leaves violence among privileged boys and youth unproblematic (Buiten & Naidoo, 2016).

Studies examining boys and male youth identifying with, practicing, or expressing alternative or subordinated forms of masculinity were scarce. While the contested and fluid nature of practices of masculinity was widely acknowledged and often sites of resistance to hegemonic masculinity examined, the work remained largely trained on boys and male youth who expressed or aspired to "hegemonic" forms of masculinity. Comparatively, little work examined boys who did not aspire to or were not capable of pursuing heteronormative forms of masculinity—lesbian, gay, bisexual, transgender, queer, and intersex (LGBTQI) boys, feminine boys, or boys who embrace alternative models of masculinity such as "caring" (Elliott, 2016; Ratele, 2015) or "nurturant" (Ratele et al., 2012) masculinities. There was also a general dearth of work on violence within LGBTQI relationships. More work considering boys' and male youth's experiences along other vectors of marginality and accounting for the diversity of their experiences as "boys" and youth as hierarchies of masculinities will be of value. Further, while there is some work on alternative masculinities—work that looks at contested meanings constructed around masculinity—it is seldom articulated with respect to understanding and addressing the experience and perpetration of and resistance to violence. Again, while there may be reasons for this, one of the potential collective representational effects (Bacchi, 2009) is to produce a largely monolithic masculine subject in conversations about gender and violence, further narrowing the scope for the cultural intelligibility of diverse masculinities in this context. This represents, in turn, a discursive effect through which "limits [are] imposed on what can be thought and said" (Bacchi, 2009, p. 15) and, therefore, on what is imagined possible with respect to interventions against violence.

4.6 Troubling Marginality and Hegemony in Research on Boys

Some work addresses the concerns we have raised and suggests an emergent pathway for research—work we draw attention to in the following section. Here, however, we wish to offer two considerations around some of the inadvertent figurations of South African boys that coalesce over time in the body of research examined. The first relates to the importance of not mistakenly representing marginalized young masculinities as hegemonic, as Ratele (2014) puts it. This results from a combined effect of (a) the profusion of research on economically and racially marginalized masculinities and violence, (b) the centering of the concept of hegemonic masculinity to understand economically and racialized marginalized masculinities[7] and their (actual or anticipated) practices of violence, and (c) the sidelining of privileged boys in research on gender and violence. The effect of these patterns in research can present an "upside down world" in which marginalized boys and youth are framed as hegemonic (Ahluwalia 2003, as cited in Ratele, 2014, p. 38). As Ratele reminds us, local gender hegemonies are marginal within the national and global capitalist patriarchy. Internally to localized spaces, some non-hegemonic identities and practices draw far less attention within research, such as caring and nurturant practices of masculinity. We see this in the dominance of a deficit discourse around black South African fathering, which frequently omits practices of care by diverse social (not just biological) fathers (Ratele et al., 2012). Non-hegemonic practices within the margin are not often subject to research (Roberts et al., 2021). Where subordinated, some alternative practices may require deeper excavation to examine, but their inclusion in studies on young masculinities and violence would be illuminating.

Further, it is important, as Laurie et al. (2021, p. 76) remind us, to "[draw] on feminist perspectives and concepts, without absorbing the category of boys into pre-existing discourses about adult men." Boys and youth are not equally positioned and require considered research and theorizing at the intersection of critical men and masculinities studies and the sociology of childhood to account for important dimensions and hierarchies regarding age. Doing this, as well as moving beyond primarily focusing on boys' expressions and pursuits of "hegemonic" masculinity, can also work to contest assumptions that "feminist critical theories are necessarily positioned against any holistic interest in boys' lives" (Laurie et al., 2021, p.76), a problem not only in the global North context in which Laurie et al. are writing but in South African contexts too.

The second main consideration we wish to raise is that a straightforward correlation between violence and marginality should not be assumed. This can be the outcome of collective patterns in the research, such as frequently researching marginal boys' and men's violence or applying an intersectional lens primarily to boys and male youth from the margin and not to other groups. It can also happen as a result of repeated conceptual connections between marginality and the pursuit of violent practices.

In terms of applying an intersectional lens, it is important to examine broader social, political, and economic contexts and histories to understand gendered identities and locations (Ratele, 2014). However, in much work on gender, there is often a tendency to do so primarily in relation to boys and men from the margin (Chandra, 2021; Ratele, 2014; Roberts & Elliott, 2020). This is a pattern in much international research, as Chandra (2021, p. 2) observes:

> ...while intersectionality can be a wonderful analytic framework for thinking about the complexities of oppression and subjectivity more broadly, it can also be highly problematic

[7] This concept is often applied in inconsistent ways, as Morrell et al. (2013) point out.

when it reproduces the expectation that [this] needs to be emphasized when talking about people of color, in a way not expected of white people.

Similarly, Roberts et al. (2021) caution that, when repeatedly applied to examine problematic constructions and practices of masculinity among men and boys "from the margin," at the expense of the application of an intersectional lens to more privileged masculinities, the "spirit" of intersectionality is undermined. That is, the intersectional theory was developed so that "inequalities are uncovered, highlighted and challenged," yet it is applied unevenly to problematic practices "in the margin."

The assumption that marginal boys' and men's use of violence is a compensation for a lost sense of power due to poverty and racism can inadvertently reinforce "prenotions" of marginalized masculinities as obdurately violent or unable to be agents of change—and in contrast, of white and middle-class boys and men as "bastions of progress" (Roberts & Elliott, 2020, p. 100). In other words, a proliferation of research focusing on marginality and violence can present a simpler correlation between the two than is the case. According to Jewkes et al.'s (2010) study, sexual violence was not highest among those with the lowest socio-economic and educational status. The relationship between marginality and masculine violence is complicated. Further research that troubles the correlation between marginality and violence can help challenge the often taken-for-granted assumptions in international research that powerful or privileged masculinities are more transformative or that emerging from marginality and accessing power will resolve violence. Further research on the transformative actualities and potential that may arise specifically from marginalities, such as caring practices among boys and men necessitated and/or enabled by social and economic conditions (Roberts et al., 2021), would contribute to troubling the assumptions of Roberts and Elliot and could help inform anti-violence interventions. As Ratele (2014) notes, there is a need to explore the transformative potential of boys from the margin.

4.7 Emerging Pathways of Research

While much work concentrated on the violent practices of black, marginalized boys and male youth and hegemonic masculinity practices within these communities, our research showed several scholars reflecting on the gaps this focus has produced and building a research agenda and body of work that address the concerns we have raised. This emerging body of work troubles the assumption that marginality is the primary producer of violent masculinity by examining non-hegemonic identities and practices of masculinity among marginalized boys and male youth and, secondly, researching violence among privileged boys and male youth. For instance, practices that reflect resistance to and rejection of hegemonic norms or engagement in caring practices and relationships are explored. Within this research, a greater level of agency in meaning-making and (re)production of gender and violence is highlighted, and boys are constructed as socially and emotionally reflexive with respect to gender

(Bhana & Mayeza, 2019; Govender et al., 2019; Helman & Ratele, 2016; Shefer, 2014; Sideris, 2004).

Many scholars flag the importance of engaging men and boys in more equitable caring relations and practices and how homogenizing representations of boys and men can limit their ability to engage in alternative practices of masculinity. For example, Gibbs et al. (2015) emphasize how expressing emotions and critical thinking around power imbalances in relationships challenge dominant forms of masculine identity. Collins (2013) explores the role of emotional reflexivity in reshaping aggressive masculinities and producing an environment of emotional self-awareness. Moosa and Bhana (2020) stress the importance of caring practices within schooling environments, which often act as sites for constructing dominant and hegemonic gender norms and developing a positive conceptualization of men in teaching roles who display a capacity for caring and understanding. Indeed, much literature discussed the importance of considering hegemonic practices and foregrounding resistance to violence and harmful hegemonic practices. Shefer (2014), for instance, advocates for the significance of work on how boys and young men resist dominant gender norms, practice alternative masculinities, and are invested in more equitable practices in their everyday life.

There is also increasing work on "other" boys. This is especially concerning boys whom their male peers regard as "unmasculine" and, as such, are subjugated to bullying, violence, and subordination but demonstrate reflexive resistance to gender norms and violent practices. Mayeza and Bhana's (2021, p. 47) recent work, for example, explores subordinated masculinities "not simply passive victims of the violence" but as demonstrating "the capacity for agency [...] evident in the ways they reflect upon how to resist and address the violent masculinities that plague them." Moreover, it considers how such boys live out complex gendered environments that are deeply inflected by age in their social and institutional location as boys. There is, as such, rich work that is already adding layers to our understanding of boys, gender, and violence, in a way that can challenge the reification of marginality as a source of violence and treats boys and young men as agentic, complex human subjects who encounter and express a range of gendered practices.

4.8 Conclusion

There are some collective gaps and areas of focus in the research that unintentionally reinscribe notions of marginal young masculinities as obdurately violent (even if that violence is cast as an outcome of marginality). However, a growing body of work contributes to challenging this assumption and to identifying and building on sites for the disruption of violent practices of masculinity in a way that recognizes and is critical of patriarchal relations while affirming variations and nuances in boys' and young men's experiences. There is a growing body of affirmative feminist boys' studies in South Africa (Laurie et al., 2021). Building on this work can productively complicate our understanding of the relationship between marginality, power, and violence—and the diverse location of young masculinities within and experiences of this. Further work on a wider range of boys and young men—for example, sexual or gender minorities, as well as economically and racially privileged boys and violence—will also be of value to address some of the concerns we have raised here about collective representations of young masculinities in South Africa and their relationship to violence.

As Bacchi (2009) reminds us, representations have effects. Therefore, it is important to critically reflect on how social problems are constructed in discourse, including within our work as scholars. Representations of social problems can shape how we come to understand and view ourselves and others—what Bacchi (2009) calls *subjectification effects*. Representations of social problems can also work to open up or close certain avenues of inquiry, as some understandings become dominant and alternative perspectives less and less speakable. Bacchi (2009) calls this the *discursive effects* of representation. In turn, this shapes policy response and subjects' lived experiences—that is, it has *lived effects* (Bacchi, 2009).

Neglecting to highlight how boys and young men resist violent masculinities and reifying the notion of marginality as necessarily violence-prone can create a self-fulfilling prophecy in which cultural constructions of poor, black boys and men are violent are being normalized and go unchallenged (*subjectification effects*). It can construct limits around the possibilities for seeing alternatives to violent expressions of masculinity within marginality (*discursive effects*). It can preclude research highlighting intervention opportunities at the sites where boys and young men are already challenging hegemonic masculinity (*lived effects*). Contributions that cite boys and male youth as part of the solution for gender equality highlight how they are equally embroiled in its pursuit as they stand to gain from its benefits (Ratele, 2014; Shefer, 2014; Shefer et al., 2015). Developing further scholarship that illustrates the role of young masculinities in gender justice and highlights the openings and entry points for gender transformation within some boys' and male youth's existing practices can help inform interventions that identify barriers to gender justice but strengths to build from.

References

Anderson, B. (2010). Coloured boys talk: Constructing heterosexual masculinities in a working class high school context. *Journal of Psychology in Africa, 20*(4), 635–645.

Bacchi, C. (2009). *Analysing policy: What's the problem represented to be?* (1st ed.). Pearson.

Bantjes, J., & Nieuwoudt, J. (2014). Masculinity and mayhem: The performance of gender in a South African boys' school. *Men & Masculinities, 17*(4), 376–395.

Bantjes, J., Kagee, A., & Meissner, B. (2017). Young men in post-apartheid South Africa talk about masculinity and suicide prevention. *South Africa Journal of Psychology, 47*(2), 233–245.

Bhana, D. (2008). Girls hit! Constructing and negotiating violent African femininities in a working-class primary school. *Discourse, 29*(3), 401–415. https://doi.org/10.1080/01596300802259160

Bhana, D. (2009). Boys will be boys: What do early childhood teachers have to do with it? *Educational Review, 61*(3), 327–339.

Bhana, D. (2015). Learning gender in the early years of schooling in South Africa. In J. Wyn & H. Cahill (Eds.), *Handbook of children and youth studies* (pp. 279–288). Springer.

Bhana, D., & Chen, H. (2020). If you a bitch, we treat you like a bitch: South African teenage boys' constructions of heterosexual masculinity. *Journal of Youth Studies, 23*(10), 1273–1292.

Bhana, D., & Mayeza, E. (2016). We don't play with gays, they're not real boys . . . they can't fight: Hegemonic masculinity and (homophobic) violence in the primary years of schooling. *International Journal of Educational Development, 51*, 36–42.

Bhana, D., & Mayeza, E. (2019). Cheese boys resisting and negotiating violent hegemonic masculinity in primary school. *NORMA, 14*(1), 3–17.

Bojuwoye, O., & Sylvester, F. (2012). Patterns of gender socialization of adolescent boys in single-mother households: Perspectives from a community in Cape Town, South Africa. *Gender, Technology and Development, 16*(2), 197–222.

Buiten, D. (2020). It's vile but is it violence? A case study analysis of news media representations of non-consensual sexual image-sharing. *Feminist Media Studies, 20*(8), 1177–1194.

Buiten, D., & Naidoo, K. (2016). Framing the problem of rape in South Africa: Gender, race, class and state histories. *Current Sociology, 64*(4), 535–550.

Buiten, D., & Naidoo, K. (2020). Laying claim to a name: Towards a sociology of gender-based violence. *South African Review of Sociology* (in press). https://doi.org/10.1080/21528586.2020.1813194

Chabaya, O., Rembe, S., Wadesango, N., & Mafanya, Z. (2009). Factors that inhibit implementation of policies on gender-based violence in schools: A case study of two districts in eastern Cape Province, South Africa. *Agenda: Empowering Women for Gender Equity, 80*, 97–108.

Chandra, S. (2021). Why do I need to talk about culture? Realising you are 'brown' in academia. *Journal of Intercultural Studies* (in press). https://www.tandfonline.com/doi/full/10.1080/07256868.2021.1987868

Chitsamatanga, B. B., & Rembe, N. S. (2020). School related gender based violence as a violation of children's rights to education in South Africa: Manifestations, consequences and possible solutions. *Journal of Human Ecology, 69*(1–3), 65–80.

Collins, A. (2013). Bullies, sissies and crybabies: Dangerous common sense in educating boys for violence. *Agenda: Empowering Women for Gender Equity, 27*(1 (95)), 71–83.

Colpitts, E. (2019). Engaging men and boys to prevent gender-based violence in South Africa: Possibilities, tensions and debates. *Revue canadienne d'études du développement, 40*(3), 423–439.

Connell, R. (1983). *Which way is up? Essays on class, sex and culture*. Allen and Unwin.

Connell, R. (1995). *Masculinities*. Cambridge.

Crenshaw, K. (1991). Mapping the margins: Intersectionality, identity politics, and violence against women of color. *Stanford Law Review, 43*(6), 1241–1299.

Dziewanski, D. (2020). Femme fatales: Girl gangsters and violent street culture in Cape Town. *Feminist Criminology, 15*(4), 438–463.

Edelstein, I. (2018). Pathways to violence propensity: Results from a two-wave study of young males in urban South Africa. *Journal of Psychology in Africa, 28*(1), 33–40.

Elliott, K. (2016). Caring masculinities: Theorizing an emerging concept. *Men and Masculinities, 19*(3), 240–259.

Gibbs, A., Jewkes, R., Sikweyiya, Y., & Willan, S. (2015). Reconstructing masculinity? A qualitative evaluation of the stepping stones and creating futures interventions in urban informal settlements in South Africa. *Culture, Health & Sexuality, 17*(2), 208–222.

Govender, K., Tucker, L. A., & Coldwell, S. (2019). Sense and sensibilities: Schoolboys talk about sex in the private conversational space. *Child & Adolescent Social Work Journal, 36*(4), 391–398.

Gqola, P. D. (2007). How the cult of femininity and violent masculinities support endemic gender based violence in contemporary South Africa. *African Identities, 5*(1), 111–124.

Gqola, P. D. (2015). *Rape: A South African nightmare*. MF Books.
Graaff, K., & Heinecken, L. (2017). Masculinities and gender-based violence in South Africa: A study of a masculinities-focused intervention programme. *Development Southern Africa, 34*(5), 622–634.
Helman, R., & Ratele, K. (2016). Everyday (in)equality at home: Complex constructions of gender in South African families. *Global Health Action, 9*, 1–13.
Jewkes, R., & Morrell, R. (2018). Hegemonic masculinity, violence, and gender equality: Using latent class analysis to investigate the origins and correlates of differences between men. *Men and Masculinities, 21*(4), 547–571.
Jewkes, R., Nduna, M., Jama-Shai, N., Chirwa, E., & Dunkle, K. (2016). Understanding the relationships between gender inequitable behaviours, childhood trauma and socio-economic status in single and multiple perpetrator rape in rural South Africa: Structural equation modelling. *PLoS One, 11*(5), 1–14.
Jewkes, R., Sikweyiya, Y., Morrell, R., & Dunkle, K. (2010). Why, when and how men rape: Understanding rape perpetration in South Africa. *South African Crime Quarterly, 34*(1), 23–31.
Kramer, S., & Bowman, B. (2021). The making of male victimhood in South African female-perpetrated sexual abuse. *Gender, Place & Culture: A Journal of Feminist Geography, 28*(6), 829–852.
Laurie, T., Driscoll, C., Grealy, L., Tang, S., & Sharkey, G. (2021). Towards an affirmative feminist boys studies. *Boyhood Studies, 14*(1), 75–92.
Mayeza, E., & Bhana, D. (2021). Boys and bullying in primary school: Young masculinities and the negotiation of power. *South African Journal of Education, 41*(1), 1–8.
Miller, J. A., Smith, E. A., Caldwell, L. L., Mathews, C., & Wegner, L. (2021). Boys are victims, too: The influence of perpetrators' age and gender in sexual coercion against boys. *Journal of Interpersonal Violence, 36*, 7–8.
Moosa, S., & Bhana, D. (2020). Men teaching young children: You can never be too sure what their intentions might be. *Oxford Review of Education, 46*(2), 169–184.
Morrell, R., Jewkes, R., & Lindegger, G. (2012). Hegemonic masculinity/masculinities in South Africa: Culture, power, and gender politics. *Men and Masculinities, 15*(1), 11–30.
Morrell, R., Jewkes, R., Lindegger, G., & Hamlall, V. (2013). Hegemonic masculinity: Reviewing the gendered analysis of men's power in South Africa. *South African Review of Sociology, 44*(1), 3–21.
Pasura, D., & Christou, A. (2018). Theorizing black (African) transnational masculinities. *Men and Masculinities, 21*(4), 521–546.
Ratele, K. (2014). Currents against gender transformation of South African men: Relocating marginality to the Centre of research and theory of masculinities. *NORMA: International Journal for Masculinity Studies, 9*(1), 30–44.
Ratele, K. (2015). Working through resistance in engaging boys and men towards gender equality and progressive masculinities. *Culture, Health & Sexuality, 17*(sup2), 144–158.
Ratele, R., Shefer, T., & Clowes, L. (2012). Talking South African fathers: A critical examination of men's constructions and experiences of fatherhood and fatherlessness. *South Africa Journal of Psychology, 42*(4), 553–563.
Roberts, S., & Elliott, K. (2020). Challenging dominant representations of marginalized boys and men in critical studies on men and masculinities. *Boyhood Studies, 13*(2), 87–104.
Roberts, S., Elliott, K., & Ralph, B. (2021). Absences, presences and unintended consequences in debates around masculinities and social change: A reply to Christofidou. *Norma: International Journal for Masculinity Studies, 16*(3), 190–199.
Rubin, J. D. (2013). Searching for certainty: Rugby and male identity in a former model C school. *Safundi, 14*(2), 135–160.
Sedite, D., Bowman, B., & Clowes, L. (2010). Perceptions of staffriding in post-apartheid South Africa: The lethal thrill of speed or the masculine performance of a painful past? *Journal of Psychology in Africa, 20*(4), 581–589.

Shefer, T. (2014). Pathways to gender equitable men: Reflections on findings from the international men and gender equality survey in the light of twenty years of gender change in South Africa. *Men & Masculinities, 17*(5), 502–509.

Shefer, T., Kruger, L. M., & Schepers, Y. (2015). Masculinity, sexuality and vulnerability in 'working' with young men in South African contexts: 'You feel like a fool and an idiot ... a loser'. *Culture, Health and Sexuality, 17*(2), 96–111.

Sideris, T. (2004). You have to change and you don't know how! Contesting what it means to be a man in a rural area of South Africa. *African Studies (Johannesburg), 63*(1), 29–49.

Walker, L. (2005). Men behaving differently: South African men since 1994. *Culture, Health & Sexuality, 7*(3), 225–238.

Wood, K. (2005). Contextualizing group rape in post-apartheid South Africa. *Culture, Health & Sexuality, 7*(4), 303–317.

Wood, K., Lambert, H., & Jewkes, R. (2008). "Injuries are beyond love": Physical violence in young South Africans' sexual relationships. *Medical Anthropology, 27*(1), 43–69.

Zufferey, C. (2014). Questioning representations of homelessness in the Australian print media. *Australian Social Work, 67*(4), 525–536.

Madeline Gerber, B.A. recently graduated Cum Laude from the University of Notre Dame with a Bachelor of Arts degree, majoring in Social Justice and Politics and International Relations. She now works in the non-government sector for an organization that seeks to strengthen rights for Aboriginal and Torres Strait Islander people, contributes to public education on Aboriginal and Torres Strait Islander perspectives, and supports self-determination. She will soon be commencing a Master's degree to analyze the extent to which anti-racist scholarship palpably contributes to racial justice in Australia for First Nations peoples. She is passionate about gender justice and has been honored for contributing to this work.

Sofi Le Berre, B.A. has recently graduated from the University of Notre Dame, Australia with Distinction, majoring in Sociology and Social Justice. She has a keen interest in discourse analysis, specifically on policy surrounding welfare in Australia and representations of racial injustice in Australian and international contexts. She seeks to continue to develop her interest in sociological research, while working in collaboration with the University of Notre Dame, Australia and the Multicultural Disability Advocacy Association as a research assistant.

Denise Buiten, Ph.D. is a Senior Lecturer in Sociology and Social Justice within the School of Arts and Sciences, University of Notre Dame, Australia. She is also a Senior Research Associate at the Department of Sociology, University of Johannesburg (UJ). Her research focuses on evolving representations of gender-based violence in media and scholarship and understanding and addressing diverse forms of gendered violence, especially those not consistently recognized as gender-based. Her recent work examines representations of technology-facilitated violence, filicide and familicide in the media, and evolving discourses around gender-based violence in scholarship.

Chapter 5
Impact of Xenophobic Violence Against Immigrant Youth Informal Traders: Evidence from Durban, South Africa

Bisimwa Timothee Makanishe and Beatrice Umubyeyi

5.1 Introduction

Xenophobic violence is one of the many social problems plaguing post-apartheid South Africa. Several studies have recorded recurring episodes of xenophobic violence over the last 27 years (Akinola, 2017; Makanishe, 2019; Misago et al., 2015). Xenophobia refers to disliking, hating, or fearing foreigners (Duncan, 2011), resulting in actions of prejudice, rejection, exclusion, discrimination, and violent attack on people based on their place of origin (Bekker & Carlton, 2010). The term "xenophobic violence" has been used by scholars to describe the recurrent episodes of attacks perpetrated against immigrants in South Africa (Mabera, 2017; Ukwandu, 2017). The main features of xenophobic violence in South Africa include "murder, assaults causing grievous bodily harm, looting, robbery, arson attacks (burning of people alive and property), displacement, intimidation and threats, harassment, eviction notices, and so on" (Misago, 2017, p. 40). Research has shown that immigrants' informal traders face several challenges, including a lack of legal status in the context of municipal by-laws as they operate in areas that are not demarcated for trade. Hence, confiscation of goods by police makes them unable to claim their stock back; fear of arrest and lack of security as immigrants are perceived to be the first targets of attack in times of protests; they also face challenges of crime and theft, harassment and demands for bribes; and arrest, detention, and physical assault/attacks. Legal documents also affect immigrants accessing bank loans to boost their businesses as most documented traders use asylum seeker permits (Human Rights Watch, 2020; Peberdy, 2016). They also face the problem of exclusionary policies, such as introducing new legislation to bar foreign nationals from certain sectors, including the small business sector. In addition, the immigrants' informal

B. T. Makanishe (✉) · B. Umubyeyi
University of KwaZulu-Natal (UKZN), Durban, South Africa

K. Naidoo et al. (eds.), *Young People, Violence and Strategic Interventions in Sub-Saharan Africa*, Clinical Sociology: Research and Practice,
https://doi.org/10.1007/978-3-031-20679-5_5

traders experience a problem with locals threatening to close their businesses and being assaulted because they are foreigners (Human Right Watch, 2020; Peberdy, 2016; Sergio Carciotto, 2020).

Many scholars who have researched migration and violence in South Africa view this violence as motivated by Afrophobia because black South Africans mostly perpetrate it against black African immigrants while non-African immigrants are generally spared from the violence (Lamola, 2018; Masenya, 2017; Mngomezulu & Dube, 2019). However, despite this likely consensus among migration scholars, there are doubts and denialism in South African government circles about whether the violence is xenophobic (Crush & Ramachandra, 2014; Makanishe, 2019). While this chapter shies away from this debate, it builds upon the emerging academic interest in the cause and impact of xenophobic violence in South Africa.

The implication of xenophobic violence among young immigrant traders in the South African informal economy has received little academic attention. The extent to which they are involved in informal trade also remains unclear. A study by Crush et al. (2017) into Zimbabwean's business activities and responses to xenophobic violence suggests that migrants unable to enter the formal economy resort to the informal economy. The study reveals that up to 30% of Zimbabwean immigrants were involved in informal trade in South Africa, with up to 75% being youth aged under 35 years. The report further reveals that many traders have experienced xenophobic violence, looting, robbery, and abuse. Studying the livelihood impact of xenophobic violence among young refugees and asylum seekers is necessary for social cohesion. Research in Sierra Leone in the context of peacebuilding shows that the lack of sustainable livelihoods can lead to disillusionment and force neglected and marginalized youth to resort to any means for survival, including violence, thus undermining the peacebuilding process (Bangura, 2016).

Unlike previous studies that have addressed the impact of xenophobic violence on the general migrant population, this study focuses on young African immigrants involved in informal trade during late 2020 and early 2021 in the Durban Central Business District (CBD). The main purpose was to explore the perceived triggers and livelihood impact of xenophobic violence experienced by participants. The study establishes the nature of informal trading activities based on participant demographics and the perceived livelihood significance thereof. It further investigates the coping strategies or survival mechanisms, including interventions by government and humanitarian organizations against the impact of the violence, which was also compounded by the emergence of the coronavirus disease (COVID-19) pandemic. The study finally offers participants' insights on how best young immigrant informal traders can be helped to rebuild their lives.

5.2 Literature Review

5.2.1 Cause of Xenophobic Attacks

Some scholars see foreign migrants as soft targets scapegoated for the "endemic poverty, joblessness, lack of shelter and basic services" and high crime levels whenever service delivery issues emerge among frustrated citizens (Misago, 2017, p. 41; Ukwandu, 2017). In this context, Misago contests a reductionist approach whereby some scholars advance competition over limited resources and employment between poor South Africans and immigrants (Mamabolo, 2015; Ukwandu, 2017) as the cause of xenophobic violence in South Africa. From this perspective, African immigrants have been accused of "stealing" jobs and overburdening South Africa's welfare systems (Mngomezulu & Dube, 2019). Misago (2017) counter-argues that this approach fails to provide a direct empirical connection between structural socio-economic factors and xenophobic violence because it does not explain why xenophobic attacks have not occurred in all poor communities. Onah (2011) seems to concur that xenophobic violence is worsened by political factors but believes the primary cause is economic. Analyzing xenophobic violence in South Africa from a political economy perspective, Misago (2017, p. 42) argues that the violence is primarily "political by other means" where complicit local leaders instigate "anonymous community members," which he also refers to as "faceless mob" or "criminals" to conduct xenophobic violence, especially in towns, townships, and informal settlements. Their political motive is to shield local leaders from accountability in respect of xenophobic violence and their failure to deliver adequate public service to their communities. Neocosmos (cited by Sharp, 2008) further argues that dividing the poor along national identities is in the interest of the South African elite. He believes that the 2008 xenophobic violence was a manifestation of a "xenophobic discourse that starts at the top, at the highest levels of the ANC-led state [...] rather than a display of xenophobic attitudes of the poor at the bottom of society" (Sharp, 2008, p. 2). He further emphasizes that xenophobia is prevalent among "the rising black elite as well as the established white elite—whose interests are the state's main concern" (Ibid., p. 2).

Besides political and structural economic factors, the literature further associates xenophobic violence with historical factors (Akinola, 2014; Kerr et al., 2019; Onah, 2011; Ukwandu, 2017). According to Akinola (2014), xenophobic attacks are the explicit manifestation of psychological fear of the unknown built over time as a result of past oppression of colonialism and apartheid. In addition, discourses of liberation struggles are often used to justify xenophobic violence (Kerr et al., 2019). Ukwandu (2017, p. 54) alludes to South Africa's "racialised past violent and the nationalist struggle against apartheid as a trigger of xenophobic violence." Quoting Tafira's view of xenophobia as "black-on-black racism," Kerr et al. (2019) indicate that the narrative and actions of struggle over basic services, such as jobs, housing, and citizenship, are raised in anti-foreigner violence across different "socio-economic and political platforms" (Ibid., p. 16).

While a direct relationship between the media and the occurrence of xenophobic violence has not been established, the media, especially the tabloid press, has been "accused of fomenting violence and exacerbating tension through inflammatory headlines and posters" (Hadland, 2010, p. 119) through which the presence of foreigners is framed as "a problem that needs to be addressed" (Okem et al., 2015. p. 80). The media is further accused of failing to provide a voice for the voiceless per the liberal imperative of the media (Hadland, 2010).

5.2.2 Impact of Xenophobic Violence

Some studies have explored the socio-economic and livelihood impact of xenophobic violence (Lelope, 2019; Nwobi et al., 2020; Rabotata et al., 2021; Tshishonga, 2015). These studies indicate that xenophobic violence harms the livelihoods of African immigrants. For example, using the Intergroup Threat Theory to investigate the socio-economic impact of xenophobic violence on Nigerians in South Africa, Nwobi et al. (2020) found that it rendered many participants homeless, unable to access education, and unemployed, and, therefore, unable to meet their basic needs. Similarly, studying the impact of xenophobic attacks on the livelihoods of Zimbabwean, Indian, and Ethiopian migrants in three South African provinces,[1] Rabotata et al. (2021) found that undocumented immigrants, particularly those located in cities, experienced the loss of income, displacement, and even deportation of immigrants due to xenophobic violence. Furthermore, from a gendered perspective, Akinola (2017) found that women and men experience xenophobia differently simply because being both foreign and female heightens people's vulnerability to xenophobic violence as they are "easily identifiable through their mode of dressing." In this context, xenophobic violence makes it extremely difficult for unskilled migrant/refugee women to engage in gainful employment and access transport due to "physical abuse and sexual harassment by taxi and bus drivers" (Ibid., p. 9745).

Noting that poor people, such as asylum seekers and refugees, who could not find wage employment depend on the economy's informal sector for their socio-economic survival, Tshishonga (2015) investigated the impact of the 2015 xenophobic violence on informal economic operations in Durban. The study found that many immigrant informal traders were forced to close or leave their businesses unattended as they ran to save their lives; hence they experienced "weakening business networks coupled with the loss of financial returns" and general socio-economic hardship (Ibid., p. 165). Similarly, Lelope (2019) investigated the socio-economic effects of xenophobic attacks on refugee entrepreneurs in Atteridgeville, South Africa. The study found that xenophobic violence resulted in the disintegration of families, destruction of businesses, and social isolation and negatively affected immigrants' physical and psychological well-being. This is confirmed by

[1] Limpopo, North-West, and Mpumalanga provinces.

Thela et al.'s (2017) investigation into the cost of Afrophobia on mental health among African migrants. The study found that mental distress was highly prevalent as nearly half (49.4%) of the respondents had symptoms of anxiety, more than half (54.6%) had depression, and nearly a quarter (24.9%) had post-traumatic stress symptoms. After adjusting the results for family separation since migrating to South Africa, the study concluded that African migrants had a high risk of developing mental health issues because of the discriminatory experiences, which hindered their smooth adjustment in South Africa. Crush et al. (2017) found that returning to the country of origin was not an attractive option for Zimbabwean immigrants when faced with challenging encounters.

5.3 Theoretical Discussion

This section provides a theoretical framework through which this study is constructed. Theories considered include structural violence and the Sustainable Livelihood Framework (SLF). Coined and introduced by Johan Galtung in the 1960s, structural violence describes a form of violence that results in harm but is caused by an unidentifiable actor (Vorobej, 2008). This is because such violence is a by-product of the historical process of social, economic, and political systems that harm people or take away human dignity and ability to meet their basic needs (Farmer et al., 2006; Zimbabwe Human Rights NGO Forum, 2014). Galtung originally framed the term "structural violence" to mean any constraint on human potential caused by socio-economic and political structures (Webb, 2019). Chronic poverty, unemployment, inequality, and political repressions compounded by weak processes of governance and maladministration, which result in the suffering of marginalized people, are manifestations of structural violence (Christie, 1997). Against this backdrop, the structural violence approach offers a model of analysis to understand the trigger or cause of xenophobic violence in South Africa. South Africa has the highest income inequality globally, with the majority of the population living in poverty and without meaningful employment.

The SLF is a well-known tool in development agency circles, noted for its usefulness in explaining factors that affect people's livelihoods (Duffy, 2015) and "planning and assessing development interventions" (Parkinson & Ramirez, 2006, p. 2). In their seminal paper, Chamber and Conway (cited by Lundy & Adebayo, 2016, p. 2) defined a livelihood as comprising "capabilities, assets (stores, resources, claims, and access) and activities required for a means of living." The SLF is useful in assessing how people strategically generate livelihoods based on the available resources and how such resources affect livelihoods at the level of individuals, households, or communities. From this perspective, this study sought to understand the livelihood outcome arising from the interaction of the livelihood vulnerability context and shocks in terms of xenophobic violence experienced by youth refugees and asylum seekers. The value of this framework is underpinned by the fact that it does not only help diagnose livelihood impacts considering the vulnerability context

Table 5.1 Illustration of livelihood asset-base

Asset	Description
Human capital	Physical, mental, and intellectual (skills) capacity of individuals to enable informal trading
Social capital	Social networks, including friends, suppliers, employers, etc., whose support enables involvement in informal trade opportunities and operations
Financial capital	Profit, savings, investment in, and reinvestment from the informal trade
Natural capital	Access to space for trading
Physical capital	Trading stand and other tangible resources used in the trading process

Source: (Authors)

in which people generate livelihoods but is also useful in gauging the necessary development interventions required to enhance available livelihood options. The vulnerability context of immigrants' informal trade activities can be determined by shocks underpinned by xenophobic violence. Interventions from individuals, governmental, and non-governmental entities are transforming structures that can enhance the capability of participants to generate meaningful livelihoods during and in the aftermath of xenophobic violence. In the context of this study, informal trade is understood as a livelihood activity underpinned by human, social, financial, natural, and physical assets available to refugee and asylum seeker youth traders in Durban (see Table 5.1).

5.4 Methodology

The chapter is based on empirical qualitative research carried out with youth immigrant informal traders in the city of Durban, Kwazulu-Natal, South Africa, between June and August 2021. For data collection, interviews were conducted with 14 youth immigrant informal traders aged between 18 and 35 (see Table 5.2). This process was guided by an interview instrument containing both open-ended and semi-structured questions to obtain detailed narratives of participants' lived experiences. Participants in this study were selected purposively and identified through the snowball sampling method. Inclusion criteria included being youth of maturity age (18–35 years), African immigrants, and informal traders in Durban CBD. The authors approached potential participants in two steps: the first step was a site visit in the Durban CBD to identify potential participants, start informal dialogues on the purpose of the study, and secure the verbal consent and contact numbers of those who agreed to participate and obtaining leads to other potential participants. Telephonic interviews were then conducted for two reasons: to lessen the duration of physical contact in adherence to COVID-19 protocols and avoid disrupting participants' commitments to their business by only conducting interviews in the evenings

Table 5.2 Participant demographics

No	Age	Sex	Education	Marriage status	Occupation (see Q3)	Country of origin	Residential status
A	24	Female	Secondary (G11)	Married	Nail cosmetician	DRC	Undocumented Asylum seeker
B	26	Female	University	Single	Fashion designer	DRC	Asylum seeker
C	30	Male	University	Single	Nail cosmetician	DRC	Asylum seeker
D	32	Male	Secondary	Married	Hairdresser	Zimbabwe	Refugee
E	30	Male	Secondary	Single	Hairdresser	Burundi	Asylum seeker
F	35	Female	College	Married	Selling clothes, shoes	DRC	Asylum seeker
G	28	Male	Secondary	Single	Haircut	Burundi	Asylum seeker
H	34	Female	Secondary	Married	Selling fruits (Banana, apples)	DRC	Refugee
I	30	Male	College	Single	Photographer	Zimbabwe	Refugee
J	35	Female	College	Married	Hairdresser	Zimbabwe	Refugee
K	27	Male	University	Single	Hairdresser	DRC	Asylum seeker
L	23	Female	Secondary	Single	Nail cosmetician	DRC	Asylum seeker
M	33	Female	University	Married	Online trading (clothing)	DRC	Refugee
N	32	Male	University	Married	IT (printing shop)	DRC	Asylum seeker

or on weekends as was deemed convenient by each participant. In total, 25 contacts were obtained, but in the end, only 14 completed the interview process. The main challenge in conducting this study was navigating the fieldwork for data collection during a pandemic and keeping participants motivated and committed to telephonic interviews against intermittent disruption due to connection problems. NVivo, a qualitative data analysis computer software package, was used to code the transcripts following a narrative approach to capture participants' voices expressing their lived experiences with xenophobic violence.

5.5 Data Analysis

5.5.1 Participants and the Nature of Their Informal Trading Activities

As shown in Table 5.2, the mean age of respondents was 29.9 years, with half being females and married. Most (8/14) had some university or college education, while the rest had attended or completed secondary education. Participants indicated that they were documented with asylum seeker permits (8) and refugee status permits (5), except for one who indicated that she was undocumented. Participants originated from Burundi, DRC, and Zimbabwe and were involved in eight forms of informal trade, with nail cosmetics and hairdressing being the most predominant. As shown in Table 5.2 above, participants from the DRC were dominant. Two factors might have determined the high number of Congolese compared to other communities: (1) when identifying those in informal trading, Congolese were many compared to other communities, and (2) there were more Congolese who were available and willing to participate in the study.

5.5.2 *Significance of Informal Trading Activities and Choice of Trading Site*

Participants regarded their occupations as important because they enabled them to meet basic needs (e.g., food, shelter, and healthcare) for survival. For example, one of them was equivocal about her job: "This occupation [nail cosmetics] is what makes me live, to pay my rent and to get food and other basic needs, such as health care, buying medication for my sinus" (Aimerence, female, 2021). Thus, informal trade occupations help participants meet basic needs and look after themselves. In addition, they spare participants from "wandering around" and engaging in unwanted activities, such as crime (Claude, male, 2021).

In this context, many participants indicated that their occupations were the only viable options to provide for their needs and support their families as the only work they knew and loved or the launchpad to a "future career." As narrated by Jeanne (Online cloth trader, female, 2021): "This job helps me to adapt to my future career to have a huge store where I sell clothes and do nails. That is why I studied business management. It helps me to survive by making ends meet". Against this backdrop, many factors underpinned participants' choice of trading sites. Some of them were trading outdoors, and others were indoors. Most of those who traded outdoors (roadside) indicated that they could not afford the rental requirement for indoor trading. However, outdoor trading often exposed traders to regular harassment from traffic police officers, so they moved from one site to another to avoid harassment. This has forced some traders to find indoor trading sites where they now pay rent following the 2020 xenophobic attacks in Durban CBD. For example, a hair cosmetician participant explained why she moved indoors: "I work on Queen Street. I chose the site because it is indoor, which makes it safe. It is not in the street" (Claudette, female, 2021).

5.5.3 Triggers of Xenophobic Violence

Participants were asked to share their views about why the recent xenophobic violence occurred. Some participants offered arguments saying that the real reasons that triggered the recent xenophobic violence were jealousy, hatred (not wanting foreigners), apartheid, politicians, and the involvement of uMkhonto we Sizwe[2] seems to be a more recent phenomenon of xenophobic violence. A hairdresser participant believed that immigrants are unwanted and dismissed the accusation that they were stealing jobs. She argued that "...in reality, we are not taking any jobs from them. If you see many of the jobs we are doing, those are the jobs that we created ourselves. We are not employed by anyone, most of us...we are not taking any jobs from anyone. What we are doing is with our knowledge and hands. They [South Africans] can do it as well" (Josephine, female, 2021). Other participants expressed similar perceptions, indicating that local South Africans were better positioned or had an advantage when accessing employment because immigrants such as refugees and asylum seekers are not able to compete with South Africans on the job market as they lacked the required documentation.

Some participants suspected that there were political forces behind the recent episode of xenophobic violence. For example, one of the participants opined that the attackers had some political backing. As she puts it, "I think they had support from the top. When I say from the top, I mean some of the government politicians were supporting this attack" (Gloria, female, 2021). The lack of adequate police intervention witnessed by participants enhanced their suspicion of political influences behind the violence. As the same participant observed, "When you watch how the police were taking a distance from us on this issue, it was clear that something was wrong or there were politicians behind this attack" (Gloria, female, 2021).

At least two participants also perceived the legacy of apartheid as a root cause of xenophobic violence. One of the participants alluded to the following: "What I saw as the big reason and cause of all of this is the historical impact of apartheid, especially what many black South African faced. This makes them feel insecure and has more hatred against themselves and other black Africans who are easy targets" (Joshua, male, 2021).

5.5.4 Economic Losses: Livelihood Impact of the 2020/2021 Xenophobic Violence in the Durban CBD

Participants alluded to the following main impacts: disruption of business, loss of income, and loss of goods and equipment.

[2]Umkhonto we Sizwe is a group of people self-identified as a political association of military veterans affiliated to the ruling party, the African National Congress (ANC).

5.5.4.1 Disruption of Business and Loss of Income

As expected, all participants indicated that they could not work and earn an income because episodes of xenophobic violence were regular, so it was unsafe to focus on doing business. This was the experience narrated by one of the hairdresser participants:

> The violence affected my opportunity to earn a living so badly, as I told you. My only occupation every day is haircutting. I wake up in the morning, Monday to Saturday, prepare myself and come to this job. I do not have any other extra job. So, during this period of attacks, no one was coming to open their tents [saloon]. . .Whenever we tried to open it, we could hear the noise that those attacks were starting. Then we ran and closed the shop. Even clients were scared to come to do their haircut. So, how can we get any money again? (Antoinette, female, 2021).

Similar stories were narrated by other participants, indicating that if they were able to attend to a client—sometimes one for the whole day—there was a high chance that the attackers "could come and take the money" (Amani, male, 2021). Even online trading was affected because it was difficult to restock goods as suppliers also had closed their businesses during xenophobic attacks. A participant expressed her frustration in this regard: "I decided to start selling clothes online, but I also struggled because businesses where I source my supplies were being attacked. For this reason, it was also difficult to buy stocks for customers" (Olina, female, 2021).

The situation was further compounded by introducing a hard lockdown because of COVID-19 in March 2021. Some participants indicated that although the nature of their business allowed them to work from home during xenophobic violence as customers could contact them telephonically, the COVID-19 lockdown compromised demand for the business. This was the case of a fashion designer participant who indicated that there was no demand for fashion design as the client had to stay at home and could not attend any events such as "going to church or parties; So they did not need designer clothes" (Innocent, male, 2021).

5.5.4.2 Loss of Goods and Equipment

Some participants indicated that they lost trading goods and equipment such as cosmetic nail products, haircutting tools, etc. For example, a hair cosmetician narrated: "They took my goods. They chased us from the stand. I was scared because it is not my country. We ran away until the violence was over. We spent one month without trading" (Jules, male, 2021). Running away meant trading goods and tools were left behind and looted by xenophobic attackers. This, for example, was the case of a hairdresser participant that stated: "During those attacks, I lost my job and all the materials such as machines for cutting hair and batteries that were helping me to charge the machines. . .Now I have started from the beginning to find other tools" (Jacques, male, 2021).

5.5.4.3 Difficulty to Meet Basic Needs

The disruption of businesses and associated income loss resulted in many immigrants' informal traders going without food. Their access to accommodation was affected as they could no longer afford to pay rental fees for their accommodation. As one of the participants narrated: "During the violent attacks, I was not working, and it was difficult to afford food and to pay rent." The participant added that he was "no longer getting enough income" as he "could not work for weeks" (Amani, male, 2021). Other participants narrated similar stories. A participant who was running a printing shop lamented that the violence had affected the future of his young family as he could no longer "afford to pay bills, rent, etc." and "life has become a problem compared to the past" (Innocent, male, 2021). Another striking example was provided by a participant, a nail cosmetician, who became indebted because he could no longer afford to buy food and pay the rental fees for his accommodation as the violence halted his ability to earn an income.

5.5.5 *Physical and Mental Impacts*

5.5.5.1 The Physical and Mental Impact

Many participants indicated that the violence affected them financially, physically, and psychologically. For example, one of them (a roadside fruit seller) shared her experience: "The violence affected me badly as I was beaten by a group of people here at the workshop while I was running with my stuff" (Gloria, female, 2021). A participant hairdresser revealed that "steel poles" were used to beat them up as groups of attackers asked them to leave their workplaces. In this context, participants also reported having been affected mentally by the xenophobic violence and its impact on their prospects for survival since their occupations were their only source of income. One of the participants, a nail cosmetician, expressed her distress: "I was so scared. I started thinking about going back to the Congo, but it has become normal because they attack us, and after a few days, it stops. So, we are now used to it, that is why I decided to stay anyway" (Olina, female, 2021).

This normalization of the situation underscores the limited livelihood options participants had. As a nail cosmetician participant narrated: "I was worried that if the violence continued, I would die because I was no longer working" (Claudette, female, 2021). In their mental distress, while some participants contemplated death, like in this case, others felt that their treatment was inhumane. For example, a young male hairdresser expressed the state of his mental health during the violence: "It also affected me mentally because of them despising and maltreating me like an animal. I am also human like them and know my rights" (Amani, male, 2021).

5.6 Coping Mechanisms

Against the impact of xenophobic violence, this study shows limited coping strategies for youth immigrant informal traders to resort to. However, it was evident that some participants adopted an integrated coping mechanism, comprising savings, other income-making strategies, a search for donations, and religiosity and spirituality.

5.6.1 Savings and Casual Income-Making Strategies

Some participants indicated that they resorted to the savings they had accumulated before the violence to meet their family's basic needs. In addition to using their savings, some adopted casual income-making strategies. For example, a fashion designer participant shared his experience: "I relied on my savings and the little I was getting from loyal customers [...] Since I also know how to do makeup, I was getting some loyal customers occasionally calling me to assist them with makeup" (Francois, male, 2021). Others reported receiving calls from loyal customers who wanted them to provide their service at home. In this context, a hairdresser explained how she survived: "I survived through my work. Sometimes, I was receiving the call from my clients to do their hair at their homes" (Claudette, female, 2021).

5.6.2 Donations from Individuals and Organizations

An integrated coping mechanism approach comprising donations from individuals and NGOs and other creative mechanisms became an important coping strategy because no single strategy was adequate. For example, the participant whose online sales occupation was halted learned how to make vetkoeks (fat cakes) using cake flour donated by the church. She then sold the vetkoek to neighbors in her flat building. She further depended on food donations and received money from her relatives abroad to pay rent. At least five participants indicated that their friends and family members or other individuals assisted them with money to pay rent. A young female roadside cloth/shoe seller depended on her husband as the violence did not affect his work (Aimerence, female, 2021). In contrast, an unmarried male hairdresser and his three roommates indicated that they depended on the leniency of their landlord when they were unable to pay the rent for their shared room, while for other basic needs "such as getting food, it was not easy" (Janvier, male, 2021).

However, this study found that while NGOs made modest efforts, no governmental intervention was reported by participants. At least three participants acknowledged receiving food donations from their churches (e.g., Grace Bible Church and

Durban Mission Church (DMC)[3]), while at least two acknowledged receiving some help from the Refugee Social Services (RSS), a Durban-based United Nations High Commissioner for Refugees (UNHCR) partner organization. A young female nail cosmetician narrated her experience with the organization: "RSS helped us get funds for new working tools to restart the business after the violence—tools like chairs, tables, nails, chemicals, and powder" (Gloria, female, 2021). However, other participants indicated that their efforts to seek help from RSS were unsuccessful. As narrated by a young male nail cosmetician: "I went to RSS to inform that we were being chased from our trading site. They advised us to look for another site, but they did not help us. We went for the second time, but they were not receiving people anymore. . .because their office was closed." (Francois, male, 2021).

5.6.3 *Suffering and Patience*

In the absence of meaningful coping strategies, at least six participants reported having no further options but suffering and exercising patience. In this respect, a male hairdresser narrated: "Survival during this period was only suffering." This is because their survival depended on them using their "art, which is to do the hair," which they could not do during xenophobic attacks because of "up and down running to save our lives" (Josua, male, 2021). The suffering was also compounded by the impact of the COVID-19 lockdown, which complicated other survival opportunities. A female cloth/shoe seller narrated a similar experience: "I could have done nothing because my work was stopped. It was very hard to survive during the first two weeks of violent attacks [. . .] we would just sleep on bread only. Another problem was not being able to pay rent" (Aimerence, female, 2021).

Because of suffering, at least two participants contemplated going back to their home countries. One of them, a male photographer from Zimbabwe, decided to return to his home country and stayed for nearly 3 months. However, those who could not afford to return to their countries, as in the case of a hairdresser participant from the Democratic Republic of Congo (DRC), ended up "absorbing and understanding" the situation, although "It was difficult to cope with the situation because I was being treated like an animal" (Olina, female, 2021).

5.6.4 *Religiosity and Spirituality*

In addition to savings, casual income-making strategies, donations, religiosity, and spirituality were important ingredients of the coping strategy mix. For example, the 24-year-old participant (nail cosmetician) who reported using her savings and

---

[3]DMC is a church that is run by Congolese immigrants in the city of Durban.

receiving assistance from RSS also reported self-encouragement and portrayed prayer as a source of strength and hope. She narrated: "what helped me is that I encouraged myself that if the violence continues, I will think of something else I can do what locals do not do. Meanwhile, I was praying, which gave me strength and hope" (Olina, female, 2021). Similarly, many participants referred to survival as the "grace of God" and "prayer." At least one participant perceived the opportunity to save before the violence as God's grace: "The small amount of saving that I had is what I managed to use—that is the grace of God I spoke about" (Jacques, male, 2021). However, others did not necessarily perceive survival by "the grace of God" as associated with savings. They simply could not explain how they survived because "it was only by the grace of God" (Innocent, male, 2021).

A similar account was narrated by the participant whose printing shop was closed for a month, but his wife received some financial donations (R800) from RSS and food donations twice from the DMC. Underpinning the reliance on religiosity and spirituality is that support from individuals and organizations was perceived as inadequate.

5.7 Recommended Interventions

Participants provided various responses on how best youth immigrant informal traders can be assisted against xenophobic violence. They mainly alluded to protection and opportunities.

5.7.1 Protection and Security

Protection from xenophobic violence was the most predominant recommendation from the participants in this study. In this context, many participants called on the South African government to intervene to stop xenophobic violence against immigrants' informal traders in Durban. As one of the participants suggested: "…government should protect us with our goods. Some of us were burnt alive with our goods, others got their goods burnt or lost; life has become difficult" (Claude, male, 2021). For example, this allegedly happened to a cloth/shoe seller participant: "I wish I could be assisted by the police who were there watching how the group of those attackers were taking my stuff and helped to bring them back. But nothing was returned to me" (Jeane, female, 2021).

Despite their frustration, some participants recommended that the "Government recognize that foreigners are human with rights like other people…and acknowledge that refugees need protection because they are here to seek protection" (Jacques, male, 2021).

Protection from xenophobic violence was perceived as crucial for peace and stability, particularly for refugees and asylum seekers to self-sustain in

South Africa. One of the participants, a roadside fruit seller refugee, unequivocally answered: "I need the government to protect us and all the small jobs we are creating to survive. It is not easy for asylum seekers to get a job in this country" (Josephine, female, 2021).

5.7.2 Opportunities

In addition to protection, participants recommended that they should be given access to opportunities. These include documentation, access to trading sites and bank credits, social grants, and education. The lack of documentation was perceived as a serious barrier to employment, self-employment, and education. One of the participants shared his struggle with trying to register his printing business despite having an asylum seeker permit: "As a foreigner who has been in this country for 10 years, working for myself, not working for someone, I need to be able to register my business and get funding. My Internet café is registered as a company that I do not even know if it is recognized. I tried to register through the normal channel but was rejected because I do not have an ID" (telephonic interview, 1 September 2021). The lack of proper identity documentation seems to be a real challenge confronting participants, including a 28-year-old barber from Burundi who shared his predicament: "Whenever you go to find any other work, they ask you to bring your ID. This is my tenth year in SA, but I am still on the asylum paper" (Jules, male, 2021).

Opportunity in terms of access to trading sites was also recommended, particularly by participants who said they lost their sites because of the recent xenophobic attacks. In this context, a nail cosmetician participant begged: "Give sites to those of us who work [outdoor] as they do for local South Africans. Instead, they removed us from the sites and gave them to Zulus. Refugees paying the municipality for their sites lost the sites that are now occupied by Zulus" (Antoinette, female, 2021).

Access to bank credits is another form of opportunity suggested by participants. Those who made this suggestion indicated that access to finance could help them improve their businesses by renting a better venue, acquiring tools, or investing in new businesses to compensate for the losses incurred during xenophobic attacks. The following responses sum it up: "I wish the government and state leaders could assist everyone who lost anything during that period of attacks to refund them what they lost. Why am I saying this, you see? During these attacks, many people lost many things. For us to get other money to start life again was not easy. You know, for many foreigners, especially refugees, it is not easy to get any loan from the banks. To get any other financial support for you to start any business is hard" (Amani, male, 2021).

Finally, access to social grants and education was perceived by some participants as mechanisms for them to supplement their "small income," have "a better life," and "go back to school" (Claudette, female, 2021).

5.8 Discussion

Looking at the demographics of participants and the nature and choice of their occupations, this study corroborates the findings by Crush et al. (2017). They found that the entry barriers to the formal sector of the economy were a push factor for immigrants into the South African informal economy. Participants in this study indicated how the lack of proper documentation did not allow them to find better jobs. In this context, self-employment in the informal economy is perceived as the most viable option to meet basic needs instead of engaging in unwanted activities, such as crime. Participants also indicated the unaffordability of rental requirements for trading indoors as their key reason for trading outdoors.

Regarding the impact of xenophobic violence and coping strategies adopted by the affected participants, this study employed the SLF to make sense of their lived experiences. From this perspective, the sustainability of livelihoods is determined by the vulnerability context and transforming structures negatively or positively affecting the livelihood asset-base, which according to Chambers, comprises human capital, financial capital, social capital, physical capital, and natural capital (Lundy & Adebayo, 2016; Makanishe, 2012).

The findings in this study suggest that the livelihoods of youth immigrant informal traders are highly vulnerable, primarily because their status as refugees and asylum seekers is a barrier to entry into the formal economy and labor market. In this study's findings, some participants complained about their failed attempts to find employment or register their businesses because of a lack of proper identity documentation since formal employers and other institutions often reject refugee and asylum seeker permits. Against this backdrop, informal trade has been the only viable livelihood option. However, this too seems to have been vulnerable to xenophobic attacks and harassment by police officers as they implement city by-laws that prohibit roadside trading.

In this study, participants narrated their experiences with xenophobic violence, including economic losses, constant business disruptions and loss of income, loss of goods and equipment, difficulty in meeting basic needs, and physical and mental impact or physical/mental distress. From a sustainable livelihood perspective, the loss of income and goods compromises financial capital in terms of earnings and investment, affecting other forms of financial capital in the form of savings and investments. This study shows that participants resorted to consuming their savings when they could no longer earn an income due to business disruptions from xenophobic attacks.

In addition, the loss of trading equipment, such as hair clippers and batteries in the case of hairdressers, compromises the physical capital on which participants' informal trade activities are based. Furthermore, the study finds that xenophobic violence potentially impacted the human capital base of participants' livelihoods. Human capital is based on two variables: health and skills. While there is no evidence that the violence affected the knowledge and skills required by participants to conduct their livelihood activities, the study findings show that they were affected physically and mentally. This health impact can impede the running of daily routines and, therefore, compromise individuals' capacity to produce their livelihoods.

In this context, the SLF suggests that transforming structures is necessary to ensure the sustainability of livelihoods (Chambers, cited in Makanishe, 2012). Transforming structures include policy and practical interventions from government and non-governmental institutions to enhance individuals' capacity to produce their livelihoods. This study shows that although some participants received some form of assistance in terms of food and finance from the faith-based and NGOs during the xenophobic attacks, such intervention was not adequate. Meanwhile, there is an alarming absence of government intervention to protect immigrant informal traders from xenophobic violence and its impacts. During attacks against immigrants, there was limited intervention of security services to protect the victims. Participants narrated their perceptions of government institutions, such as the police, supporting perpetrators rather than protecting victims. In this context, some participants relied mostly on help from individuals. In contrast, others adopted spirituality and religiosity in terms of exercising patience, prayers, and relying on the grace of God to cope with the impact of the violence. According to Villani et al. (2019, p. 1), this form of spirituality and religiosity can be "positive predictors of subjective well-being" and, therefore, an important coping mechanism for people under stressful circumstances, depending on their religious backgrounds.

5.9 Conclusion

This study sought to investigate the cause and impact of xenophobic violence during the late 2020 and early 2021 on youth immigrant informal traders in the Durban CBD. The study findings show that while informal trade is the only viable option available for immigrants in South Africa, it has been severely affected by xenophobic violence. The violence, which was perpetrated by groups of people who, according to participants, self-identified as uMkhonto we Sizwe, was triggered by structural factors embedded in historical, social, economic, and political factors.

As perceived by participants in this study, it is evident that xenophobic attitudes and economic exclusion toward immigrants, especially toward youth immigrant informal traders, in South Africa are a result of a mix of social-economic and political factors. The results from the study reveal that perpetrators blamed the victims for many problems they faced. The argument and perception behind the socio-economic factors are that foreign nationals affect the economic well-being of black South Africans. Such attitude toward black foreigners is echoed in political rhetoric where immigrants are blamed for competing with South African citizens over scarce resources, including jobs, public services, schools, infrastructures, housing, insufficient job opportunities, and informal trading opportunities. Poverty produces frustration and aggression. However, jealousy, hatred, and bitterness are directed mostly toward black foreigners, whose marginal and vulnerable status makes them easy targets.

References

Akinola, A. O. (2014). South Africa and the two faces of xenophobia: A critical reflection. *Africa Peace and Conflict Journal, 7*(1), 56–67.

Akinola, A. (2017). South Africa and the xenophobia dilemma: A gendered perspective. *Gender and Behaviour, 15*(3), 9739–9751.

Bangura, I. (2016). We can't eat peace: Youth, sustainable livelihoods and the peacebuilding process in Sierra Leone. *Journal of Peacebuilding & Development, 11*(2), 37–50.

Bekker, S., & Carlton, D. (Eds.). (2010). *Racism, xenophobia and ethnic conflict*. Creda Press.

Carciotto, S. (2020). *In the crosshairs: Foreigners in SA's informal sector*. Institute for Security Studies Today, Pretoria. Retrieved February 5, 2022 from https://issafrica.org/iss-today

Christie, D. J. (1997). Reducing direct and structural violence: The human needs theory. *Journal of Peace and Psychology, 3*(4), 315–332.

Crush, J., & Ramachandra, S. (2014). Xenophobic violence in South Africa: Denialism, minimalism, realism. *Migration Policy Series, 66*.

Crush, J., Tawodzera, G., Chikanda, A., Ramachandran, S., & Tevera, D. (2017). *South Africa case study: The double crisis – Mass migration from Zimbabwe and xenophobic violence in South Africa* (pp. 1–93, Rep.). International Centre for Migration Policy Development and Waterloo, ON: Southern African Migration Programme.

Duffy, L. (2015). Achieving a sustainable livelihood after leaving intimate partner violence: Challenges and opportunities. *Journal of Family Violence, 30*(4), 403–417.

Duncan, N. (2011). Reaping the whirlwind: Xenophobic violence in South Africa. *International Community Psychology, 3*(1), 254–271.

Farmer, P. E., Nizeye, B., Stulac, S., & Keshavjee, S. (2006). Structural violence and clinical medicine. *PLoS Medicine, 3*(10), e449. https://doi.org/10.1371/journal.pmed.00300440

Hadland, A. (2010). Shooting the messenger: Mediating the public and the role of the media in South Africa's xenophobic violence. *Africa Development, 35*(3), 119–143.

Human Rights Watch. (2020). *They have robbed me of my life. Xenophobic violence against non-nationals in South Africa*. Human Rights Watch Southern Africa.

Kerr, P., Durrheim, K., & Dixon, J. (2019). Xenophobic violence and struggle discourse in South Africa. *Journal of Asian and African Studies, 54*(7), 995–1011.

Lamola, M. J. (2018). The de-Africanisation of the African National Congress, Afrophobia in South Africa and the Limpopo River fever. *Filosofia Theoretica: Journal of African Philosophy, Culture and Religions, 7*(3), 72–93.

Lelope, L. A. (2019). *The socio-economic effects of xenophobic attacks on refugee entrepreneurs in Atteridgeville* (Doctoral dissertation, University of Pretoria).

Lundy, B. D., & Adebayo, A. G. (2016). Introduction: Sustainable livelihoods, conflicts, and transformation. *Journal of Global Initiatives: Policy, Pedagogy, Perspective, 10*(2), 2.

Mabera, F. (2017). The impact of xenophobia and xenophobic violence on South Africa's developmental partnership agenda. *Africa Review, 9*(1), 28–42.

Makanishe, B. T. (2012). *Politics of mining reforms and poverty: Informal mining suspension and its impacts on rural livelihoods in the Twangiza mining area*. Eastern DRC (Master's dissertation, University of KwaZulu-Natal).

Makanishe, B. T. (2019). Xenophobia in South Africa: When shall we call a spade a spade? *Zimbabwe Briefing*. Retrieved from https://www.zimbabwebriefing.org/single-post/2019/09/26/xenophobia-in-south-africa-when-shall-we-call-a-spade-a-spade

Mamabolo, M. A. (2015). Drivers of community xenophobic attacks in South Africa: Poverty and unemployment. *TD: The Journal for Transdisciplinary Research in Southern Africa, 11*(4), 143–150.

Masenya, M. J. (2017). Afrophobia in South Africa: A general perspective of xenophobia. *Bangladesh Sociological Society, 14*(1), 81.

Misago, J. P. (2017). Politics by other means? The political economy of xenophobic violence in post-apartheid South Africa. *The Black Scholar, 47*(2), 40–53.

Misago, J. P., Freemantle, I., & Landau, L. B. (2015). *Protection from Xenophobia: An evaluation of UNHCR's Regional Office for Southern Africa's Xenophobia Related Programmes*. The African Centre for Migration and Society. UNHCR. https://www.unhcr.org/55cb153f9.pdf
Mngomezulu, B. R., & Dube, M. (2019). Lost in translation: A critical analysis of xenophobia in Africa. *Journal of African Union Studies, 8*(2), 67.
Neocosmos, M. (2008). The politics of fear and the fear of politics: Reflections on xenophobic violence in South Africa. *Journal of Asian and African Studies, 43*(6), 586–594.
Nwobi, U. A., Nwokoma, U. B., & Uzozie, H. A. (2020). An examination of the xenophobic violence in South Africa and its impact on socio-economic lives of Nigerians in that country 2015-2019. *African Journal of Social and Behavioural Sciences, 10*(2), 4017–4421.
Okem, A., Asuelime, L., & Adekoye, R. (2015). Re-visiting xenophobia in South Africa and its impact on Africa's integration. *Africa Insight, 45*(2), 75–85.
Onah, E. I. (2011). The politics of xenophobia: Race, national groups and the anti-immigrant violence in South Africa. *IFE PsychologIA: An International Journal, 16*(2), 261–273.
Parkinson, S., & Ramirez, R. (2006). Using a sustainable livelihoods approach to assessing the impact of ICTs in development. *The Journal of Community Informatics, 2*(3). Retrieved from https://openjournals.uwaterloo.ca/index.php/JoCI/article/view/2072
Peberdy, S. (2016). *International migrants in Johannesburg's informal economy*. SAMP Migration Policy Series No. 71. SAMP: Waterloo and Cape Town.
Rabotata, E., Makhubele, J., Baloyi, T., Mafa, P., Kwakwa, M., Masilo, T., Matlakala, F., & Mabasa, A. (2021). The impact of xenophobic attacks on the livelihoods of migrants in selected provinces of South Africa. *International Journal of Criminology and Sociology, 10*, 254–259.
Sharp, J. (2008). 'Fortress SA': Xenophobic violence in South Africa. *Anthropology Today, 24*(4). https://doi.org/10.1111/j.1467-8322.2008.00597.x
Thela, L., Tomita, A., Maharaj, V., Mhlongo, M., & Burns, J. K. (2017). Counting the cost of Afrophobia: Post-migration adaptation and mental health challenges of African refugees in South Africa. *Transcultural Psychiatry, 54*(5–6), 715–732.
Tshishonga, N. (2015). The impact of xenophobia-Afrophobia on the informal economy in Durban CBD, South Africa. *TD: The Journal for Transdisciplinary Research in Southern Africa, 11*(4), 163–179.
Ukwandu, D. C. (2017). Reflections on xenophobic violence in South Africa–what happens to a dream deferred? *African Journal of Public Affairs, 9*(9), 43–62.
Villani, D., Sorgente, A., Iannello, P., & Antonietti, A. (2019). The role of spirituality and religiosity in subjective well-being of individuals with different religious statuses. *Frontiers in Psychology, 10*, 1525.
Vorobej, M. (2008). Structural violence. *The Canadian Journal of Peace and Conflict Studies, 40*(2), 84–98.
Webb, R. J. (2019). Addressing structural violence: Reforming our perspectives. *International. Academy of Practical Theory, Conference series. Iapt. CS 1*, 53–60.
Zimbabwe Human Rights NGO Forum. (2014). Structural violence and organised violence and torture in Zimbabwe, A special paper.

Bisimwa Timothee Makanishe, MA is a Ph.D. candidate in Economic History and Development Studies and holds a Master's degree in Development Studies from the University of KwaZulu-Natal (UKZN). He is currently a Research Fellow at the UKZN-based Maurice Webb Race Relations Unit and a lecturer teaching Sociology of Work at the Durban University of Technology (DUT). Previously, he had taught multiple social science disciplines, including cultural and heritage tourism, economic history and development studies, public governance, and industrial and organizational labor studies. He successfully supervised several postgraduate (Honors) research projects at UKZN. As a research fellow for the last five years, he has actively participated in implementing various research projects commissioned by different government departments and educational institutions in South Africa. His research interest is located within the broader social and economic development area as it relates to migration, labor, employment, poverty, the informal economy, livelihoods, and public policy.

Beatrice Umubyeyi, Ph.D. is a Specialist in Conflict Transformation and Peace Studies. She is a Postdoctoral Research Fellow at the University of KwaZulu-Natal (UKZN). She is also a visiting scholar at Universite de l'Afrique Sub-Saharienne in the Democratic Republic of Congo (DRC). She has published numerous articles and book chapters. Her research areas include (but are not limited to) family conflict and conflict resolution, conflict transformation, peacebuilding, migration, regional integration, and indigenous knowledge. She has teaching experience and has been a supervisor of postgraduate students. She has also attended various research conferences in Africa and abroad.

Chapter 6
Heteronormativity in Health Settings: Realities of LGBT Youth's Access to Healthcare in South Africa

Sthembiso Pollen Mkhize and Pranitha Maharaj

6.1 Introduction

South Africa's legislative and constitutional reform promises adequate healthcare for all; however, studies show that disparities and inequalities in healthcare provision are still highly prevalent (Harris et al., 2011; Mkhize et al., 2021). The Constitution of South Africa[1] offers comprehensive recognition and legal protection of lesbian, gay, bisexual and transgender (LGBT) individuals and is acknowledged as one of the most advanced and progressive globally. The Equality Clause in the Bill of Right's Section 9(3) mandates that nobody should be discriminated against based on, among other grounds, their sex, gender, or sexual orientation. Further rights enshrined in the Bill of Rights guarantee inherent dignity (Section 10), the right to life (Section 11), as well as the right to security, freedom from all forms of violence, and treatment that is inhumane or degrading (Section 12). However, these legislative commitments exist amidst pervasive and constant conservative societal attitudes, which manifest in social exclusion, stigma, and perpetuated violence in the daily lives of LGBT individuals, including in healthcare (Müller & Daskilewicz, 2019; Rispel et al., 2011).

[1] See *Constitution of South Africa (*1996*)*, Article 7(2).

S. P. Mkhize (✉)
Gauteng City-Region Observatory, University of Johannesburg, University of the Witwatersrand, Johannesburg, South Africa
e-mail: sthembiso.mkhize@gcro.ac.za

P. Maharaj
South African Research Chair in Economic Development, University of KwaZulu-Natal, Durban, South Africa
e-mail: Maharajp7@ukzn.ac.za

K. Naidoo et al. (eds.), *Young People, Violence and Strategic Interventions in Sub-Saharan Africa*, Clinical Sociology: Research and Practice,
https://doi.org/10.1007/978-3-031-20679-5_6

While South Africa has a liberal constitution that recognizes everyone's sexual orientation and gender identity (SOGI) and offers the right to access healthcare (Section 27), research shows that sexual and gender minorities continue to experience a wide array of health inequities, including inadequate coverage of preventative health services. They also face difficulties in accessing healthcare services as a result of unfriendly health providers and facilities and a non-inclusive health system that is not well equipped to meet the needs of those not conforming to "normal" forms of gender and sexuality (Ansara, 2012; Kuyper & Vanwesenbeeck, 2011; Mkhize & Maharaj, 2021; Müller, 2016). Institutionalized heteronormativity[2] in the healthcare setting treats some people as "immoral" and "deviant" as a result of their sexual orientation and gender identity and maintains the idea that cisgenderism and heterosexuality are the only "normal" forms of gender and sexuality (Ansara, 2012). Heteronormativity remains firmly intact through social structures, practices, and institutions and also serves to marginalize the "other" sexualities, leading to different forms of violence (Javaid, 2018). Studies suggest that violence is not always physical or direct but also indirect or structural, depending on the actors actively perpetuating it (Basnyat, 2017; Mkhize & Maharaj, 2020). In the context of structural violence, "actors" refer to systemic inequalities integrated into institutions, playing a significant role in shaping the structural arrangements that harm people.

Consequently, these structural arrangements result in structural violence against those on the margins of society, becoming ingrained in how society functions and denying people's basic needs (Basnyat, 2017; Galtung, 1969). Society's pervasive biases toward gender binary continue to marginalize, exclude, and structurally violate all non-heteronormative sexual (LGB) and gender (T) identities (Müller, 2016). This biasness results in failure to provide culturally competent sexual healthcare services for LGBT individuals, leading to their reluctance to visit health services, which is likely to compromise their health status and overall well-being.

Previous studies have shown that sexual and gender minority youth are reluctant to access and utilize sexual health services due to the lack of friendly and competent healthcare providers (Quinn et al., 2015; Romijnders et al., 2016). However, studies suggest that multiple layers of discrimination and marginalization experienced by LGBT individuals are not only perpetrated by healthcare providers but are deeply rooted in the heteronormativity-based health system itself, which assumes that the health needs of LGBT individuals are similar to those identifying as heterosexuals and cisgender (Cele et al., 2015; Colpitts & Gahagan, 2016). Increasing evidence on the impacts of the coronavirus disease (COVID-19) on the provision of sexual and reproductive health (SRH) care for LGBT individuals suggests that health disparities are worsening among this group, and this is likely a consequence of existing challenges that persisted prior to its emergence (Lynch & Teagle, 2020; Ruprecht et al., 2021). As South Africa continues to battle with the COVID-19 pandemic, LGBT individuals have experienced a range of barriers to accessing healthcare. Additionally, the COVID-19 pandemic has restricted access to SRH services such as

[2]M Warner *Introduction: Fear of a Queer Planet* (1991).

condoms, lubricants, human immunodeficiency virus (HIV) testing and treatment services, and hormone treatment for transgender persons and other sexual and gender minorities (Lynch & Teagle, 2020).

LGBT youth have unique sexual healthcare needs that often differ from their heterosexual counterparts, which increase their risk of sexually transmitted infections (STIs) and HIV if not met (Wood et al., 2016). These sexual healthcare needs include an enabling environment for service provision, trained staff to work competently and effectively with LGBT individuals, availability of risk behavior information, testing and counseling services provided by culturally competent staff, and initiatives to promote prevention and care for LGBT (Mprah, 2016). The heteronormative-based approach to LGBT health has rendered the unique needs and experiences of sexual and gender minorities invisible within mainstream health data, systems and policies (Bauer et al., 2009; Colpitts & Gahagan, 2016; Mulé et al., 2009). In addition, it is evident that LGBT individuals use healthcare services less frequently than their heterosexual counterparts due to the negative treatment they receive within healthcare services (Heck et al., 2006; Kuyper & Vanwesenbeeck, 2011). Given the current structure of South Africa's health system, this chapter aims to examine structural violence in the context of healthcare and draws on in-depth interviews conducted with LGBT students at a university in South Africa.

6.2 Understanding Structural Violence Confronting LGBT in Healthcare

Structural forces play a key role in perpetuating inequities in access to healthcare. "Structural violence" is a term coined by Johan Galtung and other liberation theologians in the 1960s, describing social structures as either economic, political, legal, religious, or cultural that prevent individuals from reaching their full potential (Farmer et al., 2019). Structural violence is indirect, almost invisible, but embedded in society's political and economic organizations, causing preventable suffering, often manifesting in an increasing gap between those who have influence and those who are relatively powerless (Lester, 2008). Winter and Leighton (2001) argue that structural violence produces the same degree of suffering as direct violence. However, the damage is likely to be much slower, more subtle, and less easy to repair. In most cases, structural violence is often not recognized or not taken into consideration and not given much attention. In the context of this study, structural violence refers to social, economic, and political restrictions that society places on LGBT individuals, hindering them from fulfilling their basic needs and attaining a better quality of life. These restrictions often originate from institutions that exercise considerable power (Lee, 2019).

Structural violence becomes a systematic way of exposing those on the margins of society to more discrimination, violence, and their entrapment in poverty (Farmer,

2010). LGBT constitute a diverse group of individuals with unique identities and experiences, likely to vary by gender, race, ethnicity, class, and other characteristics (Amoroto, 2016). LGBT, as members of a social minority group, often suffer from a range of socio-economic and cultural injustices (Subhrajit, 2014). They are more likely to experience prejudice, discrimination, intolerance, harassment, and violence than those who identify as heterosexual, mainly due to their sexual orientation and gender identity. In addition, their lack of social recognition influences their capacity to fully access and enjoy their rights like any other citizen. Research suggests that heteronormativity in practice and policy-level response to large-scale disasters tend to systematically ignore the needs of LGBT populations (Gaillard et al., 2017). Further, as a marginalized group, LGBT individuals remain at risk of falling through the cracks in efforts and advocacies to strengthen their access to services (Lynch & Teagle, 2020). This perpetuates the social patterns of structural violence and discrimination and directly impacts the health and well-being of sexual and gender minorities.

Violence is perpetrated against LGBT when they are seen as inferior to those who are not LGBT (Amoroto, 2016). According to Amoroto (2016), when LGBTs do not equally enjoy the same human rights and freedoms as non-LGBT citizens enjoy, or when LGBTs do not enjoy the full promise of human rights, then violence in both scenarios is also present. In Galtung's (1969) framework, there is violence against LGBT individuals if their human agency and life chances are restricted due to their SOGI. Amoroto (2016) pointed out how democracy consistently favors what it deems as the majority and, in the process, continues to undermine the minority. In this instance, since the majority of individuals in many societies identify as heterosexual, policymakers have the power to enact policies that discriminate against those who identify as non-heterosexual, justifying such policies as serving the majority's interests.

LGBT individuals continue to face numerous challenges and difficulties growing up in a heteronormative society as they are often regarded as deviant. The tremendous challenges that they encounter include ignorance, stigma, hatred, discrimination, violence, labeling, and rejection by their own families and communities, as well as other barriers, such as inequality in the workplace and health insurance sectors, the provision of substandard care, and outright denial of care because of an individual's sexual orientation or gender identity. For most, the unfortunate part is that this is their daily reality (Çinar, 2011). In health, they experience limited access to quality healthcare, and as a result, under-utilization of health services is quite severe due to systematic discrimination and marginalization against them (Mulé et al., 2009). Also, due to the historical context of HIV, being referred to as a "gay disease" (De Cock et al., 2011), the majority of research on the sexual health of the LGBT community has focused mainly on men who have sex with men (MSM), leaving behind other non-heteronormative populations such as lesbians and transgender individuals. In addition, little has been said about women who have sex with women (WSW) and the health disparities of transgender individuals. This study aims to contribute to this body of knowledge to address the issues faced by the whole LGBT community when accessing and utilizing sexual healthcare services.

6.3 Researching Experiences of LGBT Youth: Methods

Traditionally, SRH services were not directly targeting youth, creating barriers to access and use for them (Alli et al., 2013). At the same time, the youth continue to face the past stigma attached to their sexuality, and those identifying as "LGBT" face additional negative experiences when accessing SRH services as a result of their non-heteronormative identities that do not conform to hegemonic systems of heterosexuality and cisgenderism (Alli et al., 2013; Ansara, 2012). In the past, research that focused on LGBT individuals was greatly curtailed and referred to as "academic amnesia" or "academic defiance" since there was a stigma surrounding homosexuality (Ilyayambwa, 2012, p. 50; Moagi & Mavhandu-Mudzusi, 2020). This form of silence in academia about homosexuality, especially in the African context, has exacerbated violence and discrimination against LGBT youth. The growing social and health research among LGBT youth has opened discussions and conversations around dismantling and challenging heteronormativity in different spheres of life. In order to contribute to this rapidly growing field, research focusing on access and use of healthcare services among LGBT youth was conducted at a university in South Africa to examine structural violence in the context of healthcare and investigate barriers to access and use.

Information for this study relied on qualitative data from in-depth interviews with 12 university students aged between 18 and 24 years in South Africa. The small sample size is related to the difficulty in locating LGBT individuals, which has also been reported in other studies (Heckathorn, 2011; Meyer & Wilson, 2009). However, this is not a problem given that the main focus of the study was not generalisability but a better understanding of the factors influencing the utilization of healthcare services among LGBT youth. Students were recruited using purposive and snowball sampling techniques on four campuses of a university in South Africa from May to September 2018. The study was granted ethics approval by the University of KwaZulu-Natal Humanities and Social Sciences Ethics Committee, and a number of measures were taken into consideration to protect the identity and dignity of all participants. The study was conscious of not outing[3] individuals that were not ready to make their sexual orientation or gender identity public by allowing them to participate voluntarily and contact the researchers privately, conducting face-to-face interviews in a safer location proposed by them, and using pseudonyms instead of their real names. This study initially proposed conducting interviews with 12 students, aiming to interview at least 2 students from each letter of "LGBT" and the 4 remaining from any identified sexual orientation or gender identity. Overall, the researchers collected qualitative data from four gay-identifying students, three bisexual and lesbian students, and two transgender students who were sure about their gender identity, even though they had not fully transitioned. Although data saturation was not intended, this study reached a minimum sample size of at least

[3] Outing refers to an act of disclosing or publicizing an LGBT person's sexual orientation or gender identity without their consent.

12 participants, as recommended by previous studies (Braun & Clarke, 2013; Guest et al., 2006), to reach the point of saturation which is sufficient for the analysis and scale of this study. On average, each interview took 48 min and was conducted in two official South African languages, IsiZulu and/or English, as preferred by the student. As consented by the student, interviews were audio-recorded, and notes were taken to assist the researchers in flagging out important themes and identifying what was said by students, which in turn helped with probing and following up on new insightful areas that were not covered on the interview guide. The use of qualitative research methods enabled students to share their experiences explicitly when accessing and utilizing healthcare services in South Africa and identify what matters to promote the well-being of LGBT youth.

This study aimed to provide insights into the utilization of sexual healthcare services by LGBT youth in South Africa. The specific objectives are to understand the importance of sexual healthcare for LGBT youth, explore the experiences and perceptions of students when accessing and utilizing healthcare services, and identify barriers and challenges they encounter when accessing and utilizing healthcare services. This chapter focuses on barriers that students encounter when accessing and utilizing healthcare services in South Africa. During the interviews, it was clear that nine (9/12) students had expressed their sexual orientation or gender identity to healthcare providers when accessing and utilizing healthcare facilities, and three (3/12) students had never disclosed their sexual or gender identity to healthcare providers due to fear of not receiving adequate healthcare that was provided to their heterosexual counterparts. All students reported accessing and utilizing sexual health services within and outside the university. However, they had different perceptions and experiences regarding the quality of healthcare provided. The collected qualitative data had undergone three important stages of coding. The first stage entailed transcribing the data verbatim and translating interviews transcribed in IsiZulu into English to make them easy to code and understandable for reporting. The second stage included coding the transcriptions line by line to find themes and patterns within the study, while the third stage entailed categorizing the codes into salient and discrete themes. Using thematic analysis, findings are presented in the next section.

6.4 Barriers in Healthcare for LGBT Youth

Sexual and gender minorities often face several barriers in healthcare facilities, ranging from challenges obtaining quality sexual healthcare, gaps in coverage of their needs and concerns, stigma and discrimination, and unpleasant experiences with healthcare providers. The interviews identified the consequences of a heteronormative-based health system, which perpetuates structural violence and discriminatory approaches toward those who do not conform to social norms of heteronormativity. LGBT youth believe that the health system is neglectful and inconsiderate of the sexual healthcare needs and concerns of LGBT youth. In addition, the consequences of structural violence on the general well-being of

LGBT individuals manifest through denials and unavailability of SRH facilities and delays in health-seeking behaviors, putting them at substantial risk of contracting STIs and HIV.

6.4.1 Disenfranchising Health System

With vulnerable health systems across Sub-Saharan Africa (SSA), the region has faced multiple health challenges resulting from the COVID-19 pandemic (Osseni, 2020). South Africa's health system remains one of the most highly unequal systems globally, consisting of an under-resourced public health system that caters to the majority of the population and a well-resourced private health system that serves a minority who can afford to pay (Coovadia et al., 2009; Müller, 2016). It was therefore not surprising that 11 (11/12) students reported using public healthcare facilities for sexual healthcare because they are not able to afford healthcare provided in the private healthcare system. Research suggests that LGBT youth face general challenges of service and supply unavailability, long waiting times, lack of culturally competent and well-trained personnel, and limited specialized services in the public healthcare system (Müller, 2017). However, they also encounter additional barriers to access and use. Even when LGBT youth manage to access healthcare services, those provided in the public health system in South Africa often do not adequately address their particular needs (Duby et al., 2018). Lockdown restrictions during the pandemic reduced and disrupted access to basic public healthcare services, resulting in delayed health-seeking behaviors and increasing the risk of HIV for LGBT youth (Lynch & Teagle, 2020; Siedner et al., 2020). During the interviews, most LGBT students felt excluded from the public healthcare system, noting that health services are not sensitized and fully equipped to provide SRH services across the spectrum of SOGI.

> Our health system is already struggling and not fully equipped to provide specialized care for us [LGBT youth]. (Nandi, Transgender woman)

> The lack of publicity about homosexuality in public clinics makes one skeptical about the services that can be provided to you. It discourages you from thinking the system [public] is an LGBT-aware system. (Shaun, Gay)

During the interviews, they also expressed that South Africa's health system has largely ignored their right to health, as the system assumes that their sexual healthcare needs are the same as those who identify as heterosexual. Further, they mentioned that public healthcare facilities are structured to accommodate heterosexual individuals, noting exclusion and discrimination. In line with this study, Newman-Valentine and Duma (2014) found that transgender women in South Africa negotiate healthcare in a heteronormative health system, which is exclusive and assumes that a patient should be treated as either male or female. Consequently, this rigid form of binary gender identification places sexual and gender minorities in two distinct healthcare boxes, with no right to identify as "different" (Newman-Valentine & Duma, 2014). South Africa's health system continues to use gendered electronic filing systems that assign the gender of a patient according to the presented identification document (ID) (Cloete, 2017). The need for the health system to modify and amend medical consultation forms to include a non-binary gender identity was noted by students. They believed that collecting data on SOGI should happen routinely before seeing the healthcare provider, as this makes them feel like their health needs matter.

> The registration forms we complete in the healthcare facilities are not inclusive at all, and I have never been allowed to tick on a "female" box because my identification document states that I am male. (Nandi, Transgender woman)

> I think if we are allowed to write our own gender identity on the registration forms we complete every time we utilize the healthcare facilities, it would really save us time. The nurses would see and know what to expect from the person they are about to assist. (Elijah, Transgender woman)

The Constitution does not discriminate against SOGI, but the accounts of marginalization and discrimination in healthcare are not surprising. Given the continuing invisibility of the issues of SOGI in healthcare practices and the disregard to accommodate multiple sexualities in healthcare provision, this stands out negatively in implementing an equitable health system (Salerno et al., 2020). In addition, healthcare provision that is based on upholding heteronormative norms generates a hostile, stigmatizing, and discriminating healthcare environment for the "other." These access issues limit the use of sexual healthcare services and result in delayed health-seeking behaviors and not exercising their right to access healthcare, as guaranteed by the Constitution. DeMulder et al. (2020) recognize the importance of highlighting that sexual and gender identities matter and that their needs should also be prioritized within current and future COVID-19 public health responses.

6.4.2 Instilled Principles of Heteronormativity

While research suggests that multiple layers of structural violence are deeply rooted in the heteronormative-based health system (Colpitts & Gahagan, 2016), other studies show that healthcare providers also perpetuate discrimination and prejudice toward the LGBT population (Rispel et al., 2011). Africa remains the most homo- and trans-phobic continent, and a relatively large number of Africans still believe that SOGI expressions threaten African 'traditions' and 'values' (Matolino, 2017; Sutherland et al., 2016). Presently in Ghana, leaders from a Muslim church are blaming transgender people and lesbians for the growing number of COVID-19 cases in the country (Parsons, 2020). The hegemonic system of heteronormativity and social norms that regulate gender continues to police sexuality in Africa and perpetuates hate crimes and discrimination against sexual and gender minorities (Tucker, 2020). Although South Africa has progressive legislation, homo- and trans-phobia incidences are rife and persistent. Healthcare provision based on heteronormativity acts in conjunction with other forms of structural violence, generating a hostile, stigmatizing, and segregating environment in health services (Albuquerque et al., 2016). During the interviews, students expressed fear of accessing healthcare facilities for their sexual health due to discrimination and prejudice, particularly from older healthcare providers, who, in their opinion, were trained in a heteronormative education system.

> I had an STI around my anal area, and just when I was to open up to the nurse about how I contracted it, she told me I should not and made an assumption that I had same-sex sexual intercourse. She literally told me that I was committing sin. (Mthobisi, Gay)

> I visited a clinic nearby for a check-up after I had anal sex, which led to me developing an abscess around my anus. Unfortunately, I was assisted by a very judgmental nurse who told me I should stop engaging in sexual behaviors with other men. She continued saying that homosexual behaviors are against the will of God, and that is why I was still going to get sick because this is a punishment. (Ntokozo, Gay)

While students perceived healthcare providers as a barrier to accessing and utilizing sexual healthcare services, they also confirmed that some providers are very judgmental and tend to impose their religious affiliations and beliefs in the work environment. In addition, LGBT youth experienced discriminatory views from healthcare providers due to heteronormative assumptions of care that stem from inadequate health training on SOGI and diversity. This is consistent with other research suggesting that healthcare providers are strongly influenced by their own beliefs, and a patient's perceived "moral worth" impacts their provision of services (Müller et al., 2016). Training that includes the SOGI health curriculum is still limited in medical schools. A hidden curriculum, which is implicit and highly gendered, instills institutional and discriminatory values in medical students and health professionals (Müller, 2016). This was clear during the interviews, with one final-year medical student noting that in their health training, they are still deprived of a comprehensive healthcare curriculum that is specifically LGBT-related and covers how they should provide healthcare for LGBT-identifying individuals.

> They do not teach these things [LGBT-related sexual health content] in Medical School. If they do, they do not dwell much on the realities of LGBT people and issues around access and use of healthcare. (Muzi, Gay)

While young men who have sex with men and transgender youth are at high risk of contracting HIV (Lane et al., 2011; Reif et al., 2018), they lack frequent access to sexual healthcare services as a result of structural violence and marginalization by the healthcare system. Healthcare providers continue to lack relevant knowledge and skills to provide healthcare and specific health needs required by transgender people (Duby et al., 2018). Pediatricians, who are meant to provide quality care for children and youth, rarely receive training in gender-affirming healthcare, and this may lead to an insufficient understanding of the unique healthcare issues that transgender youth face, as they have inadequate knowledge of how to prescribe treatment and provide care for them (Gridley et al., 2016; Vance et al., 2015). In addition, a study conducted in South Africa found that participants identifying as transgender faced additional difficulty finding healthcare providers who render competent transgender healthcare and provide a friendly space (Luvuno et al., 2019). One transgender student in this study perceived healthcare providers to be poorly equipped to care for transgender youth. Further, this student also noted the difficulties of receiving adequate healthcare when a transgender person has not undergone gender-affirming surgery. Generally, in this context, LGBT youth are likely reluctant to visit health facilities for their healthcare needs.

> Healthcare providers are unknowledgeable and unskilled in treating and caring for our population [transgender youth]. Nurses still don't know how to address us or where to start to assist us. (Nandi, Transgender woman)

Few South African healthcare providers receive the necessary training to address sexual health concerns. This gap in training in the area of sexual health has implications for healthcare providers when assessing and treating LGBT youth (Campbell & Stein, 2014). Healthcare providers' lack of comprehensive health training in LGBT sexual health and inability to provide culturally competent care for sexual and gender minorities results in poor healthcare quality for LGBT youth. Providing explicit and holistic training that is not highly gendered and heteronormative based is essential to overcome healthcare providers' ignorance, discrimination, and prejudice against LGBT youth.

6.4.3 Persistent Cisgenderism in Health Settings

Investing in youth-friendly healthcare services has continued to be a promising approach to meeting the SRH needs of youth. However, LGBT youth remain largely unrecognized in health promotion and prevention practices, threatening their overall well-being as they are more likely to engage in risky sexual behaviors. Engaging in risky sexual behaviors puts them at a higher risk of contracting STIs, including HIV. It is always advisable to use disease prevention methods such as condoms, lubricants, dental dams, and finger cots to prevent the transmission of sexual infections.[4] Unfortunately, these methods are not well distributed in healthcare facilities, and during the interviews, students noted difficulties and challenges in accessing them. Studies show that the distribution of lubricants and other prevention methods required by LGBT youth remains poor due to a lack of availability or accessibility (Rebe et al., 2014; Romijnders et al., 2016). This situation is likely to have worsened during the COVID-19 pandemic (Lynch & Teagle, 2020). In addition, the COVID-19 outbreak continues to strain healthcare systems and further limits the provision of SRH services, especially in resource-limited areas (Nordhues et al., 2021). While the healthcare system is heteronormative-based, students emphasized that specific disease prevention methods, including lubricants and finger cots needed when engaging

[4] It is important to note that a person may be homosexual or transgender but not sexually active, while another individual may be heterosexual and engaging in anal sex; hence, prevention and sexual health needs differ based on risk, not only on SOGI.

in sexual behaviors, are not always available in healthcare facilities. In addition, 10 (10/12) students confirmed that these prevention methods tend to be hidden or not displayed publicly for them to access freely.

> The unavailability of lubricants in the campus clinic sometimes reminds me of the clinics back home, where the healthcare personnel do not even know what they are. (Sanele, Bisexual man)

> I use finger cots for sexual pleasure, but they are not available in healthcare facilities. I can only get them online or in pharmacies. (Andile, Lesbian)

During the interviews, students were also asked to mention prevention methods they use when engaging in sexual behaviors. It was clear that most students were aware of condoms and lubricants. Only two (2/12) students mentioned the dental dam, and others were curious about this prevention method. This speaks to the lack of awareness and advertising of SRH resources available to sexual and gender minorities. Using the sexuality-health education approach during the interviews, students were educated about this prevention method to encourage them to make informed decisions to maintain healthy practices when it comes to their sexual health.

> No, I never heard of a dental-what? What is that? Please tell me more about it. (Elijah, Transgender woman)

> I am aware of a dental dam, but I have never come across it in any healthcare facility I've been to. (Buhle, Lesbian)

To show that a healthcare facility is friendly and provides adequate healthcare for LGBT youth, posters, brochures, and pamphlets should be visible and publicly displayed to ensure a sense of acceptance and inclusivity. In accessing healthcare, LGBT youth are often more accepting of physical healthcare environments that make them feel comfortable, appealing, and welcoming, reflecting diversity and inclusivity (Hawke et al., 2019). However, during the interviews, at least half of the students did not perceive healthcare services as LGBT-friendly and inclusive. They mentioned that several sexual healthcare services they utilized in the past did not have posters and pamphlets on health promotion and disease prevention for the LGBT population. In addition, they emphasized that these sexual healthcare services are structured to serve and cater to the needs of heterosexual individuals because educational materials distributed in these facilities are gender binary and mostly heteronormative.

> I also think there should be posters and pamphlets in healthcare centers to show that the Department of Health is also on our side and to also assure ourselves that our needs would be met if we access these centers. (Sonke, Gay)

> By the look of things, every time you visit a healthcare facility, I actually don't think there is an attempt to assist or even cater to us [LGBT]. You know, a few posters here and there would boost our confidence and give us assurance that our needs are catered for. (Casey, Lesbian)

Often, LGBT youth may not be aware of available SRH services, which is a barrier to access. Thus, an inclusive health system that is non-heteronormative based is important in promoting the use of sexual healthcare services for LGBT youth. In addition, engaging organizations advocating for LGBT communities in developing LGBT-friendly promotional materials is essential in making the healthcare system inclusive and welcoming for LGBT youth.

6.4.4 Inherent Paternalism

"Medical paternalism" is a term that has been defined as "the interference with a person's liberty of action, justified by reasons referring exclusively to the welfare, good, happiness, needs, interest or values of the person being coerced" (Dworkin, 1972, p. 65). This term is applicable here as it unpacks the realities of transgender youth and their access to healthcare. Most individuals identifying as transgender often desire medical assistance to transition from one sex to match their gender identity. However, this process is long in South Africa, considering that health systems are drastically underfunded and struggling. In most instances, a relatively high number of transgender people usually access gender affirmation surgeries by traveling to more accepting and medically advanced countries where medical regulations concerning these types of surgeries are relatively loose (Finley, 2020). During the COVID-19 pandemic, research suggests that accessing transgender SRH services has become extremely onerous, resulting in the rescheduling of appointments due to lockdown restrictions, poor access to hormone treatment, and a long waiting list to access transgender-specific care (van der Miesen et al., 2020). In this study, one transgender student who wishes to transition noted that accessing surgical treatment is prohibitively expensive and out-of-reach for the most marginalized.

> I tried accessing hormonal and surgical therapy, only to find out that the process is financially constraining. (Nandi, Transgender woman)

Healthcare providers such as physicians, psychologists, and endocrinologists play a pivotal role in transgender-specific care, including referring transgender patients to specific medical services, diagnosing, and treating gender dysphoria, providing cross-sex hormone therapies and treatment, and serving as consultants within healthcare systems (Johnson et al., 2016). Diagnosis of gender dysphoria does not always favor transgender youth wishing to transition from one gender to another, as many of the problems in providing transgender healthcare arise from the fundamental battle between paternalism by healthcare providers and the autonomy of transgender youth. Beliefs and standards that require transgender youth to "prove" their trans-ness to transition are unfair and disrespectful to their right to life and right to access healthcare. During the interviews, transgender students shared that proving their trans-ness to healthcare providers demonstrates an inherent distrust of statements aiming to treat gender dysphoria.

> Transitioning and being a woman fully is one of my goals. But the process of proving my gender identity with medical professionals and the Department of Home Affairs is discouraging. (Nandi, Transgender woman)

> I know people who started this transition process ten years ago, but still, they have not transitioned, and their identification document contains the sex they were assigned at birth. How frustrating? (Elijah, Transgender woman)

Many health system-related factors impact transgender youth in achieving their right to life. Delaying the transition process fueled by strong paternalism is unethical, as it violates the autonomy and integrity of transgender youth wishing to transition. Healthcare providers, who do not explain treatment plans or reasons for delaying the transition process to transgender patients, put a dangerous limitation on bodily autonomy and stray into the realm of strong paternalism (Finley, 2020). The World Professional Association for Transgender Health (WPATH) aims to address the inconsistencies in the lack of education and treatment concerning the care provided to transgender people (WPATH, 2012). The WPATH treatment model assumes that all healthcare providers are fully trained to care for transgender patients. It forces transgender patients to bow to the will of healthcare providers in the hope of being permitted access to medically necessary care (Finley, 2020). However, as noted above, healthcare providers still lack appropriate and comprehensive health training in providing quality care for sexual and gender minorities.

6.5 Conclusion and Recommendations

This chapter has highlighted the inhibiting factors influencing LGBT youth to delay seeking care in South Africa. Clearly, youth who identify outside the "heteronormative box" is not entirely recognized by the healthcare system and are most likely to face structural violence, discrimination, and marginalization. During the interviews, LGBT youth shed light on barriers and challenges they face when accessing and utilizing sexual healthcare services. These included disappointment with the healthcare system and unpleasant experiences with healthcare providers. For more than a year, the COVID-19 pandemic has highlighted how health systems can entrench and perpetuate broader hegemonic and societal power hierarchies, resulting in differential health outcomes (Ahmed et al., 2020). Restricted access to healthcare across the world has hit the most vulnerable groups, including LGBT individuals, who have been adversely affected. Therefore, even though the data does not reflect the current pandemic situation, it sheds insight into the existing experience of LGBT individuals and highlights the imminent need for effective and reliable healthcare to accommodate this marginalized population. The interviews suggest that LGBT youth face structural violence in healthcare, which may ultimately discourage them from visiting sexual healthcare facilities. Generally, LGBT youth often face stigma, prejudice, and marginalization in the healthcare system in South Africa, despite the strong emphasis in the Constitution on equality for all. The findings of this study highlight the importance of raising awareness on the spectrum of sexual orientation and gender identity, applying an intersectional lens to the health system to address health inequities, and gearing healthcare programs to provide services for all. In addition, structural problems contributing to inadequate access to and the use of sexual healthcare services among individuals identifying as LGBT require structural interventions, and they should provide an integrated approach for the promotion of inclusion and diversity in the provision of healthcare. Interventions to protect sexual- and reproductive-health rights during the global crisis need to be part of an intersectional effort that takes into account vulnerabilities brought out by diverse identities and experiences, including those faced by lesbian, gay, bisexual, transgender, transsexual, queer, questioning, intersex, asexual, ally, pansexual (LGBTIQ+) individuals. Applying an intersectional lens to the health system can provide a robust way to address health inequities perpetuated by norms of heteronormativity.

References

Ahmed, F., Ahmed, N. E., Pissarides, C., & Stiglitz, J. (2020). Why inequality could spread COVID-19. *The Lancet Public Health, 5*(5), e240.

Albuquerque, G. A., de Lima Garcia, C., da Silva Quirino, G., Alves, M. J. H., Belém, J. M., dos Santos Figueiredo, F. W., et al. (2016). Access to health services by lesbian, gay, bisexual, and transgender persons: Systematic literature review. *BMC International Health and Human Rights, 16*(1), 1–10.

Alli, F., Maharaj, P., & Vawda, M. Y. (2013). Interpersonal relations between health care workers and young clients: Barriers to accessing sexual and reproductive health care. *Journal of Community Health, 38*(1), 150–155.

Amoroto, B. (2016). Structural-systemic-cultural violence against LGBTQs in the Philippines. *Journal of Human Rights and Peace Studies, 2*(1), 67–102.

Ansara, Y. G. (2012). Cisgenderism in medical settings: Challenging structural violence through collaborative partnerships. In I. Rivers & R. Ward (Eds.), *Out of the ordinary: LGBT lives* (pp. 102–122). Cambridge Scholar Publishing.

Basnyat, I. (2017). Structural violence in health care: Lived experience of street-based female commercial sex workers in Kathmandu. *Qualitative Health Research, 27*(2), 191–203.

Bauer, G. R., Hammond, R., Travers, R., Kaay, M., Hohenadel, K. M., & Boyce, M. (2009). I don't think this is theoretical; this is our lives: How erasure impacts health care for transgender people. *Journal of the Association of Nurses in AIDS Care, 20*(5), 348–361.

Braun, V., & Clarke, V. (2013). *Successful qualitative research: A practical guide for beginners*. Sage.

Campbell, M. M., & Stein, D. J. (2014). Sexual health in the South African context. *SAMJ: South African Medical Journal, 104*(6), 439–440.

Cele, N. H., Sibiya, M. N., & Sokhela, D. G. (2015). Experiences of homosexual patients' access to primary health care services in Umlazi, KwaZulu-Natal. *Curationis, 38*(2), 1–9.

Çinar, M. (2011). *They make your life like shit. Masculinity and violence against transgender people in Istanbul*. Retrieved June 28, 2021 from https://www.fu-berlin.de/sites/gpo/int_bez/frauenmenschenrechte/theymakeyourlifeshit/MelikeCinar.pdf

Cloete, A. (2017). *Do healthcare systems in South Africa provide for the healthcare needs of gay, lesbian & transgender populations?* Human Sciences Research Council.

Colpitts, E., & Gahagan, J. (2016). I feel like I am surviving the health care system: Understanding LGBTQ health in Nova Scotia, Canada. *BMC Public Health, 16*(1), 1–12.

Constitution of South Africa. (1996). Constitution of the Republic of South Africa, Act No. 108 of 1996. Parliament of the Republic of South Africa, Cape Town.

Coovadia, H., Jewkes, R., Barron, P., Sanders, D., & McIntyre, D. (2009). The health and health system of South Africa: Historical roots of current public health challenges. *The Lancet, 374*(9692), 817–834.

De Cock, K. M., Jaffe, H. W., & Curran, J. W. (2011). Reflections on 30 years of AIDS. *Emerging Infectious Diseases, 17*(6), 1044.

DeMulder, J., Kraus-Perrotta, C., & Zaidi, H. (2020). Sexual and gender minority adolescents must be prioritised during the global COVID-19 public health response. *Sexual and Reproductive Health Matters, 28*(1), 1804717.

Duby, Z., Nkosi, B., Scheibe, A., Brown, B., & Bekker, L. G. (2018). Scared of going to the clinic: Contextualising healthcare access for men who have sex with men, female sex workers and people who use drugs in two South African cities. *Southern African Journal of HIV Medicine, 19*(1), 1–8.

Dworkin, G. (1972). Paternalism. *The Monist, 56*, 64–84.

Farmer, P. (2010). On suffering and structural violence: Social and economic rights in the global era (1996, 2003). In H. Saussy (Ed.), *Partner to the poor* (pp. 328–349). University of California Press.

Farmer, P. E., Nizeye, B., Stulac, S., & Keshavjee, S. (2019). Structural violence and clinical medicine. *The Social Medicine Reader, 2*(3), 156–169.

Finley, C. (2020). *Paternalism and autonomy in transgender healthcare*. Honors dissertation, Butler University.

Gaillard, J. C., Gorman-Murray, A., & Fordham, M. (2017). Sexual and gender minorities in disaster. *Gender, Place & Culture, 24*(1), 18–26.

Galtung, J. (1969). Violence, peace and peace research. *Journal of Peace Research, 6*, 167–191.

Gridley, S. J., Crouch, J. M., Evans, Y., Eng, W., Antoon, E., Lyapustina, M., et al. (2016). Youth and caregiver perspectives on barriers to gender-affirming health care for transgender youth. *Journal of Adolescent Health, 59*(3), 254–261.

Guest, G., Bunce, A., & Johnson, L. (2006). How many interviews are enough? An experiment with data saturation and variability. *Field Methods, 18*(1), 59–82.

Harris, B., Goudge, J., Ataguba, J. E., McIntyre, D., Nxumalo, N., Jikwana, S., & Chersich, M. (2011). Inequities in access to health care in South Africa. *Journal of Public Health Policy, 32*(S1), S102–S123.

Hawke, L. D., Mehra, K., Settipani, C., Relihan, J., Darnay, K., Chaim, G., & Henderson, J. (2019). What makes mental health and substance use services youth friendly? A scoping review of literature. *BMC Health Services Research, 19*(1), 1–16.

Heck, J. E., Sell, R. L., & Gorin, S. S. (2006). Health care access among individuals involved in same-sex relationships. *American Journal of Public Health, 96*(6), 1111–1118.

Heckathorn, D. D. (2011). Comment: Snowball versus respondent-driven sampling. *Sociological Methodology, 41*(1), 355–366.

Ilyayambwa, M. (2012). Homosexual rights and the law: A South African constitutional metamorphosis. *International Journal of Humanities and Social Science, 2*(4), 50–58.

Javaid, A. (2018). Out of place: Sexualities, sexual violence, and heteronormativity. *Aggression and Violent Behavior, 39*, 83–89.

Johnson, L., Shipherd, J., & Walton, H. M. (2016). The psychologist's role in transgender-specific care with US veterans. *Psychological Services, 13*(1), 69.

Kuyper, L., & Vanwesenbeeck, I. (2011). Examining sexual health differences between lesbian, gay, bisexual, and heterosexual adults: The role of sociodemographics, sexual behavior characteristics, and minority stress. *Journal of Sex Research, 48*(2–3), 263–274.

Lane, T., Raymond, H. F., Dladla, S., Rasethe, J., Struthers, H., McFarland, W., & McIntyre, J. (2011). High HIV prevalence among men who have sex with men in Soweto, South Africa: Results from the Soweto Men's study. *AIDS and Behavior, 15*(3), 626–634.

Lee, E. O. J. (2019). Responses to structural violence: The Everyday ways in which queer and trans migrants with precarious status respond to and resist the Canadian immigration regime. *International Journal of Child, Youth and Family Studies, 10*(1), 70–94.

Lester, K. (2008). *Encyclopedia of violence. Peace, and conflict*. Elsevier.

Luvuno, Z. P., Ncama, B., & Mchunu, G. (2019). Transgender population's experiences with regard to accessing reproductive health care in Kwazulu-Natal, South Africa: A qualitative study. *African Journal of Primary Health Care & Family Medicine, 11*(1), 1–9.

Lynch, I., & Teagle, A. (2020). The COVID-19 impact on sexual- and reproductive-health rights and gender-based violence. *HSRC Review, 18*(2), 36–37.

Matolino, B. (2017). Being gay and African: A view from an African philosopher. *Phronimon, 18*, 59–78.

Meyer, I. H., & Wilson, P. A. (2009). Sampling lesbian, gay, and bisexual populations. *Journal of Counselling Psychology, 56*(1), 23.

Mkhize, S. P., & Maharaj, P. (2020). Structural violence on the margins of society: LGBT student access to health services. *Agenda, 34*(2), 104–114.

Mkhize, S. P., & Maharaj, P. (2021). Meeting the sexual health needs of LGBT youth: Perceptions and experiences of university students in KwaZulu-Natal, South Africa. *Journal of Social Service Research, 47*(1), 56–72.

Mkhize, S. P., de Kadt, J., Naidoo, Y., & Parker, A. (2021). Health. In J. de Kadt, C. Hamann, S. P. & A. Parker (Eds.), *Quality of life 6 (2020/21) Survey: Overview report* (Section 7). Gauteng City-Region Observatory (GCRO).

Moagi, L. A., & Mavhandu-Mudzusi, A. H. (2020). *Violence against LGBT (QI) persons in Africa.* The Palgrave Handbook of African Women's Studies.

Mprah, A. (2016). Sexual and reproductive health needs of LGBT: Commentary. *African Journal of Reproductive Health, 20*(1), 16–20.

Mulé, N. J., Ross, L. E., Deeprose, B., Jackson, B. E., Daley, A., Travers, A., & Moore, D. (2009). Promoting LGBT health and well-being through inclusive policy development. *International Journal for Equity in Health, 8*(1), 1–11.

Müller, A. (2016). Health for all? Sexual orientation, gender identity, and the implementation of the right to access to health care in South Africa. *Health and Human Rights, 18*(2), 195.

Müller, A., Röhrs, S., Hoffman-Wanderer, Y., & Moult, K. (2016). You have to make a judgment call: Morals, judgments and the provision of quality sexual and reproductive health services for adolescents in South Africa. *Social Science & Medicine, 148*, 71–78.

Müller, A. (2017). Scrambling for access: Availability, accessibility, acceptability and quality of healthcare for lesbian, gay, bisexual and transgender people in South Africa. *BMC International Health and Human Rights, 17*(1), 1–10.

Müller, A., & Daskilewicz, K. (2019). *Are we doing alright? Realities of violence, mental health, and access to healthcare related to sexual orientation and gender identity and expression in East and Southern Africa: Research report based on a community-led study in nine countries.* COC Netherlands.

Newman-Valentine, D. D., & Duma, S. E. (2014). Transsexual women's journey towards a heteronormative health care system: Gender and equity. *African Journal for Physical Health Education, Recreation and Dance, 20*(Suppl 1), 385–394.

Nordhues, H. C., Bhagra, A., Stroud, N. N., Vencill, J. A., & Kuhle, C. L. (2021, April). COVID-19 gender disparities and mitigation recommendations: A narrative review. In *Mayo Clinic proceedings.* Elsevier.

Osseni, I. A. (2020). COVID-19 pandemic in sub-Saharan Africa: Preparedness, response, and hidden potentials. *Tropical Medicine and Health, 48*(1), 1–3.

Parsons, V. (2020). Muslim leaders of Ghana blame coronavirus on 'transgender and lesbianism'. *Again. Pink News.* Retrieved from https://www.pinknews.co.uk/2020/03/27/ghana-coronavirus-muslim-mission-pandemic-transgender-lesbian-homophobia/

Quinn, G. P., Sutton, S. K., Winfield, B., Breen, S., Canales, J., Shetty, G., et al. (2015). Lesbian, gay, bisexual, transgender, queer/questioning (LGBTQ) perceptions and health care experiences. *Journal of Gay & Lesbian Social Services, 27*(2), 246–261.

Rebe, K. B., De Swardt, G., Berman, P. A., Struthers, H., & McIntyre, J. A. (2014). Sexual lubricants in South Africa may potentially disrupt mucosal surfaces and increase HIV transmission risk among men who have sex with men. *South African Medical Journal, 104*(1), 49–51.

Reif, S., Wilson, E., & McAllaster, C. (2018). Perceptions and impact of HIV stigma among high risk populations in the US Deep South. *Journal of HIV and AIDS, 4*(2), 1–7.

Rispel, L. C., Metcalf, C. A., Cloete, A., Moorman, J., & Reddy, V. (2011). You become afraid to tell them that you are gay: Health service utilization by men who have sex with men in South African cities. *Journal of Public Health Policy, 32*(1), 137–151.

Romijnders, K. A., Nyoni, J. E., Ross, M. W., McCurdy, S. A., Mbwambo, J., Kok, G., & Crutzen, R. (2016). Lubricant use and condom use during anal sex in men who have sex with men in Tanzania. *International Journal of STD & AIDS, 27*(14), 1289–1302.

Ruprecht, M. M., Wang, X., Johnson, A. K., Xu, J., Felt, D., Ihenacho, S., et al. (2021). Evidence of social and structural COVID-19 disparities by sexual orientation, gender identity, and race/ethnicity in an urban environment. *Journal of Urban Health, 98*(1), 27–40.

Salerno, J. P., Devadas, J., Pease, M., Nketia, B., & Fish, J. N. (2020). Sexual and gender minority stress amid the COVID-19 pandemic: Implications for LGBTQ young persons' mental health and well-being. *Public Health Reports, 135*(6), 721–727.

Siedner, M. J., Kraemer, J. D., Meyer, M. J., Harling, G., Mngomezulu, T., Gabela, P., et al. (2020). Access to primary healthcare during lockdown measures for COVID-19 in rural South Africa: An interrupted time series analysis. *BMJ Open, 10*(10), e043763.

Subhrajit, C. (2014). Problems faced by LGBT people in the mainstream society: Some recommendations. *International Journal of Interdisciplinary and Multidisciplinary Studies, 1*(5), 317–331.

Sutherland, C., Roberts, B., Gabriel, N., Struwig, J., & Gordon, S. (2016). *Progressive prudes: A survey of attitudes towards homosexuality & gender non-conformity in South Africa*. Human Sciences Research Council.

Tucker, A. (2020). Geographies of sexualities in sub-Saharan Africa: Positioning and critically engaging with international human rights and related ascendant discourses. *Progress in Human Geography, 44*(4), 683–703.

van der Miesen, A. I., Raaijmakers, D., & van de Grift, T. C. (2020). You have to wait a little longer: Transgender (mental) health at risk as a consequence of deferring gender-affirming treatments during COVID-19. *Archives of Sexual Behavior, 49*, 1395–1399.

Vance, S. R., Jr., Halpern-Felsher, B. L., & Rosenthal, S. M. (2015). Health care providers' comfort with and barriers to care of transgender youth. *Journal of Adolescent Health, 56*(2), 251–253.

Warner, M. (1991). Introduction: Fear of a queer planet. *Social Text*, 3–17.

Winter, D. D., & Leighton, D. C. (2001). Structural violence. In D. J. Christie, R. V. Wagner, & D. D. Winter (Eds.), *Peace, conflict, and violence: Peace psychology in the 21st century*. Prentice-Hall.

Wood, S. M., Salas-Humara, C., & Dowshen, N. L. (2016). Human immunodeficiency virus, other sexually transmitted infections, and sexual and reproductive health in lesbian, gay, bisexual, transgender youth. *Pediatric Clinics, 63*(6), 1027–1055.

World Professional Association for Transgender Health. (2012). *Standards of care for the health of transsexual, transgender, and gender nonconforming people [7th version]*. WPATH Publications.

Sthembiso Pollen Mkhize, M.A. is a Junior Researcher at the Gauteng City-Region Observatory (a partnership between provincial and local governments, the University of Johannesburg, and the University of the Witwatersrand in South Africa). He holds a Master's degree in Population Studies from the University of KwaZulu-Natal and his research agenda extends across multiple constructs that lie at the heart of promoting quality of life and well-being, health, social justice, inclusion, and visibility for marginalized individuals.

Pranitha Maharaj, Ph.D. is a Professor and DSI/NRF SARChI Chair in Economic Development at the School of Built Environment and Development Studies, University of KwaZulu-Natal, Durban. She holds a DSI-NRF-funded Ph.D. from the London School of Hygiene and Tropical Medicine and has written extensively on the sexual and reproductive health of young people.

Chapter 7
"Secure the Bag": Young Women's Agencies Toward Better Versus Bare Realities During COVID

Sinethemba Sidloyi

7.1 Introduction

"Securing the bag" refers to an economic instrumentality among young women through which women draw money and fashionable items toward a better lifestyle using transactional sexual relationships with blessers.[1] This economic activity is different from sex work. Sex work can be broadly defined as a business transaction in which sex is exchanged for money between a client and a service provider outside of an intimate relationship (Makhakhe, 2017). On the other hand, transactional sexual relationships with blessers are intimate relationships in which men (usually older and married) financially support a younger woman in exchange for sex and companionship (Moodley & Ebrahim, 2019; Nayar, 2016; Wojcicki, 2002). Research interest in this phenomenon dates back to earlier conceptualizations of sugar daddies and notions of the so-called "Minister of Transport/Finance," terms that were used to describe older men's socio-economic roles in young women's lives (Singatha, 2020). The concepts also reflect the centrality of money and material benefits in women's intimate relationships (Shefer & Strebel, 2013). Transactional sexual relationships continue in present-day South Africa through the notion of the blesser, as illustrated in Fig. 7.1.

Through the help of websites such as blesserfinder.com and Blesser Finder South Africa (SA) that promise young women a "key to financial freedom," young women are able to connect online with prominent blessers. Blesser Finder SA has a

[1] Blessers are usually married, rich men who spend money on young women, buying expensive gifts and taking them on local and international holidays, such as Dubai, in exchange for sexual favors.

S. Sidloyi (✉)
University of Johannesburg, Johannesburg, South Africa
e-mail: ssidloyi@uj.ac.za

K. Naidoo et al. (eds.), *Young People, Violence and Strategic Interventions in Sub-Saharan Africa*, Clinical Sociology: Research and Practice,
https://doi.org/10.1007/978-3-031-20679-5_7

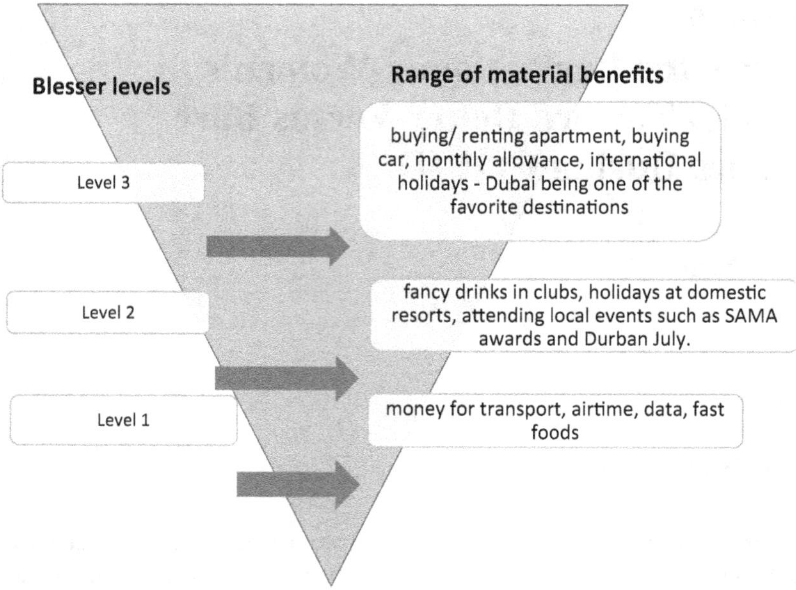

Fig. 7.1 Blesser levels and respective benefits (NB: Level 1 benefits were mostly accessed during COVID-19 due to travel restrictions, work restrictions for those not in essential services, and job losses)

WhatsApp number to which young women can send their details and are connected to blessers, receiving a transport allowance to meet the blesser once they agree to a relationship. This social media site clearly states that it has no age restriction and has a following of more than 3000 people, with requests for blessers consistently observed. In addition to social media platforms such as blesserfinder.com, young women meet with prominent blessers in nightclubs and other social spaces where they can receive expensive alcohol paid for by men (Zawu, 2020).

Scholars in other countries note a transactional sexual relationship trend similar to the South African blesser trend (see Hawkins et al., 2009; Masvawure, 2010; Mensah, 2020; Mixon, 2018; Nayar, 2016; Sidloyi, 2021; Wojcicki, 2002; Zembe et al., 2013). For example, Mensah (2020, p. 547) proposes a growing pursuit of a lifestyle that portrays affluence, economic freedom, and social power among young women in Nigeria. The lifestyle is fuelled by the association of material consumption with independence, choice, and prestige, some of the aspirations visible among young women of varying economic backgrounds. A similar view is shared by Masvawure (2010, p. 861), who maintains that there is a desire for flashiness that is displayed by young women in Zimbabwe, underlying their consumption of fashionable items such as clothing. These luxury items enhance young women's social status and set them apart from those who do not have access to such items. Hence, as Masvawure (2010, p. 864) suggests, the pressure to be fashionable is not unique to young women from financially disadvantaged backgrounds. Instead, this pressure is shared across economic backgrounds, demonstrating how images of affluence are communicated through the media in ways that shape young women's choices. The young women's different economic positions inform the range of material benefits that young women access depending on the blesser level (see Fig. 7.1).

Hawkins et al. (2009, p. 173) made a similar observation in their study of young women in Maputo, Mozambique, recognizing that young women idealized a lifestyle that is driven by pursuits of trendy clothes, drinking beverages in exclusive bars, riding in expensive cars, and owning the latest cell phones. The young women thus interpret these material desires as a symbol of freedom, affluence, and independence, demonstrating that the lifestyle goals they aspire to are shaped by this belief that material goods will give them social power and social status. Similarly, in a study among female college students in the United States, Mixon (2018) observed that many female students are turning to transactional sexual relationship forms of financing their livelihoods. Consequently, young women enter into potentially lucrative romantic arrangements with older males, referred to as sugar daddies, many of whom they connect with online using dating sites such as seeking.com. Seeking.com is a dating site that was created specifically to connect American sugar babies, sugar daddies, and sugar mommas in 2006, subsequently expanding in 2010 to Canada, Australia, the United Kingdom, and other parts of Europe. To date, this site has approximately 20 million users who connect from more than 100 countries worldwide. However, as a result of the controversy over the term "sugar daddy," it is stated on the website that the term is no longer used to describe members. Nevertheless, seeking.com, similar to the Blesser Finder SA site, continues with its aim to connect young women with wealthy and generous romantic partners, living up to its motto that life is too short to settle.

Nayar (2016) observes the same phenomenon of sugar daddies in the United States; the women involved in transactional sexual relationships embrace the economic underpinnings of their instrumental use of intimacy and beauty. However, they also raise romantic connotations that indicate a refusal to see their relations as work and, therefore, are solely driven by market logic. The above discussion indicates that the intertwining of financial instrumentality and intimate sexual love makes transactional relationships complex to unpack because the intimate relationship aspect distinguishes blesser sexual relations from sex work. Nonetheless, it does not diminish the centrality of money and material benefits in the blesser sexual relationships as these relationships would not continue without them (Howell & Vincent, 2014; Leclerc-Madlala, 2004; Wojcicki, 2002). Therefore, the emphasis on intimacy safeguards the blessees from the stigma that tends to be associated with sex work. At the same time, young women continue to benefit materially through transactional sexual relationships.

The noted complexity of transactional sexual relationships, as well as their common use as an economic agency among young women, makes it essential for scholars to continue exploring transactional sexual relationships. It also becomes important to examine how this phenomenon changes over time and how it manifests in ways informed by constructions of the varying societal spaces in which it is exercised. The importance of investigation would be very useful during the current coronavirus disease (COVID-19) pandemic, which has exposed persistent socio-economic disparities in township livelihoods, reminding us how women in these communities are interconnected through conflicting experiences of financial disadvantage (Khwela-Mdluli & Beharry-Ramraj, 2020; Leburu-Masigo & Kgadima, 2020).

In the absence of a COVID-19 vaccine in March 2020, when we went into lockdown, the South African government pronounced that going into quarantine would be the response to curb the spread of the Coronavirus. This led to a drastic alteration in the day-to-day lives of individuals, as many had to work from home, students were studying from home, and efforts were being made to maintain social distance (Leburu-Masigo & Kgadima, 2020). However, township spaces continued to be busy with many people not adhering to the lockdown regulations, as children continued playing on the streets and alcohol consumption carried on as usual. This created the impression that townships were the same as before the COVID-19 pandemic. Nevertheless, this supposed normality was however met with contrasting financial realities. As a result, the lockdown's negative consequences, such as job losses, strenuous working conditions for essential workers (e.g., nurses), and disrupted schooling for students, soon became a reality for many people in these locations (Dlamini, 2021).

It is within the socio-economic disadvantages of the lockdown where an increase in gender-based violence (GBV) was noted by both media and scholars who cited being trapped at home with abusive partners and being isolated from people and resources of support as possible causes of the increase (see Channon, 2020; Dlamini, 2021; Leburu-Masigo & Kgadima, 2020; Lefafa, 2020; Mbunge, 2020; Radebe, 2020; UN Women, 2020a, 2020b). As Mlambo (2020) suggested, South Africa reported 87,000 GBV cases during the lockdown's first 7 days. Subsequently, Statistics South Africa (Stats SA) indicated that approximately 33,899 births occurred to mothers aged 17 years and younger in 2020/2021. In addition, over 600 children aged 10–13 gave birth; of these young women, 499 gave birth in 2020, indicating the sexual vulnerability of young women in South African spaces (Statistics South Africa, 2021a, b). The above-mentioned occurrences unearth the persistence of gender inequality that is still widespread in South African society underlying violent masculinities through which young women are subject to various emotional, sexual, financial, and physical abuse. With the above views in mind, the objective of this chapter is to examine how the Ngangelizwe and Alexandra Townships as socio-economic spaces influence young women's approaches to transactional sexual relationships. This discussion aims to unpack how young women in these two townships "secure the bag" toward meeting their lifestyle goals, uncovering how the COVID-19 pandemic and the resultant lockdown affected the women's instrumentalities.

7.2 Approach to Study

The objective of understanding the socio-economic instrumentalities of young women made it imperative to employ qualitative research methods. Qualitative methods enable researchers to understand the experiences and underlying meanings of lived experiences through the research participant's perspective (Naidoo, 2015). This is because qualitative research provides ways to examine individuals or social groups within the context in which their realities are constructed while also allowing space for participants to share their experiences through their own voices. Hence, Fossey et al. (2002) suggest that qualitative methods are useful for eliciting contextual information that improves understanding of social groups, providing researchers with in-depth information from which they can generate knowledge about social reality.

Within the above-discussed conceptualization of qualitative research techniques, an ethnographic approach was utilized since I wished to be close to the participants and how they negotiated their lifestyle choices. Closeness meant spending time with participants in their homes, visiting nightclubs and other social spaces where they interact with others, and having recurring in-depth conversations with them. The engagement with participants over an extended period enabled understanding of the young people through their voices during discussions and by observing their patterns as they went to school and work, met with friends, and carried on their daily tasks through which their realities were negotiated. Since the study aimed to understand the young women within their township space, ethnography was ideal also because it enabled access to observe and learn about the township space from the participants. The learning occurred during interactions with the young women as they sat outside their homes with their friends passing time and when attending social functions in the neighborhood with the participants. As Hathaway (1995, p. 545) suggests, ethnography enables an understanding of how cultures work and affect the people who belong to them. Thus, access to the township spaces (Ngangelizwe Township, Mthatha, and Alexandra Township, Gauteng) as well as the subjective lives of participants become an important aspect of ethnographic studies.

7.3 Data Collection Process

Having gained access to Ngangelizwe Township, I identified approximately 20 young women who met the sample criteria, aged approximately 21–29 years, female, and present- and long-term residences of Ngangelizwe Township. The sample size was motivated by an interest in spending quality time with each participant to gain in-depth access to their lived experiences rather than examining large numbers of people. All the identified participants spoke isiXhosa and English interchangeably, with some using local terminology/slang. I, fluent in isiXhosa and English, engaged with the participants in both languages while relying on the participant's explanation of the local terminology they sometimes used. As a result, the recorded conversations with participants were held in English and isiXhosa. Where isiXhosa was used, I translated it into English during transcription. The participants were primarily identified based on observations made during social activities such as attending funerals, church, and clubbing; observations suggesting these young women carried rich information that could be valuable for the study. To build on the accounts of young women in township spaces during the COVID-19 lockdown period, I gained access to participants in Alexandra Township in the Gauteng province through the social workers positioned at the Alexandra police station. The social workers became an entry into a snowballing sampling method through which ten young women were identified and interviewed.

Due to the lockdown travel restrictions, Alexandra Township was convenient as a field of study, which did not allow me to travel to the Eastern Cape Province, where Ngangelizwe Township is located. The option was to visit a nearby site whose socio-economic features were similar to those of Ngangelizwe Township. Alexandra Township was identified because of its noted likeness to Ngangelizwe Township. From the interaction and conversations with Alexandra residents, I recognized a need to examine young women's lived experiences during COVID-19 while reflecting on the prior study on lived experiences of young women in Ngangelizwe Township, Mthatha. At this site, I observed gendered enactments in participants' routines while listening to details of the young women's lived experiences from childhood until the present, recording the in-depth conversations in English, isiZulu, and Sotho—languages that I can speak and read. During ethnographic encounters in Alexandra Township, I abided by the lockdown protocols. As such, data collection occurred during Level One lockdown, where people were allowed to meet in small groups. Sanitizers and masks were made available to participants during meetings.

7.4 Data Analysis and Interpretation

A thematic data analysis approach was utilized, which entails a number of steps, as Creswell (2013) has illustrated. During the data analysis and interpretation phases, close attention was paid to the heterogeneous realities of the young women as informed by the varying periods in which data were collected (pre- and during the pandemic). I identified themes that emerged from the discussions as read on transcripts and observation notes. While drawing out the themes, I paid attention to how young women's realities were shaped similarly and differently by their township spaces. Attention was also paid to the unique ways its geographic locations and socio-economic structuring shape the two township spaces. The following lived experiences of young women were unearthed, with a focus on the economic actions of the young women toward meeting their lifestyle aspirations. The themes that were identified in this study are: Intimate relationships are a gateway into better socio-economic experiences; Township spaces as influences on young women's economic agencies; Transactional sexual relations as shaped by township intersectionality; and

Securing the bag within vulnerabilities. These themes are used to deliberate on young women's economic agencies—grounding the instrumental actions of the women within the intersectional structuring of their township spaces.

7.5 Intimate Relationships Are a Gateway to Better Socio-economic Experiences

From the narratives, it became clear that the desire for material gain underlies these young women's expectations of intimate relationships. In fact, young women enter into intimate relationships with men not only for love and companionship but also as a means to better their socio-economic circumstances since they are not able to afford certain luxuries on their own, as reflected in the following statements by the participants in this study:

> Of course, I date for love, but I cannot date a broke man. A man must make means and be able to make things happen. When I need money to stay this pretty, for example, he must be able to make a plan.—Aphelele (23, 1 child, unemployed).

> A man must spoil his woman. A man must spend on you because if he is not spending on you, then who is he spending on?—Akhona (20, 1 child, student).

> An ideal boyfriend for me is a person who has a source of income, one who is not stingy, and one who understands that it's expensive to be a woman. There are clothes, there is makeup, and there is social life, you know.—Busi (26, 2 children, unemployed).

> Money is very important in a relationship, sisi (sister). It's such a deal-breaker. Yho, ngubani ofuna uhlupheka enendoda [who wants to struggle, yet they have a man?].—Sbongile (27, 1 child, unemployed).

> I wouldn't date someone who is not working. Maybe because I am working too, but I really would not. Unless they lost a job while we were dating and they are seriously looking for another one. But to go and date someone who is not working, no way.—Yonela (26, 1 child, employed).

The above statements by research participants indicate that having money is important when young women consider intimate relationship partners. The man's willingness to use his money to provide for the lifestyle desires of the young women is equally important, as indicated by Akhona's utterances that a man must spoil his woman. The importance of money in young women's intimate relationships is similarly documented by Mampane (2018), who maintains that young women tend to rely on their intimate partners to meet financial needs that their parents are unable to meet—suggesting that transactional sexual relationships serve as an economic mechanism that buffers young women from poverty-related experiences by mostly drawing Level 1 blesser benefits as indicated in Fig. 7.1.

Mavhandu-Mudzusi (2019) and Zawu (2020) maintain that blesser–blessee relationships are a preferred economic means through which young women rise to a better socio-economic status. According to Mavhandu-Mudzusi (2019), blessers provide young women with economic benefits such as apartments, clothing, cell phones, and airtime, which denote Levels 2 and 3 blesser benefits (see Fig. 7.1), but also offer feelings of safety and security that result from dating men who can pose as father figures when the need arises. Thus, in addition to recognizing the prevalence of transactional sexual relationships, it is crucial to uncover young women's different needs and desires that lead them into this socio-economic strategy rather than assuming that it is only about exchanging money and material gifts. Singatha (2020) and Sidloyi (2021) suggest that unless there is an understanding of the reasons why young women engage in transactional relationships and how these reasons are influenced by societal structuring, researchers will not be able to provide suitable solutions to the vulnerabilities such as GBV experiences that young women are faced with in these blesser–blessee relations.

7.6 Townships Spaces as Influences on Young Women's Economic Agencies

As reflected in the above discussion, intimate relationships are conceptualized as a doorway to a better life. The meanings of better vs. bare life are shaped by the young women's township views of which items are fashionable and therefore sought after. This means that young women's economic agencies through intimate relationships are influenced mainly by pressure to fit within societal perceptions of affluence and social status, as reflected in the following extracts:

> Girls want to slay [slay is a compliment given to girls who are dressed in style/well]. *They want to be recognized, and they want to be seen. Like, for me, it's about wanting to feel good because when I look beautiful, and someone sees and compliments me, then I feel seen.*— Aphiwe (22, 2 children, student).

> There are social trends, you know. I want to slay. I mean, I want the good life. I cannot only see it on Facebook. I must experience it. You know what they say, moss: YOLO [you only live once].—Chuma (23, 1 child, employed).

> I guess for many of us it's FOMO [fear of missing out]. We want to be like other children. You know, when you open Instagram and see what other people are getting from their men, and you are here with someone who does not even take you out? That's not nice. You wonder why not me?—Sasa (21, no children, student).

> Girls here want to be like Boity and Minnie Dlamini [television personalities/celebrities]. To the extent that they sometimes forget that those girls have money, and we don't. Not the kind of money that they have.—Babes (21, no children, student).

> Kukuthanda izinto [it's liking things]. People do not want nice things to pass them. There is that love for fashion; even though people know they cannot afford it, they still want to conform. They put pressure on themselves to wear this and that like others, yet they know their backgrounds do not allow them. We are not all like Bonang and these people on TV, but we push to live like them.—Nomhle (25, 1 child, unemployed).

> Sometimes it's wanting to fit in, you know. I'm just thinking of the pressure when you are going to school, and you sort of want to be okay or Fridays, going out with friends. There are

> those kinds of social experiences, but sometimes you just get charmed by a guy, and one gift leads to more gifts, and it ends up being like that.—Zaza (22, 1 child, student).

As indicated by the participants above, peer pressure often drives young women to desire materials they cannot afford. The pressure, signified by expressions such as FOMO (fear of missing out), YOLO (you only live once), and Ukuthanda izinto (liking things), is perpetuated by social media images where trends are continuously showcased and glamorized. The participants' views are indicative of observations by scholars such as Chohan and Langa (2011), Meel (2011), and Singatha (2020), who argue that peer pressure is instigated by social media influencers who constantly update images of their "soft life."[2] Therefore, social media influence, coupled with gender inequality through which men tend to have more money than women, makes the intimate relationship a quicker gendered pathway for women to access the "soft life" that is displayed. This, together with the constant availability of older men who want to spend their money on younger women, perpetuates an uneven power relationship through reliance on transactional sex.

7.7 Transactional Sexual Relations as Shaped by Township Intersectionality

Prior gendered experiences shape young women's intimate relationships. This means that the young women's agentic actions are also unconsciously adopted social actions that are informed by the intersections of race, gender, class, and age that underlie the township spaces in which the women live (Sidloyi, 2021). The intersections are reflected in the following descriptions by participants in this study:

> Boys, especially dating someone your age, is just too messy because they are so disrespectful towards women. You end up fighting. They cheat, they lie, they have no money, so you go through so much pain for nothing.—Asanda (21, no children, employed).

> I don't know if age really matters, but I just do not date boys my age anymore, and I do not date in my neighborhood at all. Boys here are rude and violent, and they don't even spoil you. I only date people who are ten years older than me and more, and I go for guys from town and all these other places, you know.—Chuma (23, 1 child, employed).

> I dated this boy who was my age, and he had so many girlfriends, and whenever I tried to talk to him about it, he would just be so rude. I got tired. I tried a couple of boys my age, and I kept on experiencing abuse and disrespect. I then decided to go for older men, and for me, they treat me better, and I also get to be spoiled with gifts.—Babes (21, no children, student).

> You have to open your eyes when you choose whom you sleep with. Don't just be with someone who can't do anything for you; otherwise, you will struggle, and no one wants to struggle.—Aphelele (23, 1 child, unemployed).

---

[2] "Soft life" is an expensive, comfortable lifestyle that requires no stress. It is signified by spending lots of money and looking good.

The above experiences of participants indicate that the choice to enter into relationships with older men is not only influenced by young women's material desires. Instead, it is a decision that materialized from prior problematic intimate relationship experiences with younger men; hence Asanda's description of it as "messy." The messy description is characterized by experiences of being cheated on, abused, and disrespected. In addition to enduring abuse, the women did not usually receive desired money or gifts, thus suggesting that the relationships did not benefit the young women in any way. Therefore, within these experiences, Aphelele maintains that one has to open their eyes when choosing whom to relate to, proposing that it is better to be intimate in a relationship with material benefits.

The above expressions by participants indicate that young women's choice of intimate relationships with blessers is devised as an economic strategy with awareness of the emotional cost of intimate relationships, which is abuse and infidelity. This mindfulness suggests that entering into transactional sexual relationships is an economic strategy devised by young women who are acutely aware of intimate relationships' risks and benefits. This positions young women as active agents rather than victims in their relationships, even though their agency coexists with experiences of vulnerability. The vulnerability is produced by the broken system of systemic injustices and patriarchy within which the young women's agentic choices are negotiated.

This view is similarly shared by scholars such as Hunter (2002), who suggests that transactional relationships are agencies that young women approach not as passive victims but with power and to access economic influence through their image as an asset to negotiate. Thus, the young women who employ this economic mechanism do so in ways that tend to both challenge and reproduce patriarchal structures. This refers to such relationships' contradictory and complex nature (see Selikow & Mbulaheni, 2013). The women tactfully present their bodies in ways that appeal to men sexually to get their attention, the overall goal being to receive the material goods they so desperately want. These tactics are in line with what Leclerc-Madlala (2004) suggests, in that transactional sexual practices may act as signifiers of modern life in how young women use sexual relationships to reflect their freedom to choose their sexual partners and their image while using their appearance to draw the material benefits they want from men.

The above views suggest that drawing from transactional sexual relationships is grounded within gendered societal structuring of social-economic spaces and should be recognized as such rather than viewed only as a subjective socio-economic decision that young women of certain socio-economic backgrounds make. In so doing, interventions that focus on the vulnerabilities of young women in transactional sexual relationships may be able to challenge the structural issues such as gender inequality that informs access to resources, as well as address how the effects manifest differently in the lived experiences of young women. This perspective is similar to one maintained by scholars such as Anthias (2012), Beames and Telford (2013), Collins (1990), Crenshaw (1989), and Faragó (2016), who uncovered the realities of women as shaped within locations that are underpinned by deep-seated coexisting gendered experiences of advantage and disadvantage.

7.8 Securing the Bag Within Vulnerabilities

The above views of participants indicate that young women enter into intimate relationships with clear socio-economic goals in mind. Additionally, they use their prior relationship experiences to guide their interactions and inform their expectations of new relationships. It is within their awareness that they draw resources from their intimate partners—suggesting that they "secure the bag" with certain socially constructed "rules of engagement." A similar view is shared by Masenya (2017), who maintains that a blessee is usually a young adult, who can be a university student from a rich or a poor household, and who does not see themselves as victims in their transactional relationship but rather as securing the bag from their blesser, thus bringing a liberal view of young women who recognize intimate relationships as spaces of socio-economic negotiation. Participants in the following descriptions indicate these economic rules of engagement:

> Let me give you an example of a blesser. I once dated a married man, and he would give me money and take me with him to his business meetings, but I would go shopping during the day when he was with his business associates. Then, when he was done, he would send a driver to fetch me, and we would have fun and sex like a normal couple. He gave me money, that man, and he took me on holidays and lots of business trips. But we broke up because he started catching feelings [falling in love] and was jealous when I was not available because I was with my boyfriend. That was a blesser because we were both together just for money and pleasure but no commitment or plans for the future.—Nono (23, 2 children, employed).

> But, who really wants to wait for month-end to get money when they can get it faster? There is a constant need for money, and sometimes waiting is hard, especially if you know that what you are waiting for is not even enough to meet the needs that you have. It's not a lie that we all want money, but some just don't like to admit it.—Busi (26, 2 children, unemployed).

> The trick is not to catch feelings and just remember that this person has a wife and probably has other girlfriends too. Especially here because there are only a few tender boys here. So if you catch feelings, you will not even enjoy the money and gifts because you start looking for commitment. These men are not dating for marriage. Some are married; it's just for fun.—Soso (22 yrs, 1 child, unemployed).

The above statements by Nono, Busi, and Soso suggest a clear understanding of the "rules" of the game. Soso elaborates on the "rules" of the game, so to speak, by explaining the importance of "not to catch feelings," i.e., not becoming emotionally involved as one must remember what is at stake. This indicates the awareness of the limits within which young women engage in transactional sexual relationships, thus treating the relationships differently by accepting the wife's or other potential girlfriend's presence. However, the boundaries are not equally respected by men in these relationships, as indicated by Nono, whose blesser became emotionally attached and possessive even though he had prior knowledge of her "other" boyfriend.

This suggests that securing the bag occurs in a context of unstable gendered power imbalances in which young women have room to negotiate, although their negotiations have boundaries beyond which there are vulnerabilities. The vulnerabilities are currently informed by the socio-economic stress resulting from the impact of the present COVID-19 pandemic, which continues to see many people losing their jobs as businesses can no longer function as usual under the range of lockdown restrictions. This is exacerbated by travel restrictions, which interfere with the usual traveling together on business trips where young women like Nono would be hosted in hotels and enjoy a good time while the blesser attends business meetings. Therefore, the young women suggest that they depend more on their men for money within the socio-economic changes following lockdown restrictions. This is because, during the COVID-19 lockdowns, young women could no longer work in restaurants, clubs or do the hair of other students to gain some money as they would have before lockdown. The pandemic thus increased their reliance on their blessers, who provided them with money for data, airtime, chocolates, flowers, and alcohol, among other gifts, as indicated in the following extracts:

> We are stuck, if you know what I mean. We are meant to live indoors, but there is no life indoors for us because there is nothing to do indoors. That is why you see so many people on the streets, even during the lockdown. We meet our partners and friends, and we have places here where we go chill and have fun because our life is out in the streets.—Lelo (28, no children, unemployed).

> I haven't worked since lockdown because the salon was closed, so I depend on my partner for money, you know. My partner comes through for me even though he complains that things aren't as they were with his businesses. It's mostly money that he gives, and he'd say I must go buy what I want.—Tomi (29, 2 children, employed).

> He gives me money, more like an allowance, because I need data and airtime and because alcohol is more expensive since people charge lockdown prices. We don't go out as usual, but we try to have fun, so for that, he gives me money. For my birthday, he brought me flowers, chocolates, and other gifts, so we tried to keep things going.—Sentle (28, 1 child, unemployed).

The negative effect of the lockdown is also how it sparks abusive emotional outbreaks that are fuelled by episodes of mistrust that erupt within the young women's intimate relationships, as indicated in the following statements by participants:

> Sometimes I would say I can't see you today and he starts saying, oh, so you found someone else. It's as if I'm hunting for the next man kind of thing. And you hear the change in the tone of voice. Then I laugh and say, no, it's not like that. He then forces us to come even if it's a few minutes and those few minutes end up being a drive to a lodge and whatever else, you know.—Busi (26, 2 children, unemployed).

> The problem is how the guy becomes all about himself. Like how they want to find you every time he calls on the phone. Like how they want you to be available when they want you even though you have your own life and schedule. Those lead to disagreements and can be violent because he feels like you are now using him.—Aphelele (23, 1 child, unemployed).

> When a man gives you money, they often believe that it gives them the right to control you in a way. Especially blessers since they give you lots of money although they are not all controlling. You see it in how they somehow want to dictate your availability. Sometimes in a romantic way, he says, get ready I'm coming over, but deep down, you know he just wants to see if he can get me anytime he wants.—Nono (23, 2 children, employed).

> For me, it was things like condom use and him thinking he can see me whenever he decides, yet I cannot call him anytime because he has a family, you know. I remember this one whom upfront told me we wouldn't use it. So now I carried the burden of having to make sure I don't fall pregnant, you know. I know other girls have the same experience of not having that power to negotiate condom use with them. Yet we know if you fall pregnant, it's your burden, so it's a matter of injection.—Chuma (23, 1 child, employed).

The above-mentioned experiences of participants suggest that risk-taking behaviors of transactional sexual relationships continue to enable young women to secure the bag within the changed context of COVID-19. However, the benefits are met with negative effects such as exposure to vulnerabilities that come with living out the precariously instrumental lifestyle under socio-economic conditions unfavorable to women. For instance, the dependence on men for money creates an impression that women are now men's possessions and owe them something in exchange for the money they give. As a result, subtle forms of emotional abuse persist, given the power imbalances in the relationships, with men having more room for negotiation over things that impact women's bodies and well-being (for example, condom use). These vulnerabilities are noted by scholars such as Dlamini (2021), Mavhandu-Mudzusi (2019), and Zawu (2020), who maintain that the number of young women subjected to sexual, emotional and/or physical violence perpetrated by an intimate partner has increased during the lockdown as the options for accessing money diminished through increasing job losses and the resultant increase in unemployment. The above discussion indicates that securing the bag through transactional sexual relationships is not simply a subjective economic strategy but a socio-economic agency influenced by the intersectional structuring of township spaces in which young women who draw from these agencies are situated. The discussion subsequently indicates that the young women's transactional sexual instrumentalities are not static, but they constantly change to fit within the context in which the young women find themselves.

7.9 Conclusion

The above discussion aimed at uncovering how young women "secure the bag" through blesser–blessee relationships. It sought to unearth how young women's instrumentalities continue to be influenced by COVID-19 and the consequent lockdown measures aimed at curbing the spread of the virus. The accounts of young women illustrated that blesser–blessee relationships are a socio-economic strategy that is devised from an agentic positioning rather than from a victim standpoint. Young urban women form relationships with financially well-off men to attain images of glamour by actively using their sexuality to acquire products that reflect high-social lifestyles and satisfy "wants" instead of meeting needs. The discussion subsequently showed that COVID-19 interrupted day-to-day routines that made young women depend more on men than ever before, as many women could not engage in the usual economic strategies through which they got money to meet their lifestyle goals. The financial benefit from men for money, data, airtime, and alcohol, among other things, was, however, met with episodes of emotional abuse in instances where the men would not be able to reach the women on the phone. This means that by giving money and gifts, there was an increase in men's control over women, perpetuating patriarchal power imbalances. Therefore, drawing from transactional sexual relationships in the above manner reflects the young women's use of their sex appeal to seduce wealthy men and acquire social and economic influence in return. This negotiation of sexual agency is done within the vulnerabilities that are informed by gendered power imbalances that underlie the increase in young women's experiences of GBV in South Africa. The young women's sexual agency is compromised within the deeply patriarchal context, as reflected by the various forms of abuse that are instigated to limit young women's sexual assertiveness. Therefore, while securing the bag is employed as an agentic economic action, it also locks young women in cycles of financial dependence on men. With COVID-19's resultant job losses, increase in youth unemployment, and peer pressure forcing many young women to "secure the bag" through transactional sexual relations, the question remains: how do women break free from financial reliance on transactional sexual relations?

References

Anthias, F. (2012). Intersectional what? Social divisions, intersectionality and levels of analysis. *Ethnicities, 13*(1), 3–19.

Beames, S., & Telford, J. (2013). Pierre Bourdieu: Habitus, field and capital in rock climbing. In C. J. E. Pike & S. Beames (Eds.), *Outdoor adventure and social theory* (pp. 77–87). Routledge.

Channon, A. (2020). *GBV: A complex problem that demands considered responses from social investors*. Retrieved July 29, 2021 from https://www.dailymaverick.co.za/opinionista/2020-06-28-gbv-a-complex-problem-that-demands-considered-responses-from-social-investors/

Chohan, Z., & Langa, M. (2011). Teenage mothers talk about their experience of teenage motherhood. *Agenda: Empowering Women for Gender Equity, 25*(3), 87–95.

Collins, P. H. (1990). *Black feminist thought: Knowledge, consciousness and the politics of empowerment.* Harper Collins.

Crenshaw, K. (1989). Demarginalizing the intersection of race and sex: A black feminist critique of antidiscrimination doctrine, feminist theory and antiracist politics. *University of Chicago Legal Forum, 1*(8), 139–167.

Creswell, J. W. (2013). *Qualitative inquiry & research design: Choosing among five approaches* (3rd ed.). Thousand Oaks.

Dlamini, N. J. (2021). Gender-based violence, twin pandemic to COVID-19. *Critical Sociology, 47*(4–5), 583–590.

Faragó, L. (2016). The social (sociological) turn in the discourse about space. *Romanian Review of Regional Studies, xii*(1), 3–12.

Fossey, E., Harvey, C., McDermott, F., & Davidson, L. (2002). Understanding and evaluating qualitative research. *Australian and New Zealand Journal of Psychiatry, 36*, 717–732.

Hathaway, R. S. (1995). Assumptions underlying quantitative and qualitative research: Implications for institutional research. *Research in Higher Education, 36*, 535–562.

Hawkins, K., Prince, N., & Mussa, F. (2009). Milking the cow: Young women's construction of identity and risk in age-disparate transactional sexual relationships in Maputo, Mozambique. *Glob Public Health, 4*(2), 169–182.

Howell, S., & Vincent, L. (2014). Licking the snake – The I'khothane and contemporary township youth identities in South Africa. *South African Review of Sociology, 42*(2), 60.

Hunter, M. (2002). The materiality of everyday sex: Thinking beyond 'prostitution'. *African Studies, 61*(1), 99–120.

Khwela-Mdluli, N., & Beharry-Ramraj, A. (2020). The effect of covid-19 on working women in South Africa. *Gender & Behaviour, 18*(4), 16501–16512.

Leburu-Masigo, G. E., & Kgadima, N. P. (2020). Gender-based violence during the covid-19 pandemic in South Africa: Guidelines for social work practice. *Gender & Behaviour, 18*(4), 16612–16622.

Leclerc-Madlala, S. (2004). *Transactional sex and the pursuit of modernity*. Centre for Social Science Research Working Paper 68. University of Cape Town.

Lefafa, N. (2020). Covid-19 lockdown provides 'perfect storm' for SA's GBV crisis. *Health-E News*. Retrieved July 29, 2021 from https://health-e.org.za/2020/04/29/covid-19-lockdown-provides-perfect-storm-for-sas-gbv-crisis/

Makhakhe, N. F. (2017). *Inner-city female sex workers in Durban South Africa: A qualitative inquiry*. Master of Social Science dissertation (Health Promotion). University of KwaZulu Natal.

Mampane, J. N. (2018). Exploring the "blesser and blessee" phenomenon: Young women, transactional sex and HIV in rural South Africa. *SAGE*, 1–9.

Masenya, M. (2017). Reading Proverbs 7 in the context of female 'blessers' and sugar mamas in South Africa. *Journal of Contextual Hermeneutics in Southern Africa, 116*(2), 120–132.

Masvawure, T. (2010). I just need to be flashy on campus: Female students and transactional sex at a university in Zimbabwe. Culture, health and sexuality. *An International Journal of Research, Intervention and Care, 12*(8), 857–870.

Mavhandu-Mudzusi, A. H. (2019). Are "Blessers" a refuge for refugee girls in Tshwane, the capital city of South Africa? A phenomenographic study. *Journal of International Women Studies, 20*(2), 257–270.

Mbunge, E. (2020). Effects of COVID-19 in south African health system and society: An explanatory study. *Diabetes Metabolic Syndrome, 14*(6), 1809–1814. https://doi.org/10.1016/j.dsx.2020.09.016

Meel, A. (2011). *Teenage pregnancy among high school girls in Mthatha, South Africa*. Masters dissertation, (Public Health), Walter Sisulu University: Mthatha.

Mensah, E. O. (2020). When you open your legs, you eat: The discourse of transactional sex among female youth in Nigeria. *Sexuality and Culture, 24*(3), 543–560.

Mixon, F. G. (2018). Sugar daddy u: Human capital investment and the university-based supply of 'romantic arrangements'. *Applied Economics, 51*(9), 956–971.

Mlambo, S. (2020). *SAPS received 87 000 gender-based violence calls during first week of lockdown – Cele*. IOL. Apr 2, 2020. Retrieved July 29, 2021 from https://tebogofoundation.org/saps-received-87-000-gender-based-violence-calls-during-first-week-lockdown-cele/

Moodley, P., & Ebrahim, S. (2019). #Blesser: A critical evaluation of conceptual antecedents and the allure of a transactional relationship. *Acta Academia, 51*(2), 21–40.

Naidoo, K. (2015). Family biography, fertility and memory-making in an AIDS-affected South African site. *The History of the Family, 20*(1), 106–121.

Nayar, K. I. (2016). Sweetening the deal: Dating for compensation in the digital age. *Journal of Gender Studies, 26*(3), 335–346.

Radebe, B. (2020). GBV continues to be at the forefront during COVID-19. GBV continues to be at the forefront during COVID-19. *SABC News*. Retrieved July 29, 2021 from https://www.sabcnews.com/sabcnews/gbv-continues-to-be-at-the-forefront-during-covid-19/

Selikow, T., & Mbulaheni, T. (2013). I do love him but at the same time I can't eat love: Sugar daddy relationships for conspicuous consumption among urban university students in South Africa. *Agenda, 27*(2), 86–98.

Sidloyi, S. (2021). Townships as intersectional spaces of gendered economic vulnerability among young women. *Rajagiri Journal of Social Development, 13*(2), 147–158.

Singatha, N. M. (2020). *An ethical assessment of the structural agency of the blessee in the 'Blesser-Blessee' phenomenon*. Masters' dissertation (School of Religion, Philosophy, and Classics). University of KwaZulu Natal.

Shefer, T., & Strebel, A. (2013). Deconstructing the 'sugar daddy': A critical review of the constructions of men in intergenerational sexual relationships in South Africa. *Agenda, 26*(4), 57–63.

Statistics South Africa. (2021a). *Mid-year population estimates*. P0302. Retrieved from https://www.statssa.gov.za/publications/P0302/P03022021.pdf

Statistics South Africa. (2021b). *Statistical Release. P0305. Recorded live birth 2020*. Retrieved from http://www.statssa.gov.za/publications/P0305/P03052020.pdf

UN Women. (2020a). *The shadow pandemic: Violence against women and girls and COVID-19, New York, USA*. Retrieved July 29, 2021 from https://www.unwomen.org/en/digital-library/multimedia/2020/4/infographicccovid19-violence-against-women-and-girls

UN Women. (2020b). *COVID-19 and ending violence against women and girls*. Retrieved September 14, 2021 from https://www.unwomen.org//media/headquarters/attachments/sections/librar/publications/2020/issue-brief-covid19-and-ending-violence-against-women-and-girls-en.pdf?la=en&vs=5006

Wojcicki, J. M. (2002). She drank his money: Survival sex and the problem of violence in taverns in Gauteng Province, South Africa. *Medical Anthropology Quarterly, 16*, 267–293.

Zawu, R. (2020). *The rise and normalization of blessee/blesser relationships in South Africa: A post-colonial feminist analysis*. Master of Arts (International Studies). Stellenbosch University.

Zembe, Y. Z., Townsend, L., Thorson, A., & Ekström, A. M. (2013). Money talks, bullshit walks, interrogating notions of consumption and survival sex among young women engaging in transactional sex in post-apartheid South Africa: A qualitative enquiry. *Globalisation and Health, 9*(28), 1–16.

Sinethemba Sidloyi , Ph.D., completed a doctorate in Sociology at the University of Johannesburg, focusing on the lives, livelihoods, and daily struggles of black, working-class women. She holds a BSocSci degree in Human and Societal Dynamics (UOFS) and Honours and Master's degrees in Gender Studies (University of Pretoria). She taught Sociology at the University of KwaZulu-Natal and guest lectured at the Humboldt University of Berlin. She has published in peer-reviewed journals and presented papers at local and international conferences. Her research interests entail studying women's gendered and lived experiences in township spaces.

Chapter 8
Youth Challenges in Namibia During COVID-19: Engaging Joblessness, Violence, and E-Learning

Immaculate Mogotsi, Maria Kaundjua, and Nelago Indongo

8.1 Introduction

The coronavirus disease (COVID-19) and harsh lockdown regulations have impacted the well-being of the youth globally (Álvarez-Iglesias et al., 2021; Singh et al., 2020). The COVID-19 pandemic has also caused significant mortality and morbidity, creating daunting health and socio-economic challenges. The restrictive measures that have been put in place by many countries to contain the spread of the virus may negatively affect access to essential sexual and reproductive health (SRH) services, particularly by adolescents living in low- and middle-income countries (LMICs) and fragile settings (Meherali et al., 2021). Young people are especially affected by the closure of social spaces, including schools, community centers, and health clinics, where many of them receive comprehensive education on SRH and services. Past research has shown that disruptions in education are extremely harmful to young people, especially girls, in terms of lost earnings and education and increased vulnerability to gender-based violence (GBV), early marriages, unintended pregnancy, and female genital mutilation (UNICEF, 2021). The pandemic has also brought about significant disruption in everyday life, with wider socio-economic implications globally. Several countries around the world

I. Mogotsi (✉)
Multidisciplinary Research Services, University of Namibia, Windhoek, Namibia
e-mail: imogotsi@unam.na

M. Kaundjua
Department of Social Sciences, University of Namibia, Windhoek, Namibia
e-mail: mbkaundjua@unam.na

N. Indongo
Centre for Research Services, University of Namibia, Windhoek, Namibia
e-mail: nkanime@unam.na

K. Naidoo et al. (eds.), *Young People, Violence and Strategic Interventions in Sub-Saharan Africa*, Clinical Sociology: Research and Practice,
https://doi.org/10.1007/978-3-031-20679-5_8

introduced lockdown measures to try and curb the spread of COVID-19 and subsequently flatten the curve. Job losses are likely to be experienced in micro, small, and medium enterprises (MSMEs) (Onyeaka et al., 2021; Simon et al., 2021). Emerging evidence (Behera et al., 2021) shows that MSMEs are "overrepresented" in sectors most affected by COVID-19, including non-food manufacturing and services such as accommodation and food, retail and wholesale trade, travel, and transport sectors in which barriers to entry are relatively low. MSMEs provide the bulk of jobs and are particularly hit across Africa, where informal firms dominate employment.

Against this background of stress and uncertainty, many young people may resort to violence to address issues (M'jid, 2020; Onyeaka et al., 2021). Youth violence is one of the most severe forms of violence, with violent behavior triggered by what is happening in the broader environment. Violence among young people can also be driven by problems in family dynamics, peer relationships, and neighborhood or community "gangsters." Both fatal and non-fatal assaults involving young people contribute greatly to the global burden of premature death, injury, and disability. Youth violence deeply harms its victims, their families, friends, and communities.

Each of these requires attention when effective change is needed to improve the quality of life among young people and their families. This chapter aims to better understand the impact of young people's chronic exposure to community violence on their emotional, behavioral, substance use, and academic function, with an overarching goal to identify malleable risks and protective factors. Specifically, this chapter examines the extent to which protective factors influence changes in violent crimes in communities and how these changes are sustained over time. The chapter is a desk review, relying on secondary data and policy documents. It is envisaged that this chapter will contribute to interventions that provide anti-violence initiatives, services, and mediation during the COVID-19 pandemic.

8.2 Situational Analysis of Namibian Youth

Namibia has one of the youngest and fastest-growing populations in southern Africa. Sixty-two percent of the working-age adults in the country are between the ages of 15 and 34 (the age group broadly defined as "youth"), and projections indicate that the number could double by 2045 (Ighobor, 2013). The national population pyramid for Namibia has a very broad base illustrating young people and a very narrow apex representing a small proportion of elderly people who are aged 60 years and older. The Namibia Statistics Agency (NSA) revealed that there are 876,908 youth aged 15–34 in Namibia, of which 310,854 (35.4%) are employed and 265,770 (30.3%) are unemployed. This means that the labor force in these age groups totals 576,624 persons, giving a labor force participation rate (LFPR) of 65.8% (Namibia Statistics Agency, 2019). The overall youth unemployment rate is 46.1%, an increase of 2.7% compared to the youth unemployment rate of 43.4% reported in 2016. Female youth experience a higher unemployment rate (48.5%) compared to their male counterparts

(43.7%) (Namibia Statistics Agency, 2019). Of even greater concern is that youth unemployment in the country appears to be on the increase.

High youth unemployment rates represent both widespread personal misfortune for individuals and a lost opportunity for critical national and global economic development. High numbers of economically frustrated youth may also contribute to social instability. According to the NSA, youth unemployment rates differ substantially between regions. While youth unemployment in Namibia is high overall, there is considerable variation across regions. The northern regions of Kunene, Zambezi, Ohangwena, Omusati, and Kavango West have particularly high youth unemployment rates (above 50%) (NSA, 2019). Urban-rural disparities in youth unemployment are also evident; while unemployment among the urban youth is 38%, this figure is much higher among the youth in rural areas at 52% (Namibia Statistics Agency, 2019). The highest youth unemployment rate recorded in Zambezi and Kunene regions is due to fewer economic activities taking place in these two regions. Kunene and Zambezi are some of the regions that are still underdeveloped, and their key development sector is tourism and agriculture.

Young Namibians at a youth dialog to celebrate the 25th anniversary of the International Conference on Population and Development (ICPD) and United Nations Population Funds (UNFPA's) 50th anniversary, attended by more than 100 youth from the nation's 14 regions, called on the Namibian Government and its partners to continue implementing the ICPD Programme of Action, for young people in particular. They made this call to recognize the diversity of Namibian youth disproportionately affected by sexual and reproductive health and rights (SRHR) issues. Young people called for strengthening their SRHR, especially for young people in rural areas and those with disabilities. In addition, they called for access to sexual reproductive health information and services, including condoms in schools, to allow them to make informed choices (UNFPA, 2019, 25 June).

Young people in much of Sub-Saharan Africa are highly vulnerable to human immunodeficiency virus (HIV) infection. Research shows that many adolescent girls and young women remain unaware of their HIV-positive status for years (Kharsany & Karim, 2016; Toska et al., 2020). With an overall adult HIV prevalence of 11.5%, Namibia is facing one of the largest HIV epidemics in Africa, and young people aged 20–34 years constitute one of the groups at the highest risk of HIV infection (Ministry of Health and Social Services, 2019, p. 53). Reaching the affected adolescent girls and young women as well as the affected young men remains a national challenge. However, the government has achieved some milestones in addressing several youth matters through the introduction of youth-friendly sexual and reproductive health services programs, through initiatives such as the Determined, Resilient, Empowered, AIDS-free, Mentored, and Safe (DREAMS) project (USAID, 2019).

Alcohol and drug abuse remain a concern, especially among young Namibian men (Bishwajit & Yaya, 2018; Peltzer & Pengpid, 2018). Young people are at risk because there are concerns that Namibia could be one of southern Africa's major cocaine traffic routes (Ananias et al., 2019). Alcohol consumption constitutes an emerging social problem among adolescents and youth in Namibia, with one study estimating that 53.5% of youths aged 13–30 use alcohol (Barth & Hubbard, 2009). Alcohol and drug consumption among the youth exacerbate many social problems, including HIV risk-taking, fighting, trouble with the police, and violence among school-going youth. With the onset of COVID-19- in Namibia, the livelihoods of many households were affected (Marenga & Amupanda, 2021).

8.2.1 Poverty and Youth Unemployment

The concepts of poverty and unemployment are intertwined. Both could be viewed as the source and/or an outcome of inequality. However, poverty is much broader and represents multiple deprivations of an individual. In fact, employment status is only one of the indicators under the living standard dimension, which is also only one of the three dimensions in the assessment of the Multidimensional Poverty Index (MPI) in the Human Development Index (United Nations Development Programme, 2019). For this reason, unemployment rates can be viewed as signifiers of the presence of high-income inequality. However, they cannot be claimed as the main cause of inequality itself, especially in unequal socio-economic structures (Moťovská, 2018). For example, Mulama and Nambinga's (2017, p. 4) analysis of youth unemployment in Namibia revealed that regions with the lowest regional Gini coefficients scored among the worst in terms of youth unemployment—Ohangwena with over 55% of youth unemployment and Omusati with 55%.

During the Namibia Intercensal and Demographic Survey (NIDS) in 2016, 52% of households reported wages and salaries as the main source of income. A large number of households in urban areas (70.2%) depended on wages and salaries as their main source of income relative to only 29.6% in rural areas (NSA, 2017b). Despite the critical importance of wages and salaries on the survival of households in Namibia, the findings from NSA (2019) revealed a high unemployment rate among the youth.

Parallel to other Southern African countries, unemployment in Namibia also has a gender dimension as the rates for females in all age groups below 50 years are higher than for males in the same age groups, with an overall female unemployment rate of 34.3% as compared to 32.5% for males (NSA, 2019). The high unemployment rate in the country, in particular youth unemployment, might have psychological impacts associated with frustrations, shame, depression, and low self-esteem among the youth and may contribute to high reports of self-directed and interpersonal violence such as suicide, theft, and murder, as well as social unrest (Kaapanda, 2007; Mulama & Nambinga, 2017). A high unemployment rate for females is also a cause of grave concern as women become more dependent on males for their livelihood, which puts them at risk of domestic violence and intimate partner violence (IPV).

The causes of youth unemployment are attributed to many factors. These factors vary across global regions and countries. Still, there are some factors on which there seems to be a fair amount of consensus. The most significant conjunctions on the causes of youth unemployment are poor/lack of education and poor macroeconomic growth or development. For example, the International Labor Organization (ILO) Report on Youth Unemployment in Africa (ILO, 2020a) states that any strategy to increase good quality youth employment requires macroeconomic and political stability and adequate infrastructure. The ILO (2020a) report further stressed that the strategies that aim to increase youth employment should not rely solely on supply-side measures aimed exclusively at enhancing the skills of the young workforce. The report concludes that more highly skilled young people will not find a market for their talents without the basic conditions for quality employment creation and growth. The report also asserts that the macroeconomic and political instability and inadequate infrastructure may explain the existence of an excess supply of tertiary graduates in a number of African countries and some other countries, which has led to a fall in the returns to tertiary education in the continent over the last decade (Ibid.).

However, the ILO (2020a) report also acknowledged the critical role of skills gaps and general issues relating to education and training in youth unemployment. The report further emphasized that education should prepare the youth for work and equip them with the appropriate competencies required in the job market (Ibid.). Moreover, higher and better levels of education can facilitate entry into better jobs; less qualified young people cite a lack of these as a major obstacle to finding decent work (ILO, 2020a).

Findings from the NSA (2019) also show a link between unemployment and educational attainment. The unemployment rate is significantly lower among people who are currently at university (27.8%), hold university diplomas and degrees (14.3%), and have post-graduate qualifications (9.5%), with a combined rate of 51.5%. The highest figures for unemployment were recorded amongst people with junior secondary (40.1%) and primary (34.6%) education, with a combined unemployment rate of 74.7%. Interestingly, the unemployment rate of persons with no formal education stands at 28.6%, much lower than those with primary and junior secondary education. However, the ILO (2020b) suggests that in low-income countries, highly educated workers may find it more difficult to find a suitable job since skilled jobs are scarce, but once they do, the chances are that it will be a high-quality job. On the contrary, unskilled people with no education may be ready to accept any job offer and are more likely to be in informal and insecure employment.

8.3 COVID-19 Precautionary Measures and Regulations

By mid-August 2021, more than 208,470,375 coronavirus cases had been confirmed worldwide, with more than 4,377,979 fatalities (World Health Organization, 2021). Namibia had 122,699 cases and 3288 deaths during the same period (World Health Organization, 2021). After the first confirmed cases in 2020, the Namibian head of state declared a State of Emergency (SOE) in the country on March 17, 2020, to mitigate the spread of the virus. A lockdown of two regions followed this: the Khomas Region (including the nearby towns of Rehoboth and Okahandja) and the

Erongo Region for 21 days until April 17, 2020 (Shangula, 2020b). The two regions, as ports of international entry, were considered to be exposed to international travelers. They also had the highest COVID-19 caseload.

Like many countries, Namibia imposed restrictions requiring physical distancing varying from 1.5 m–2 m, and social gatherings such as churches, schools, and public concerts were prohibited. Similarly, sports facilities such as stadiums, gyms, playgrounds, and park use were also barred (Republic of Namibia, 2020a; Shangula, 2020a). All public and private workers were to remain at home, which entailed remote working or temporary closure for non-essential services. These COVID-19 measures necessitated the closure of national borders and restriction of movement between regions. The government also implemented a dusk-to-dawn curfew in all 14 regions. Markets and bars were prohibited from trading (Shikongo, 2020, March 24). Until May 2020, only critical and essential workers/services were permitted to operate as per the circular published in the Government Gazette (Republic of Namibia, 2020a). The COVID-19 regulations have been adapted since the first COVID-19 cases were recorded in Namibia until 2021, when Namibia experienced its third COVID-19 wave. Depending on the severity of cases and fatalities in specific regions, COVID-19 measures were adapted accordingly.

Several strategies were put into place to halt the spread of COVID-19; these include the compulsory wearing of masks, hand hygiene, and social distancing (Shangula, 2020b). Vaccination campaigns were rolled out; COVID-19 tests to enter Namibia and quarantining positive COVID-19 test results were all measures put in place to control this novel pandemic. Big data analysis and proactive tests with smart contact tracing were used to contain infected patients effectively (Shangula, 2020b).

8.4 Implications of COVID-19 Regulations on Youth Activities

Though healthy youth are less vulnerable to COVID-19, there remains genuine concern about the transmission of the virus, especially the spread to older people and those with comorbidities (Lee et al., 2020; Moore et al., 2020). COVID-19 has led to significant changes in daily life for the youth and their families, adversely impacting their livelihood (Chazovachii, 2020). Namibian youth can be categorized as either school-going, out-of-school, employed, or unemployed. COVID-19 regulations also implied that most youths were no longer attending school and other institutions of learning, with face-to-face lessons replaced by home-schooling and online learning activities. During the initial response to the COVID-19 outbreak, recommendations for physical distancing, behavior restrictions, and overall instructions to stay home meant that for most youth, their healthy routines, including healthy movement behaviors and opportunities to spend time outdoors, were all haltered.

Though these measures benefit the fight against the spread of COVID-19, they put severe pressure on citizens and the country's economy and burden on household dynamics. This had implications for the relations between the youth and their parents, siblings, and greater family members with whom they are in lockdown (Gittings et al., 2021; Shabir & Aijaz, 2020). The closure of all public spaces, the restrictions on physical contact with their peers, and the message to stay at home took away important social learning spaces for most young people (Lips, 2021). Not only were the youth affected by the movement restriction imposed on them by the regulations, but they also had to adjust to the new norms of staying at home. The lockdown required Namibians to stay home except for seeking food, essential services, or movement to and from work for those considered essential workers.

8.4.1 COVID-19 and Its Effect on SGBV Among the Youth

It is important to consider the unintended consequences of staying at home. Globally, several studies highlighted the surge of domestic violence during the COVID-19 lockdown (Dekel & Abrahams, 2021; Kourti et al., 2021; Kumar, 2020; Nesset et al., 2021). Kumar (2020) highlighted that sociologists contend domestic violence increases when families spend more time together.

Krug et al. (2002, p. 5) define violence as "the intentional use of physical force or power, threatened or actual, against oneself, another person, or against a group or community, that either results in or has a high likelihood of resulting in injury, death, psychological harm, mal-development or deprivation." Krug et al. (2002) further classify violence into three (3) broader categories, namely (a) self-directed violence, (b) interpersonal violence, and (c) collective violence.

Violence is a global phenomenon that affects all countries to a lesser or larger extent. It is reported to be one of the leading causes of death worldwide. Besides its impact on the health and well-being of populations, violence also has a tremendous economic cost in terms of expenditures on service provision, loss of income, and decreased productivity (Breuer, 2021). According to the World Bank Report (2016), the global economy's annual cost of GBV against women is estimated to be $12 trillion. Breuer (2021) estimated the loss of economic output due to GBV for both men and women in Namibia at N$2.9 billion, which is 1.64% of the 2018 GDP. Illustrating the skewed distribution of sexual and gender-based violence (SGBV) in Namibia, Breuer (2021) further reports that women bear a share of 1.63% of the above, while men only encounter 0.01% of the overall losses.

According to Mercy et al. (2017), global violence has become increasingly interpersonal and tied with criminal activity, particularly in urban areas. Similarly, interpersonal violence is the most common category of violence in Namibia, entrenched in the history of colonialism, apartheid, and patriarchal systems (Edwards-Jauch, 2016). These social structures created unequal power relations, unequal access to goods and services, and opportunities among Namibian racial groups and between men and women. The unequal distribution of advantages is built into social, economic, and political structures, which govern the daily lives and manifests in challenges such as poverty, unemployment, lack of access to land, rapid urbanization coupled with the housing shortage and lack of access to other basic municipality services such as water, electricity, and sanitation. Due to these structural arrangements, domestic violence, intimate partner violence (IPV), and baby dumping were high in Namibia even before the COVID-19 pandemic (NSA, 2014). However, interpersonal violence, such as intimate partner violence (IPV) and elder and child abuse, is likely to be underreported as it usually occurs (though not exclusively) in private homes.

In addition to interpersonal violence, community violence (exercised between unrelated individuals who may or may not know each other) is also common in Namibia. Martin (2017) indicates that crime rates in Namibia, particularly violent ones, continue to escalate. For example, the national crime statistics further indicate that within the Namibian Police Force for the years 2014 and 2015, a total of 93 juvenile arrests were made countrywide, and an additional 45 arrests were made from January to March 2016 (Martin, 2017). The statistics further indicate that most arrests were related to residential housebreakings, assault with the intent to do grievous bodily harm, theft, rape, and common assault (Martin, 2017).

Namibia's youth violence and crime are economically motivated (Martin, 2017). For example, a report by a local newspaper implied that the high unemployment rate amongst the youth motivates them to engage in offenses such as housebreaking, armed robberies, car theft, stock theft, and money laundering (Sinvula, 2014, December 12). Similarly, the Ministry of Safety and Security (2016) also identified housebreaking with intent to steal and stock theft as offenses mostly committed by offenders under its care. These types of crimes are committed with the hope of salvaging goods that can be sold to purchase food and other necessities (Ministry of Safety and Security, 2016).

The Namibia Statistic Agency (2014) also indicated that domestic violence is an endemic problem in Namibia but also corroborates that it might be the most underreported form of violence against both women and men and girls and boys (NSA, 2014). According to NSA (2014), 33% of ever-married women aged 15–49 years have experienced physical, sexual, and/or emotional violence from their partner. Thirty-two percent of adolescent girls aged 15–19 and 35% of young girls aged 20–24 have experienced physical violence from their partner. Moreover, 6% of women reported experiencing physical violence during pregnancy, which is predominant among young women aged 15–24 (NSA, 2014). Similarly, a study by Bikinesi et al. (2017) at Outapi Clinic in Northern Namibia found that 10.1% of pregnant women had experienced IPV during their lifetime, 9.1% in the last 12 months, and 8.0% had experienced IPV during their then pregnancy. Emotional abuse was the most common type of IPV, followed by financial, physical, and sexual abuse (Bikinesi et al., 2017).

According to NSA (2014), the prevalence and the non-reporting trend of SGBV and IPV are exacerbated by societal attitudes that condone SGBV. For example, 28% of women and 22% of men aged 15–49 interviewed in NSA (2014) justified beating as an acceptable way for the husband to discipline his wife. The Government of Namibia has enacted several legal frameworks to protect survivors and punish the perpetrators of SGBV and IPV. They are among others: the Married Persons Equality Act (No. 1 of 1996); Combating of Rape Act (No. 8 of 2000); Combating of Domestic Violence Act (No. 4 of 2003); Maintenance Act (No. 9 of 2003), and Children Status Act (No. 6 of 2006) (Legal Assistance Center, 2021). Despite these legal frameworks' existence, the patriarchal system, strengthened by cultural beliefs, reduces women's control over their lives, making it extremely difficult for some women to use the law. Traditional values and norms, reinforced by western patriarchy, remain strong in most of Namibia and reinforce gender roles (Ambunda & de Klerk, 2008). Hence, SGBV is deeply rooted in socio-cultural norms which undermine women's decision-making power and low self-esteem and contribute to poor health outcomes (NSA, 2014). On the contrary, in some Namibian societies, being male is associated with taking risks, being tough, aggressive, and having many sexual partners (Edwards-Jauch, 2016). As a result, violence becomes a normalized act to the youth as most of them are socialized in this normative system where violence is encouraged and/or practiced.

8.4.2 COVID-19 Amplifies Youth Violence

According to Krug et al. (2002), violence by young people is one of the most visible in society. Around the world, newspapers and the broadcast media daily report violence by gangs, in schools, or by young people on the streets. Krug et al. (2002) further state that the youth are the main victims and perpetrators of such violence as they are easily recruited into gangs. Nevertheless, the report also states that youth violence does not only harm its victims but also their families, friends, and communities. The effects of youth violence are seen not only in death, illness, and disability but also in their quality of life. These findings are also confirmed by the World Bank Report on Gender Equality (World Bank, 2016) and Breuer (2021), who highlighted the ripple effect of violence. They indicated that violence adds greatly to the costs of health and welfare services, including treatment of injuries, counseling, child protection centers, SGBV safety homes, juvenile courts, life skills, rehabilitation programs, etc. Furthermore, violence also reduces productivity due to illness related to injuries to the victim and incarceration of the perpetrators. It also decreases property value in areas with a high prevalence of violence, disrupts a range of essential services, and generally undermines the fabric of society (Breuer, 2021; World Bank, 2016). Youth violence also incurs an economic cost to the family due to legal and bail costs, loss of income due to the incarceration of the perpetrator, and death of the victim. The families also experience psychological and emotional effects of trauma, stress, depression, and shame. The World Bank (2016) report further states that youth violence on utmost occasions is (though not always) connected to other social problems such as absenteeism and dropping out of school, substance abuse, compulsive lying, reckless driving, and high rates of sexually transmitted diseases.

IPV with femicide, which is euphemistically referred to as "passion killing" in Namibia, has been on the increase. According to Melber (2020), these cases are mainly attributed to low self-esteem among men, material dependence (mostly women's dependency on men), intergenerational sexual relations, poor coping mechanisms, and failure to handle rejection in intimate sexual relations. Consequently, suicide is also a daily occurrence in Namibia. The persistent trend of femicide and young women continuously going missing led to a countrywide protest by young women and some male supporters as well as the lesbian, gay, bisexual, transgender, queer and intersex (LGBTQI) groups early in October 2020. The protest, which came to be known as the "#ShutItAllDown" movement, was triggered by the discovery of female human remains in a coastal town that was suspected to be that of Shannon Wasserfall, a young woman in her 20s who was reported missing in April 2020. The protest, which started on social media, went viral with posters by young people in the streets, demanding the President declare a state of emergency over violence against women and female homicide. In addition, the protesters were also demanding armed response units and special training for police officers in handling GBV cases. Africanews (2020) reported that the Namibian Police Force and Special Reserve Force fired rubber bullets, teargas, and used batons to subdue around 400 youth protesters of the "#ShutItAllDown" movement, mostly young women who were chanting slogans such as "no justice, no peace" as they were demanding for more accountability on the side of the state to address prevailing incidences of SGBV in Namibia. Twenty-six activists were detained, although charges against them were later dropped (Becker, 2021). The reaction of the police in this instance shows that the protest of "#ShutItAllDown" was labeled as organized collective violence by the youth and tied to criminality. After the police action, some of the youth took to social media and, in desperation, tweeted statements such as:

> You protest, (you) face law enforcement harassment and arrest.

Another youth tweeted,

> you stay (home) you are being abused; you leave home you get murdered; you go to the police, they victim blame, lose case document or arrive too late.

Contrary to reports from many other parts of the world like France and the United States, the Namibian Police reported fewer cases of SGBV per month, with 175 cases reported following the first COVID-19 pandemic lockdown (Africanews, 2020; UN Women and UNFPA, 2021). However, it should be noted that fewer reported cases with the police should not necessarily be interpreted as a reduction in SGBV. COVID-19 restrictions pose a challenge to victims of domestic violence to access places of safety and psychosocial support services (Uzobo & Ayinmoro, 2021). Domestic violence offenders generally try to isolate their victims by keeping them away from their relatives, co-workers, and psychosocial support providers, including law enforcement personnel. Therefore, the vulnerability of SGBV victims who stay at home increases during a lockdown.

Having the youth and adults at home all day long may increase family conflict as houses and communities are more crowded than usual. Victims of domestic violence may find themselves more isolated from the community during this time. They may find it harder to access places of safety and other psychosocial support services while their abusers are nearby (Abramson, 2020).

As mentioned earlier in this chapter, domestic violence and IPV are generally underreported. These phenomena could be amplified during lockdowns, where the victim is likely locked up with the perpetrator. SGBV and particularly domestic and IPV cases can only be revealed through confidential interviews. For example, most respondents interviewed in the Rapid Gender Assessments (RGAs) conducted in East and Southern Africa felt that incidences of SGBV had increased during the COVID-19 pandemic, with nearly four in ten women (38%) and men (39%) in the sub-region indicating that they knew at least one person who had been a victim of SGBV during the COVID-19 lockdown (UN Women and UNFPA, 2021). Arguably, violence intersects with youth unemployment.

8.4.3 *Effect of COVID-19 on Youth Joblessness*

With the emergence of the COVID-19 pandemic, governments placed safety regulations and measures such as lockdowns, travel restrictions, the closing of the workplace, businesses etc., in place to minimize the risk of transmission from outside and among the citizens. Though these regulations and measures are beneficial in minimizing the spread of the COVID-19 virus, they can negatively affect countries and households' economies. The United Nations (UN) assessed the "Socio-Economic Impact of COVID-19 in Southern Africa" and raised the concern that COVID-19 aggravated the already high unemployment situation in Southern Africa as both the formal and informal sectors were expected to deteriorate even further (UN Economic Commission for Africa, 2020). In countries such as Namibia, the youth who comprise the largest population composition was the hardest hit.

Like most countries, the Government of the Republic of Namibia responded to observable economic effects due to the COVID-19 pandemic. On April 1, 2020, the Minister of Finance announced the Stimulus and Relief Package (SRP) to address the negative effects of the first 21-day lockdown (March 27 to April 16, 2020) (Republic of Namibia, 2020b). The economic effects resulted from constraints at both global and national levels (Ajambo, 2020). SRP is a targeted fiscal stimulus aimed to protect the most vulnerable (particularly labor), whose spending could hopefully boost aggregate economic activity (Ajambo, 2020). Namibia's SRP endeavors to provide relief to the most vulnerable, especially those whose livelihoods may have been lost. Provisions were also made for the relaxation of labor regulations to avoid major retrenchments and business closures by allowing employers to negotiate a 20% (40% for the worst-hit industries) temporary reduction of salaries and wages during the crisis (Republic of Namibia, 2020b).

Despite the government's efforts to amend labor regulations to mitigate against retrenchment because of the protracted COVID-19 lockdown, most industries resorted to retrenching their staff to protect their companies from bankruptcy. On the other hand, those in tourism, entertainment, and hospitality are completely closed. A few industries opted to temporarily reduce salaries in line with the government's amendment that relaxed labor regulations to avoid major retrenchments. Some industries implemented rotational work to avoid crowding and simultaneously reduced working hours. These measures aggravated the economic hardship of the youth, who were mostly unemployed, with no housing or land tenure/or ownership (NSA, 2014). Görlich et al. (2013) argued that the youth are more vulnerable to negative changes in the labor market because youth employment tends to be super-cyclical. It fluctuates stronger than adult unemployment. Several factors contribute to this higher cyclical volatility; young workers usually have lower job protection. In addition, they are most likely to have gained less job-specific experience and expertise. Gittings et al. (2021) add that the youth are likely to be unskilled and inexperienced workers. Young professionals are also likely to be last employed and, therefore, first to be retrenched when companies are downscaling. Moreover, since (young) women tend to occupy more temporary, seasonal, part-time jobs than men, they are most adversely impacted. The closing of barbershops, hair salons, bars, and shebeens is also more likely to affect young women who are mostly employed or self-employed in these sectors. In addition, restrictions on public gatherings, for instance, negatively impact those who are self-employed and depend on such gatherings.

The impact of the COVID-19 pandemic, particularly in terms of income losses (due to salary cuts, retrenchments, closure of business, increment of food prices due to reduction in supply, sickness, and death of breadwinners), has led to food insecurity in the context of already fragile urban households who highly rely on wages and salaries for their livelihoods. This had implications for the relations between the youth and their parents, sibling, and greater family members with whom they are in lockdown (Gittings et al., 2021; Shabir & Aijaz, 2020). Unemployment and financial stress can trigger tension in the household and perpetuate violence between intimate partners or parents and their dependent adult children. Furthermore, increased economic hardships of households may lead to more pressure on adolescents to find work rather than return to school during the post-COVID-19 recovery phase (UN Women & UNFPA, 2021). In some regions, the effects of COVID-19 could also increase the risk for girls to engage in risky sexual behavior, including transactional sex and early marriage.

Many youths have lost the ability to earn an income, and they do not have a buffer in the form of social grants. As part of the SRP, a once-off emergency income grant of N$750.00, equivalent to US$50.37, was issued to all unemployed Namibians aged 18 to 59 years or those who had lost their jobs (Republic of Namibia, 2020b). Another targeting criterion was that the recipient did not receive any other existing social grants. The N$750.00 is slightly above the upper bound poverty line of N $520.8 estimated for the Namibia Household Income and Expenditure Survey (NHIES) (NSA, 2017b). This means the income grant could barely cover the basic needs of an average household during the 21 days of lockdown. In addition, it might not cushion other necessities during that month and subsequent months. Namibia is characterized by a large informal economy and informal employment. Results from the Namibia Labour Force Survey (NLFS) 2016/17 show that about 57.7% of the employed population are in informal employment. The percentage was higher for females at 61.2% relative to 54.1% for males in informal employment. Informal employment is widespread in rural areas where more than 80% of the employees are employed (NSA, 2017a). These figures imply that only a small number of the employed population in the formal sector and formal employment in Namibia could benefit from the Tax-back loan scheme under the SRP.

Self-employed young people selling vegetables, reusable and washable face masks, roasted meat, and other traditional delicacies on the streets of Windhoek report that they now spend more hours vending than before the COVID-19 pandemic. They share the sentiment that COVID-19 restrictions took away their livelihoods in 2020, and they find it hard to recover their businesses and feed their families (XinhuaNet, 2021). As there is an over-reliance on wages and salaries in urban households, the loss of jobs, salary cuts, and loss of business during COVID-19 lockdowns have eroded income in many households and threatened food security and nutrition. This can lead to intra-household conflicts and clashes associated with physical, mental, and psychological violence and evictions. Marenga and Amupanda (2021) also documented the economic challenges resulting from COVID-19, which had pushed many individuals to resort to loans, friends, and family support to provide for their livelihoods.

Economic uncertainties place particular stressors on the youth, particularly those who are breadwinners and those with young children. Within Namibia's cultural and religious domains, families expect young men to provide for their families (Legal Assistance Center, 2017). However, the inability to acquire some form of employment as a result of the COVID-19 lockdown contributes to stressors that can trigger violent behaviors. For some people, such precarious conditions push them into petty crimes of pickpocketing, burglaries, or car break-ins as a means of survival. Before COVID-19 lockdown restrictions, these youth categories were already economically disadvantaged (Namibia Statistics Agency, 2019). However, due to the prohibition of non-essential movements and gatherings, informal trading activities, and the scaling down of many industries during the lockdown, the youth could not leave their homes to seek work or do business. Consequently, the COVID-19 restrictions exacerbated the economic hardship for the majority of young people.

Martin (2017) also supported the view that Namibia's youth violence and crime are economically motivated. For example, a report by a local newspaper implied that the high unemployment rate amongst the youth motivates them to engage in offenses such as burglary, armed robbery, car theft, stock theft, and money laundering (Sinvula, 2014, December 12). Similarly, the Ministry of Safety and Security (2016) also identified housebreaking with intent to steal and stock theft as offenses mostly committed by offenders under its care. These types of crimes are committed with the hope of salvaging goods that can be sold to purchase food and other necessities (Ministry of Safety and Security, 2016).

The living conditions of many young people in Namibia remain precarious. Many COVID-19 prevention measures (to wash hands, self-isolate, and physical distance) assume basic living conditions and access to essential services (e.g., water, space)

(Wilkinson, 2020). However, many of these strategies will not be possible to the same degree in developing countries and especially in informal urban settlements. With a high prevalence of unemployment among the youth in Namibia, many do not own houses, and a substantial number reside in informal settlements (Namibia Statistics Agency, 2014). These areas are generally densely populated with inadequate household water and sanitation and little or no waste management. In addition, people here endure a lack of basic services and cannot secure tenure and house ownership (NSA, 2014; Wilkinson, 2020). Due to the proximity of the structures, the concept of a "household" in informal settlements can be flexible, with people moving between homes and sharing food or sleeping space. Therefore, control strategies and responses based on assumptions about household units may not be feasible (Wilkinson, 2020). Poor ventilation and confined spaces increase transmission risk due to limited air circulation. Water points and toilets are also shared, posing risks for spatial distancing and isolation. For example, spatial distancing is compromised when queuing to collect water or using a toilet. Waste disposal is often inadequate, and waste in the street poses several biohazard risks, including potentially COVID-19 (Ibid.).

Water subsidies were introduced as part of the Government SRP, recognizing the water shortage in informal settlements. Subsidized by NamWater and the local authorities, water subsidies aimed to ensure that water points were kept open without requiring community members to purchase water during lockdowns. In order to increase the number of water points, water tanks were erected in informal settlements (Ajambo, 2020). The water subsidy brought some relief in relation to access to water, but unfortunately, it did not address the challenges of queuing for such services, spacing, and poor waste management.

8.4.4 Land and Housing Needs Among the Youth

The right to adequate housing is guaranteed under international human rights law. Nakuta (2021) pointed out that this right, like many other economic, social, and cultural rights, is not expressly recognized in the Namibian Constitution. However, Nakuta (2021) argues that these rights should be binding in the country as Namibia ratified some of the major human rights instruments that recognize this right. Article 25 of the UN Universal Declaration of Human Rights affirms the right to adequate housing as it states, "Everyone has a right to a standard of living adequate for the health and well-being of himself and of his family, including food, clothing, housing and medical care and necessary social services…"

During the 2013/14 Namibian Demographic Health Survey (NDHS), men and women were asked to indicate whether they own land or housing alone, jointly, or both alone and jointly. Overall, 75.5% of women and 59.7% of men reported that they did not own land; similarly, 64.9% of women and 42.7% of men indicated that they did not own a house (NSA, 2014). The report showed a significant positive correlation between land ownership and the age of respondents. For both sexes, the proportion of those who did not own land or a house decreased by age. The analysis further indicated that urban dwellers were more likely not to own land or housing than those living in rural areas (NSA, 2014). Today, Namibia's demand for land and housing is increasing, mainly among the youth (UNDP, 2019). Moreover, compared to other countries in the region, house prices are very high and unaffordable in Namibia, especially for young adults. This trend has resulted in unrest and protests among the youth who are demanding cheaper, affordable land and house prices (UNDP, 2019).

Equally, early in August 2021, violent clashes were also reported between police officers and some Windhoek residents (mostly youth in the low-income category) who had illegally occupied land and erected their makeshift housing structures (shacks) in the Otjomuise and Tobias Hainyeko constituencies on the outskirt of the capital city, Windhoek. The agitated land grabbers reacted by throwing rocks and hurling insults as they questioned the motives of police officers who were demolishing their shacks. The police retaliated with teargas and by shooting rubber bullets, and some land grabbers were arrested. The illegal land occupants justified their actions by claiming that most had lost their jobs and informal businesses due to COVID-19. They also argued that they had been waiting too long on the authorities to allocate land to them. They further indicated that they could also not afford the price of decent houses, and the cost of rent is exorbitant (Nambadja in The Namibian Newspaper of 09 August, 2021; Tjitemisa, in the New Era Newspaper of 12 August, 2021). For example, during media interviews with the youth whose informal shelters were demolished by the police in Otjomuise in August 2021, the illegal land occupants stated that COVID-19 had rendered them homeless. Some of them stated that they were evicted from family homes as family members could no longer sustain them together with their young children. Those who were renting were evicted due to defaults on their rent payments.

A combination of higher unemployment rates and lack of access to land and housing among women renders them powerless and dependent on men. Namupala et al. (2021) found that the lack of secure housing and tenure increases women's vulnerability to domestic violence and that low-income women in urban informal settlements often do not have the legal means to remain in their homes after reporting a violent partner. This scenario could be more pronounced among the youth, and Namupala et al. (2021) argue that COVID-19 lockdowns exacerbated the situation. Without access to land and housing, most of the youth in Namibia, even up to age 35, live with parents, relatives, friends, or intimate partners. On the other hand, most urban dwellers live in an informal settlement with no legal security of tenure over the land where they erect their homes and often face forced evictions by the local authority.

8.4.5 Implications of COVID-19 Regulations on Youth Education

Education is one of the deciding factors for poverty alleviation and economic growth. However, governments of developing countries struggle to meet the demand for quality education, and Namibia is no exception (Mässing, 2017). According to UNESCO estimates of April 2020, a total of 124 million learners in East and Southern Africa (ESA) have been affected by school closures due to the COVID-19 pandemic (UN Women and UNFPA, 2021). The study in ESA raised concerns that the COVID-19 pandemic will deepen the crisis in the sub-region for girls and boys of school-going age as school closures negatively impact continuity and motivation levels. The study in ESA further states that the scenario may even be exacerbated for many girls for whom accessing school and staying in school have been difficult even under normal circumstances. Furthermore, the pandemic reduces the likelihood of them continuing their education during the recovery period. In 2020, the Ministry of Education, Arts and Culture in Namibia also revealed that a total of 25,235 pupils across the country had not returned to school and could not be traced after the lockdown (Republic of Namibia, n.d.).

8.4.5.1 COVID-19 Lockdowns and Closure of Schools and Tertiary Institutions in Namibia

Youth of school-going age and those at tertiary institutions also experienced a halt to their learning as COVID-19 regulations required that educational institutions be closed. Since the detection of the first two cases of COVID-19 on March 14, 2020, the Government of the Republic of Namibia announced a 21-day full lockdown. Due to the ban on all large gatherings, all schools from early child development (ECD) centers, primary and secondary schools, and tertiary institutions were closed. Since then, ECD centers and schools have been moving between full closure, distance learning, and face-to-face teaching. Rotational face-to-face learning was also introduced in schools with big classes. However, tertiary institutions remained closed and introduced online learning and teaching (e-learning) via information and communication technology (ICT).

8.4.5.2 Opportunities and Challenges to Effective E-Learning in Namibia During COVID-19

E-learning is formally defined as: "...electronically mediated asynchronous and synchronous communication for the purpose of constructing and confirming knowledge" (Mässing, 2017, p. 1). The mode of e-learning is also not completely new in Namibia's education system. For example, e-learning has been in place at the University of Namibia (UNAM) through its Center for Open, Distance and eLearning (CODEL) since 2016, when the Center for External Studies and Center for eLearning and Interactive Multimedia were merged (University of Namibia, 2017). However, e-learning was not fully rolled out to all programs until the emergence of COVID-19. During the lockdowns, schools and tertiary institutions resolved that learning should be halted but continued through other learning modes. Some government schools required teachers to send schoolwork to the learners, while others agreed to follow online schooling (Republic of Namibia, n.d.). Each of these modes of learning brought opportunities and challenges. Some schools made copies of learning materials for parents to collect at schools to teach their children. These modes of learning required parental involvement. There was no guarantee that learners could comprehend the educational materials without adult support. Those who resolved to online teaching faced technical challenges, which are not unique to Namibia. Some learners and students in tertiary institutions did not have computers, laptops, or mobile phones compatible with e-learning (Gervasius, 2020; Kaisara & Bwalya, 2020). Learners and students from low-income backgrounds and rural areas had no access to electricity or a stable Internet connection, and most youth could not afford data and ICT devices (Gervasius, 2020). A study by Kaisara and Bwalya (2020) at the Namibia University of Science and Technology (NUST) reveals that challenges faced by e-learning users were not only limited to technology but also social. Some respondents indicated that their home environments were not conducive to learning (Ibid.). Kaisara and Bwalya (2020) underscore the fact that Namibia is still one of the most unequal societies in the world. As such, a number of students enrolled for higher education reside in crowded high-density locations without running water, electricity, and Internet connections, thus making learning and studying extremely difficult. A study by the UN Economic Commission for Africa in Southern Africa also argues that poor and rural-based students who were already vulnerable to falling behind will face even more hurdles to keep pace with the elite, with no chance to pursue tertiary education (UN Economic Commission for Africa, 2020).

Another challenge in e-learning is ICT literacy; teachers and learners need additional training. New ICT users find it difficult to log in and navigate platforms such as Moodle (Kaisara & Bwalya, 2020). This finding is consistent with the statement from the respondents in Angula and Mutelo's study (2021), who indicated that the adoption and implementation of e-learning had been a challenge in Namibian educational institutions due to the lack of ICT knowledge to utilize e-learning platforms. Hence, it takes time for staff to acquaint themselves with the new technology adopted or implemented (Ibid.). Both lecturers and students also faced challenges in adapting and adopting new communication systems via Microsoft Teams and Zoom services (Angula & Mutelo, 2021). Students at NUST also expressed a feeling of isolation and loneliness in the process of e-learning. They raised concerns about a lack of motivation usually derived from interaction with their peers (Kaisara & Bwalya, 2020). Kaisara and Bwalya (2020) also identified isolation as a challenge students face when learning through e-learning in Ghana. Therefore, they argue that it is pertinent that e-learning offerings deliberately cultivate a culture of collaboration amongst e-learning students via WhatsApp, Zoom, Microsoft Teams, email, and SMS.

8.4.5.3 Consequences of School Closures on the Youth

The cancelation of face-to-face learning and teaching accompanied by a migration to online learning brought certain challenges. Despite online learning providing a degree of flexibility, students raised the concern that they hardly found time to do their academic work due to many other commitments. A UNAM student interviewed by Hamutenya and Silavwe (2020) indicated that most students had difficulties studying at home as parents expected them to do their home chores first. Hence, the home environment is not the most conducive for studying due to several distractions such as noise and disturbances from other cohabitants, which also trigger conflicts in close interpersonal relationships.

The effect of COVID-19 lockdowns with the accompanying closure of schools and institutions of higher learning and the introduction of e-learning created fear, depression, uncertainty, and a feeling of powerlessness among the youth in Namibia. This can be explained by what Émile Durkheim refers to as "anomie." Anomie describes a scenario of absence, breakdown, confusion, or conflict in the norms of society (Marshall, 1998). Durkheim argues that anomie creates a psychological state of powerlessness and may lead to aggression and violence, often including self-destructive behavior such as suicide.

Moreover, more than 3000 girls fell pregnant when schools closed and did not return when schools reopened in September 2020 (Nembwaya and Erastus, 2020). Of grave concern is that some of the schoolgirls were impregnated by close family members (Ibid.). This report corroborates the findings from the UN Women and UNFPA (2021) study conducted in ESA. The study's findings suggest that the pandemic has increased girls' risk of engaging in risky sexual behavior and becoming victims of sexual violence and exploitation (UN Women and UNFPA, 2021). The study by the UN Women and UNFPA (2021) further reports that SGBV had increased, especially during the lockdown, as the drivers of SGBV like economic strain, substance abuse, and being in a confined environment became more pronounced.

Young women in Namibia generally have difficulty accessing SRH services due to the normative system of gender inequality. The dissonance between existing laws and what is culturally desirable is still real (Kaundjua et al., 2014). While this challenge could be addressed in sex education forums and life skills programs at school, school closures resulted in the separation of girls from life skills teachers and the safety of hostels. This made them prone to sexual abuse and exploitation in the confinement of the household.

8.4.6 Implications of COVID-19 on Youth's Access to Sexual and Reproductive Health (SRH)

Namibia's health services are twofold: private (serving 18% of the population with medical aid) and public (serving the remaining 82%). This, in part, is due to the country's high-income inequality. Access to healthcare is comparably good, with 76% of the population living within a 10 km radius of a healthcare facility (Christians, 2020). However, only 18% of the population is covered by medical aid funds. As a result, the remaining 82% of the population is covered by the public health system or out-of-pocket (OOP) expenditure in the private sector (Ibid.). Higher unemployment rates among the youth imply that most cannot afford medical aid and lack OOP to access healthcare in the private sector (NSA, 2019). Young people also encounter obstacles in accessing healthcare services in the public sector due to crowded health facilities and distance, especially in rural areas.

Findings of the Rapid Gender Assessments (RGAs) conducted in East and Southern Africa (ESA) for COVID-19 also suggest that women were more likely to be ill and less likely to be covered by medical aid than men in all the countries in ESA, except Malawi (UN Women & UNFPA, 2021). Consequently, women suffer and die from health complications as they do not seek healthcare timely and miss follow-up appointments for services such as family planning, maternal and child health, counseling, and antiretroviral therapy. Women may also be subjected to physical and mental torture by male partners who control the usage of medical aid. To assess women's decision-making autonomy, the NSA (2014) collected information on women's participation in three household decisions: their healthcare, major household purchases, and visits to family or relatives. The findings indicate that about 75% of married women aged 15–49 were involved in all three decisions. Nevertheless, the proportion of women involved in all three decisions increases with age—from 54% in the youngest age group to 78% in the oldest age group. These findings suggest that married young women are less likely to be involved in the decision of their partners, including their health. Young women's decision-making autonomy on health issues may also decrease during the COVID-19 epidemic as families were sometimes cut off from healthcare services, security, and other social support systems during lockdowns.

Contraceptive shortages were also experienced in 2020 during lockdown as a result of border closures (Mbathera et al., 2020, 19 May). This situation further worsened incidences of unwanted pregnancies among the youth. Access to contraceptive services has been a challenge for women and girls who need these services the most. Namibian Sun (2021, 26 April) highlighted how some health facilities closed down or only provided limited services to women and girls. As a result, many women and girls skip important medical check-ups for fear of contracting COVID-19. Due to contraceptive shortages, health authorities advised girls and women to abstain from sex to prevent unwanted pregnancy. Such advice from health authorities is oblivious to the unequal gender relations between men and women and the difficulties women experience in negotiating safe sexual practices with their sexual partners. Sexual power imbalances are more pronounced in intergenerational sexual relations. The complex interplay between power and gender is crucial for understanding who controls when, where, and how sex takes place in intergenerational sexual relationships (Mshweshwe, 2020). The power imbalance and gender inequality in intergenerational sexual relations perpetuate GBV. In most instances, young girls and young women are involved in intergenerational sexual relations, commonly termed the "sugar daddy" phenomenon. Given the power imbalances in these relationships, most young people do not have the sexual negotiation skills to demand safe sex.

8.5 Call to Action to Address Youth Vulnerabilities Resulting from COVID-19

In this section, a few recommendations are laid out to improve youth wellness during COVID-19. Incorporating youth engagement strategies is important in ensuring a youth-friendly strategy on matters pertaining to education disruptions, prevention of SGBV, addressing youth unemployment, and access to SRH services.

Studies have shown that retaining contact with friends and pursuing leisure activities are key to the well-being of many young people. Financial worries emanating from job losses and low economic activities also indicate young people's stressors. Hence, having an undisturbed place at home becomes very important for young people's well-being during a pandemic or lockdown. A study conducted in Germany confirmed the importance of feeling protected for young people and living in an atmosphere where they are supported in their homes (Lips, 2021). Home environments that lack emotional, physical, and psychosocial support and a feeling of protection at home can be extremely distressing for the youth. To safeguard the well-being of young people, they must inform policymakers about the impact of COVID-19 on their overall well-being (Lips, 2021). The rights of young people are enshrined in the Africa Youth Charter, Namibian National Youth Policy, and many international instruments, which make it mandatory for their voices to be considered in all matters that are of concern to them. Hence, caution must be taken that the prevailing COVID-19 crisis does not reverse these hard-earned rights. Lips (2021) cautions that a critical eye must be kept on youth inclusion and the importance of finding suitable means of making their perspectives public and assessing whether the formats designed to protect their rights to participation can stand up to the COVID-19 crisis.

Having access to SGBV prevention information is pivotal in saving lives. Therefore, SGBV prevention information and helplines are shared widely through various platforms such as newspapers and social media. Traditional mediums can also be explored to ensure the youth know whom to reach out to. For example, announcements through radios and local structures such as regional council offices, sports clubs, churches, and traditional authorities could reach the youth. NGOs such as

Childline/Lifeline have been running helplines and online support platforms; this ought to be expanded or established to reach the youth as an audience. It is critical to keep these helplines and information channels open during and after the peak of COVID-19.

One way to tackle the negative ways of coping with COVID-19 that may exacerbate the risk of violence is by placing constraints on the sale of alcohol. Alcohol consumption among the youth has been seen to escalate youth violence. During the first lockdown, Namibia banned the sale of alcohol nationally to reduce the risk of violence in the home to curtail COVID-19. Accessing shelters and other places of safety during the pandemic is important in safeguarding lives. These shelters accommodate survivors to escape abusers temporarily. However, given the COVID-19 regulations that restrict movement and enforce curfews, there is a need to amend COVID-19 regulations to allow individuals in situations of domestic violence to leave the family home. Furthermore, there is a need to expand SGBV services to be easily accessible. COVID-19 quarantine limits individual mobility and freedom of movement. However, several initiatives can be rolled out to enhance access to violence-related services. These initiatives can vary from setting up temporary violence-related services near shopping malls where women are likely to be already visiting. Importantly, violence-related services for the youth must be classified as "essential" and not locked down due to COVID-19.

The causes of youth poverty and unemployment in Namibia are multidimensional. Therefore, policies and programs in poverty reduction and employment creation should take a multi-sectoral approach. Multi-sectoral approach interventions must include all stakeholders, including the government, private sector, informal sector, credit institutions, and youth groups. These interventions should also focus on institutional building for the youth and other marginalized and vulnerable groups to ensure sustainability even in a pandemic. While Namibia has quite a number of social protection programs, none of them are directly targeting the youth. Hence, there is a need to target social protection programs that can cushion the youth in times of calamities.

Although the overall unemployment rates in Namibia are high, they are more pronounced among younger individuals, women, people with no education or lower levels of education, those residing in rural areas, and other marginalized communities (NSA, 2019). Therefore, job creation programs need to particularly target these vulnerable groups. Poverty reduction programs should foster and create a favorable environment for young women entrepreneurs and finance youth-led self-employment initiatives. A lack of skills and educational mismatch were highlighted as contributors to youth unemployment (ILO, 2020a; Kaapanda, 2007). Therefore, youth intervention should focus on transforming the educational and training system to match it with the demands of current labor market interventions.

E-learning seems to be a viable option to safeguard access to education amidst the COVID-19 pandemic. However, the implementation of e-learning is threatened by a lack of ICT infrastructure and the capacity of teachers and learners to access and use e-learning. Currently, e-learning is limited to predominantly urban schools and institutions of high learning. Public higher education institutions have basic e-learning infrastructure, although bandwidth and student capacity to access teaching and learning might be a challenge (Gervasius, 2020). In order to embrace and benefit from e-learning, the Namibian Government and its development partners have to develop clear and equitable guidelines for educational budget allocations and invest in ICT infrastructure and training.

References

Abramson, A. (2020). *How COVID-19 may increase domestic violence and child abuse. National crises ramp up stress among couples and families. Psychologists identify the risks and point to resources that can help*. American Psychological Association.

Africanews. (2020). *Namibia governor calls for action against gender-based violence.* Retrieved from https://www.africanews.com/2020/11/24/namibian-governor-calls-for-action-against-gender-based-violence//

Ajambo, E. (2020). *COVID-19. An emerging development challenge, but opportunity for the sustainable development goals (SDGs) in Namibia*. United Nations-Namibia.

Álvarez-Iglesias, A., Garman, E., & Lund, C. (2021). Effects of COVID-19 on the economy and mental health of young people in South Africa: Opportunities for strengthening social protection programmes by integrating mental health. *South Africa Journal of Psychology, 51*(2), 199–204. https://doi.org/10.1177/00812463211015348

Ambunda, L., & de Klerk, S. (2008). Women and custom in Namibia: A research overview. In O. C. Ruppel (Ed.), *Women's rights and customary law in Namibia: A conflict between human and cultural rights?* (pp. 43–81). Basler Africa.

Ananias, J., Makhubele, J., Hasheela, M. W., Tiberia, N. I. H., Freeman, R. J., Mafa, P., Matlakala, F., Chilwalo, N., Frank, R., & Svinurai, A. (2019). Views of teachers and hostel matrons on the landscape of substance abuse amongst the youth in the northern region of Namibia. *Global Journal of Health Science, 11*(5), 133–143. https://doi.org/10.5539/gjhs.v11n5p133

Angula, N., & Mutelo, S. C. (2021). The usage of e-learning challenges in the Namibia educational institutions: A Namibian experience during COVID-19. *International Journal of Smart Computing and Information Technology, 1*, 1-4. doi.org/10.54646/bijscit.007 BOHR Publishers www.bohrpub.com

Barth, K., & Hubbard, D. (2009). *Alcohol and youths: Suggestions for law reform*. LAC.

Becker, H. (2021). #ShutItAllDownNamibia: Young Namibians are hitting the streets against gender-based violence and colonial legacies in Namibia. *Journal of Social Justice, 1*, 184–191.

Behera, M., Mishra, S., & Mohapatra, N. (2021). COVID-19 pandemic and micro, small and medium enterprises (MSMEs): Policy response for revival. *Small Enterprises Development, Management & Extension Journal, 47*(3), 213–228.

Bikinesi, L. T., Mash, R., & Joyner, K. (2017). Prevalence of intimate partner violence and associated factors amongst women attending antenatal care at Outapi Clinic, Namibia: A descriptive survey. *African Journal of Primary Health Care & Family Medicine, 9*(1), e1–e6. https://doi.org/10.4102/phcfm.v9i1.1512

Bishwajit, G., & Yaya, S. (2018). Prevalence of alcohol and tobacco use among men and women in Namibia. *International Journal of Environmental Research and Public Health, 16*(1), 59–70. https://doi.org/10.3390/ijerph16010059

Breuer, S. (2021). *Economic analyses on the cost of gender-based violence in Namibia.* ZÖSS Discussion Paper, No. 86, Universität Hamburg, Zentrum für Ökonomische und Soziologische Studien (ZÖSS).

Chazovachii, B. (2020). Understanding strategies for resilient livelihoods by Masvingo urban's vulnerable groups during the Covid-19 pandemic in Zimbabwe. *African Journal of Governance & Development, 9*(1.1), 139–159.

Christians, F. (2020). Country profile – Primary healthcare and family medicine in Namibia. *African Journal of Primary Health Care & Family Medicine, 12*(1), a2242. https://doi.org/10.4102/phcfm.v12i1.2242

Dekel, B., & Abrahams, N. (2021). *I will rather be killed by Corona than by him.* Experiences of abused women seeking shelter during South Africa's COVID-19 lockdown. *PLoS One, 16*(10), 1–15 e0259275. https://doi.org/10.1371/journal.pone.0259275

Edwards-Jauch, L. (2016). Gender-based violence and masculinity in Namibia: A structuralist framing of the debate. *Journal for Studies in Humanities and Social Sciences, 5*(1), 49–62.

Gervasius, N. (2020). *Compulsory e-learning in Namibia's public schools: A commendable idea marred by the digital divide?* Association of Progress and Communication (APC).

Gittings, L., Toska, E., Medley, S., Cluver, L., Logie, C. H., Ralayo, N., Chen, J., & Mbithi-Dikgole, J. (2021). Now my life is stuck! Experiences of adolescents and young people during COVID-19 lockdown in South Africa. *Global Public Health, 16*(6), 947–963. https://doi.org/10.1080/17441692.2021.1899262

Görlich, D., Stepanok, I., & Al-Hussami, F. (2013). *Youth unemployment in Europe and the world: Causes, consequences and solutions.* Institut für Weltwirtschaft Kiel Institute for the World Economy.

Hamutenya, P., & Silavwe, W. (2020). *COVID-19 complicates students' lives.* Campus News, University of Namibia.

Ighobor, K. (2013). *Africa's youth: A ticking time bomb or an opportunity*? Africa Renewal E-Magazine, http://www.un.org/africarenewal/magazine/may-2013/

International Labour Organisation. (2020a). *Report on employment in Africa (Re-Africa): Tackling the youth employment challenge.* ILO Regional Office for Africa.

International Labour Organisation. (2020b). *Education pays off, but you have to be patient.* ILO Harmonized Microdata collection.

Kaapanda, R. N. (2007). *The role of the ministry of youth, national service, sport and culture in reducing youth unemployment in Namibia with special focus on the Urban Khomas region* (Master's thesis). University of Namibia.

Kaisara, G., & Bwalya, K. J. (2020). Investigating the E-learning challenges faced by students during Covid-19 in Namibia. *International Journal of Higher Education, 10*(1), 308–318. https://doi.org/10.5430/ijhe.v10n1p308

Kaundjua, M., Kauari, L., & Mufune, P. (2014). Young people's perceptions of sex and relationships in northern Namibia. *International Journal of Child, Youth and Family Studies, 5*(2), 279–295.

Kharsany, A. B., & Karim, Q. A. (2016). HIV infection and AIDS in sub-Saharan Africa: Current status, challenges and opportunities. *The Open AIDS Journal, 10*, 34–48. https://doi.org/10.2174/1874613601610010034

Kourti, A., Stavridou, A., Panagouli, E., Psaltopoulou, T., Spiliopoulou, C., Tsolia, M., Sergentanis, T. N., & Tsitsika, A. (2021). Domestic violence during the COVID-19 pandemic: A systematic review. *Trauma, Violence & Abuse*, 15248380211038690. Advance online publication. 1–27. https://doi.org/10.1177/15248380211038690

Krug, E. G., Dahlberg, L. L., Mercy, J. A., Zwi, A. B., & Lozano, R. (Eds.). (2002). *World report on violence and health.* World Health Organization.

Kumar, A. (2020). COVID-19 and domestic violence: A possible public health crisis. *Journal of Health Management, 22*(2), 192–196. https://doi.org/10.1177/0972063420932765

Lee, P. I., Hu, Y. L., Chen, P. Y., Huang, Y. C., & Hsueh, P. R. (2020). Are children less susceptible to COVID-19? *Journal of Microbiology, Immunology, and Infection, S1684–1182*(20), 30039–30036. https://doi.org/10.1016/j.jmii.2020.02.011

Legal Assistance Center. (2017). *Namibia gender analysis 2017 prepared for the delegation of the European Union to Namibia.* Legal Assistance Centre.

Legal Assistance Center. (2021). *Current laws in force in Namibia* (as of 20 December 2021). Windhoek.

Lips, A. (2021). The situation of young people at home during COVID-19 pandemic. *Childhood Vulnerability, 3*, 61–78. https://doi.org/10.1007/s41255-021-00014-3

Marenga, R., & Amupanda, J. S. (2021). The coronavirus and social justice in Namibia. *Politikon, 48*(2), 206–225. https://doi.org/10.1080/02589346.2021.1913803

Marshall, G. (1998). *A dictionary of sociology*. Oxford University.

Martin, M. (2017). *Juvenile justice: A Namibian overview. Resource material,* Series No. 101. UNAFEI.

Mässing, C. (2017). *Success factors and challenges for e-learning technologies in the Namibian higher education system: A case study of the University of Namibia*. Bachelor's degree Project in Information Systems Level ECTS Spring Term Year. University of Skövde.

Mbathera, E., Nembwaya, H., Cloete, L., Kahiurika, N., & Kooper, L. (2020, May 20). Contraception disaster hits Namibia. *The Namibian*.

Meherali, S., Adewale, B., Ali, S., Kennedy, M., Salami, B., Richter, S., Okeke-Ihejirika, P. E., Ali, P., da Silva, K. L., Adjorlolo, S., et al. (2021). Impact of the COVID-19 pandemic on adolescents' sexual and reproductive health in low- and middle-income countries. *International Journal of Environmental Research and Public Health, 18*, 13221. https://doi.org/10.3390/ijerph182413221

Melber, H. (2020). *#ShutItDown in Namibia-the fight against gender-based viol*ence. The Conversation.

Mercy, J. A., Hillis, S. D., Butchart, A., Bellis, M. A., Ward, C. L., Fang, & Rosenberg, M. L. (2017). Interpersonal violence: Global impact and paths to prevention. In C. N. Mock, R. Nugent, & O. Kobusingye (Eds.), *Injury prevention and environmental health* (3rd ed.). https://www.ncbi.nlm.nih.gov/books/NBK525208/. https://doi.org/10.1596/978-1-4648-0522-6_ch5

Ministry of Health and Social Services. (2019). *Namibia population-based HIV impact assessment (NAMPHIA) 2017: Final report*. Ministry of Health and Social Services.

Ministry of Safety and Security. (2016). *NCS quarterly reports for the period 01 April 2015–31 March 2016*. Namibian Correctional Service.

M'jid, N. M. (2020). Hidden scars: The impact of violence and the COVID-19 pandemic on children's mental health. *Child and Adolescent Psychiatry and Mental Health, 14*, 33–35. https://doi.org/10.1186/s13034-020-00340-8

Moťovská, N. (2018). *Unemployment: The cause of inequality? A qualitative and quantitative case study analysis of income inequality in Namibia* (Master's thesis). International Institute of Social Studies.

Moore, S. A., Faulkner, G., Rhodes, R. E., Brussoni, M., Chulak-Bozzer, T., Ferguson, L. J., Mitra, R., O'Reilly, N., Spence, J. C., Vanderloo, L. M., & Tremblay, M. S. (2020). Impact of the COVID-19 virus outbreak on movement and play behaviors of Canadian children and youth: A national survey. *International Journal of Behavioral Nutrition and Physical Activity, 17*, 85. https://doi.org/10.1186/s12966-020-00987-8

Mshweshwe, L. (2020). Understanding domestic violence: Masculinity, culture, traditions. *Heliyon, 6*(10), e05334. https://doi.org/10.1016/j.heliyon.2020.e05334

Mulama, L., & Nambinga, V. (2017). *Namibia's untapped resource: Analysing youth unemployment.* National Planning Commission. https://www.npc.gov.na/?wpfb_dl=311

Nambadja, C. (2021, August 09). Namibia: We are tired of empty promises. *The Namibian*. https://allafrica.com/stories/202108090736.html

Namibia Statistics Agency. (2014). *Namibia demographic and health survey 2013*. Namibia Statistics Agency.

Namibia Statistics Agency. (2017a). *Namibia inter-censal demographic survey 2016 report*. Namibia Statistics Agency.

Namibia Statistics Agency. (2017b). *Namibia household income and expenditure survey (NHIES) 2015/2016 report*. Namibia Statistics Agency.

Namibia Statistics Agency. (2019). *Namibia labour force survey 2018 report*. Namibia Statistics Agency.

Namibian Sun. (2021, 26 April). Teen pregnancies surge during lockdown. *Namibian Sun*.
Namupala, N., Nangolo, E., & Edwards-Jauch, L. (2021). Women's access to urban land and housing: Implications for human rights and gender justice. *Namibian Journal of Social Justice, 1*, 141–191.
Nakuta, J. B. (2021). The right to adequate housing in Namibia: A right not vindicated in Namibia. *Namibian Journal of Social Justice, 1*(202), 22–43.
Nembwaya, H., & Erastus, N. (2020, November 20). 3 300 schoolgirls pregnant after COVID-19 lockdown. *The Namibian.* https://www.namibian.com.na/206504/archive-read/3-300-schoolgirls-pregnant-after-COVID-19lockdown
Nesset, M. B., Gudde, C. B., Mentzoni, G. E., et al. (2021). Intimate partner violence during COVID-19 lockdown in Norway: The increase of police reports. *BMC Public Health, 21*, 2292. https://doi.org/10.1186/s12889-021-12408-x
Onyeaka, H., Anumudu, C. K., Al-Sharify, Z. T., Egele-Godswill, E., & Mbaegbu, P. (2021). COVID-19 pandemic: A review of the global lockdown and its far-reaching effects. *Science Progress*. https://doi.org/10.1177/00368504211019854, 104, 003685042110198
Peltzer, K., & Pengpid, S. (2018). Concurrent alcohol and tobacco use among school-going adolescents in Namibia: Prevalence and risk factors. *Journal of Psychology in Africa, 28*(2), 141–146. https://doi.org/10.1080/14330237.2018.1455317
Republic of Namibia. (2020a). *Public health COVID-19 general regulations: Amendment* (Government Notice 235 of 2020). Republic of Namibia.
Republic of Namibia. (2020b). *Launch statement emergency income grant of the economic stimulus and relief package*. Ministry of Finance.
Republic of Namibia. (n.d.). *Guidelines for schools in Namibia. On the prevention and management of COVID-19*. Ministry of Education, Arts and Culture.
Shabir, A. L., & Aijaz, A. (2020). COVID-19 pandemic – An African perspective. *Emerging Microbes & Infections, 9*(1), 1300–1308. https://doi.org/10.1080/22221751.2020.1775132
Shangula, K. (2020a). *Update by Dr Kalumbi Shangula, minister of health and social services on COVID-19 in Namibia*. Ministry of Health and Social Services.
Shangula, K. (2020b). *Countrywide lockdown on account of COVID-19 pandemic*. Ministry of Health and Social Services.
Shikongo, A. (2020, March 24). Partial lockdown in effect from Friday. *The Namibian*. https://www.namibian.com.na/199422/archive-read/Partial-lockdown-in-effectfrom-Friday
Simon, J., White, R. G., van der Boor, C., & Łaszewska, A. (2021). Impacts of the Covid-19 lockdown and relevant vulnerabilities on capability well-being, mental health and social support: An Austrian survey study. *BMC Public Health, 21*, 314.
Singh, S., Roy, D., Sinha, K., Parveen, S., Sharma, G., & Joshi, G. (2020). Impact of COVID-19 and lockdown on mental health of children and adolescents: A narrative review with recommendations. *Psychiatry Research, 293*, 113429. https://doi.org/10.1016/j.psychres.2020.113429
Sinvula, J. I. (2014, December 12). Unemployment in Namibia – A major challenge. *New Era*. https://www.newera.com.na/2014/12/12/unemployment-namibia-major-challenge/
Tjitemisa, K. (2021, August 12). Chaos in the city. *New Era*. https://neweralive.na/posts/chaos-in-the-city
Toska, E., Laurenzi, C. A., Roberts, K. J., Cluver, L., & Sherr, L. (2020). Adolescent mothers affected by HIV and their children: A scoping review of evidence and experiences from sub-Saharan Africa. *Global Public Health, 15*(11), 1655–1673. https://doi.org/10.1080/17441692.2020.1775867
UNICEF. (2021). *Impact of COVID-19: Adolescent well-being and mental health*. UNICEF.
UN Economic Commission for Africa. (2020). *Socio-economic impact of COVID-19 in Southern Africa*. UN Economic Commission for Africa.
United Nations Development Programmes. (2019). *Namibia national development report*. UNDP.
UNFPA East and Southern Africa. (2019, June 25). We want improved sexual and reproductive health. Youth people in Namibia call for support to ICPD agenda. Retrieved from https://esaro.

unfpa.org/en/news/we-want-improved-sexual-and-reproductive-health-%E2%80%93-young-people-namibia-call-support-icpd-agenda
UN Women & UNFPA. (2021). *The impact of COVID-19 on women and men.*
University of Namibia. (2017). | CODeL | eLearning. University of Namibia. http://www.unam.edu.na/codel/elearning
USAID. (2019). *Performance evaluation of Namibia's dreams program.* Global Health Program Cycle Improvement Project.
Uzobo, E., & Ayinmoro, A. D. (2021). Trapped between two pandemics: Domestic violence cases under Covid-19 pandemic lockdown: A scoping review. *International Quarterly of Community Health Education.* https://doi.org/10.1177/0272684X211022121
Wilkinson, A. (2020). Local response in health emergencies: Key considerations for addressing the COVID-19 pandemic in informal urban settlements. *Environment & Urbanization, International Institute for Environment and Development (IIED), 503*, 32(2), 503–522. https://doi.org/10.1177/0956247820922843. www.sagepublications.com
World Bank. (2016). *Gender equality, poverty reduction, and inclusive growth.* World Bank.
World Health Organization. (2021). Situation report. Corona virus (COVID-19). Coronavirus disease (COVID-19) weekly epidemiological update and weekly operational update.
XinhuaNet. (2021, April 04). *Business as usual for traders in Namibia amid Easter holiday.* www.XinhuaNet.com

Immaculate Mogotsi, Ph.D. is a Senior Research Fellow at the Multidisciplinary Research Services at the University of Namibia (UNAM) and is responsible for the Gender Training and Research Program. She holds a Bachelor's degree in Social Work and Community Development from UNAM and a Master of Arts degree in Women and Development Studies from the International Institute of Social Studies in the Netherlands. She recently defended her Doctoral studies in Sociology at UNAM. Her main research and lecturing interests cover gender-based violence, women empowerment, sexual and reproductive health and rights, and feminist theories. She has been instrumental in introducing an M.A. program in Gender and Development at UNAM.

Maria Kaundjua, M.A. is a Senior Lecturer in the Department of Social Sciences at the University of Namibia (UNAM). She holds a Master's degree in Population and Development Studies from the Institute of Social Studies (ISS) in The Hague, Netherlands. Her current research interests are mortality analyses, the social aspect of health and disability, and social aspects of climate change and variability.

Nelago Indongo, DPhil is an Associate Professor in the Department of Computing, Mathematical and Statistical Sciences and Director of the Centre for Research Services at the University of Namibia (UNAM). She holds a DPhil in Sociology. Her research focuses on statistical and demographic analysis of issues affecting population structure and distribution. Her research contributes to understanding the sexual and reproductive health needs and rights of young people, especially teenagers. She is interested in examining aspects concerning urbanization, well-being, and disaggregation by gender. Her research outputs have contributed to national debates on exclusive breastfeeding and maternity leave, which resulted in policy reviews and program interventions, especially on maternal and child health and adolescents' reproductive health.

Chapter 9
Catalyzing Action on Intimate Partner Violence Against Pregnant Adolescent Girls and Young Women in Zambia

Eugene Krupa, Albert Manasyan, Kate Woodman, Nobutu Muttau, and J. Anitha Menon

9.1 Introduction

Intimate partner violence (IPV) is a serious, ongoing problem affecting the lives of adolescent girls and young women (AGYW) in Zambia, across Africa, and worldwide. While contributing factors are challenging to address, effective strategies are emerging. This chapter explores the causes and impact of IPV in Zambia and globally and the useful tools and strategies for addressing them and inhibiting future occurrences. We integrate learnings from our recent action research project in

E. Krupa
School of Public Health, University of Alberta, Edmonton, AB, Canada

Catalyst Research and Development Inc., Edmonton, AB, Canada
e-mail: ekrupa@ualberta.ca

A. Manasyan
Division of Neonatology, University of Alabama at Birmingham, Birmingham, AL, USA

Department of Reproductive, Maternal, Newborn, and Child Health, Centre for Infectious Disease Research in Zambia, Lusaka, Zambia
e-mail: Albert.Manasyan@cidrz.org

K. Woodman
Catalyst Research and Development Inc., Edmonton, AB, Canada
e-mail: kwoodman@catalystrandd.com

N. Muttau
Department of Reproductive, Maternal, Newborn, and Child Health, Centre for Infectious Disease Research in Zambia, Lusaka, Zambia
e-mail: Nobutu.Muttau@cidrz.org

J. A. Menon (✉)
Department of Psychology, University of Zambia, Lusaka, Zambia

Department of International Studies, American University of Sharjah, Sharjah, UAE

K. Naidoo et al. (eds.), *Young People, Violence and Strategic Interventions in Sub-Saharan Africa*, Clinical Sociology: Research and Practice,
https://doi.org/10.1007/978-3-031-20679-5_9

Lusaka, Zambia, as a case study to illustrate the consequences of IPV in pregnant women and an effective strategy to address it (Menon et al., 2019).

The chapter illuminates the environments facilitating IPV globally and in Sub-Saharan Africa (SSA) and the resulting impacts on child marriage, pregnancy, and human immunodeficiency virus (HIV). Secondly, we examine the impact of the coronavirus disease (COVID-19) on IPV, including maternal and child health services and maternal and perinatal outcomes, and highlight the importance of timely and effective IPV interventions, including diagnosis and prevention. Thirdly, the chapter outlines the prevalence of IPV in Zambian communities, including its driving factors and lessons learned based on findings from a recent case study in Zambia. Furthermore, we outline the two key World Health Organization (WHO) frameworks (ecological and INSPIRE) used to outline an intersectional view of the forces that shape social identities, power relations, and dynamics contributing to violence. In Sect. 9.4, we detail the Danger Assessment (DA) instrument and associated “Safety Planning,” which we have adapted to a Zambian context and integrated with routine primary (antenatal) care. Section 9.5 discusses the impact of the DA tool in Zambia, following study findings. In Sect. 9.6, we summarize lessons learned from the Zambian study using the INSPIRE framework and propose strategies and approaches to consider to address IPV in Zambia and globally. Finally, in Sect. 9.7, we conclude the chapter by highlighting the findings and the proven and effective tools available for facilitating access to services and assisting victims of IPV, where women from LMIC settings bear the overwhelming burden.

9.2 Background: IPV Globally and in Africa

9.2.1 Violence Against Women and Youth in Sub-Saharan Africa

IPV perpetrated against women and youth is a human rights violation and is considered a major global public health, medical, and societal problem with negative consequences on the victim’s physical, psychological, sexual, and reproductive health (Berhanie et al., 2019). Globally, 30% of women experience gender-based violence (GBV), with the highest prevalence in developing countries (WHO, 2013). The most common type of GBV is IPV, a multi-faceted challenge linked to various health consequences, including poor perinatal outcomes (Rahman et al., 2013). IPV includes the sexual, physical, and emotional abuse and controlling behavior perpetrated by intimate partners (WHO, 2012).

IPV prevalence is double in developing countries as compared with developed countries (27.7% vs. 13.3%) (Azene et al., 2019). Countries in Africa report the highest levels of IPV globally, with 45.6% of women having experienced violence and 11.9% sexual assault from their partners throughout their lifetime (Devries et al., 2013; WHO, 2013). IPV is the most common societal problem in SSA, with an overall prevalence of 36% (WHO, 2013). In South Africa, IPV accounts for 10.9%

of disability-adjusted life years (DALY) (Norman et al., 2010). Furthermore, 50% of South African women who die are killed by their intimate partners, representing the highest rate of femicide in the world (Abrahams et al., 2009).

9.2.2 Risk Factors of IPV

In Africa, IPV risk factors for women and youth include socio-economic conditions such as low level of education, unemployment, as well as cultural beliefs that attest to men's dominant role in marriage (Morrell et al., 2012). Such patriarchal beliefs sustain community tolerance of IPV, leading to many unreported cases (Boonzaier, 2005). In many countries in SSA, the community endorses a man's privilege to discipline his wife physically (Uthman et al., 2009). Evidence shows an association between women's household decision-making capacity and IPV (Ahinkorah, 2018). Polygamy, common in SSA, is also a key determinant of IPV. The chances of the wives experiencing IPV are higher in a polygamous marriage than in a monogamous one (Amo-Adjei & Tuoyire, 2016; Behrman, 2019).

The high prevalence of HIV in Africa has also been linked with IPV, with the direction of a relationship being highly contested. Some scientists argue that IPV increases exposure to HIV, while others argue that an HIV-positive status increases their susceptibility to IPV (Karim & Baxter, 2016; WHO, 2013). HIV-positive women and youth disclosing their HIV status to their intimate partners were also found vulnerable to IPV (Karim & Baxter, 2016). In a culture of female subordination prevalent in many African countries, HIV status and socio-economic factors increase the risk of violence for pregnant women and youth (Shamu et al., 2011).

Child marriage is also a known risk factor for IPV (Rahman et al., 2014). Early literature identified those girls who married before the age of 18 as twice as likely to report being physically abused or threatened by their husbands than those who married later. They were also three times more likely to report being forced to have sex without their consent (Rahman et al., 2014). An associated factor is teenage pregnancy, which can be a consequence of child marriage and/or IPV.

9.2.3 Consequences of IPV During Pregnancy

Globally, 214 million women become pregnant every year, of which almost 50% are unintended pregnancies (Bearak et al., 2020; WHO, 2020b). In developing regions, 770,000 adolescent girls below the age of 15 and 21 million girls aged 15–19 become pregnant, of which 12 million give birth (Darroch et al., 2016; UNFPA, 2015). Adolescent pregnancies remain a global public health concern in developed and developing countries, driven mainly by poverty and a lack of education. While globally, we have seen an 11.6% decline in the adolescent-specific fertility rate in the past 20 years, there is a big disparity between high-income and low- and middle-income countries (LMIC) and within regions (Ganchimeg et al., 2014). However, despite this decline, the number of childbirths among adolescent girls has not declined due to the growing population of girls aged 15–19 (UN DESA, 2017).

Women and youth in abusive relationships may believe that pregnancy protects them from violence, and they might expect their partner to be more sympathetic toward them. However, pregnancy may give rise to insecurities in jealous men who doubt their paternity and their partner's fidelity. Young women between the ages of 15–24 years are more vulnerable to psychosocial challenges due to several and partly overlapping reasons, including developmental immaturity, low self-esteem, poor negotiation skills, and limited financial resources (Burch & Gallup, 2004; Ickovics et al., 2011).

While the prevalence of IPV during pregnancy ranges from 1% to 28% globally, it is as high as 57% in Africa (Azene et al., 2019). According to the UNICEF, 2018 report for Zambia, 59% of adolescent girls (15–19) were either pregnant or had been pregnant (UNICEF, 2018). Teenage and young adulthood years are important periods in which the foundations for a woman's future health and life are formed (Sawyer et al., 2012). Experiencing IPV during this developmental phase can affect the trajectory of future sexual behavior and tolerance of violence. Zambia reports that fewer than 25% of Zambian women believed that a married woman could refuse to have sex with her husband, even if he had shown infidelity and was infected with HIV. Further, only 11% thought a woman could ask her husband to use a condom in these circumstances (UNFPA, 2008). Our study data indicated that 33% of pregnant women reported being choked by their partner. Almost half the participants reported being beaten by their partner while pregnant.

Experiencing violence during pregnancy has a profound negative impact on maternal health and fetal growth and development. An exacerbating risk factor associated with IPV is unwanted or unplanned pregnancies (WHO, 2011). IPV during pregnancy could lead to adverse maternal and fetal outcomes (Groves et al., 2015). Adverse perinatal outcomes include preterm birth, low birth weight, developmental delays, perinatal death, and miscarriage (Pavey et al., 2014; Shah et al., 2010). Adverse maternal outcomes can be categorized into mental health (i.e., anxiety, depression/postpartum depression, thoughts of suicide, including smoking, drinking, and use of drugs), physical health (i.e., physical injury—broken bones, cuts, burns), and sexual and reproductive health outcomes (i.e., obstetric complications, preterm labor, and sexually transmitted infections) (Groves et al., 2015; Ludermir et al., 2010). Such outcomes are due to the direct trauma to the pregnant woman's body and the continuous stress affecting the child's growth and development. Studies have found that children born to women experiencing IPV during pregnancy are at increased risk of language and neurological delays (Udo et al., 2016). Furthermore, it has been shown that children witnessing IPV show changes in the intelligence quotient (IQ), cognitive functions, and socio-emotional development (Mueller & Tronick, 2019).

IPV also has various psychological, social, and physical consequences. Women experiencing IPV in SSA were likely to report psychological distress, high levels of depression, post-traumatic stress disorder, and suicidal ideation (Nguyen et al., 2019). Women were less likely to report any forms of GBV due to shame, financial dependency on their partner, fear of retaliation, lack of law enforcement, and normalizing of GBV by the community (WHO, 2012). Underreporting subsequently challenges accurately determining the rate of IPV and effectively addressing it. IPV is also associated with the transmission of HIV and sexually transmitted diseases (Seth et al., 2010; Weiss et al., 2008).

9.3 COVID-19 and IPV: One Pandemic Within Another

Globally, pandemic lockdowns have led to an upsurge in IPV, recording a 33% increase in Singapore, 30% in France, and 300% in China (Fawole et al., 2021). During self-isolation or quarantine periods, women continued to report high rates of IPV by their marital partners. The loss of jobs negatively impacted household incomes (Taub, 2020). Demand for victim shelter also increased. One study found that up to 25% of women who delivered during the COVID-19 pandemic experienced a form of IPV, the most common form being emotional abuse, followed by sexual and physical abuse (Muldoon et al., 2021).

Despite the evidence base for the impact of IPV on pregnant women and newborns, studies in high-, middle-, and low-income countries are still scarce (Naghizadeh et al., 2021). This exacerbates access to possible solutions to curb the high rates of IPV during this pandemic. Timely IPV diagnosis and prevention strategies during emergencies are crucial and should be a public health priority (Naghizadeh et al., 2021). Two studies have been published evaluating the impact of COVID-19 on IPV against pregnant women (in Iran and Ethiopia) (Naghizadeh et al., 2021; Teshome et al., 2021). Both studies found a significant increase in emotional (32.8–72%), sexual (12.4–49%), and physical (4.8–30%) abuse while pregnant. The studies further found that factors associated with IPV were reduced spousal income, alcohol use, and drugs (Naghizadeh et al., 2021; Teshome et al., 2021).

In LMIC settings, the emergence of the COVID-19 pandemic negatively impacted the already strained healthcare system, affecting the quality and reducing the uptake of antenatal (ANC) and postnatal care (PNC) services, setting back the decades of work done to improve maternal, newborn, and child health outcomes (Patabendige et al., 2021). Consequently, findings show that maternal and perinatal outcomes have worsened during the COVID-19 pandemic globally, with a significant increase in maternal mortality and stillbirth rates but no change in preterm birth rates (Chmielewska et al., 2021). Additionally, an increase in maternal depression rates was recorded as evaluated by the mean Edinburgh Postnatal Depression Scale (Ceulemans et al., 2020; Saeed & Wemakor, 2019). A recent modeling work found that maternal deaths can rise between 17% and 43% due to barriers associated with movement restrictions, economic challenges, fear of being infected while at the facility, and an overburdened healthcare system following the COVID-19 pandemic (Smriti et al., 2020).

A study in Ethiopia found that during the COVID-19 pandemic, mothers who lived less than 30 min away from the health facility or who had higher education were more likely to attend ANC at a health facility than those who lived more than 90 min away or were less educated (Temesgen et al., 2021). A significant reduction in postnatal care services was recorded in a Rwanda study, similar to findings from Guinea and Sierra Leone during the Ebola crisis (Wanyana et al., 2021). Furthermore, COVID-19 service-related disruptions have impacted not only the elderly but also the already struggling under-5 years immunization programs. A recent UNICEF report found that 23 million children—3.7 million more than in 2019—missed out on life-saving vaccines in 2020 (UNICEF, 2021). Such disruptions can lead to vaccine-preventable outbreaks, risking the re-emergence of diphtheria, measles, and other life-threatening yet preventable illnesses (UNICEF, 2020). Such has already been witnessed in Guinea, Liberia, and Sierra Leone as a result of the Ebola outbreak in 2014–2015, which led to a spike in measles from 2.7 per one million to 11.5 per one million (Masresha et al., 2020).

Prior to the pandemic, IPV was highly prevalent among women in Zambia (Central Statistical Office (CSO) [Zambia], 2014). COVID-19 catalyzed the existing pandemic of violence against women (Fawole et al., 2021). Many people were asked to work from home, and others were laid off and lost income. Restricted movement or lockdowns left victims of IPV trapped at home with their abusers. The COVID-19 measures imposed by the government may have slowed the spread of the SARS-COV-2 virus but exacerbated IPV (Everjoy Mahuku, 2020). In light of this, the Zambian government intensified its efforts to fight IPV by joining the rest of the world in commemorating the annual awareness campaign "16 Days of Activism" under the theme: "Orange The World: Fund, Respond, Prevent, Collect" (GWI, 2020). In addition, the government reaffirmed its commitment to strengthening IPV response services at the local and national levels in the context of COVID-19 (UNW, 2020). Results of the actions were not yet available at the time of writing.

The COVID-19 pandemic caused additional hardship and challenges for those at risk of IPV. It led to restricted movement and increased exposure to abusers, isolation from social supports, reduced family income causing financial stress, and issues with access to health facilities. Therefore, policies and programs, including healthy public policies, and policies and programs associated with COVID-19, should be carefully designed, evaluated, and adjusted so they do not add to the challenge of those at risk of IPV.

9.4 Addressing IPV: Lessons from a Zambian Study

9.4.1 A Lusaka, Zambia Case Study on IPV and Pregnant Adolescent Girls and Young Women

In Zambia, violence and sexual coercion in marital relationships are common, with the prevalence increasing among AGYW aged 15–24 (Plan, 2005). Zambian youth experience various forms of IPV: 22% sexual violence, 21% emotional violence, and 16% physical violence (Kusanthan et al., 2015). Zambia has one of the highest child marriage rates globally, with about 42% of women between 20 and 24 years being married by 18 years of age (Vision, 2015).

This chapter references knowledge from a demonstration case study implemented in Lusaka, Zambia, funded by Grand Challenges Canada (GCC) (Menon et al., 2019). The intervention provided meaningful learning about pregnant AGYW who experienced IPV and attended ANC clinics through a randomized controlled trial. The key to this learning was data from the DA process and instrument (see Sect. 9.5). The project involved those attending clinics who screened positive for IPV, ANC nurses, and local community health workers (CHWs). Since its completion in 2019, the key findings have been elevated among stakeholders within the Government of Zambia, who are now considering policy changes to include the DA instrument and process as standard ANC practice.

9.4.2 WHO Violence Prevention Frameworks

Of the many frameworks of dynamics contributing to violence among youth, especially females, two WHO frameworks are particularly helpful in organizing action for positive change in policies and practices:

1. The ecological framework identifies risk factors for violence against children and youth at four levels—individual, close relationships, community, and societal (WHO, 2022).
2. The INSPIRE framework outlines strategies and approaches for policies and practices (WHO, 2020a).

Collectively, these inform an intersectional view of the forces that shape an individual's social and power identities, creating the tensions and power differentials contributing to violence. In this chapter, we utilize these models to inform and organize our understanding of the experience of pregnant AGYW who experience IPV.

The WHO's Violence Prevention Alliance has created an ecological framework to understand the environments that facilitate violence and how the various types of violence interact (see Fig. 9.1). It shows that no single factor can fully explain why some populations or groups are vulnerable to violence or not. Instead, violence is understood as the outcome of interaction among many factors across individual, relationship, community, and society levels. This model encompasses the dimensions of interpersonal violence, including IPV.

We apply the WHO ecological framework to explore the factors driving IPV in the Zambian community at the individual, relational, community, and societal levels, and in our study communities in particular (see Fig. 9.1).

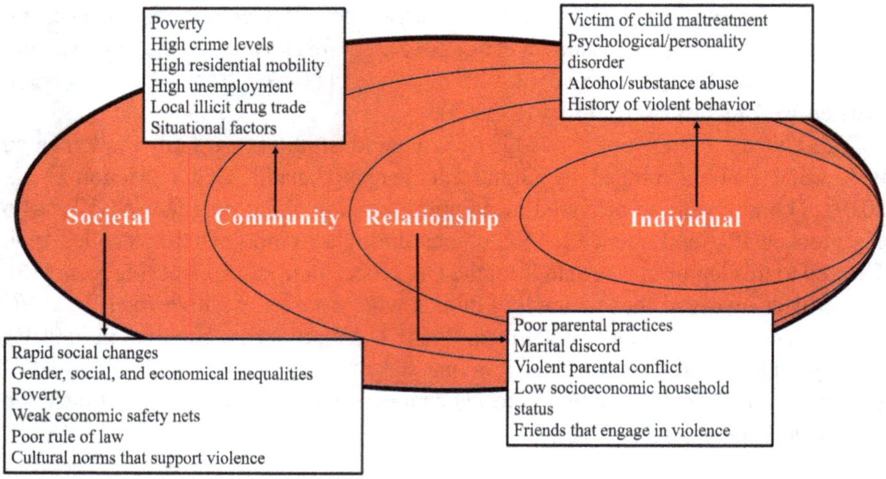

Fig. 9.1 The WHO's ecological framework for violence: examples of risk factors at each level

9.4.3 Factors Driving IPV in Zambian Communities

Societal Level The four project communities evolved in a period of rapid social change. As elsewhere in Africa and globally, the promise of increased income drew millions from rural agricultural communities to Lusaka, Zambia's capital. Many migrants sought low-cost shelter in informal, unstructured communities, which tended to have little or no services. Traditional cultures and societal expectations were carried along with this migration, bringing many positive factors such as community cohesiveness and caring. However, risk factors for violence also arrived and persisted: male privilege and dominance of voice, gender roles and limitations, low aspirations for jobs requiring training, low interest in education for girls (thus low attainment), teen marriage, early pregnancy, and low sense of self-worth and agency. Employment prospects were and continue to be variable. Many slipped into poverty without capital, education, training, or economic safety nets, and women remained financially dependent.

Community Level The communities in our study did not experience extraordinary violent crime rates. The major factors driving violence in our study communities are poverty, cultural/societal expectations, oppression of women and girls, uncertainty in support, and a low sense of personal agency in dealing with violence. In contrast, IPV rates, when reported and recorded, indicate high prevalence. Similarly, unemployment and alcohol consumption rates are high compared to rural communities and middle-class urban areas. In the study communities, violence against women and girls was common and considered normal and acceptable, even expected by some. Police and social structures are under-resourced and ill-prepared to act, so they could not be counted on for consistent support. The health system and local clinics are similarly challenged. Overwhelmed with the day-to-day needs of large populations served by small clinics, they were without resources to address IPV directly. The tremendous shortage of health and social service professionals means many core functions are possible only with the assistance of community health volunteers (CHVs) or minimally paid and trained CHWs. Impoverished communities have few resources to assist victims or perpetrators in addressing historical patterns and transitioning to violence-free relationships. Creating positive and sustainable change ultimately requires attending to the Social Determinants of Health (SDoH) and strategic action to develop healthy public policies, community action, and re-design health services.

Close Relationships (Family and Friends) Many of those residing in the communities had extensive and important social support. However, there were inconsistencies as well; societal and community dynamics played out in relationships between intimate partners that tend to be violent. The larger dynamics can be barriers to expected support from family and friends—for both victims and perpetrators. Women and youth victims bear most of the diagnosable harm due to IPV. However, the social context of the perpetrator is essential to consider in the Zambian context. The traditions and wounds they carry can result in violent behaviors. Many of those who experienced violence have limited education and poor-paying jobs. Most have few people or services that would help them understand their situation and the harm caused, and fewer, if any, would find services or support to transition to a violence-free life.

Individuals Most women and youth identified in the screening process lived in impoverished households. A history of normalizing violence was prevalent, as was the sense of low power and agency. All enrolled were pregnant females, and most reported that the pregnancy was not intended. One-fifth of the participants in the study reported consuming alcohol during pregnancy; alcohol use among men is also a common phenomenon in Zambia and is associated with an increase in perpetuating violence. A history of violence with others is also an established factor of violence with the partner. About one-third of the respondents reported that their partners had encountered violence with family members, and 26% reported that their partners had encountered violence with friends. It would be necessary for the women to recognize the individual factors that put them at risk of violence to address it effectively. Our intervention facilitated this process.

It is crucial to recognize the complex environments that influence the way IPV presents in SSA, along with the pandemic-level prevalence of incidents. Understanding these realities and applying the WHO's ecological framework provides a model that clarifies and informs the development of appropriate and effective interventions. Further, the consistent application of this approach has significant implications for developing a database to support public health and other sectors with policy development. Risk factors for individuals of particular interest in our research were cultural male dominance, child marriage, and pregnancy.

It is important that the government of Zambia develop a policy basis and supports housing IPV incidents. Those designing policies and programs should consider the acute needs of victims, the "upstream" needs and challenges faced by victims and perpetrators, their cultural and economic context, and the multiple levels of factors illustrated in the WHO's ecological model. Innovations have attempted to increase personal empowerment, build the capacity to achieve and sustain financial and social independence, and address toxic masculinity, mental health, and alcohol use. Key implications lie in implementing interventions, which need to be harmonized to cover key identified factors. Further, evaluation to collect significant data would inform the assessment of those interventions. Lessons learned could be used to support the emerging IPV suite of policies.

9.5 Danger Assessment (DA) and Safety Planning to Prevent IPV

Accurately describing IPV threats in abusive relationships is critical to making them visible and "real" to victims. Accurate assessment illuminates violence and facilitates opportunities to create plans for safety or escape as appropriate for the victim's circumstances. Assessing risk from the victim's perspective, while unique in a sector dominated by perpetrator risk assessment, has proven to be effective decision-making support for both the survivor and service provider. The DA, a well-researched and validated instrument used in our study to address IPV in pregnant women, assesses the risk for intimate partner homicide and is proven to be an effective predictor of reassault (Campbell, 2004; Campbell et al., 2009). The tool is available freely for clinical and research use (Campbell, 2004).

Beyond the DA's capacity to support the woman fleeing violence and provide the service provider with a clear understanding of her unique risks, the data arising is of relevance to policymakers. A two-part tool involving both a calendar-based assessment of the frequency and type of abuse and the 20-item instrument results in a robust understanding of how IPV is presented and experienced. When analyzed in aggregate, the comprehensive data derived from this tool provides policymakers with a clearer, evidence-informed understanding of what policy gaps may exist in providing services and supports to the sector—and creating safe spaces for AGYW to thrive in the non-violent future.

Implementation requires the practitioner to adopt a collaborative and relational approach that creates space for the woman to share her voice and direct experience with her intimate partner (Graham et al., 2021). Together, they create and review a calendar of prior experiences of violence, indicating the approximate days she experienced abuse (physical, emotional, spiritual, financial, etc.) and the severity of that abuse (using a five-point Likert scale). They then work through the 20-item instrument, containing questions exploring proven indicators, including abuse during pregnancy, and requiring a "yes" or "no" response. Standardized scoring for the DA ranges from −3 to 37; responses are calculated and located within one of four defined risk categories: variable, increased, severe, and extreme danger (Campbell et al., 2009).

The benefits of accurate IPV information available through utilizing the DA tool

- Provides a qualitative description of violence against women that may otherwise remain hidden
- Provides ongoing data on incidence, causes, and consequences of IPV
- Supports the development of priority prevention strategies based on risk factors identifiable in the data
- Enables early interventions based on emerging trends and problem areas
- Provides a baseline against which the impact of intervention efforts can be measured
- Offers a profile of prevalence and characteristics of IPV and associated risk factors

*Adapted from "What are the benefits of accurate epidemiological information?" from WHO Preventing IPV and sexual violence against women: taking action and generating evidence (*WHO, 2010*).*

Once the two-part DA process is completed, the practitioners have a solid basis of information for discussion to support the woman's empowerment by developing a strategy unique to her circumstances. The data reported holds the potential to build the survivor's capacity to find safety for herself and the children in her care. She will better understand her risk, identify and consider self-care options that work for her, and take protective actions that are appropriate and effective (Graham et al., 2021). The DA supports mitigation actions by providing information that the practitioner can use to contextualize risk and co-develop a safe pathway to a non-violent future with the woman or youth.

The psychometric properties of the DA instrument indicate the validity of the tool and its predictive accuracy, as established in the United States and elsewhere. As an evidence-based instrument, the DA contributes to interrupting violence and improving the health and safety of persons experiencing IPV (Sigalla et al., 2017). For example, the most recent test for internal consistency reliability found alphas ranging from 0.60 to 0.86 (Graham et al., 2021). Concurrent validity of the DA has been established as related to other risk-assessment measures, reflecting appropriate levels of severity across different groups of women from Latina, European, and African American communities. The predictive validity has been researched (e.g., sensitivity: correct identification of reassault, severely reassault, or IPH; specificity: correct identification of no reassault, severely reassault, or IPH). Using ROC analyses has indicated the probability of correctly identifying a case with a particular outcome (Douglas et al., 2008; Graham et al., 2021).

The DA has been adapted for use in a variety of contexts (e.g., healthcare settings, women's shelters, law enforcement) and populations (e.g., immigrant women, indigenous women, and same-sex couples) (Campbell & Messing, 2017; Messing & Thaller, 2014; Wang, 2015). Similar to these research projects, the DA was adapted for use in Zambia. Not surprisingly, justice systems in the United States, United Kingdom, and Canada have validated the DA score as evidence in court. In addition, health systems globally have used the DA, or the DA-5 (a validated, shortened form of the instrument) as a screener in emergency departments. Finally, globally, women's emergency shelters use the instrument as part of the intake process (Graham et al., 2021).

The DA is a useful tool to support safety planning for women, including pregnant women and girls. The instrument works well for triage, providing a risk-informed context for preventative intervention. The information provided in the calendar and the risk assessment from the 20-item scale enable the woman and practitioner to discuss, in concrete terms, what is the best pathway to an evidence-informed transition to safety. Because the discussion is based on the woman's self-assessed risk and the feedback can be immediate, the resulting safety plan is unique to her and relevant to what she needs. Typically, the plan includes, but is not limited to: planning an escape route, packing an emergency bag, storing money, making copies of important documents, and making arrangements for domestic animals (Bader et al., 2019). In the framework of the Zambia case study, the nurses and community health workers followed best practice steps (touchstones of usability, safety, and acceptability) to ensure participant safety in the research project (Anderson et al., 2017).

9.6 Impact of the Danger Assessment Tool in Zambia

Adapting the DA for use in Zambia achieved what the study authors hoped—it offered support to pregnant AGYWs attending the ANC intervention sites in Lusaka by providing them with clear information about the level of risk they faced. Participants were invited to talk with the ANC nurse after a positive response to the screening question. Completing the DA at two points (pre- and post-birth) afforded a critical opportunity for the pregnant woman or youth to understand her risk, the risk of the children in her care, and the newborn child. The second DA session further supported her in goal attainment, safety planning, and understanding her pathway for a non-abusive future.

Using the DA with pregnant AGYW resulted in positive and safety-promoting opportunities. The following activities proved supportive for the AGYW engaged in the intervention:

- Processing the DA results with skilled and trained healthcare workers
- Completing calendar and safety planning activities
- Receiving information on local, supportive resources
- Visits by the local community health worker

In addition, the ANC and community health providers affirmed the relevance and utility of the DA system as an essential intervention with pregnant AGYW, despite the extra demands it placed on their time in busy clinics. These practitioners recommended the integration of the DA as routine practice at ANCs. Participation in this intervention revealed the importance of addressing IPV to improve maternal and newborn health outcomes.

Using DA and safety planning tools has proven to help identify and mitigate IPV in youth and adults. Most importantly, DA and safety planning has helped victims understand their situations, increase their sense of agency, self-efficacy, and empowerment, and effectively act to create positive and sustainable change. Extending the use of the DA process beyond the ANC, for instance, in addition to validation for use in emergency shelters, these tools have been valued and validated in the courts and health systems and have been successfully adopted within various contexts and populations.

This section summarizes actions to consider when forming an inter-sectoral, multi-level strategy for populations, especially adolescent youth in impoverished urban communities. As the WHO's ecological framework suggested and our experience confirmed, the root causes of IPV are in the social environment. The "upstream" influence of intersectional factors or social determinants of health sets the scene for specific health and injustice issues, including IPV. Therefore, to reduce and eliminate IPV and its impacts, policy- and decision-makers need to consider ways to address the upstream, intersectional root causes and create the support needed to enable current victims (and perpetrators) to achieve a violence-free future.

9.7 Using the INSPIRE Framework to Address Study Findings in Zambia

The WHO's INSPIRE framework (see Fig. 9.2) was originally developed for child abuse but is generally also applicable to IPV. It provides a model for integrating ecological thinking with learning about specific contexts and organizing interventions that would address current issues and upstream, intersectional factors. The letters of the acronym helped to organize planning in seven categories. Approaches for each category are suggested, and key sectors are identified.

What follows are "letter-by-letter" examples of how the INSPIRE framework was used to organize thinking and engage partners from many sectors to discuss our study findings, as well as several notes on rural and remote communities and current policies receiving advocacy. Readers will also find references to approaches in rural and remote communities.

I—Implementing and Enforcing Laws Throughout our study and work in knowledge mobilization, we were impressed at the level of interest shown by leaders in the justice sector, which includes the police. Judges were strongly motivated to secure evidence for prosecuting perpetrators and appropriate follow-up action. Similarly,

Strategy	Approach	Sectors	Cross-cutting activities
Implementation and enforcement of laws	• Laws banning violent punishment of children by parents, teachers or other caregivers • Laws criminalizing sexual abuse and exploitation of children • Laws that prevent alcohol misuse • Laws limiting youth access to firearms and other weapons	Justice	Multisectoral actions and coordination
Norms and values	• Changing adherence to restrictive and harmful gender and social norms • Community mobilization programmes • Bystander interventions	Health, Education, Social Welfare	
Safe environments	• Reducing violence by addressing "hotspots" • Interrupting the spread of violence • Improving the built environment	Interior, Planning	
Parent and caregiver support	• Delivered through home visits • Delivered in groups in community settings • Delivered through comprehensive programmes	Social Welfare, Health	
Income and economic strengthening	• Cash transfers • Group saving and loans combined with gender equity training • Microfinance combined with gender norm training	Finance, Labour	Monitoring and evaluation
Response and support services	• Counselling and therapeutic approaches • Screening combined with interventions • Treatment programmes for juvenile offenders in the criminal justice system • Foster care interventions involving social welfare services	Health, Justice, Social Welfare	
Education and life skills	• Increase enrolment in pre-school, primary and secondary schools • Establish a safe and enabling school environment • Improve children's knowledge about sexual abuse and how to protect themselves against it • Life and social skills training • Adolescent intimate partner violence prevention programmes	Education	

Fig. 9.2 WHO INSPIRE framework

police leaders were motivated to re-examine their practices when responding to IPV and raise standards for dealing with violence in all forms. Improving these services requires considerable resources for retraining and increasing staff available for investigation and documentation. It also requires a significant shift for police and community residents. These only increase incrementally and require more time before change can be detected.

Policy: With strong interest from the judiciary, laws for IPV are in place or development. However, further progress is needed on enforcement but will require additional personnel, training, and monitoring resources.

N—Norms and Values The authors have worked with several Zambian non-governmental organizations (NGOs), including faith-based organizations, that are active and skilled in girl and women empowerment, addressing gender inequalities, and preventing IPV (e.g., YWCA, ZCCP-Kwatu, Caritas/Catholic Development and Peace, Bwafwano). In addition to direct support, they advocate with leaders to change social norms regarding violence. They may also work to address upstream factors (i.e., intersectional, social determinants of health) that set the scene for IPV or its prevention. These include promoting education for girls, employment, income generation to address poverty, awareness of cultural and historical factors, etc.

Some authors have worked extensively with traditional governments and intersectoral Safe Motherhood Action Groups (SMAGs) in rural and remote communities. Traditional governments can be quite effective partners in facilitating change in attitudes. Community-based groups like SMAGs bring diverse sectors together in a coalition. They were formed to reduce maternal and infant death in childbirth but have typically embraced roles in preventing IPV. The authors have appreciated the significant influence involvement in sports and other new opportunities, such as in developing computer literacy, has on both girls' empowerment and boys' respect for girls and women.

Policy: Many NGOs do excellent work in this area and deserve broader support in design, implementation, and evaluation. Community sensitization is underway, and bystander interventions are more common but need further resources and champions. Assessment processes and data are needed to identify targets and develop mitigation strategies in all communities.

S—Safe Environments The NGO initiatives described above also led to creating safe environments, including shelters. The main problem is that the NGOs are typically not working in many areas, so services and support vary. The ideal would be for governments to progressively take more responsibility for safe environments, but this is difficult in a low-resource country setting.

P—Personal Support CHW and CHV mandates can be very broad or focused. These cadres developed across SSA due to shortages of health professionals, and many tasks shifted to CHWs and CHVs with the arrival of HIV/AIDS. CHWs and CHVs are ideally situated and skilled to communicate with individuals on their safety plans and are skilled in their approaches. They liaised with the range of support called for in a safety plan (e.g., NGOs, police) to ensure helpful support and provide essential direct social support.

Although women and their newborns bear most of the diagnosable harm due to violence, perpetrators often have experienced violence and resort to harmful behavior. Many have limited education, poor-paying jobs, abuse alcohol, and experience mental health issues. Understandably, they develop low self-esteem, dysfunctions, and negative behaviors that characterize individuals with that history. In the absence of psychosocial and economic empowerment to overcome these challenges, their trajectories are difficult to influence. The authors have seen promising practices in some low-resource communities. One example is a "men's club" that provides informal social support to perpetrators in reducing alcohol use/dependency and choosing non-violent futures.

Policy: Increased attention to CHW and CHV training and activities would go a long way to improve personal support for those fleeing IPV.

I—Income and Economic Strengthening Government programs have increased over the last decade but are unable to get to all or most of those in need of economic empowerment. No government programs were known in our study communities. However, there were several examples of NGOs that worked to address upstream factors (i.e., intersectional, social determinants of health) that set the scene for IPV or its prevention. These include promoting education (especially for girls) and facilitating high educational attainment, building employability and entrepreneurial skills, awareness of cultural and historical factors, etc.

Policy: Resources are needed to transition to scale to ensure that any girl or woman in Zambia has options for financial independence to escape IPV.

R—Response and Support Services In our study, we identified few formal, government-funded supports. Primary care centers, ANCs, and police stations were typically under-resourced. There were no systematic approaches to identifying and addressing violence in core services. Pregnant AGYW would normally visit the ANC three times before delivery, so ANC was ideally situated to screen for violence and offer support and referral. We provided nurses and community workers with training and tools to screen for and respond to pregnant AGYW experiencing violence. Staff effectively and successfully conducted the DA and safety planning processes with clients. These processes helped AGYW to become more aware of their level of danger. It increased awareness and understanding of the power differentials and male dominance and supported an increased sense of agency and self-efficacy. Participants reported an increased sense of empowerment to act for their futures and that of their children. Early outcomes showed this was happening for most women and girls.

Policy: Many communities are without counseling professionals. Pre-service training is possible, but even with adequate resources, a strategy for scaling up will likely need to include trained community workers, similar to CHW. In addition, pastoral care options should be explored, and clergy provided with awareness and training sessions.

E—Education and Life Skills Historically, families have directed education resources to males. Girls' schooling was often disrupted and reduced for a variety of economic, cultural, and social reasons. Impoverished families with few resources after housing and food may choose to direct these to enable male children to advance in school and keep girls to work at home. These family realities may be coupled with cultural shaming for adolescent girls and/or discouragement and low expectations for attainment (i.e., a narrative saying education is of little use for one destined to remain a cook, housekeeper, and childcare worker). In population-scale surveys, young women in impoverished urban and rural communities have much lower literacy, numeracy, and educational attainment rates. Collectively, these exacerbate power differentials and increase tensions arising from early marriage, pregnancy, and financial dependence. Change in recent years is due to inspiring and enabling youth to seek equity. However, cultural momentum continues long after changes in education occur.

Policy: The importance of continuing school as a protective factor cannot be overstated. Much remains to be done to increase the number of teaching staff and bring schools and teachers up to higher efficiency for learning. Targeted action has increased girls' enrolment and attainment, boys' and girls' sense of empowerment and self-worth, and awareness of relationship dynamics and IPV. There is considerable interest in training, and progress has been made in creating access to digital opportunities. However, considerable resources will be required to build educational capacity to enable all to achieve their potential.

9.7.1 Other Health and Social Policy Recommendations

We offer these recommendations but also understand that policies need to be customized to national and regional realities, and they require resources to implement, evaluate, and improve.

(a) *Conceptualize the "health system" as broader than healthcare services and consider determinants of health and violence*: Like all efforts to address health issues, IPV has upstream determinants and results from inequities or intersectional dynamics that lead to power and resource differentials. These block attempts to end violence against girls and women. Action on healthy public policies (i.e., the focus of the following section) and inter-sectoral collaboration are essential for positive, sustainable change.
(b) *Reorient and support local health services*: to ensure effective diagnosis and action to contribute to violence-free lives. This includes DA, safety planning, and referral to local resources, ideally for victims and perpetrators. Progress requires additional health professionals, community workers, and resources to train and sustain them.
(c) *Develop/use effective tools* and processes for the following:

- Facilitating diagnosis (i.e., screening and DA)
- Referral to effective support (safety planning and referral to the community)
- Data gathering for local decision-making, including the ability to provide updates to inform national and provincial-level policy
- Mapping community assets for violence prevention

(d) *Convene NGOs and government ministry collaboration*: Facilitate collaboration to create appropriate services, support victims and perpetrators of violence, and address upstream determinants.

9.8 Conclusion

While IPV occurs in all settings and among men and women, the overwhelming burden of IPV is borne by women in LMIC settings. Being pregnant provides the context for IPV and seriously threatens women's and unborn babies' health. The child's exposure to IPV in-utero and after delivery can impact their physical, developmental, and emotional well-being in both the short and long term. We suggest a need for comprehensive, multi-sectoral, long-term collaboration between governments and civil society at all levels of the ecological framework. We introduced a DA tool and process in four low-income community ANC clinics. This facilitated access to and the provision of specialist GBV services and support for pregnant women and girls in Zambia. This enabled preventative risk assessment for project participants by guiding safety planning and empowering them with information and learning about their situation. The DA intervention was innovative for the Zambian health sector, and the findings indicate the intervention was effective at individual and policy levels. The data was disseminated to inform health and justice policy decisions and NGO decisions for improving, sustaining, and scaling up services. This is the first step toward a community-based and sustainable intervention to address IPV in pregnant women in Zambia. Further work is required to reach out to a larger population and provide support services.

References

Abrahams, N., Jewkes, R., Martin, L. J., Mathews, S., Vetten, L., & Lombard, C. (2009). Mortality of women from intimate partner violence in South Africa: A national epidemiological study. *Violence and Victims, 24*(4), 546–556.

Ahinkorah, B. O., Dickson, K. S., & Seidu, A. A. (2018). Women decision-making capacity and intimate partner violence among women in sub-Saharan Africa. *Arch Public Health, 76*, 5.

Amo-Adjei, J., & Tuoyire, D. A. (2016). Do ethnicity and polygyny contribute to justification of men beating women in Ghana? *Women & Health, 56*(1), 48–64.

Anderson, J. C., Glass, N. E., & Campbell, J. C. (2017). Conducting clinically based intimate partner violence research: Safety protocol recommendations. *Nursing Research, 66*(5), 405–409.

Azene, Z. N., Yeshita, H. Y., & Mekonnen, F. A. (2019). Intimate partner violence and associated factors among pregnant women attending antenatal care service in Debre Markos town health facilities, Northwest Ethiopia. *PLoS One, 14*(7), e0218722.

Bader, D., Dumount-Smith, C., Guruge, S., Nepinak, J., Porteous, T., Campbell, M., Straatman, A. L., & Dawson, M. (2019). *Creating safety plans with vulnerable populations to reduce the risk of repeated violence and domestic homicide*. Canadian Domestic Homicide Prevention Initiative.

Bearak, J., Popinchalk, A., Ganatra, B., Moller, A. B., Tuncalp, O., Beavin, C., et al. (2020). Unintended pregnancy and abortion by income, region, and the legal status of abortion: Estimates from a comprehensive model for 1990-2019. *The Lancet Global Health, 8*(9), e1152–e1161.

Behrman, J. A. (2019). Polygynous unions and intimate partner violence in Nigeria: An examination of the role of selection. *Journal of Marriage and Family, 81*(4), 905–919.

Berhanie, E., Gebregziabher, D., Berihu, H., Gerezgiher, A., & Kidane, G. (2019). Intimate partner violence during pregnancy and adverse birth outcomes: A case-control study. *Reproductive Health, 16*(1), 22.

Boonzaier, F. (2005). Woman abuse in South Africa: A brief contextual analysis. *Feminism & Psychology, 15*(1), 99–103.

Burch, R. L., & Gallup, G. G. (2004). Pregnancy as a stimulus for domestic violence. *Journal of Family Violence, 19*(4), 243–247.

Campbell, J. (2004). *Danger assessment*. Retrieved from www.dangerassessment.org/DA.aspx

Campbell, J. C., & Messing, J. T. (2017). *Assessing dangerousness, domestic violence offenders and child abusers*.

Campbell, J. C., Webster, D. W., & Glass, N. (2009). The danger assessment: Validation of a lethality risk assessment instrument for intimate partner femicide. *Journal of Interpersonal Violence, 24*(4), 653–674.

Central Statistical Office (CSO) [Zambia], M. o. H. M. Z., ICF International. (2014). *Zambia demographic and health survey 2013–14*. Central Statistical Office, Ministry of Health, and ICF International.

Ceulemans, M., Hompes, T., & Foulon, V. (2020). Mental health status of pregnant and breastfeeding women during the COVID-19 pandemic: A call for action. *International Journal of Gynaecology and Obstetrics, 151*(1), 146–147.

Chmielewska, B., Barratt, I., Townsend, R., Kalafat, E., van der Meulen, J., Gurol-Urganci, I., et al. (2021). Effects of the COVID-19 pandemic on maternal and perinatal outcomes: A systematic review and meta-analysis. *The Lancet Global Health, 9*(6), e759–e772.

Darroch, J. W. V., Bankole, A., & Ashford, L. S. (2016). *Adding it up: Costs and benefits of meeting the contraceptive needs of adolescents*. Guttmacher Institute.

Devries, K. M., Mak, J. Y., Garcia-Moreno, C., Petzold, M., Child, J. C., Falder, G., et al. (2013). Global health. The global prevalence of intimate partner violence against women. *Science, 340*(6140), 1527–1528.

Douglas, K. S., Reeves, K. A., & Weir, J. (2008). *HCR-20 violence risk assessment scheme: Overview and annotated bibliography*. Retrieved from http://kdouglas.files.wordpress.com/2006/04/annotate10%2D%2D24nov2008.pdf

Everjoy Mahuku, K. L. Y., & Karl Deering, B. M. (2020). *Rapid gender analysis for COVID 19 East, Central and Southern Africa*. Retrieved August 26, 2021, from https://reliefweb.int/report/angola/care-rapid-gender-analysis-covid-19-east-central-and-southern-africa

Fawole, O. I., Okedare, O. O., & Reed, E. (2021). Home was not a safe haven: Women's experiences of intimate partner violence during the COVID-19 lockdown in Nigeria. *BMC Womens Health, 21*(1), 32.

Ganchimeg, T., Ota, E., Morisaki, N., Laopaiboon, M., Lumbiganon, P., Zhang, J., et al. (2014). Pregnancy and childbirth outcomes among adolescent mothers: A World Health Organization multicountry study. *BJOG, 121*(1), 40–48.

Graham, L. M., Sahay, K. M., Rizo, C. F., Messing, J. T., & Macy, R. J. (2021). The validity and reliability of available intimate partner homicide and reassault risk assessment tools: A systematic review. *Trauma Violence Abuse, 22*(1), 18–40.

Groves, A. K., Moodley, D., McNaughton-Reyes, L., Martin, S. L., Foshee, V., & Maman, S. (2015). Prevalence, rates and correlates of intimate partner violence among south African women during pregnancy and the postpartum period. *Maternal and Child Health Journal, 19*(3), 487–495.

GWI. (2020). *Eliminating gender-based violence through women-led strategic advocacy for systemic change. 16 days of activism against gender-based violence.* Graduate Women International.

Ickovics, J. R., Reed, E., Magriples, U., Westdahl, C., Schindler Rising, S., & Kershaw, T. S. (2011). Effects of group prenatal care on psychosocial risk in pregnancy: Results from a randomised controlled trial. *Psychology & Health, 26*(2), 235–250.

Karim, Q. A., & Baxter, C. (2016). The dual burden of gender-based violence and HIV in adolescent girls and young women in South Africa. *South African Medical Journal, 106*(12), 1151–1153.

Kusanthan, T., Mwaba, S. O. C., & Menon, J. A. (2015). Factors affecting domestic violence among married women in Zambia. *Journal of Education, Society and Behavioral Science, 12*(2), 1–13.

Ludermir, A. B., Lewis, G., Valongueiro, S. A., de Araujo, T. V., & Araya, R. (2010). Violence against women by their intimate partner during pregnancy and postnatal depression: A prospective cohort study. *Lancet, 376*(9744), 903–910.

Masresha, B. G., Luce, R., Jr., Weldegebriel, G., Katsande, R., Gasasira, A., & Mihigo, R. (2020). The impact of a prolonged Ebola outbreak on measles elimination activities in Guinea, Liberia and Sierra Leone, 2014-2015. *Pan African Medical Journal, 35*(Suppl 1), 8.

Menon, J. A., Krupa, G., Kusanthan, T., Mwaba, S. O. C., & Woodman, K. (2019). *Assessing and addressing risk of antenatal attendees: Catalyzing action on violence against pregnant women and adolescent girls in Lusaka, Zambia.* Report submitted to Grand Challenges Canada: Grand Challenges Canada.

Messing, J. T., & Thaller, J. (2014). Intimate partner violence risk assessment: A primer for social workers. *The British Journal of Social Work, 45*(6), 1804–1820.

Morrell, R., Jewkes, R., & Lindegger, G. (2012). Hegemonic masculinity/masculinities in South Africa: Culture, power, and gender politics. *Men and Masculinities, 15*(1), 11–30.

Mueller, I., & Tronick, E. (2019). Early life exposure to violence: Developmental consequences on brain and behavior. *Frontiers in Behavioral Neuroscience, 13*, 156.

Muldoon, K. A., Denize, K. M., Talarico, R., Boisvert, C., Frank, O., Harvey, A. L. J., et al. (2021). COVID-19 and perinatal intimate partner violence: A cross-sectional survey of pregnant and postpartum individuals in the early stages of the COVID-19 pandemic. *BMJ Open, 11*(5), e049295.

Naghizadeh, S., Mirghafourvand, M., & Mohammadirad, R. (2021). Domestic violence and its relationship with quality of life in pregnant women during the outbreak of COVID-19 disease. *BMC Pregnancy and Childbirth, 21*(1), 88.

Nguyen, K. H., Padilla, M., Villaveces, A., Patel, P., Atuchukwu, V., Onotu, D., et al. (2019). Coerced and forced sexual initiation and its association with negative health outcomes among youth: Results from the Nigeria, Uganda, and Zambia violence against children surveys. *Child Abuse & Neglect, 96*, 104074.

Norman, R., Schneider, M., Bradshaw, D., Jewkes, R., Abrahams, N., Matzopoulos, R., et al. (2010). Interpersonal violence: An important risk factor for disease and injury in South Africa. *Population Health Metrics, 8*, 32.

Patabendige, M., Gamage, M. M., & Jayawardane, A. (2021). The potential impact of COVID-19 pandemic on the antenatal care as perceived by non-COVID-19 pregnant women: women's experience research brief. *Journal of Patient Experience, 8*, 2374373521998820.

Pavey, A. R., Gorman, G. H., Kuehn, D., Stokes, T. A., & Hisle-Gorman, E. (2014). Intimate partner violence increases adverse outcomes at birth and in early infancy. *The Journal of Pediatrics, 165*(5), 1034–1039.

Plan. (2005, February 16, 2015). *Gender-based violence: A situation in Chadiza, Chibombo, Mansa and Mazabuka.* Retrieved August 07, 2021, from http://www.norad.no/en

Rahman, M., Hoque, M. A., Mostofa, M. G., & Makinoda, S. (2014). Association between adolescent marriage and intimate partner violence: A study of young adult women in Bangladesh. *Asia-Pacific Journal of Public Health, 26*(2), 160–168.

Rahman, M., Nakamura, K., Seino, K., & Kizuki, M. (2013). Does gender inequity increase the risk of intimate partner violence among women? Evidence from a national Bangladeshi sample. *PLoS One, 8*(12), e82423.

Saeed, N., & Wemakor, A. (2019). Prevalence and determinants of depression in mothers of children under 5 years in Bole District, Ghana. *BMC Research Notes, 12*(1), 373.

Sawyer, S. M., Afifi, R. A., Bearinger, L. H., Blakemore, S. J., Dick, B., Ezeh, A. C., et al. (2012). Adolescence: A foundation for future health. *Lancet, 379*(9826), 1630–1640.

Seth, P., Raiford, J. L., Robinson, L. S., Wingood, G. M., & Diclemente, R. J. (2010). Intimate partner violence and other partner-related factors: Correlates of sexually transmissible infections and risky sexual behaviours among young adult African American women. *Sexual Health, 7*(1), 25–30.

Shah, P. S., Shah, J., & Knowledge Synthesis Group on Determinants of Preterm, L. B. W. B. (2010). Maternal exposure to domestic violence and pregnancy and birth outcomes: A systematic review and meta-analyses. *Journal of Women's Health (2002), 19*(11), 2017–2031.

Shamu, S., Abrahams, N., Temmerman, M., Musekiwa, A., & Zarowsky, C. (2011). A systematic review of African studies on intimate partner violence against pregnant women: Prevalence and risk factors. *PLoS One, 6*(3), e17591.

Sigalla, G. N., Rasch, V., Gammeltoft, T., Meyrowitsch, D. W., Rogathi, J., Manongi, R., et al. (2017). Social support and intimate partner violence during pregnancy among women attending antenatal care in Moshi municipality, Northern Tanzania. *BMC Public Health, 17*(1), 240.

Smriti, P., Saugat, K., & Madhusudan, S. (2020). Access to maternal health services during COVID-19. *Europasian Journal of Medical Sciences, 2*(0).

Taub, A. (2020). A new COVID-19 crisis: Domestic abuse rises worldwide. *New York Times*. Retrieved August 3, 2021, from https://www.nytimes.com/2020/04/06/world/coronavirus-domestic-violence.html

Temesgen, K., Wakgari, N., Debelo, B. T., Tafa, B., Alemu, G., Wondimu, F., et al. (2021). Maternal health care services utilization amidst COVID-19 pandemic in West Shoa zone, Central Ethiopia. *PLoS One, 16*(3), e0249214.

Teshome, A., Gudu, W., Bekele, D., Asfaw, M., Enyew, R., & Compton, S. D. (2021). Intimate partner violence among prenatal care attendees amidst the COVID-19 crisis: The incidence in Ethiopia. *International Journal of Gynaecology and Obstetrics, 153*(1), 45–50.

Udo, I. E., Sharps, P., Bronner, Y., & Hossain, M. B. (2016). Maternal intimate partner violence: Relationships with language and neurological development of infants and toddlers. *Matern Child Health Journal, 20*(7), 1424–1431.

UN DESA, S. D. (2017). *SDG Indicators: Global database*.

UNFPA. (2008). *National action plan on gender-based violence*.

UNFPA. (2015). *Girlhood, not motherhood: Preventing adolescent pregnancy*. UNFPA.

UNICEF. (2018). *UNICEF Zambia annual report 2018*. UNICEF.

UNICEF. (2020). *Vaccination coverage estimates data visualization*. Retrieved August 3, 2021, from https://data.unicef.org/resources/immunization-coverage-estimates-data-visualization/?utm_source=newsletter&utm_medium=email&utm_campaign=WUENIC%20dashboard

UNICEF. (2021). *COVID-19 pandemic leads to major backsliding on childhood vaccinations, new WHO, UNICEF data shows*.

UNW. (2020). *In Focus: 16 days of activism against gender-based violence*. Retrieved from https://www.unwomen.org/en/news/in-focus/end-violence-against-women

Uthman, O. A., Lawoko, S., & Moradi, T. (2009). Factors associated with attitudes towards intimate partner violence against women: A comparative analysis of 17 sub-Saharan countries. *BMC International Health and Human Rights, 9*, 14.

Vision, W. (2015). *A situation report on child marriages in Zambia*.

Wang, P. L. (2015). Assessing the danger: Validation of Taiwan intimate partner violence danger assessment. *Journal of Interpersonal Violence, 30*(14), 2428–2446.
Wanyana, D., Wong, R., & Hakizimana, D. (2021). Rapid assessment on the utilization of maternal and child health services during COVID-19 in Rwanda. *Public Health Action, 11*(1), 12–21.
Weiss, H. A., Wasserheit, J. N., Barnabas, R. V., Hayes, R. J., & Abu-Raddad, L. J. (2008). Persisting with prevention: The importance of adherence for HIV prevention. *Emerging Themes in Epidemiology, 5*, 8.
WHO. (2010). *Preventing intimate partner violence and sexual violence against women: Taking action and generating evidence*. WHO.
WHO. (2011). *Intimate partner violence during pregnancy*. WHO.
WHO. (2012). *Understanding and addressing violence against women: Intimate partner violence*. World Health Organization.
WHO. (2013). *Global and regional estimates of violence against women: Prevalence and health effects of intimate partner violence and non-partner sexual violence*. World Health Organization.
WHO. (2020a). *Global status report on preventing violence against children*. WHO.
WHO. (2020b). *New estimates show worldwide fall in unintended pregnancies since 1990–1994*. Retrieved August 3, 2021, from https://www.who.int/news/item/23-07-2020-new-estimates-show-worldwide-fall-in-unintended-pregnancies-since-1990-1994
WHO. (2022). *The violence prevention alliance approach*. Retrieved January 17, 2022, from https://www.who.int/groups/violence-prevention-alliance/approach

Eugene Krupa, Ph.D., C.E., is a Co-Principal and Senior Consultant with Catalyst Research and Development and Adjunct Professor at the University of Alberta, School of Public Health, Canada. He has developed and researched many innovations in prevention and population health in Canada and Zambia. Most often, initiatives address social and environmental root causes or determinants of health and well-being. He has worked with many inter-agency and inter-sectoral collaboratives on interpersonal violence (family/gender-based/intimate partner), chronic and infectious diseases, and mental health and addictions. Much of his attention has been on healthy child development and building resiliency with families in the early and teen years in the context of communities. Frameworks for analysis and action are typically intersectional, inter-agency, and inter-sectoral. Approaches build local capacity to collaborate and understand upstream factors and then use knowledge to create and sustain positive change in policies and practices.

Albert Manasyan, M.D., has more than ten years of experience in reproductive, maternal, newborn, and child health, leading complex global health programs in Sub-Saharan Africa, managing cross-functional and multi-national teams, and providing strategic direction in government and nonprofit environments. He is an Associate Professor at the University of Alabama at Birmingham (UAB), based in Zambia. He was seconded to work at the Centre for Infectious Disease Research in Zambia (CIDRZ), where he set up and headed the Department of Reproductive, Maternal, Newborn, and Child Health. His primary research focuses on novel community and health facility models to reduce maternal and neonatal mortality, emphasizing perinatal mortality among preterm infants. Furthermore, he has led research on early infant diagnosis of HIV, safe motherhood, post-partum hemorrhage, sexually transmitted infection (STI) screening among adolescents and pregnant women, and cervical cancer, including the use of artificial intelligence. He has published numerous manuscripts and contributed to developing several national guidelines related to his field of expertise.

Kate Woodman, Ph.D., C.E., is a Co-Principal and Senior Consultant with Catalyst Research and Development. She frequently undertakes research and evaluation in Canada and abroad in the Intimate Partner Violence sector. She worked with the Lusaka, Zambia team on a project to support pregnant women and youth fleeing violence, introducing them to Dr. Jacquelyn Campbell's widely used Danger Assessment tool. Previously, she worked with the group implementing the first World Conference on Women's Shelters (2008), which led to the creation of the Global Network of Women's Shelters (https://gnws.org). Currently, she supports efforts in Canada on human trafficking (https://lila.help) and continues to publish, present, and advocate in support of efforts to make a difference for women and children fleeing violence.

Nobutu Muttau, B.A. is an Assistant Study Coordinator at the Centre for Infectious Disease Research in Zambia (CIDRZ). She holds a B.A. degree in Development Studies and Psychology from the University of Zambia. She has five years of experience in proposal/grant writing and coordinating research studies on maternal and newborn health and HIV under the Department of Reproductive, Maternal, Newborn, and Child Health. Her primary research interest is using Social and Behavioral Science in public health practice. She currently coordinates water, sanitation, and hygiene (WASH) projects under the Social and Behavioral Science unit at CIDRZ. She served as part of the COVID-19 Hygiene Hub, a technical advisory grant setup by the London School of Hygiene and Tropical Medicine (LSHTM). LSHTM established the hub to support actors in low- and middle-income countries (LMICs) to rapidly design evidence-based hygiene interventions to combat COVID-19 and contribute to national hygiene prevention efforts.

J. Anitha Menon, Ph.D. is a Professor of Health Psychology in the Department of Psychology, University of Zambia, and the Chairperson of the University of Zambia Committee on human immunodeficiency virus/acquired immunodeficiency syndrome (HIV/AIDS). She is also the Founding President of the Psychology Association of Zambia. She is now a Visiting Professor at the American University of Sharjah, UAE. She holds a Ph.D. in Psychiatry/Health Psychology from the University of Nottingham. For more than 27 years, she has been actively involved in various research and service-related projects. Her primary research interest pertains to the issue of HIV and well-being, adolescents' psychological well-being, and gender-based violence issues. She has also been involved in and led various national and international research projects and has been the team leader for several. She is the recipient of many prestigious international awards, such as the Labour Day Award from the University of Zambia for Innovation and Excellence (2014), the U.K. Alumni Award for Professional Achievement (2018), and African Women Leaders (2019).

Chapter 10
Males' Experiences of Gender-Based Violence in Sub-Saharan Africa (SSA): A Review of Literature

Dumsani Gumede, Manono Luthuli, Siphesihle Hlongwane, Kingsley Orievulu, Ntombizonke Gumede, and Oluwafemi Adeagbo

10.1 Introduction

Gender-based violence (GBV) is an abuse of human rights that occurs regardless of culture, socio-economic status, or religion and varies in frequency, form, and extent from country to country (Abrahams et al., 2014). It is a global public health problem that poses challenges to human health, with a higher prevalence in developing countries (Esther, 2020; Mutisya, 2018). The United Nations (UN) defines GBV as "any act of gender-based violence that results in or is likely to result in physical, sexual, economic or mental harm or suffering to women, including threats of such acts, coercion or arbitrary deprivation of liberty, whether occurring in public or in private life" (Muluneh et al., 2020, p. 1). GBV is enacted under many different manifestations, such as the relationship between the perpetrator and the victim, i.e., intimate partner violence (IPV) which is most common or non-IPV, or by type of act of GBV, i.e., physical, sexual, economic, or emotional violence directed at someone because of their biological sex or gender identity (Muluneh et al., 2020; Potter et al., 2021). GBV is a profound human rights violation and has major social and developmental impacts on survivors of violence, their families, communities, and society more broadly (Kassa, 2021; Schulz, 2018). On an individual level, GBV can have psychological, behavioral, and physical consequences for survivors (Mshweshwe, 2020).

D. Gumede (✉) · M. Luthuli · S. Hlongwane · K. Orievulu · N. Gumede
Africa Health Research Institute, KwaZulu-Natal, South Africa
e-mail: dumsani.gumede@ahri.org

O. Adeagbo
Department of Community and Behavioral Health, College of Public Health, University of Iowa, Iowa, IA, USA
e-mail: oluwafemi-adeagbo@uiowa.edu

K. Naidoo et al. (eds.), *Young People, Violence and Strategic Interventions in Sub-Saharan Africa*, Clinical Sociology: Research and Practice,
https://doi.org/10.1007/978-3-031-20679-5_10

In Sub-Saharan Africa (SSA), GBV remains a public health, human rights, and development issue despite significant laws enacted to curb abuse in various countries (Muluneh et al., 2020). In many parts of SSA, there is poor access to formal psychosocial or even medical support, and many survivors are unable to access the help they need (Carpenter, 2006, 2017; Zarkov, 2017). Survivors' families and loved ones can also experience indirect trauma, and many do not know how to provide effective support. Violence also has significant economic consequences, as high rates of GBV place a heavy burden on the health and criminal justice systems (Okeke-Ihejirika et al., 2019). The psychological impacts of GBV may include post-traumatic stress disorder (PTSD), depression, complex trauma, and generalized anxiety disorders (Rennison & Addington, 2018; Sadock et al., 2015). The behavioral impacts of GBV may include alcohol abuse, suicidal ideations, low self-esteem, living in fear, and isolation (Edition, 2013; Rennison & Addington, 2018; Sadock et al., 2015). The physical impacts of GBV may include head injuries, back pains, loss of hearing, loss of eyesight, damage to internal organs, and cardiovascular problems (Krug et al., 2002; Edition, 2013; Sadock et al., 2015; Stubbs & Szoeke, 2021). Given these consequences, one may argue that the costs of GBV are high.

Most available literature from SSA focuses on violence against females (both heterosexual and homosexual) and children, with little focus on males' experiences (Hlongwa et al., 2020). Furthermore, most of these studies focused on small-scale studies such as provinces and districts, in particular countries that could overestimate the prevalence of GBV (Muluneh et al., 2020). These small-scale studies cannot be generalized to the wider population, and country-specific statistics are sparse. However, understanding the males' perceptions and experiences of GBV can assist with identifying appropriate interventions to deal with GBV.

Limited studies have collectively and systematically examined the perceptions and experiences of GBV in varying forms among males in SSA countries. Most of these small-scale studies have portrayed males as perpetrators of GBV (Ganou, 2021; Peacock & Barker, 2014). The introduction of the coronavirus disease (COVID-19) measures such as lockdown may have increased IPV, which is associated with increased unemployment, substance abuse, and reduced economic status during the pandemic (Moreira & Pinto da Costa, 2020; Evans et al., 2020).

Risk factors for GBV are assessed at the individual, community, and policy levels across the world. At the individual and family level, these risk factors include suffering abuse as a child, witnessing family violence, attitudes that perpetuate violence, gender inequalities, hypermasculinity, hostility toward powerless individuals, desire for power and control in relationships, and experiencing poor parenting as a child (Ameh et al., 2012; Christensen, 2019). At the community level, social norms and cultural practices exist within the communities that label males as the perpetrators of violence and hold skepticism that males could be victims as well (Ali & Naylor, 2013; Christensen, 2019). Some social policies that increase the risk of GBV among males include limited access to health services, protection services, helplines, and shelters because these services exclusively target female victims (Christensen, 2019). This review is, therefore, designed to provide more comprehensive insight into male experiences to foster more informed programming and policies on GBV locally, regionally, and globally.

10.2 Methods

This review was conducted using the Preferred Reporting Items for Systematic Reviews and Meta-Analysis (PRISMA) guidelines across all 48 SSA countries (McInnes et al., 2018; Moher et al., 2009). We conducted a literature search across ten electronic databases, namely EBSCOhost, Education Resource Information Center (ERIC), Google Scholar, PubMed, Sabinet, Cumulative Index to Nursing and Allied Health Literature (CINAHL), Medical Literature Online (Medline), ScienceDirect, JSTOR, and Science Citation Index websites. The search focused on studies linked to male experiences and perceptions of GBV from January 2010 to July 2021. We chose 2010 as our starting date due to perceptions that the focus on male abuse has largely become more substantive over the past decade. We relied on both peer-reviewed studies and grey literature, including unpublished but relevant literature due to the dearth of literature on male experiences of GBV. These included articles, theses, books, reports, commentaries, and abstracts published in English. The keywords searched were perceptions of GBV among males in SSA, males' experiences of GBV in SSA, males' experiences of IPV, and males' perceptions of psychological and emotional aggression. The keywords were chosen based on prior assumptions, and some were also inferred from the literature. The authors used a combination of keywords to search for relevant literature and then created a database containing all the reviewed articles. The authors also looked at references and relevant reviews to find literature.

We imported the retrieved articles into the Mendeley reference management software and screened for and removed duplicates. We also screened article titles, abstracts, locations of study, years of publication, and the overarching scope of the articles to identify those in proximity to the focus of this study. We examined both qualitative and quantitative articles. However, we omitted studies that were not in

Table 10.1 Eligibility criteria

Inclusion criteria	*Exclusion criteria*
• GBV (sexual, physical, and emotional/psychological violence) among males. • Only studies from SSA. • Published and grey literature (unpublished articles), books, theses, reports, commentaries, and conference abstracts. • Published material between 2010 and 2021. • Studies involving males. • Qualitative and quantitative studies. • Only studies conducted or written in English.	• All studies were published before 2010 and published in another language. • Articles that did not have a full text or abstract. • Studies focused on both males and females but did not report separately. • Studies were conducted outside the SSA region.

SSA or were not published in the English language. While we focused on studies reporting male experiences of various facets of GBV, those articles with incomplete text and those published before 2010 were excluded. Table 10.1 shows the inclusion and exclusion criteria used in this review.

10.2.1 Data Analysis and Synthesis

Methodological rigor for this review was attained by having all authors critically appraise the methodological validity of the studies that met the inclusion criteria. Authors used the "Confidence in the Evidence from Reviews" (GRADE-CERQual) approach, which aims to systematically determine the level of confidence to place in individual qualitative literature review findings based on four components: (1) limitations of each relevant study, (2) adequacy of data in each relevant study, (3) the coherence of each relevant study, and (4) the overall relevance of each study to the review aims (Guyatt et al., 2011; Lewin et al., 2015; Munthe-Kaas et al., 2019). All the studies that met the selection criteria underwent the initial screening questions, indicating whether further methodological quality appraisal was feasible. Retrieved articles were screened for titles, year, country, and language of publication, and those that were not relevant to the topic were removed. We incorporated peer-reviewed and grey literature published in English from 2010 to 2021, focusing on male-related experiences and narratives of GBV. Following this, relevant articles were summarized. Common themes of the research topic were drawn from this exploratory process and reorganized into a coherent framework. Supplementary literature was consulted to explain the developing themes further. The information provided for a content analysis of the prominent themes, and the perceptions of GBV among males in SSA, males' experiences of GBV in SSA, males' experience of IPV, males' perceptions of psychological and emotional aggression in countries within the SSA region.

10.3 Key Findings and Discussion

Eighty-seven articles and reports were found in the initial search from all databases. After excluding 49 articles that were not relevant to our study, 38 articles remained for screening. Screening by title led to the exclusion of eight articles. Further reading of abstracts for 29 full-text articles led to the exclusion of a further 10 articles. Finally, 21 articles met the inclusion criteria. Those that met the criteria include 11 quantitative studies and eight qualitative studies. The flow chart of excluding studies is presented in Fig. 10.1.

A common denominator among most of the studies reviewed is their use of the term "GBV" as an umbrella term for domestic violence, intimate partner violence, sexual violence, and any other psychological violence that reinforces unequal power

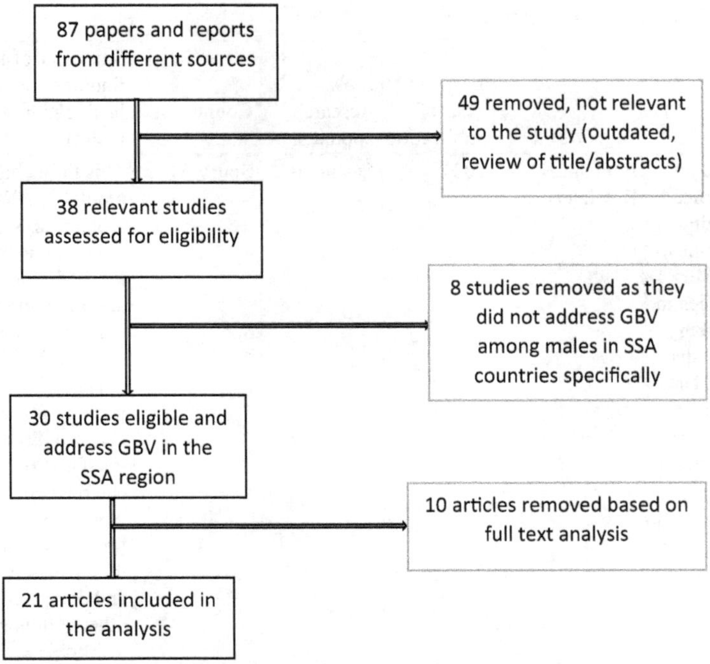

Fig. 10.1 Flow chart for research study selection process

relationships between gender identities and expressions. Most studies focus on GBV against females (particularly IPV), while there is sparse literature on the experiences of males as victims and the reasons behind males' perpetration of violence (Perrin et al., 2019). Thus, a relatively small number of articles (21) were found to be relevant for this manuscript. The details of the articles finally reviewed and included are presented in Table 10.2.

Overall, GBV predictors include socio-demographic factors, individual factors, and family factors. Ten studies reported socio-economic factors as predictors of GBV, while eight cited individual factors (Muluneh et al., 2020). Eight of the studies reported predictors due to partner/spouse's habits, and only two studies reported family-related predictors. Seven studies reported predictors due to previous experience. Lower educational status, being married, being involved in sex work, having experienced abuse in the past, substance abuse by a partner, having a gender-biased attitude, being younger than their partner, lower socio-economic status, urban residence, having a promiscuous partner, and poor social support were found to be predictors of male experiences of GBV. Perpetrator factors identified include sexual history, previous experience of abuse, educational status, substance use, gender-biased attitude, and having experienced abuse from one's mother (Akamike et al., 2019; Muluneh et al., 2020). It is important to understand men's experiences of violence and the causes and consequences of GBV among men. Key themes from the literature review are discussed below.

Table 10.2 Studies that were reviewed

Title	Author/s	Year of publication	Research approach	Country of study	Summary of key findings and justification for inclusion
Intimate Partner Violence and Shifting Masculinities: African Men's Experiences in Johannesburg (Doctoral dissertation, University of Johannesburg (South Africa).	Emmanuel Rowlands	2021	Qualitative	South Africa	This thesis highlighted a number of issues around GBV against men. The author focused more on IPV and masculinities, but many issues were discussed and explained. This was relevant for our review because it provided insight into how African men conceptualize manhood and IPV's impact on African men's masculinities and compared this to other continents such as Europe.
Gender Dimensions of the COVID-19 Pandemic	Carmen de Paz, Miriam Muller, Ana Maria Munoz Boudet and Isis Gaddis	2020	Qualitative	Global	This article highlighted what implications the COVID-19 pandemic had for males and females with regard to three dimensions: education, economic conditions, and agency. This was relevant for our review because the literature suggests that these three dimensions also affect how GBV occurs.
Understanding the relationship between male gender socialization and gender-based violence among refugees in SSA	M Whitney Fry, Asheley C Skinner and Stephanie B Wheeler	2017	Mixed Methods	SSA	This article told us how aspects of culture, language, religion, gender roles, and role models, or lack thereof, shape young men's views of females and gender relations in general. This was relevant for our review because it provided insight into how young men's socialization influences their acts and perspectives of violence.

(continued)

Table 10.2 (continued)

Title	Author/s	Year of publication	Research approach	Country of study	Summary of key findings and justification for inclusion
"Chasing a leopard out of the homestead": Mundurume's task in the era of HIV and AIDS	Julius Mutugi Gathogo	2012	Quantitative	Kenya	This study seeks to understand the role of the Kenyan man in the country's fight against the HIV/AIDS disease. This study was relevant for our review because it described the gendered roles of males and females and how these roles can cause and fight against HIV/AIDS as well as other epidemics such as GBV
Gender-based violence: the effect of gender-based violence on men in Clermont township	Jabulani Blessing Msomi	2011	Mixed Methods	South Africa	This study investigated the risk factors and outcomes of GBV against males in a township in the Province of KwaZulu-Natal in South Africa. This study was relevant for our review because it discussed how men experience violence in relationships, why they do or do not report it, the context of GBV in the community, and strategies used by men to protect themselves against GBV.
Violence in SSA schools: A scoping review protocol	Delarise Maud Mulqueeny, Senzokuhle Mpumelelo Nkabini and Sabelo Abednego Nxumalo	2020	Qualitative	SSA	This article mapped literature on violence in SSA schools. This was relevant for our review because it set the scene with regard to how various kinds of violence unfold within schools in SSA. We looked specifically for discussions from male perspectives with regard to violence in schools.

(continued)

Table 10.2 (continued)

Title	Author/s	Year of publication	Research approach	Country of study	Summary of key findings and justification for inclusion
Powerful Discourse: Gender-Based Violence and Counter-Discourses in South Africa	Kunle Oparinde and Rachel Matteau	2021	Qualitative	South Africa	This article critically examines how language is being used to combat and expose the issue of GBV in South Africa. This was relevant for our study because it highlighted commonly held perspectives and narratives of GBV, which tend to ignore males' perspectives of males on this issue.
COVID-19 is no excuse to regress on gender equality.	Vyn Young Park and Ancilla Marie Inocencio	2020	Qualitative	Global	This article sought to discuss the gendered impact of the COVID-19 pandemic. This was relevant for our research because it revealed how much of the policy response addressing the resulting gender inequalities and challenges had focused only on women as victims.
Gender-Based Violence. The Encyclopedia of Peace Psychology.	Olivera Simic	2011	Qualitative	East and Central Africa	This manuscript sought to discuss the shift in perspectives from GBV as a family matter to a societal issue that has implications for human rights and public health. This was relevant for our review because it discussed the role males are understood to play in the GBV narrative.

(continued)

Table 10.2 (continued)

Title	Author/s	Year of publication	Research approach	Country of study	Summary of key findings and justification for inclusion
Patriarchal practices in everyday life: Toward a gendered struggle against domestic violence	Tsoaledi D. Thobejane	2012	Qualitative	South Africa	This article discussed how common patriarchal practices influence the experience of domestic violence for males and women. This was important for our review because it highlighted how patriarchy affects the reality of domestic violence for both males and females in South Africa.
Gender-based violence against men: a muted reality	Tsoaledi D. Thobejane, Ntshengedzeni V. Luthada, and Lobelo D. Mogorosi	2018	Qualitative	South Africa	This article investigates GBV perpetrated by women against men. This was relevant for our review because the manuscripts revealed how GBV perpetrated by men against women is underreported due to the stigma of men being victims of violence at the hands of women.
The missing "C": Sexual violence against children in SSA	Chi Chi Undie, Saiqa Mullick and Ian Askew	2013	Qualitative	Sub-Saharan Africa	This manuscript highlights how policy and literature have neglected the issue of violence against children in developing countries in SSA. This paper was relevant for our review because it emphasized the need for more inclusive policy and literature with regards to the experience of violence whereby adult women are not the only victims acknowledged.

(continued)

Table 10.2 (continued)

Title	Author/s	Year of publication	Research approach	Country of study	Summary of key findings and justification for inclusion
Burden and Characteristics of Domestic Violence among Males in SSA Setting	N Ameh, S.O Shittu, M.A. Abduli, S.B. Bature and O.O. Oyefabi	2012	Quantitative	Nigeria	This paper examined the prevalence and characteristics of domestic violence in which men are the victims. This study was relevant for our review because it revealed the nature of violence that men generally experience and their subsequent help-seeking behaviors.
Social norms and beliefs about gender-based violence scale: a measure for use with gender-based violence prevention programs in low-resource and humanitarian settings	Nancy Perrin, Mendy Marsh, Amber Clough, Amelie Desgroppes, Clement Yope Phanuel, Ali Abdi, Francesco Kaburu, Silje Heitmann, Masumi Yamashina, Brendan Ross, Sophie Read-Hamilton, Rachael Turner, Lori Heise, and Nancy Glass	2019	Mixed Methods	Somalia and South Sudan	This paper sought to examine social norms and beliefs about GBV. This paper was relevant for our review because it revealed commonly held beliefs and social norms that place males as people who are not susceptible to GBV.

10.3.1 Males' Experience of GBV in SSA

While the general discourse of GBV perceives women and young children as victims, men also bear an array of violence committed against them. For example, some men reported violence from their intimate partners, such as having hot water or oil poured over them while they were sleeping, chopping off men's genitals, being insulted in front of children, whipping, and other forms of physical and verbal abuse (Gathogo, 2012; Thobejane et al., 2018). However, GBV among males is underreported across SSA mainly due to misconceptions about males' experience of GBV, perceptions of power and control in gendered relations, cultural grooming, unresolved childhood trauma linked to violence, poor knowledge of conflict resolution strategies among males and females, and perceptions of manhood and masculinity, which are socially constructed and fluid in different settings and plural (Apperley, 2015; Christian et al., 2011; Perrin et al., 2019; Wirtz et al., 2014). Often, black African men are groomed using violence in homes and communities with an emphasis on toxic masculinity that promotes the ideology that "strong men" do not cry irrespective of their pain or any abuse they may experience (Barker & Ricardo, 2005, p. 27; Paluck et al., 2010; Mshweshwe, 2020). However, this cannot be applied to all African males.

The predominant ideas in these studies about males as victims of GBV centered around how often these male victims failed to report their experiences because of the fear of being embarrassed or labeled as "useless man," "weak," "coward," or "women wrapper" (Chitando & Chirongoma, 2012). Some studies showed that IPV, verbal and psychological abuse toward males from females as a result of cultural differences, and the inability to argue productively were common (Dutton, 2011; Heilman & Barker, 2018; Perrin et al., 2019). This is usually aggravated by wives, girlfriends, or in-laws, where males are ridiculed or called names, particularly where women have more resources (e.g., financial or social class) than men. Several studies have shown that life experiences, psychological characteristics, and disorders, such as adverse childhood experiences (ACE), past experiences of violence, unresolved traumas, gender identity, racial identity, socio-economic background, personality disorder, and attachment disorder play a key role in the perpetration of violence by both males and females (Dutton, 2011; Lee et al., 2021; Mutisya, 2018; Muluneh et al., 2020). However, some studies on men's experiences of GBV were limited to physical and sexual violence in homosexual relationships, with little on emotional, physical, and psychological violence in both sexual and non-sexual relationships (Eves, 2010; Kiss et al., 2020). It was also noted that many scholars had ignored males' experiences in GBV research in the SSA region (Mosavel et al., 2012; Van Hout & Mhlanga-Gunda, 2018). Scholarly works presenting men as perpetrators only complicate GBV disclosure for men who had been abused by their partners or in-laws (Mahlori et al., 2018). There is a notable gap in GBV literature geared toward male victims, as most scholars have primarily focused on females and children (Chynoweth et al., 2017). Again, most GBV cases against men were underreported across SSA, mainly due to misconceptions about masculinity (Perrin et al., 2019; Strebel et al., 2006).

Although many studies address the issue of GBV from different perspectives, the most prominent perspective has been the case of GBV against women because women are more likely to experience violence (Oparinde & Matsha, 2021). However, Thobejane et al. (2018) argue that there is a muted reality of GBV against men because men do not speak out about their experiences of violence, especially intimate partner violence, because of the stigma attached to being a victim of such violence. The authors further elaborate that there is a masculinity expectation in almost all societies that if a man is in pain, he is not allowed to show his pain or cry, as this is indicative of weakness as a man. This expectation of masculinity makes it difficult for most men to report violence committed against them, fearing that they will lose their gender identity as a "strong and masculine male" in a predominately patriarchal society.

10.3.2 Causes and Permutations of GBV Among Males in the SSA Region

According to Piccard (2011), GBV occurs because of normative role expectations and unequal power relationships between genders in society. The causes of GBV among males in the SSA region are complex and deeply rooted in social, cultural, economic, and institutional factors (Antonowicz, 2010; Simic, 2011). In addition, there is an acknowledgment in the literature that GBV among males is caused by an interplay of individual, community, economic, cultural, and religious factors interacting at different levels of society (Krug et al., 2002; Msomi, 2011). For Heise et al. (2002), some factors that influence GBV at an individual level include growing up in a home characterized by violence, which becomes normalized later in life as a means of communication, and having an absent father or a father who is not a positive role model. The expectations associated with different genders vary from society to society and over time. Social and cultural norms that imbed patriarchal gender relations often perpetuate discrimination against males as the perpetrators of GBV and contribute to the systemic GBV in most SSA countries (Beninger, 2013; Mshweshwe, 2020; Mulqueeny et al., 2020). Also, violence may be structural and affects men differently. Structural violence is "where violence is built into structures, appearing as unequal power relations and, consequently, as unequal opportunities" (Piccard, 2011, p. 2). This occurs when certain groups, classes, genders (e.g., women and girls), or nationalities have privileged access to goods, resources, and opportunities over others and when this unequal advantage is built into the social, political, and economic systems that govern their lives. Because of how this violence is built into systems, political and social change is needed over time to identify and address structural violence among women and men.

Dutton and White (2013) argued that GBV is often framed as a "woman issue" or "violence against women," and frequently, literature refers to GBV as intimate partner violence or domestic violence. This notion often disregards that males can be victims of GBV and generates a perception that males are perpetrators of violence and more capable of inflicting injury or causing harm to their partners. This belief is called the "gender paradigm," which leads to male victims being met with disbelief when attempting to get protection or access services. This "gender paradigm" was consistently reinforced by several studies on "male perpetrators" and "female victims" (Lysova et al., 2020; Wallace et al., 2019). This makes it difficult to understand the causes of GBV affecting males. They find it difficult to locate services specific to their needs as helplines and shelters are exclusively for female victims (Christensen, 2019). There has long been a stereotype that a man is strong and dominant, and a woman is weak and submissive (Mshweshwe, 2020; Thobejane, 2012). According to Thobejane (2012), these stereotypes have resulted in many violent acts against men going unreported and unpunished. The male gender socialization in SSA leads to GBV perpetration patterns (Fry et al., 2019). Evidence from multiple studies such as Park and Inocencio (2020) and Undie et al. (2013) show that while this analysis is true, it does, however, only portray one side of the coin. While male gender socialization dictates that men should be strong and dominant, in cases where this socialization does not manifest, men fear ridicule from all spheres of society, resulting in muted responses to violence committed against them. Similarly, Oparinde and Matsha (2021) articulate that the discourse in social practice ultimately underpins and shapes structural and ideological power relations in society. Thus, violence against men is barely reported due to stigma dictating that this is not a societal issue compared to violence against women.

Thobejane et al. (2018, p. 5) elaborate that "female-to-male" domestic violence is a catastrophe that has always existed but has never been given the attention it deserves, like domestic violence perpetrated against women. Similarly, violence against men has been trivialized as it is influenced by social and gender stereotypes that define men as "alpha males" and "heads of households," who are supposed to be strong defenders of families and other dependents. Therefore, the premise that men are strong and dominant protectors inadvertently perpetuates the trivialization of violence against men as it is assumed that males are strong enough to defend themselves against any form of violence. The general gendered identity of females as gentle and fragile that needs to be protected by males posits that it is unlikely or impossible for females to be violent toward males. The reality, however, is that men also experience various kinds of violence, just like women.

10.3.3 GBV Legislations in SSA Region

SSA is home to a substantial gender divide encompassing numerous aspects of life (Horvath et al., 2009; Shoola, 2014). Though this divide is a historical reality for SSA, the current process of globalization presents both negative and positive impacts on the gender divide. The SSA region predominantly subscribes to a patriarchal system that is embedded in cultures, social norms, and how males are groomed (Shoola, 2014). This often leads to most of the laws regarding GBV leaning toward the protection of women rather than looking at GBV as an issue that can affect any gender, including males (Mpani & Nsibande, 2015; Mshweshwe, 2020). The right to equality and non-discrimination, irrespective of gender or perception of whether any gender is more suited to perpetuating GBV, is a fundamental right protected in all human rights instruments. However, women often enjoy preferential treatment when it comes to GBV issues. According to Barad and Slattery (2007), preferential treatment in the case of GBV is a form of a human rights violation that legislation should seek to address. While history suggests males are likely to be the perpetrators of GBV, states should strive to formulate policies that protect all within their jurisdiction.

In recent years, most SSA governments have taken important actions to address GBV, recognizing its detrimental impact on their citizens and the country's progress. However, accurate statistics on GBV against males are difficult to obtain for many reasons. For example, most incidents of GBV are not reported, and countries with developed laws seem to focus more on females as victims while males are identified as perpetrators (Dunkle et al., 2013). The majority of extant laws seem to focus on rape, sexual assault, and domestic violence among females while some scholars note that males experience sexual victimization, especially from other males are understudied and underreported (Mills et al., 2015). It is noteworthy that boys and young males are often subjected to abuse from older males under the guise of grooming, teaching, and discipline, and this contributes to shorter lifespans for males as this often results in conflict, death, or creates hatred which further perpetuates GBV (Van Der Veur et al., 2007). It was noted that most Southern African Development Community (SADC) countries had done much more than the rest of the SSA countries in developing laws and legislation to fight GBV. For example, in 1997, SADC made a declaration on gender and development in its 1998 addendum on preventing and eradicating violence against women and children (Mapuva, 2014; Nedziwe, 2020). This declaration was designed to combat GBV and evaluate how laws can effectively address the challenges of violence against women (van Eerdewijk & van de Sand, 2014).

Furthermore, other laws include the SADC Protocol on Gender and Development, the SADC Strategy to address GBV and GBV in situations of armed or other forms of conflict, and the Ten-Year SADC Strategic Plan of Action on Combating Trafficking in Persons, especially women and children (Juda-Chembe, 2019; Union, 2009). Although these laws are confined to violence against women, while it recognizes that males (both men and boys) sometimes are victims of GBV, they seem to focus on rape, sexual assault, and domestic violence against women (Kilonzo et al., 2009; Keesbury & Askew, 2010). Fearon and Hoeffler (2014) and Ahinkorah (2021) found that the most common types of violence in the SSA region were IPV, domestic violence, sexual assault, and human trafficking; hence these laws tend to be directed to deal with them, ignoring other types of violence. Addressing the failure of a legal system to effectively investigate, prosecute, and charge claims for GBV, i.e., sexual assault, domestic violence, or in another form, requires action on numerous fronts. Introducing legislation that appears good on paper will not suffice to bring about a change of approach without political and social initiatives designed to implement that legislation. Thus, while the most current legislations are necessary to reduce the menace of GBV, they are not sufficient as they are mainly female-oriented. Developing inclusive legislation (irrespective of one's gender and sexual orientation) is crucial to eliminating GBV. Concerted efforts must be taken to sensitize relevant public officials, i.e., police officers, judges, lawyers, healthcare workers, etc., about males' experiences of violence and how they can apply GBV-related laws and policies effectively. For example, in the case of Kenya, it has been reported that victims reporting GBV experience cultural, procedural, and bureaucratic hurdles before assistance is provided (Barad & Slattery,

2007). Also, most of the efforts are focused on response; however, response efforts need to be complemented by prevention programming and policy development.

10.3.4 COVID-19 Pandemic and GBV in SSA

According to Mittal and Singh (2020), violence has generally increased in the face of pandemics. A rapid gender analysis report on COVID-19 produced by CARE and International Rescue stated that it was expected that GBV would rise amid the COVID-19 pandemic and quarantines. The report consequently recommended enhancing and building existing services for victims of GBV. The report further emphasized the need to strengthen online services to provide psychological support and legal aid services, especially in HIV hyper-endemic countries (Mittal & Singh, 2020). The COVID-19 pandemic has led to disruptions in global social and economic activities. While the early narrative described COVID-19 as the "great equalizer," asserting that the virus can infect anyone, policymakers must understand that the effects of COVID-19 will not be the same for everyone. As previously experienced from various epidemics, COVID-19 malignantly impacted groups who are most vulnerable and amplified any existing inequalities across SSA countries, communities, households, and individuals. This highlights the existing gender inequalities in the economic sphere in SSA and summarizes how the COVID-19 pandemic could affect those who are most vulnerable. The advent of COVID-19 has exacerbated the already high incidence of GBV (De Paz et al., 2020).

The most common type of GBV among males during the COVID-19 pandemic appears to be psychological abuse, as many men in the region have lost income and have failed to provide for their families. Interestingly, this type of violence was the most frequent before the COVID-19 pandemic and is a common form of abuse against men (Mittal & Singh, 2020). Evidence suggests a complex relationship between COVID-19-specific stressors, such as health anxiety and intolerance of uncertainty, GBV, and mental health issues (Opanasenko et al., 2021). COVID-19 stressors might directly trigger the mechanism of aggression and cause physical or psychological violence and associated mental health implications for victims, or it might be mediated by pre-existing mental health issues experienced by perpetrators (Opanasenko et al., 2021).

10.3.5 Prognosis: Roles of Key Stakeholders in Eradicating Violence

Violence is complex and requires multilevel approaches by various stakeholders (e.g., government, individuals, and civil societies) at different levels (e.g., micro, meso, and macro) to eradicate GBV (Dlamini, 2021; Okeke-Ihejirika et al., 2019).

Stakeholders, such as government, civil society, and individual citizens, are important actors in creating awareness and/or eradicating violence against individuals:

The role Government Gender inequality contributes significantly to GBV. Governments should strive to use land, employment opportunities, economic opportunities, quality education, health, proper sanitation, and safety to benefit all citizens equally to reduce gender inequality and, therefore, GBV (Dlamini, 2021). This can be achieved by government accountability, meaningful social participation, and non-discriminatory laws (Zamora et al., 2018). Governments are legally obligated to address the problem of GBV through a range of measures, including developing inclusive legislation to combat GBV against anyone (male or female and other sexual and gender minorities) and evaluate how laws can effectively address the challenges associated with GBV against all genders.

The role of Civil Society Organizations Civil society organizations plays important roles in building strong advocacy and awareness about GBV. As Dlamini (2021, p587) proposes, advocacy work should include 'bringing all stakeholders together, sensitizing and engaging the private sector on ways to identify and respond to GBV, including among males, addressing gender inequality, partnership with media and faith-based leaders to challenge gender stereotypes, and engaging law enforcement agencies' to respond adequately without stigmatizing the victims. Collaborations among organizations of different civil societies (including community-based organizations) will give birth to a platform where inclusive interventions are co-created, thus making it easier for more groups of society to take ownership of the interventions (Dlamini, 2021). Although some countries (e.g., South Africa, Kenya and Botswana) have instituted different innovative initiatives to address the increase in GBV, others that have not yet done so (e.g., Nigeria and Sierra Leone) can draw on their experience, especially how they can respond to men experiencing violence without fear of stigmatisation or discrimination.

The role of Individual Citizens It is important to recognize informal ways of collective action in people's lived realities. Continued work is needed with communities to understand their innovative ways of addressing gender inequalities and how this knowledge can be transfered into policy to curb the GBV scourge especially among males. Collective action (formal and informal) does not necessarily translate into a 'gender transformative' movement.

Approaches to addressing GBV can be divided into response and prevention. Response services aim to support and help survivors of violence in various ways (for instance, medical help, psychosocial support, and shelter). Prevention initiatives aim at how GBV can be prevented from happening. Response services can, in turn, prevent violence from occurring or reoccurring. Major strides are being made internationally on how to best respond and provide services for survivors of violence. The World Health Organization (WHO) provides guidelines that describe an appropriate health sector response to violence, including providing post-rape care and training health professionals to provide these services (WHO, 2013). However, it does not recommend routine case identification in health services where violence exposure is a reality but stresses the importance of mental health services for GBV victims.

As discussed, there seems to be no consensus on the best way to confront GBV. However, increasing public awareness will drive further efforts to fight this injustice and inequalities, especially for men experiencing or who have experienced violence. This means that culturally sensitive awareness campaigns should be directed at both males and females to combat GBV effectively.

10.4 Conclusion

The literature reviewed reveals that males can be victims of GBV; therefore, it is important to establish support networks and encourage them to report their experiences with law enforcement agencies to obtain help. An inter-sectoral approach is necessary to address the problem of GBV. Community engagement, including stakeholder engagement, is also vital in addressing GBV. From the foregoing, it has been established that males are also victims of GBV, but they are underreported in the literature. Thus, more studies need to be conducted to understand male experiences of GBV and how they can be addressed.

Our review shows a yawning gap in the academic literature about males' experiences of violence in SSA. The vast majority of literature only discusses males as perpetrators of violence and females as the victims of violence in society. More academic discourse could inform law and policy reform to provide males with more protection as victims of violence in SSA. In addition, further research into males' perceptions and experiences of violence is needed to show that men are also victims of GBV. This will provide new insights into why some men act in a violent manner, which could thus help in finding ways to eradicate GBV.

10.5 Study Limitations and Strengths

This review aimed to provide insights into a previously under-investigated issue, i.e., GBV against males. There are, however, several limitations. First, we found that GBV is a very complex issue. Most GBV amongst males is often not reported in the literature for various reasons, including cultural reasons, fear of humiliation, grooming young males, etc. We justified focusing on GBV against males, not as a justification for males' perpetration of violence, nor are we implying that GBV against women and children is not happening and should be ignored. However, we are trying to raise awareness for the underrepresented voice so that inclusive approaches to dealing with GBV can be developed. The major strength of this review is its insights into an ignored topic in SSA. Furthermore, the dearth of documented literature on men's experience and perceptions of GBV severely limited our search, and the majority of searched literature was repeated from different sites searched.

References

Abrahams, N., Devries, K., Watts, C., Pallitto, C., Petzold, M., Shamu, S., & García-Moreno, C. (2014). Worldwide prevalence of non-partner sexual violence: A systematic review. *The Lancet, 383*(9929), 1648–1654.

Ahinkorah, B. O. (2021). Polygamy and intimate partner violence in sub-Saharan Africa: Evidence from 16 cross-sectional demographic and health surveys. *SSM-Population Health, 13*, 100729.

Akamike, I. C., Uneke, C. J., Uro-Chukwu, H. C., Okedo-Alex, I. N., & Chukwu, O. E. (2019). Predictors and facilitators of gender-based violence in sub-Saharan Africa: A rapid review. *Journal of Global Health Reports, 3*.

Ali, P. A., & Naylor, P. B. (2013). Intimate partner violence: A narrative review of the biological and psychological explanations for its causation. *Aggression and Violent Behaviour, 18*(3), 373–382. https://doi.org/10.1016/j.avb.2013.01.003

Ameh, N., Shittu, S. O., Abdul, M. A., Bature, S. B., & Oyefabi, O. O. (2012). Burden and characteristics of domestic violence among males in a sub-Saharan African setting. *Nigerian Journal of Medicine, 21*(4), 412–415.

Antonowicz, L. (2010). *Too often in silence: A report on school-based violence in West and Central Africa*. UNICEF, Plan West Africa, Save the Children Sweden West Africa and ActionAid.

Apperley, H. (2015). Hidden victims: A call to action on sexual violence against men in conflict. *Medicine, Conflict and Survival, 31*(2), 92–99.

Barad, E., & Slattery, E. (2007). *Gender-based violence laws in sub-Saharan Africa*. Report prepared for the Committee on African Affairs of the New York City Bar.

Barker, G., & Ricardo, C. (2005). *Young men and the construction of masculinity in sub-Saharan Africa: Implications for HIV/AIDS, conflict, and violence*. World Bank.

Beninger, C. (2013). Combating sexual violence in schools in sub-Saharan Africa: Legal strategies under regional and international human rights law. *African Human Rights Law Journal, 13*(2), 281–301.

Carpenter, R. C. (2006). Recognizing gender-based violence against civilian men and boys in conflict situations. *Security Dialogue, 37*(1), 83–103.

Carpenter, R. C. (2017). *Recognizing gender-based violence against civilian men and boys in conflict situations*. The Criminology of War.

Chitando, E., & Chirongoma, S. (2012). *Redemptive masculinities: Men, HIV, and religion*.

Christian, M., Safari, O., Ramazani, P., Burnham, G., & Glass, N. (2011). Sexual and gender-based violence against men in the Democratic Republic of Congo: Effects on survivors, their families and the community. *Medicine, conflict and survival, 27*(4), 227–246.

Christensen, M. C. (2019). Using photovoice to address gender-based violence: A qualitative systematic review. *Trauma, Violence, & Abuse, 20*(4), 484–497.

Chynoweth, S. K., Freccero, J., & Touquet, H. (2017). Sexual violence against men and boys in conflict and forced displacement: Implications for the health sector. *Reproductive Health Matters, 25*(51), 90–94.

De Paz, C., Muller, M., Munoz Boudet, A. M. & Gaddis, I. (2020). Gender dimensions of the COVID-19 pandemic.

Dlamini, J. N. (2021). Gender-based violence, twin pandemic to COVID-19. *Critical Sociology, 47* (4–5), 583–590.

Dunkle, K. L., Jewkes, R. K., Murdock, D. W., Sikweyiya, Y., & Morrell, R. (2013). Prevalence of consensual male-male sex and sexual violence, and associations with HIV in South Africa: A population-based cross-sectional study. *PLoS Medicine, 10*(6), e1001472.

Dutton, D. G. (2011). *Rethinking domestic violence*. UBC Press.
Dutton, D. G., & White, K. R. (2013). Male victims of domestic violence. *New Male Studies: An international journal, 2*(1), 5–17.
Edition, F. (2013). Diagnostic and statistical manual of mental disorders. *American Psychiatric Assoc, 21*.
Esther, O. (2020). Gender-based violence in workplaces: A critical examination of its implications in the contemporary society. *EVAIA: International Journal of Ethics and Values, 1*(2).
Evans, M. L., Lindauer, M., & Farrell, M. E. (2020). A pandemic within a pandemic—Intimate partner violence during Covid-19. *New England Journal of Medicine, 383*(24), 2302–2304.
Eves, R. (2010). Masculinity matters: Men, gender-based violence and the AIDS epidemic in Papua New Guinea. *Civic Insecurity: Law, Order and HIV in Papua New Guinea, 1*, 2010.
Fearon, J., & Hoeffler, A. (2014). *Benefits and costs of the conflict and violence targets for the post-2015 development agenda*. Conflict and violence assessment paper, Copenhagen Consensus Center, 1–65.
Fry, M. W., Skinner, A. C., & Wheeler, S. B. (2019). Understanding the relationship between male gender socialization and gender-based violence among refugees in Sub-Saharan Africa. *Trauma, Violence, & Abuse, 20*(5), 638–652.
Gathogo, J. (2012). Chasing a leopard out of the homestead: Mundurume's task in the era of HIV and AIDS'. *Redemptive masculinities: Men, HIV and religion*, 447–470.
Ganou, S. (2021). *Sexual and gender-based violence in the Democratic Republic of Congo: The role of men and masculinities*.
Guyatt, G. H., Oxman, A. D., Kunz, R., Woodcock, J., Brozek, J., Helfand, M., Alonso-Coello, P., Glasziou, P., Jaeschke, R., Akl, E. A., Norris, S., Vist, G., Dahm, P., Shukla, V. K., Higgins, J., Falck-Ytter, Y., Schünemann, H. J., & GRADE Working Group. (2011). GRADE guidelines: 7. Rating the quality of evidence—Inconsistency. *Journal of Clinical Epidemiology, 64*(12), 1294–1302.
Heilman, B., & Barker, G. (2018). *Masculine norms and violence: Making the connections*. Promundo.
Heise, L., Ellsberg, M., & Gottmoeller, M. (2002). A global overview of gender-based violence. *International Journal of Gynaecology and Obstetrics, 78*, S5–S14.
Horvath, E., Zukani, M., Eppel, D., Kays, M., Konare, A., Park, Y. S., Pischalnikova, E. Y., Stankard, N., & Zingher, T. (2009). *Gender-based violence laws in sub-Saharan Africa*.
Hlongwa, M., Mashamba-Thompson, T., Makhunga, S., Muraraneza, C., & Hlongwana, K. (2020). Men's perspectives on HIV self-testing in sub-Saharan Africa: A systematic review and meta-synthesis. *BMC Public Health, 20*(1), 1–13.
Juda-Chembe, K. (2019). The scourge of human trafficking in the SADC region as hindrance to development: A legal analysis. *Comparative and International Law Journal of Southern Africa, 52*(2), 234–252.
Kassa, H. (2021). Gender summit? *New agenda: South African Journal of Social and Economic Policy, 2021*(80), 34–35.
Keesbury, J., & Askew, I. (2010). *Comprehensive responses to gender-based violence in low-resource settings: Lessons learned from implementation*.
Kilonzo, N., Ndung'u, N., Nthamburi, N., Ajema, C., Taegtmeyer, M., Theobald, S., & Tolhurst, R. (2009). Sexual violence legislation in sub-Saharan Africa: The need for strengthened medico-legal linkages. *Reproductive Health Matters, 17*(34), 10–19.
Kiss, L., Quinlan-Davidson, M., Pasquero, L., Tejero, P. O., Hogg, C., Theis, J., Park, A., Zimmerman, C., & Hossain, M. (2020). Male and LGBT survivors of sexual violence in conflict situations: A realist review of health interventions in low-and middle-income countries. *Conflict and Health, 14*(1), 1–26. https://doi.org/10.1186/s13031-020-0254-5
Krug, E. G., Mercy, J. A., Dahlberg, L. L., & Zwi, A. B. (2002). The world report on violence and health. *The Lancet, 360*(9339), 1083–1088.

Lee, K. A., Sacco, P., & Bright, C. L. (2021). Adverse childhood experiences (ACEs), excessive alcohol use and intimate partner violence (IPV) perpetration among Black men: A latent class analysis. *Child Abuse & Neglect, 121*, 105273. https://doi.org/10.1016/j.chiabu.2021.105273

Lewin, S., Glenton, C., Munthe-Kaas, H., Carlsen, B., Colvin, C. J., Gülmezoglu, M., Noyes, J., Booth, A., Garside, R., & Rashidian, A. (2015). Using qualitative evidence in decision making for health and social interventions: An approach to assess confidence in findings from qualitative evidence syntheses (GRADE-CERQual). *PLoS Medicine, 12*(10), e1001895.

Lysova, A., Hanson, K., Hines, D. A., Dixon, L., Douglas, E. M., & Celi, E. M. (2020). A qualitative study of the male victims' experiences with the criminal justice response to intimate partner abuse in four English-speaking countries. *Criminal Justice and Behavior, 47*(10), 1264–1281.

Mahlori, X. F., Byrne, D. C., & Mabude, L. A. (2018). Perceptions of gender-based violence among university staff: Interim results. *SAGE Open, 8*(3), 2158244018800163.

Mapuva, J. W. M. (2014). The SADC regional bloc: What challenges and prospects for regional integration? *Law, Democracy & Development, 18*, 22–36.

Mills, E., Shahrokh, T., Wheeler, J., Black, G., Cornelius, R., & Van Den Heever, L. (2015). *Turning the tide: The role of collective action for addressing structural and gender-based violence in South Africa* (No. IDS Evidence Report; 118). IDS.

Mittal, S., & Singh, T. (2020). Gender-based violence during COVID-19 pandemic: A mini-review. *Frontiers in Global Women's Health, 1*, 4.

Moher, D., Liberati, A., Tetzlaff, J., Altman, D. G., & Prisma Group. (2009). Preferred reporting items for systematic reviews and meta-analyses: The PRISMA statement. *PLoS Medicine, 6*(7), e1000097.

Moreira, D. N., & Pinto da Costa, M. (2020). The impact of the Covid-19 pandemic in the precipitation of intimate partner violence. *International Journal of Law and Psychiatry, 71*, 101606. https://doi.org/10.1016/j.ijlp.2020.101606

Mosavel, M., Ahmed, R., & Simon, C. (2012). Perceptions of gender-based violence among South African youth: Implications for health promotion interventions. *Health Promotion International, 27*(3), 323–330. https://doi.org/10.1093/heapro/dar041

Muluneh, M. D., Stulz, V., Francis, L., & Agho, K. (2020). Gender based violence against women in sub-Saharan Africa: A systematic review and meta-analysis of cross-sectional studies. *International Journal of Environmental Research and Public Health, 17*(3), 903.

Munthe-Kaas, H. M., Glenton, C., Booth, A., Noyes, J., & Lewin, S. (2019). Systematic mapping of existing tools to appraise methodological strengths and limitations of qualitative research: First stage in the development of the CAMELOT tool. *BMC Medical Research Methodology, 19*(1), 1–13.

Mutisya, R. K. (2018). *Effects of a psychosocial intervention on gender-based violence, antepartum depression, general health and adoption of safety behaviours in pregnant women in Kisumu County, Kenya* (Doctoral dissertation, JKUAT-COHES).

McInnes, M. D., Moher, D., Thombs, B. D., McGrath, T. A., Bossuyt, P. M., Clifford, T., Cohen, J. F., Deeks, J. J., Gatsonis, C., Hooft, L., Hunt, H. A., Hyde, C. J., Korevaar, D. A., Leeflang, M. M. G., Macaskill, P., Reitsma, J. B., Rodin, R., Rutjes, A. W. S., Salameh, J.-P., et al. (2018). Preferred reporting items for a systematic review and meta-analysis of diagnostic test accuracy studies: The PRISMA-DTA statement. *JAMA, 319*(4), 388–396.

Mpani, P., & Nsibande, N. (2015). Understanding gender policy and gender-based violence in South Africa: A literature review. *Soul City Institute of Health & Development Communication*, 1–53.

Msomi, J. B. (2011). *Gender based violence: The effect of gender-based violence on men in Clermont township* (Doctoral dissertation).

Mshweshwe, L. (2020). Understanding domestic violence: Masculinity, culture, traditions. *Heliyon, 6*(10), e05334. https://doi.org/10.1016/j.heliyon.2020.e05334

Mulqueeny, D. M., Nkabini, S. M., & Nxumalo, S. A. (2020). *Violence in sub-Saharan African schools: A scoping review protocol.*

Nedziwe, C. L. (2020). Rethinking SADC: A mixed actor approach to collective policymaking on external relations 1. In *African foreign policies* (pp. 210–227). Routledge.
Okeke-Ihejirika, P., Salami, B., & Amodu, O. (2019). Exploring intimate partner violence from the perspective of African men: A meta-synthesis. *Aggression and Violent Behaviour, 46*, 98–108.
Opanasenko, A., Lugova, H., Mon, A. A., & Ivanko, O. (2021). Mental health impact of gender-based violence amid COVID-19 pandemic: A review. *Bangladesh Journal of Medical Science*, 17–25.
Oparinde, K., & Matsha, R. M. (2021). Powerful discourse: Gender-based violence and counter-discourses in South Africa. *Cogent Arts & Humanities, 8*(1), 1911035.
Paluck, E. L., Ball, L., Poynton, C., & Sieloff, S. (2010). *Social norms marketing aimed at gender based violence: A literature review and critical assessment*. International Rescue Committee.
Park, C. Y., & Inocencio, A. M. (2020). *COVID-19 is no excuse to regress on gender equality*.
Peacock, D., & Barker, G. (2014). Working with men and boys to prevent gender-based violence: Principles, lessons learned, and ways forward. *Men and Masculinities, 17*(5), 578–599.
Perrin, N., Marsh, M., Clough, A., Desgroppes, A., Phanuel, C. Y., Abdi, A., Kaburu, F., Heitmann, S., Yamashina, M., Ross, B., Read-Hamilton, S., Turner, R., Heise, L., & Glass, N. (2019). Social norms and beliefs about gender-based violence scale: A measure for use with gender-based violence prevention programs in low-resource and humanitarian settings. *Conflict and Health, 13*(1), 1–12.
Piccard, S. (2011). *Masculinities and gender-based violence in conflict and post-conflict settings-addressing gap in violence against men*.
Potter, L. C., Morris, R., Hegarty, K., García-Moreno, C., & Feder, G. (2021). Categories and health impacts of intimate partner violence in the World Health Organization multi-country study on women's health and domestic violence. *International Journal of Epidemiology, 50*(2), 652–662.
Rennison, C. M., & Addington, L. A. (2018). Comparing violent victimization experiences of male and female college-attending emerging adults. *Violence Against Women, 24*(8), 952–972.
Sadock, B. J., Sadock, V. A., & Ruiz, P. (2015). *Synopsis of psychiatry: Behavioural sciences, clinical psychiatry*. Wolters Kluwer.
Simic, O. (2011). *Gender-based violence. The encyclopaedia of peace psychology*.
Schulz, P. (2018). Displacement from gendered personhood: Sexual violence and masculinities in northern Uganda. *International Affairs, 94*(5), 1101–1119.
Shoola, T. (2014). The effect of the sub-Saharan African gender divide on the rights and status of women in a globalized world. *International Research Scape Journal, 1*(1), 7.
Stubbs, A., & Szoeke, C. (2021). The effect of intimate partner violence on the physical health and health-related behaviors of women: A systematic review of the literature. *Trauma, Violence, & Abuse*, 1524838020985541.
Strebel, A., Crawford, M., Shefer, T., Cloete, A., Henda, N., Kaufman, M., Simbayi, L., Magome, K., & Kalichman, S. (2006). Social constructions of gender roles, gender-based violence and HIV/AIDS in two communities of the Western Cape, South Africa. *SAHARA: Journal of Social Aspects of HIV/AIDS Research Alliance, 3*(3), 516–528.
Thobejane, T. D. (2012). Patriarchal practices in everyday life: Towards a gendered struggle against domestic violence. *Southern African Journal for Folklore Studies, 22*(2), 37–43.
Thobejane, T. D., Luthada, N. V., & Mogorosi, L. D. (2018). Gender-based violence against men: A muted reality. *Southern African Journal for Folklore Studies, 28*(1), 1–15.
Union, A. (2009). *Gender policy*. African Union.
Undie, C., Mullick, S., & Askew, I. (2013). *The missing 'C': Sexual violence against children in sub-Saharan Africa*. Research Watch.
van Eerdewijk, A., & van de Sand, J. (2014). Violence against women and southern African advocacy on the SADC gender protocol. In *Gender equality norms in regional governance* (pp. 193–217). Palgrave Macmillan, London.
Van Der Veur, D., Ohana, Y., Titley, G., Buldioski, G., & Schneider, A. (2007). *Gender matters: A manual on addressing gender-based violence affecting young people*. Council of Europe.

Van Hout, M. C., & Mhlanga-Gunda, R. (2018). Contemporary women prisoners' health experiences, unique prison health care needs and health care outcomes in sub–Saharan Africa: A scoping review of extant literature. *BMC International Health and Human Rights, 18*(1), 1–12.

Wallace, S., Wallace, C., Kenkre, J., Brayford, J., & Borja, S. (2019). Men who experience domestic abuse: A service perspective. *Journal of Aggression, Conflict and Peace Research., 11*, 127.

Wirtz, A. L., Pham, K., Glass, N., Loochkartt, S., Kidane, T., Cuspoca, D., Rubenstein, L. S., Singh, S., & Vu, A. (2014). Gender-based violence in conflict and displacement: Qualitative findings from displaced women in Colombia. *Conflict and Health, 8*(1), 1–14.

World Health Organization. (2013). *Responding to intimate partner violence and sexual violence against women: WHO clinical and policy guidelines*. World Health Organization.

Zamora, G., Koller, T. S., Thomas, R., Manandhar, M., Lustigova, E., Diop, A., & Magar, V. (2018). Tools and approaches to operationalize the commitment to equity, gender and human rights: Towards leaving no one behind in the sustainable development goals. *Global Health Action, 11*(sup1), 75–81.

Zarkov, D. (2017). *The body of the other man* (pp. 327–344). Routledge.

Dumsani Gumede, Ph.D. is a Social Scientist at Africa Health Research Institute, KwaZulu-Natal, South Africa. He obtained a doctoral degree (Ph.D.) in Public Health, Master of Commerce degree in Leadership Studies, and BSc degree in Physiotherapy, all from the University of KwaZulu-Natal (UKZN), South Africa. His research interests include health promotions, health systems, process evaluation, mentoring, human immunodeficiency virus/acquired immunodeficiency syndrome (HIV/AIDS), gender, and youth (https://orcid.org/0000-0001-8739-6033).

Manono Luthuli, MCom is a Senior Social Science Research Assistant at the Africa Health Research Institute, KwaZulu-Natal, South Africa. He holds a Master of Commerce degree in Leadership Studies and a Bachelor of Social Science (Honours) degree in Psychology from the University of KwaZulu-Natal, South Africa. His research interests include men's sexual reproductive health, mental health, and adolescent health (https://orcid.org/0000-0002-3376-3261).

Siphesihle Hlongwane, M.A. is a Research Professional at the Africa Health Research Institute, KwaZulu-Natal, South Africa. He holds a Master of Development Studies degree and a Bachelor of Social Science degree in Geography and Environmental Management from the University of KwaZulu-Natal (UKZN), South Africa. His research interests include the health promotion of sexual reproductive health in young people (https://orcid.org/0000-0001-9858-8866).

Kingsley Orievulu, Ph.D. is a Research Associate at the Africa Health Research Institute (AHRI), KwaZulu-Natal, South Africa. He is also a Research Fellow at the Centre for Africa-China Studies (CACS), University of Johannesburg (UJ), South Africa. He holds a Ph.D. in Development Studies at the University of the Witwatersrand (Wits), South Africa, focusing on multilateral institutions, development interventions, and local experiences of such interventions. His current works focus on ethical issues in research during disasters and public health emergencies, the social dimensions of vaccine hesitancy in urban and rural settings, and climate change-linked environmental stressors and public health with a specific focus on drought impacts on human immunodeficiency virus (HIV) treatment in under-resourced contexts. Recent publications include *Drought and HIV treatment adherence in Africa*; *Economic, social and demographic impacts of drought on treatment adherence among people living with HIV in rural South Africa: A qualitative analysis*; *Institutional responses to drought in a high HIV prevalence setting in rural South Africa*; and *Age of consent: A case for harmonizing laws and policies to advance, promote and protect adolescents' sexual and reproductive health rights.*

Ntombizonke Gumede, Ph.D. is a Research Scientist at the Africa Health Research Institute (AHRI), Social Science and Research Ethics, and a Ph.D. candidate at the Department of Anthropology and Sociology of the University of Western Cape (UWC). Before joining AHRI, she was a Ph.D. researcher at the Human Sciences Research Council (HSRC) in the Human and Social Development (HSD) research program in Pretoria. She holds an M.A. in Social Science in Sociology (the narrative study of lives) from the University of the Free State (UFS). She has worked for the National Research Foundation (NRF), and as an academic facilitator, she was responsible for integrating developmental competencies with academic outcomes to equip students to achieve academic success in higher education for extended curricula in the Faculty of Humanities, Sociology Department, UFS. She has coordinated and managed projects and is experienced in designing, implementing, and analyzing qualitative and quantitative research. Her areas of research specialization include family-related issues, social demography and epidemiology, sexual and reproductive health, rights, justice and freedom, and migration.

Oluwafemi Adeagbo, Ph.D. is an Assistant Professor in the Department of Community and Behavioral Health at the University of Iowa College of Public Health in the USA. He is an applied socio-behavioral scientist with academic training in multiple social science disciplines (B.A. [Hons] Philosophy, M.A. in Migration Studies, and Ph.D. in Sociology). He is a Visiting Professor in the Department of Sociology at the University of Johannesburg (UJ), South Africa, and an Honorary Senior Research Fellow at the University College London. He has extensive research experience working collaboratively with local and international institutions on HIV-related research in South Africa, Nigeria, Zambia, and the USA. He is interested in global health, stigma reduction interventions, human immunodeficiency virus/acquired immunodeficiency syndrome (HIV/AIDS), social aspects of health, social justice, gender and sexualities, implementation science, and the evaluation of complex interventions. He was recently recognized by the African Academy of Science (2021) and the South African National Research Foundation (NRF) (2019) for his scientific contributions.

Chapter 11
Youth Exclusion and Violence as Intervention: The EndSARS Protest as Metaphor in Nigeria

Olayinka Akanle and Goodluck Uzieyi

11.1 Introduction

The purpose of this chapter is to explore the End Special Anti-Robbery Squad (EndSARS) protest as a narrative (metaphor) of youth exclusion and their determined/coordinated response through the demand for improved inclusion, focusing on mobilization against police brutality in Nigeria. Even though the protest started peacefully and was not designed to be violent and disruptive/destructive ab initio, it later turned violent and remained a definitive occurrence in the history of Nigeria. The protest also remains a major showcase in Africa and globally. Going forward, it is certain that it will be impossible to account for Nigeria's development, democracy, governance, human security, policing, youthhood, and social inclusion/exclusion without strategic reference to and accommodation of the EndSARS protest that happened in October 2020 (Uwazuruike, 2022). The EndSARS protest was an epochal and historically defining incident in Nigeria. It was a powerful moment in Nigeria, and it is important to take account of this to build an understanding of youthhood and social exclusion/inclusion not only in Nigeria but in Africa (Akanle, 2022). There are many crucial lessons to be drawn from the EndSARS experience in Nigeria, and these lessons are relevant for Nigeria, Africa, and the world at large. This is the major remit and interest of this chapter. This chapter is based on an extensive review of secondary data/literature and autoethnography. The lived experiences on the ground and primary insights of the authors in the contexts of

O. Akanle (✉)
Department of Sociology, Faculty of The Social Sciences, University of Ibadan, Ibadan, Nigeria

Department of Sociology, Faculty of Humanities, University of Johannesburg, Johannesburg, South Africa

G. Uzieyi
Department of Sociology, University of Ibadan, Ibadan, Nigeria

K. Naidoo et al. (eds.), *Young People, Violence and Strategic Interventions in Sub-Saharan Africa*, Clinical Sociology: Research and Practice,
https://doi.org/10.1007/978-3-031-20679-5_11

youthhood, human security, societal developments, and democratic/governance inclusion/exclusion realities of Nigeria were very relevant and engaging issues discussed in this chapter.

Although state agents violently quashed the protest, this was not without serious after-effects. After the protest was violently suppressed, the Lagos Judicial Panel of Enquiry was constituted by the government of Lagos state (the epicenter of the protest) with clear Terms of Reference to unravel the trajectories, ramifications, and consequences of the protest, including deaths (Uwazuruike, 2022). The panel submitted its report to the Lagos state government 1 month after concluding its 1-year-long investigative sitting, where many witnesses testified, and evidence was reviewed—including textual, audio, and video evidence. The report was submitted privately to the government in November 2021 but leaked on social media immediately. After many denials by agents of the government, the panel held/concluded that the army and police were at the protest grounds with live bullets and that people were massacred with live ammunition during the protest. Governments have since rejected the reports and unleashed state-sponsored propaganda against the report and members of the panel even when the public and international stakeholders have consistently hailed the report and the courage of members of the panel to uphold the truth and accuracy in the face of state-sponsored intimidation during the sittings and thereafter (Uwazuruike, 2022).

Although there were seeming controversies (especially from government/state actors) about whether people were killed and the actual number of people killed during the protest, the 309-page report given by the *Lagos State Judicial Panel on Restitution for Victims of SARS Related Abuses and Other Matters* addressed and confirmed the truth behind such controversies and, as a result, quenched such controversies. It was massive, organized, and led by the youth of Nigeria online and physically. It was sustained over many days and unprecedentedly in terms of coordination and demand for accountability in Nigeria and Africa. It highlighted a keen demand for better youth inclusion and responsible governance, just as there were casualties. Regardless of its generated controversies, the panel report remains the only generally acceptable and widely popular report on the EndSARS protest. It documented a *massacre* numbering over 40 deaths traceable to Lekki Toll Gate in Lagos. Lekki Toll Gate represented the epicenter of the protest in Lagos. According to the *Lagos State Judicial Panel on Restitution for Victims of SARS Related Abuses and Other Matters,* at least 48 were casualties of the Lekki incident. According to the 309-page report, among the 48 unarmed protesters, many were shot dead, and others were injured with bullets or assaulted by security forces at the Lekki toll gate on October 20, 2020.

The EndSARS protest was in response to widespread youth exclusion and abuses in Nigeria, especially from the Special Anti-Robbery Squad (SARS) of the Nigerian Police Force as an enforcement arm of government. Thus, the SARS is the epitome/signpost/flagship of youth abuses and exclusion in Nigeria, and the #EndSARS protest is the flagship counteraction by the youths against youth oppression, exclusion, and galvanized collective action against corruption, misrule, and government irresponsibility in Nigeria. As the youths are widely excluded from government, economy, society, and institutions, they face excruciating survival challenges in Nigeria and Africa and literally find themselves severely inhibited. As a result, the youth face serious and debilitating challenges in Nigeria (Tade, 2020) and Africa generally, even though they are the most dominant sociodemographic group on the continent and in African countries (Fayehun & Isiugo-Abanihe, 2020). This is now commonly known as the demographic youth bulge of Africa, which has the capacity to be a gain or threat to countries and the continent depending on whether it is efficiently managed or not (Fayehun & Isiugo-Abanihe, 2020). If well managed, the youth bulge can be a demographic gain. If poorly managed, however, the youth bulge will be the greatest burden and the most dangerous undoing of Africa as a collective continent and of African nations individually.

The situation of youths' exclusion is highly precarious in Nigeria, particularly given its massive population, years of misgovernance, corruption, poverty, insecurity, unemployment, and the massive youth bulge. Nigeria is a country that has the highest population in Africa, with over 200 million people, with the youths accounting for not less than 70% of the total population (Akanle, 2019). Nigeria is endowed with various human and natural resources, but the country's development has been severely hindered due to poor governance, massive corruption, and slow economic growth. As a result, unemployment and poverty are prevalent in Nigeria. Over the years, there has been a great increase in people living in poverty in Nigeria. As asserted by the World Poverty Clock (a Web tool produced by World Data Lab), the number of people living in extreme poverty in Nigeria has increased from 86.9 million in 2018 to 93.7 million in 2019 (Daniel, 2019). Unemployment and poverty are best described as the nurturers of youth crime, as most of the crimes in the country are committed by young people (Ezemenaka, 2021). Most youth crimes and violence can be traced to factors such as political alienation, economic exclusion, and socio-economic hardship (Akanle et al., 2019; Akanle, 2022). These exclusionary and alienating elements largely culminated in the EndSARS protest.

The EndSARS protest brings to focus the youth's interrogatory and vehement response capabilities that cannot be underestimated in understanding youthhood, exclusion, and development in Africa and particularly Nigeria (Agbalajobi, 2020; Ikuteyijo, 2021). Youth exclusion is institutional, structural, and systemic in nature. It manifests through the instrumentation of the inimical social, economic, cultural, psychological, and political monopolies of the significant other older adults who maintain strangleholds on the existing societal arrangements (Dambo, 2021; Akanle, 2022). Any society that holds the view that its youth is its future will always develop policies and programs that will secure the current and future of the youth and ameliorate their exclusion thresholds and challenges. These appear far-flung in Nigeria based on the trajectories and manifestations of the realities. In any society where youth are perceived as liabilities, without any workable plan or program in place to get the best out of youth, protest, violence, and youth-led disruptions are certain (Akanle & Shittu, 2021). In the following sections, this chapter discusses how the EndSARS protest erupted/developed, metamorphosed, and became a metaphor for ending corruption, bad governance, police brutality, unemployment, poverty and so on. Finally, the chapter draws out the lessons learned/to be learned through the protest.

11.2 Context of Youth Exclusion in Nigeria

Although youth unemployment is a global phenomenon and widespread in Africa, youth unemployment is gargantuan in Nigeria, with the majority of the youths in Nigeria being unemployed without any likelihood of employment in sight (Odunlami & Akanle, 2021; Tade, 2020). Unemployment happens when people willing to work cannot find suitable and payable jobs at a given period (Akpan, 2015). In Nigeria, many youths are ready to work, but there are no suitable jobs to earn a decent living (Ajaegbu, 2012; Tade, 2020). Many able and competent youths are roaming the streets of Nigeria in search of jobs/economic opportunities to earn decent livelihoods. It is indeed challenging for youths in Nigeria to earn a decent living in the face of excruciating unemployment. It is, in fact, more likely that a young person will be unemployed and live in poverty in Nigeria than the other way around (Odunlami & Akanle, 2021). The ultimate implications of this massive unabating, near-hopeless unemployment situation and harsh economy in Nigeria are youths' frustrations and hopelessness and the likelihood of violent reactions against perceived irresponsible governments and apathetic significant older adults. An important flipside of the huge youth unemployment problem in Nigeria is that the few economic opportunities available are appropriated and highjacked through kinship and social networks of the rich, powerful, and politically connected against the more populous common woman who lacks social and kinship clout and connections. This, in turn, brews frustrations and tensions (Akanle & Nwaobiala, 2020).

Often, the few available jobs also do not match the training of the youths. As a result, there is a massive case of skills mismatch in Nigeria's youth and unemployment conundrum (Akanle, 2021; Tade, 2020). The continuous problem of unemployment troubling the current youths of this generation in Nigeria is a serious threat to the socio-economic and political advancement of society (Akanle et al., 2019; Tade, 2020). Very few government programs address the gargantuan unemployment in Nigeria, but they are generally ineffective. Many of such interventions are mere window-dressing and tokens within unsustainable frameworks of social protection programs, as in the NPower program, which is the main youths' empowerment program initiated by the Nigerian government. Reasons include incompetence, nepotism and cronyism, corruption, and over-politicization, among others. For instance, in the year 2020, the federal government launched a special public work program to reduce the unemployment rate in Nigeria, hoping that about 1000 Nigerians from each of the 744 local governments would be engaged in the program. Regrettably, the program did not take off after much media glamour and glitterati, largely due to political arm-twisting among state actors. The program aimed to employ unskilled laborers with a monthly salary of ₦20,000 (about USD$36). Strikingly, it was discovered that Ph.D. holders and not less than 200 Master's degree holders were among the applicants for social protection jobs with a monthly salary of ₦20,000 (about USD$36). This demonstrates the enormity and frustrating level of unemployment in the country. Hence, most of these applicants are young people (often graduates) who are desperate to exit poverty and unemployment.

As of the second quarter of 2020, data from the National Bureau of Statistics (NBS) show Nigeria's unemployment rate as 27.1%. NBS (2018[1]) revealed that the unemployment rates in Nigeria in 2017 and 2018 were 20.42% and 23.13%, respectively, and most of these were youths. According to Ajufo (2013), about 4.5 million youths who are graduates enter the labor market without any hope of getting a job every year. Therefore, unemployment has become a very serious problem in Nigeria, particularly among the youths. In order to meet their daily needs, many youths get involved in dubious ways such as fraud, cybercrime, banditry, drug peddling, kidnapping, violence, prostitution, and so on (Anthony, 2013). The number of youths going into cybercrime (*yahoo yahoo*) is on the rise daily as they are being driven to see this as a quick way of building alternative livelihoods (Akanle & Shadare, 2020). According to Afeez and Ojo (2021), cybercrimes are of different classes in Nigeria; they range from *Yahoo boys* (cyber criminals) and their 419 Internet frauds, hacking, software piracy, pornography, credit score card or automatic teller machine (ATM) fraud, denial of service attack, virus dissemination, phishing, cyber plagiarism, cyber-stalking, cyber-defamation, etc.

In the 1970s and 1980s, poverty among youths was not a serious issue due to the full grips of agricultural activities in society coupled with the low effect of urbanization and migration. As a result, youths did not pose a social problem. However, due to the high negative effect of urbanization and migration, poverty has continued to grow among the youths. Urbanization has become mainly demographically driven in Nigeria, without proportionate socio-economic benefits and dividends to the urban settings. Hence, the high rate of unemployment and poverty is on the increase. However, poverty among the youths is not a thing of today. As from the mid-1980s, as occasioned by Structural Adjustment Program (SAP), poverty has been on the steady rise. The state of poverty among the youths is increasing. Poverty is widespread in Nigeria, and the youths suffer higher poverty rates due to deep-seated systemic exclusion from the society's functional socio-economic and political fabrics. There are various reasons why poverty amongst the youths is still on the rise. There is an increasing demand for workers with specialized skills that can only be provided by world-class institutions, which Nigeria lacks. The higher the levels of education and skill sets, the higher the earnings. Due to the forces of globalization and technological advances, new skills are needed in all working environments for greater productivity and to meet societal needs. According to the World Development Report (2007), the growing demand for skills has increased the value of further education and made it more important for growth. What then happens in a country like Nigeria with a poor educational system and retrogressed educational

[1] Please see https://www.worldbank.org/en/programs/lsms/brief/nigeria-releases-new-report-on-poverty-and-inequality-in-country. Accessed 17/06/2022.

infrastructures for the youths? Indeed, in many countries, building a workforce with higher-order skills is an important part of improving the climate for investment, acquiring competitive edges, and generally maintaining growth ramifications for sustainable (youth) poverty elimination. Many youths live in poverty because of their inability to acquire higher education for higher skills.

Government negligence toward educational development is a major way poverty is growing among the youths. The lack of inclusiveness of youths in governmental functions has given birth to youths with low morale for education. Many youths in Nigeria now consider education a scam and a waste of time. This is because of the many cases of youth unemployment, even among those youths who graduated with first-class degrees. As a result, unfortunately, many youths have created a popular slogan for education in Nigeria: "Education is a Scam." These kinds of collective sentiments are regrettable because, logically, education aims to enlighten, empower, stimulate creative thinking, and equip people with the required skills to either work for themselves or public or private entities and to escape poverty and the poverty trap. However, Nigerian governments have indulged in aggravated youth negligence over the years and have failed to provide such competitive education for the teeming youths in the country. Even the educational budgetary allocation by the government cannot drive educational development in Nigeria. In developed societies, high consideration is given to education in terms of budgetary allocation. For example, Singapore allocates 20% of its National Expenditure Budget for education, while Nigeria allocates 8%. Therefore, it is not surprising that Nigeria's educational and national developments stagnate while Singapore and Malaysia, for instance, continually progress (Oluwadamilare, 2016). The neglect of education and associated undervalued certificates have led to the erroneous consideration of education as a scam among the teeming youths. The implication is that youths facing adversity are easily manipulated by societal pressures and appropriated and deployed by political elites with dubious and opportunistic intentions.

Youth exclusion from governance is the demonstrative hallmark of systemic exclusion relative to the youths in Nigerian society. In other words, apart from youths' unemployment and poverty, youths' exclusion from governance is another major challenge confronting the youth in Nigeria. Very few youths are in governmental positions, and a negligible proportion in government are for political tokenism, window dressing, and appendages (Udalla, 2011). The youths represent the largest demographic percentages translating to huge political and voting resources. Yet, they are the most excluded when it comes to voting, governance, occupation and execution, policy formulations, and institutional strengthening. The general notion of governments is that youths have nothing much to offer and are lethargic and dependent. Hence, governments expect and prefer unvarying respect and silence from the youths, and any attempt to question their authority, they weaponize traditions to avoid accountability (Tade, 2020). This notion of the youths as lazy and immature for governance was further popularized and aggravated by the president of Nigeria, President Mohammadu Buhari, during the Commonwealth Business Forum in London. In contrast, previous governments of President Olusegun Obasanjo and others, at different times, maintained that the youths were not ready for leadership. This notion belies youth exclusion from governance in real terms and times. Governments and political elites that hold unfavorable views of young people do not include them in programs, policies, and governance.

The exclusion of youths from governance in Nigeria is seemingly designed and championed by the old political elites who desire to hold on to power and resist any generational shifts toward the youths. The perception of power by the old Nigerian political elites is that power is biologically and socially hereditary. The political leaders believe they are more experienced than the youths and, therefore, more legitimate and competent to govern. Therefore, the older generation opines they are more entitled to hold on to power even against the youths. Senators, for instance, usually spend 16 years holding the same positions and later contest for a gubernatorial seat. After completing 8 years in that office, they return to seek gubernatorial offices and (if possible) contest the presidency; thus, the process of political circulation and round-tripping continues unending as the old political class remains in governance while the youths are shut out of governance perpetually. That is the typical political cycle of Nigerian political leaders. They believe in holding power until they die. This gives no room for the youths to explore and exploit their governance potential. The three arms of government (executive, judiciary, and legislature) are complete reflections and manifestations of youths' exclusion in Nigeria. In President Buhari's administration, for instance, the youngest minister in charge of the Ministry of Humanitarian Affairs, Disaster Management and Social Development, Sadiya Umar Farouq, is 43 years of age. There is no single individual below the age of 35 in the administration. Even though there is a popular saying that "youths are the leaders of tomorrow," such a saying is a myth in Nigeria as older people hold deep sway in governance to the chagrin of the youths.

TIn Nigeria, the exclusion of youths from governance is institutional and systemic in nature. The deliberate exclusion of the youths from governance is legitimized through the constitution by adopting an age benchmark (15–35 years) as criteria for contesting political offices in Nigeria (Akanle & Fageyinbo, 2019). In Nigeria, the age criteria to seek elective positions is 35 years and above. This is a clear indication that the youths are not designed to be a part of governance in Nigeria. Recently the "Not Too Young to Run Bill" was signed into law to accommodate the youths into governance in response to youths' agitations. Whether the *Not Too Young to Run* law will be effective in driving youths' inclusion in governance or not, time will tell. However, the prognoses may not be too positive based on the impacts of many years of strategic disempowerment of the youths in a nation with very expensive and lopsided political processes and systems.

Apart from the age criteria used to exclude the youths from governance, the political parties have also acted as instruments of youth exclusion for youths aspiring to hold political offices in Nigeria. The high cost of purchasing nomination forms in the political parties in Nigeria is prohibitive and an indirect message to the youths that national politics is not for the young people but for the "recycled" leaders. They have gathered enormous wealth over time to perpetuate themselves in governance. In 2019, the presidential nomination form of the All-Progressive Congress (APC) was 45 million nairas (N45,000,000/$108,302.49), while that of the People's

Democratic Party (PDP) was 12 million nairas (N12,000,000/$28,863.79). The gubernatorial nomination form for APC was 22 million, 500,000 nairas (N22.5 m/ $54,119.61), and the one of PDP was 6 million nairas (N6m/$14,431.90). An average visionary youth will not easily be able to access this kind of money to buy such expensive forms to be involved in governance. Moreover, even if they were able to buy the forms with the help of supporters, they would still require additional funds for campaigning, and the overall electioneering process remains extremely expensive. This is a clear indication that the youths' exclusion from governance is systematic and institutional in Nigeria.

There are also situations where many youths engage in self-systematic exclusion from governance based on principles and self-convictions. That is, some youths also sometimes exclude themselves from governance because of the issue of godfatherism. The issue of godfatherism is discouraging the youths from participating in governance. Godfathers see politics and governance as business. If they support a person, the person must 'dance to their tune' through governance or financial returns. Disinterest in keeping to the terms and conditions of godfathers and instead of remaining original and true to themselves make many conscious youths stay out of governance processes. Such principled youths believe their time will come when they objectively participate in governance and make original positive changes through governance rather than being used within the current problematic political and governance systems and processes.

A very unfortunate twist to youth exclusion in Nigeria is the issue of systemic negative youth profiling and police harassment. In fact, this is the flagship and the immediate cause of the End SARS protest. That is, many older generation discourses dominate debates and suggest that young people are all scammers and criminals. This makes older people and law enforcement agents, including the police, rough handle an average youth, including seizing their phones, laptops, and gadgets. Arguably, at the societal level, there is an insufficient effort to genuinely understand contemporary works and lifestyles of young people that may contradict traditional African culture and conception of work (especially given influences due to globalization and information technology). It is noteworthy that broader perceptions of youth—of society and law enforcement officers—determine the unfavorable treatment of young people in significant ways. Stereotypes persist and can have very negative consequences. For example, when an average police officer or even general adults see any youth with a laptop, fine/exotic/clean car, or iPhone, there are assumptions that the young person must be a thief or a cybercriminal and must be arrested, extorted, extra-judicially killed or detained. Nigeria is a society where youths are perceived and treated as liabilities with no plan or program to get the best out of them. Policies put in place more often than not serve to frustrate their innovations and survival ingenuity.

Interestingly, the remits of youths' perception have great consequences on youths' culture (lifestyle). If the perception is good, the youth's culture in such a society is more likely to be great in the final analysis, and it can also go the other way round if the perception is obnoxious. Thus, extreme care is needed in avoiding labeling and profiling/stigmatizing the youths if they are to contribute positively and effectively to sustainable development. While many developed countries have great plans for their youths' development not because they are the richest but because they know that the youths are their future, many countries in Africa, particularly Nigeria, appear to have no design and plan to build this generational cohort in a meaningful way. This lack of planning, and regard for youth development, accounts for much of the violence being witnessed across Africa and Nigeria (Ukeje & Iwilade, 2012). To note is the fact that if Nigeria continues to exclude and negatively profile its young people, violence and protests will continue to be legitimized and also gain momentum.

Youths now have common survival belief systems to navigate the murky social, economic, and policing systems peculiar to their youth subculture. They have common beliefs, norms, and values that they create to assist and enable them to survive the harsh conditions of Nigeria. For instance, one of such beliefs is "*street smartness*." It is believed that for youths to survive the unfavorable economy, negative profiling, and exclusion, they must be *street smart*. With this belief, many graduates go into vocational training, which formal schools do not offer, to acquire the necessary skills to become entrepreneurs. Some who believe the state has failed them see no reason to acquire additional skills. Consequently, they define their street smartness and focus on survival rather than growth, improvement, and social networking. The state and community's stereotypical view of the youths has given birth to systematic harassment and brutalization of youths who are seen to be *successful* by the police and general Nigerian security architecture. The Nigerian Police, especially its now disbanded Special Anti-Robbery Squad (SARS), has been central in driving much of these stereotypical and negative constructions of young people. During the EndSARS protest, there were few attempts to understand the issues being raised, but an aggressive attempt to suppress the mobilization due to stereotypical views of young people and annoyance at their demands for inclusion. There were reported cases of strayed bullets injuring innocent citizens, sexual assaults, mistaken identity, extrajudicial killings, illegal detentions, extortion, traumatization, and tortures.

11.2.1 The EndSARS Protest

The police are central to maintaining law and order in society. However, because of the profound civil interfacing of the police, they tend to have much more to do in managing and maintaining social stability and equilibrium. This can be overwhelming given the enormous responsibilities of maintaining social order in the face of a paucity of funds, shortage of personnel, resources, and facilities available to the police, particularly in Nigeria, given rising crimes and insecurity. Thus, due to the different duties and responsibilities of the Nigerian Police Force, a special unit was carved out to combat armed robbery and other serious crimes in Nigeria. This special unit was named SARS. It was established in 1992 as one of the 14 units in the Force Criminal Investigation and Intelligence Department (Okeshola & Mudaire, 2013).

Other units were established in the police to combat social crimes and reduce social problems right from the end of the civil war in 1970. They are, for instance, the counterterrorism unit, special tactical squad, force intelligence unit, intelligence response team, and so on. All these units have been functioning in society since their establishment, but the citizens of Nigeria frown at the functionality and reputation of SARS in society due to their brutality, excessive use of force, corruption, and general highhandedness. SARS' human rights abuses were numerous and severally documented on social media, including videos and posts/chats (Ujene & Orji-Egwu, 2018; Uwazuruike, 2022).

According to Amnesty International (2016), SARS was responsible for human rights violations, degrading treatment, cruelty, and widespread torture of the people they were meant to protect. Moreover, some of these human rights abuses range from shooting or killing detainees, threats of execution, and other physical, financial, and emotional abuses (Amnesty International, 2016, 2020a, 2020b). The youths were mostly the victims of human rights violations (Ikuteyijo, 2021; Tade, 2020). Hence, Amnesty International (2020a) documented that SARS carried out 82 extra-judicial killing and abuse cases between January 2017 and May 2020. According to Iwenwanne (2018), about 101,500 people have been killed in custody with no justice for the victims. The extrajudicial killings, torturing, human rights violations, and many other cases of abuse led to a call by the citizens, especially the youths, to disband SARS. That later translated into the global viral hashtag #EndSARS.

The EndSARS campaign started on Twitter in 2016 by Segun Awosanya, popularly known as Segalink, inciting the authority of the police to reform the police unit. However, in the end, nothing was done (Iwenwanne, 2018). A petition was signed by 10,195 people in 2017 and submitted to Nigerian National Assembly to demand the disbandment of SARS (Mansur, 2017). The campaign for scrapping SARS gained momentum via social media - and then in physical form when people came out *en masse* to protest. The protest took place in more than ten states in Nigeria and overseas (including in America and the United Kingdom) to the extent that it became a global issue and many celebrities tweeted in support. However, rather than the police overhauling its special unit or scrapping it due to popular demands, the police responded that those protesting and agitating for scrapping SARS were armed robbers who saw the unit's operation as a threat to their criminal activities. Nevertheless, when the agitations and the demands of the people became intense, the then Inspector General of the Nigerian Police, Ibrahim Idris, had no option but to order the reorganization and reformation of the special police unit, SARS (Adewole, 2017). This was the first wave of the EndSARS protest led and driven by technology by the youths in the first instance. However, the reform was not total and very ineffective as the extrajudicial killings, extortion, and other forms of abuses by SARS continued. In order to further push for reduction and/or an end to police brutality, Nigerian rapper Michael Ugochukwu Stephen, popularly known as Ruggedman (a youth), released a song titled "Is Police Your Friend" in 2018. The song went viral, but nothing was done to address the issues raised by Ruggedman, which was a call for reforms in the police, particularly SARS.

On 3 October 2020, the second wave of EndSARS protest started on Twitter when a video of a SARS officer seen shooting a youth in Delta state trended. The police allegedly killed the youth, and this brewed anger on social media as the video went viral (Okon, 2020). Two days later, a 20-year-old up-and-coming musician, Daniel Chibuike, was allegedly abused and killed by the same SARS (Lambo, 2020). On October 8, 2020, the second wave of nationwide offline protests began after years of bottled anger and sentiments toward the police from the videos and pictures displaying police extortion, harassment, extrajudicial killing, and human rights violation. As the protest gained momentum, the Nigeria Police Force tried to throw the protest into disorder by shooting unarmed protesters using water cannons and teargas and arresting demonstrators (BBC, 2020a, 2020b; Busari et al., 2020). As a result, the protest became intensified with protesters calling for the reformation and accountability of the special police unit, SARS. Gradually the focus of the protest changed from EndSARS to end bad government because they later discovered that SARS is a problem to society. In contrast, bad governance is the root of the problem, and as a result, EndSARS became a metaphor for ending bad leadership, corruption, insecurity, nepotism, infrastructural decay, and so on. The protesters later became aware that part of the reason police engage in extortion and abuse is due to the very low salaries of the police. The EndSARS protesters, therefore, added the need for better welfare of the police to the objectives of the protest.

The protest continued peacefully for several days and was mainly led by Nigerian youths, celebrities, and some activists. It is important to point out that the protest had no leader, and the protesters were decentralized. The youths' bond, energy, and determination to end SARS and bad governance were so strong that they were at major junctions in all the states where protests took place. The young people cooked, ate, organized at the protest grounds, improvised ways of charging their phones and electronic gadgets, and then live-streamed events for local and international followers. The determination to use social media was so firm that about 28 million tweets with the hashtag EndSARS were recorded on Twitter (Kazeem, 2020). The protest was peaceful for about 4 days until it turned bloody. As of October 13, 2020, the fifth day of the offline protest, about ten unarmed protesters were killed (Kazeem, 2020). On October 20, 2020, it was alleged that one of the greatest unarmed protester massacres occurred at Lekki Tollgate Lagos. The bloodbaths and disruption of the protest by provocateurs and the armies led to the end of the EndSARS protest. The protesters' major strategy was to ensure there was no leader of the protest. The government has ended many protests in the past by either arresting the key leaders of such protests or bribing the leader(s) with a huge sum of money. For the EndSARS protest, there was no one to arrest, hold accountable and/or bribe. Despite the fact that there was no known leader(s) of the protest, the protest was very organized and peaceful for so many days (Al Jazeera, 2020a; Aluko, 2021; Anthony, 2020; BBC, 2020a, 2020b, 2020c; Bode, 2020; Bidemi, 2020; Olufemi, 2020; Premium Times, 2020; Al Jazeera, 2020b; Stephanie & Nimi, 2021; Premium Times, 2020; Al Jazeera, 2020c). After seeing the determination of the youths to continue the protest and noting the economic setbacks the protest caused the country, the Nigerian government dissolved the Special Anti-Robbery Squad (SARS). Despite the disbandment of the Special Anti-Robbery Squad (SARS), the youths refused to stop the protest. They warned the government that disbanding SARS was just one of the many demands, and they would not stop the protest until all their demands were met. The protesters made five new demands for the government to meet before stopping the protests. The five (5) demands were: Immediate release of all arrested protesters, justice for all deceased victims of police brutality through compensation for their families, setting up an independent body to oversee the investigation and prosecution of all reports of police misconduct, in line with the new Police Act, psychological evaluation and retraining (to be confirmed by an independent body) of all disbanded SARS officers before they can be redeployed, and finally, increase police salary so that they are adequately compensated for protecting the lives and property of citizens (Nasir, 2021; Adewole, 2017). The Nigerian government acceded to the demands and took immediate steps to address them, such as forming a new unit called S.W.A. T to replace SARS. Also, some states set up judicial panels to systematically examine the allegations of police brutality (Ikuteyijo, 2021; Nasir, 2021; Tade, 2020; Uwazuruike, 2022).

11.3 The (Social) Media, the Diaspora, and International Community

Social media played the most significant role in mobilizing and sustaining the EndSARS protest. In fact, it would have been impossible to have the protest without social media. Social media proved itself as a real effective agent of socialization competent in motivating ideas and galvanizing actions through the transfer of information, norms, beliefs, and values within and across generations (Akanle et al., 2021a, b). Other media systems, including traditional ones like television stations, radio stations, and newspapers, were not left out. Daily activities of the protest were publicized on radio, television stations, and in newspapers. Information spread through the media and was made available in different languages to update all sectors on the occurrences relating to the protest. Different articles were also published in different media outlets in the country to enlighten people on the direction of the protest. The traditional and social media became the leader, catalysts, and machinery for disseminating information and ideas surrounding the EndSARS protest. Traditional and social media were the effective invisible leaders of the protest as people could be anywhere in their living rooms and offices and still effectively join and drive the protest. As stated, social media particularly played a pivotal role as it created the platforms for social media influencers and the diaspora, who were able to spread anti-exclusionary narratives to propel and sustain the protest effectively.

MMobilizations of youths to the physical and virtual venues of the protest were made possible by social media, especially Twitter (Agbalajobi, 2020; Dambo, 2021; Fayehun & Isiugo-Abanihe, 2020; Ikuteyijo, 2021; Tade, 2020; Uwazuruike, 2022).

Twitter was the de facto planning and meeting center for the protesters. They went there to get the latest information about the protest and the next steps to take. It also served as a vehicle of coordination during the demonstrations. Twitter was used to feed and update the young protesters with the latest information surrounding the protest, which led to the success of the peaceful protest for days before the infiltration of provocateurs and the Nigerian army that led to the end of the protest. Hence, Twitter also acted as a mobilizing force by amplifying the voices of the protesters with hashtags like; #EndPoliceBrutality, #EndSARS, #EndSARSNow, #SARSMustEnd and so on. The amplified voices of the demonstrators got the attention of the state, its agents, and international communities. The hashtag, #EndSARS, was one of the top trending hashtags worldwide, with over 2 million tweets.

The mobilization of the youths during protests and their domination of the Internet space was made possible due to the large population of youths utilizing the Internet. According to the Nigeria Communications Commission (NCC), there were 122 million Internet users at the time in Nigeria (NCC, 2019). Also, according to Fasunwon (2019), of the 2.7 billion active Facebook users, significant proportions (17 million) are Nigerians. This is significant and led to the success of the EndSARS protest. There is no doubt that the youths have the highest number of Internet users in the country due to their population size. According to NOIPolls (2019), in the six geopolitical zones of Nigeria, the youths have the highest number of Internet users, ranging from 18 to 35 years of age. Due to their large number of users, they were able to overpower the Internet space to their own advantage in achieving their goals. For instance, when few demonstrators converged for demonstrations, they used Twitter to share their strategic locations, and within a few minutes, the small number would turn to hundreds.

The protest at Lekki toll gate, Lagos, Nigeria, was a typical demonstration of the power of social media. On October 12, 2020, a call was made on Twitter to close down the Lekki toll gate, which was the major transit point of Lagos since Lagos was the epicenter of the protest. The call led to the disruption of the city, leading to a long line of traffic jams that shut down the city. As a result, the Lagos State Governor, Babatunde Sanwoolu, was forced to address the protesters a few hours later. The use of the Internet and social media for the protest also restricted the counteractions of the government and its agents. Since the government knew its forceful counteractions could be made known to the public and the international communities through the help of the same social media, it exercised restraints even though the state eventually damned all consequences and embarked on propaganda followed by excessive use of force to quell the protest.

The Nigerian diaspora appreciated and related to the protest to solve the country's more fundamental problems, including bad governance and youth exclusion. The diaspora was very involved in the protest, and many took it personally for various reasons, including discrimination and maltreatment they faced in their countries of destination and their intention to return if things improved in Nigeria. Even though they are in the diaspora, many have families, kinship and social networks, and investments in Nigeria. They are, therefore, to some agree, still attached to Nigeria.

Thus, when the opportunity of the EndSARS protest presented itself through the agitations of the youths, the diaspora related to this opportunity to express their suppressed anger toward the poor leadership and underdevelopment of the country. They gave their support through physical/online demonstrations or/and financial donations to help achieve the purpose of the protest.

11.4 The Youths and EndSARS Protest in the Era of COVID-19: Lessons for Nigeria and Africa—Concluding Remarks

It was striking that the EndSARS protest was organized during the COVID-19 pandemic ravaging the whole country and the world. The youths dared and neglected the COVID-19 protocols issued by the Nigeria Center for Disease Control (NCDC) in pursuit of their goals to end the exclusionary and oppressive conduct of the government through the protest. Most of the physical protesters were ready to do whatever it took to constantly move the protest to achieve its aims. Many protesters were not afraid of paying heavy prices for their actions because of their entrenched exclusion and frustrations with the system. Despite the killing of some protesters by the Nigerian police and army, the protesters did not stop the protest (Chinedu, 2021; Emmanuel, 2021). The resoluteness behind the Nigerian youths' protest was arguably similar to the Indian farmers' protest/movement and the Black Lives Matter (BLM) protest in the United States of America during the COVID-19 pandemic (Lopez, 2020; Neyman & Dalsey, 2021). The COVID-19 pandemic that hit India and the United States of America was more than most countries in the world, yet it did not deter the farmers' movement and the BLM protesters. While the farmers emphatically stated that whether they contract the coronavirus or not, the "black laws" will still kill them (Jaskiran, 2021), just as the BLM protesters insisted racial exclusion was even more dangerous than the COVID-19 pandemic (Neyman & Dalsey, 2021; Lopez, 2020). The youths' determination and resilience were far greater than any fear of COVID-19 contagion and fatalities. During the protest, there were outright violations of the COVID-19 protocols. A major protocol guiding against COVID-19 contagion and fatalities is physical distancing premised on 'small' physical gatherings. This was never observed during the protests as hundreds of youths gathered. The protesters deliberately disobeyed the guidelines of physical distancing in protest against the instructions of a state that had lost credibility in their eyes.

There are many important lessons to be learned in this epochal protest, and these lessons are essential for Nigeria and Africa. First, through the protest, the youths made effective landmark and epochal statements against social exclusion, maltreatment, oppression, injustices, bad leadership, corruption, and intimidation, thereby asserting a broad political impact. Youths across the country (and elsewhere) gathered despite the ravaging COVID-19 pandemic to fight for freedom, justice, and good governance. Through the protest's conception, process, and outcomes, a major lesson is that dispassionate followership will never give the citizens the desired social change. Dispassionate followership means the inability and unwillingness of citizens to do something about their exploited and alienated circumstances. The followership in Nigeria has been a docile one to an extent, including the youths. The youths have complained about their circumstances over the years but seldom publicly voice their complaints. The EndSARS protest was the first of its kind and objectively epochal. The EndSARS protest was a radical departure from the status quo. Through traditional- and social media, a level of political consciousness was achieved amongst the youths.

Arguably, the youth as a generational category have developed a class consciousness through mass protest. This transformation has influenced an understanding that there are some problems, which can only be solved through protest and confrontations rather than through docile means. Even though the youths did not get all they demanded, the protest led to some important fundamental social and political changes. For instance, SARS, the major cause of the protest, was disbanded. It also had great effects on the Nigerian Police Force in general, particularly regarding cautioning the policy. The protest also clearly demonstrated to the police and political leaders that they no longer have a monopoly over the means of violence and that the youths can force change. The protest also changed the orientation of the government toward the masses. They learned that passivity and compliance of the followers should not be seen as eternal weakness or a fixed state.

The protest showed the interesting technological and innovative competitive edges and competencies of the youths with the help of the Internet. Since the youths are technologically savvy, they raised more than 4 million nairas (N4,000,000 [Naira]/$4862 USD) for two physically challenged youths in less than 24 h during the protest. This was thus far a feat impossible and unprecedented even for the government. The protesters, through the help of a non-governmental organization (NGO), Feminist Coalition, were able to raise #77,190,350.11/ $187160.59 USD) and also used technology companies like Flutterwave to raise #10,262,703/ $24945.11 USD) (Charles, 2020). Moreover, when the government started freezing the protesters' accounts, they raised money through other means like cryptocurrency. This shows that the youth are creative, strategic, innovative, and technologically savvy.

The EndSARS protest clearly showed the resilience and creativity of the Nigerian youth to solve complex problems. They were able to think outside the box to get innovative ideas in order to achieve their goals. The EndSARS protest revealed that the youths have great energy that can be transformed into national and continental development assets. Any government that lacks accountability and transparency creates an opportunity for anarchy and, in cases, rebellion from the followers, especially the youth. No society can grow and make progress without great governance, accountability, and transparency. Therefore, the government of Nigeria should not see the protest cynically as a youth attempt to destroy the country's unity but rather a call for greater inclusion, coherence, transparency, and accountability in every sphere and institution.

Against the background of continued/persistent youth exclusion, misgovernance, corruption, poverty, unemployment, injustices, and highhandedness of law enforcement officials—including the police—in Nigeria, even with the EndSARS, only time will tell if there will be another EndSARS protest in Nigeria soon. If lessons are not learned, an EndSARS protest in the near future may be more wide-ranging, fundamental, destructive, and bloodier. Such protest may turn out to be an affirmative generational and class action that may affect the existential scaffoldings of the country. It is, therefore, high time that the Nigerian government, elites, and everyone in Nigeria, Africa, and the world build more objective and robust views of the protest and strategically engage to effectively and inclusively address the fundamental problems that led to the protest in the first place. To avert more damaging EndSARS protest(s) in the nearest future, the time to act inclusively, pragmatically, sustainably, and objectively is now. Strategic and sustainable youth inclusion is key to peace, progress, justice, growth, and development.

References

Adewole, K. (2017). *SARS reform is the best alternative to #EndSARS*. The cable. Retrieved February 18, 2020 from https://www.thecable.ng

Afeez, A. S., & Ojo, A. O. (2021). Impact of social media on police brutality awareness in Nigeria. *International Journal for Management and Modern Education, 1*(1), 14–27.

Agbalajobi, D. (2020). *Why #EndSARS protests are different, and what lessons they hold for Nigeria. Conversation*. Retrieved February 18, 2020 from https://theconversation.com/why-endsars-protests-are-different-and-what-lessons-they-hold-for-nigeria-148320

Ajaegbu, O. (2012). Rising youth unemployment and violent crime in Nigeria. *American Journal of Social Issues and Humanities, 2*, 315–321.

Ajufo, B. I. (2013). Challenges of youth unemployment in Nigeria: Effective career guidance as a panacea. *African Research Review, 7*(1), 307–321.

Akanle, O. (2019). Youth restiveness, national security and development in Nigeria. In I. P. Onyeonoru & A. A. Atere (Eds.), *Security and Society in Nigeria* (pp. 1–14). Ibadan University Press.

Akanle, O. (2021). *The precariousness of right to inclusive quality education: Incessant strikes, IT deficits, infrastructural gaps and knowledge production in Nigerian public universities*. Paper presented at unequal world conference. The right to education – Transforming the world through inclusive quality education. January 24–25, 2021.

Akanle, O. (2022). *Youth exclusion and empowerment in the contemporary global order: Contexts of economy, education and governance*. Emerald Publishing Limited.

Akanle, O., Ademuson, A. O., & Omotayo, A. (2019). Incubation hubs and development in Southwestern Nigeria. *Ilorin Journal of Sociology, 11*(2), 248–260.

Akanle, O., & Fageyinbo, K. T. (2019). European football clubs and football betting among the youths in Nigeria. *Soccer and Society, 20*(1), 1–20.

Akanle, O., Fayehun, O. A., & Oyelakin, S. (2021a). The information communication technology, social media, international migration and migrants' relations with kin in Nigeria. *Journal of Asian and African Studies, 56*(6), 1212–1225.

Akanle, O., Nwanagu, G. C., & Akanle, O. E. (2021b). Social media among distant spouses in South Western Nigeria. *African Journal of Science, Technology, Innovation and Development, 13*(3), 347–355.

Akanle, O., & Nwaobiala, U. R. (2020). *Disabling normativities in post Covid-19 Nigeria: Contexts, fragilities, stabilities and gendered role dynamics of female breadwinning.* Paper presented at the 1st African Research Universities Alliance (ARUA) Centre of Excellence for unemployment and skills development international conference, 2020. University of Lagos, Nigeria, 2–4 December 2020.

Akanle, O., & Shadare, B. R. (2020). Why has it been so difficult to counteract cybercrime in Nigeria: Evidence from an ethnographic study. *International Journal of Cyber Criminology, 14*(1), 21–43.

Akanle, O., & Shittu, O. S. (2021). The unending development question of Nigeria. *European Journal of Development Research, 34*, 321–342.

Akpan, D. A. (2015). Youth's unemployment and illiteracy: Impact on national security, the Nigerian experience. *International Journal of Arts and Humanities, 4*(14), 62–71.

Al Jazeera. (2020a). *#EndSARS: Nigerians protest against police brutality.* www.aljazeera.com. Aljazeera Media Network.

Al Jazeera. (2020b). *Lekki shooting: Army admits troops deployed, denies opening fire.* www.aljazeera.com. Al Jazeera Media Network.

Al Jazeera. (2020c). *Nigerian police beat, arrest protesters at site of Lekki shooting.* www.aljazeera.com. Al Jazeera Media Network.

Aluko, O. A. (2021). Leadership and governance crisis in Nigeria: The case of the #Endsars protest. *Journal of Public Administration and Governance, 11*(2), 246–257.

Amnesty International. (2016). *You have signed your death warrant: Torture and other ill treatment by Nigeria's special anti-robbery squad (SARS).* London: AFR 44/4868/2016.

Amnesty International. (2020a). *Nigeria: Killing of #EndSARS protesters by the military must be investigated.* Retrieved February 22, 2020, from https://www.amnesty.org/en/latest/news/2020/10/killing-of-endsars-protesters-by-the-military-must-be-investigated/

Amnesty International. (2020b). Nigeria police continue to torture with impunity. www.amnesty.org

Anthony, A. (2020). *Video indicates security officials provide cover for hoodlums attacking #EndSARS protesters in Abuja.* Retrieved February 22, 2020 from https://businessday.ng/news/article/video-indicates-security-officials-provide-cover-for-hoodlums-attacking-endsars-protesters-in-abuja/

Anthony, A. A. (2013). Youths' unemployment and crime in Nigeria: A nexus and implications for national development. *International Journal of Sociology and Anthropology, 5*(8), 350–357.

BBC News. (2020a). SARS ban: Two dead in Nigeria police brutality protests. *BBC News*, 12 October 2020.

BBC News. (2020b). *Nigeria SARS protest: Army chief denies firing live bullets at protesters in Lagos.* Retrieved February 22, 2020 from https://www.bbc.com/news/world-africa-54947999

BBC News. (2020c). *Nigeria's Lekki shooting: What has happened so far at Lagos judicial panel.* Retrieved February 22, 2020 from https://www.bbc.co.uk/news/world-africa-55099016

Bidemi, A. (2020). *#EndSARS: How hoodlums razed Oyo police stations, stole weapons.* Retrieved February 24, 2022 from https://www.premiumtimesng.com/news/headlines/424586-endsars-how-hoodlums-razed-oyo-police-stations-stole-weapons.html

Bode, A. (2020). *Hoodlums hijack #EndSARS protests in Lagos.* Retrieved March 15, 2020 from https://www.vanguardngr.com/2020/10/over-30-lives-perish-25-police-stations-60-cars-burnt-as-hoodlums-overrun-lagos/

Busari, S., Orji, S., & Salaudeen, A. (2020). *Nigerians take to the streets in protests against controversial police unit accused of brutality.* Retrieved June 17, 2022 from https://edition.cnn.com/2020/10/09/africa/nigeria-police-sars-police-brutality-intl/index.html

Charles, M. (2020). *4 lessons to learn from #EndSARS protests.* Retrieved June 17, 2022 from https://www.dataphyte.com/latest-reports/governance/4-lessons-to-learn-from-endsars-protests/

Chinedu, A. (2021). *Nigeria panel finds army, police killed peaceful protesters.* Retrieved June 17, 2022 from https://www.usnews.com/news/world/articles/2021-11-16/nigeria-panel-finds-army-police-killed-peaceful-protesters

Dambo, T. H. (2021). Young Nigerians turned to twitter on the night of the Lekki shootings: What that tells us. *The Conversation*. Retrieved February 18, 2020 from https://theconversation.com/young-nigerians-turned-to-twitter-on-the-night-of-the-lekki-shootings-what-that-tells-us-170554

Daniel, I. (2019). *The menace of extreme poverty*. Retrieved February 22, 2022 from https://www.vanguardngr.com/2019/06/the-menace-of-extreme-poverty/

Emmanuel, A. (2021). *Army shot unarmed protesters in Lagos 'massacres'- leaked report.* Retrieved June 17, 202 from https://www.vanguardngr.com/2019/06/the-menace-of-extreme-poverty/

Ezemenaka, K. E. (2021). Youth violence and human security in Nigeria. *Social Sciences, 10*(7), 267. https://doi.org/10.3390/socsci10070267

Fasunwon, A. F. (2019). Social media and political mobilisation in Nigeria. *Journal of Research and Innovation in Social Science, 3*(12), 224–230.

Fayehun, F., & Isiugo-Abanihe, U. (2020). #EndSARS: How Nigeria can tap into its youthful population. *The Conversation*. Retrieved February 18, 2020 from https://theconversation.com/endsars-how-nigeria-can-tap-into-its-youthful-population-148319

Ikuteyijo, L. (2021). Nigeria's police: Few promises of reform have been kept a year after #EndSARS protests. *The Conversation*. Retrieved February 18, 2020 from https://theconversation.com/nigerias-police-few-promises-of-reform-have-been-kept-a-year-after-endsars-protests-170028

Iwenwanne, V. (2018). *Civic tech startups take on Nigeria's struggle for justice*. Devex. Retrieved June 17, 2022 from https://www.devex.com/news/civic-tech-startups-take-on-nigeria-s-struggle-for-justice-93751

Jaskiran, K. C. (2021). Indian farmers' strike continues in the shadow of COVID-19. *The Conversation.* Retrieved June 17, 2021 from https://theconversation.com/indian-farmers-strike-continues-in-the-shadow-of-covid-19-159454

Kazeem, Y. (2020). *How a youth-led digital movement is driving Nigeria's largest protests in a decade.* Retrieved June 17, 2022 from https://finance.yahoo.com/news/youth-led-digital-movement-driving-041734596.html

Lambo, D. (2020). Angry youths protest as cop shoots Rivers musician dead. *Punch Newspaper.* Retrieved June 17, 2022 from https://punchng.com/angry-youths-protest-as-cop-shoots-rivers-musician-dead/

Lopez, G. (2020). *The effect of Black Lives Matter protests on coronavirus cases, explained coronavirus cases are increasing, but Black Lives Matter protests may not be to blame. Here's why.* Retrieved June 17, 2022 from https://www.vox.com/2020/6/26/21300636/coronavirus-pandemic-black-lives-matter-protests

Mansur, I. (2017). *Trending: Nigerians say enough is enough, it is time to #EndSARS*. Retrieved June 17, 2022 from https://www.thecable.ng/nigerians-say-end-sars-police-brutality

Nasir, A. (2021). *Analysis: #EndSARS: Five months after, is the Nigerian government meeting protesters' demands.* Retrieved February 18, 2020 from https://www.premiumtimesng.com/news/headlines/455674-analysis-endsars-five-months-after-is-the-nigerian-govt-meeting-protesters-demands.html

National Bureau Statistics (NBS). 2018. *Unemployment/Underemployment Report.* Retrieved August 12, 2021 from https://nigerianstat.gov.ng/elibrary?queries[search]=unemployment

Nigerian Communications Commission (NCC). (2019). *NCC hinges Nigeria's 122 million internet users' protection on effective governance*. Retrieved February 18, 2020 from https://www.ncc.gov.ng/stakeholder/media-public/news-headlines/614-ncc-hinges-nigeria-s-122-million-internet-users-protection-on-effective-governance

Neyman, G., & Dalsey, W. (2021). Black lives matter protests and COVID-19 cases: Relationship in two databases. *Journal of Public Health, 43*(2), 225–227.

Odunlami, P., & Akanle, O. (2021). *The youth unemployment quagmire of Africa: Graduates in artisanal sector of Southwestern Nigeria.* Paper Presented at the 2nd ARUA Centre of Excellence for Unemployment and Skills Development International Conference, Cape-Town, South Africa. Theme: The drive for innovative solutions to youth unemployment in Africa: policy and practice imperatives. Cape Town, South Africa. 24–26 August 2021.

Okeshola, F., & Mudaire, P. (2013). Community policing in Nigeria: Challenges and prospects. *American International Journal of Contemporary Research, 3*, 134–138.

Okon, D. (2020). *Nigerians insist on disbandment of SARS as IGP bans killer police unit for third time.* Retrieved February 18, 2020 from https://businessday.ng/features/article/nigerians-insist-on-disbandment-of-sars-as-igp-bans-killer-police-unit-for-third-time/

Olufemi, A. (2020). *#EndSars: Lawyers, activists condemn Nigerian government for freezing accounts of protesters.* Retrieved February 18, 2020 from https://www.premiumtimesng.com/news/headlines/424971-endsars-lawyers-activists-condemn-nigerian-govt-for-freezing-accounts-of-protesters.html

Oluwadamilare, O. (2016). *Fixing Nigeria's education for global competitiveness.* Retrieved June 17, 2022 from https://guardian.ng/features/fixing-nigerias-education-for-global-competitiveness/

Premium Times. (2020). #EndSARS: Sanwo-Olu confirms two deaths from Lekki shooting. *Premium Times*, 22 October 2020.

NOIPolls. (2019). *Social Media Poll Report 2019.* Retrieved June 17, 2022 from https://noi-polls.com/wp-content/uploads/2019/11/Social-Media-Poll-Report.pdf

Stephanie, B., & Nimi, P. (2021). Nigerian police arrest protesters at Lekki shooting site. *CNN.* Retrieved June 17, 2022 from https://edition.cnn.com/2021/02/13/africa/nigeria-endsars-lekki-protests-intl/index.html

Tade, O. (2020). #EndSARS: What it feels like to be in the shoes of a young Nigerian. *The Conversation.* Retrieved February 18, 2020 from https://theconversation.com/endsars-what-it-feels-like-to-be-in-the-shoes-of-a-young-nigerian-148377

Udalla, E. A. (2011). Exclusion of the youth from governance and the implications for Africa's developmental democracy. *The Nigerian Experience,* April 4, 2011. Retrieved June 17, 2022 from https://ssrn.com/abstract=1905246

Ujene, I. G., & Orji-Egwu, A. O. (2018). Information communication technology as a tool for social control: A study of Nigeria's #ENDSARS. *Journal of Human Capital Development, 11*(2), 1–16.

Ukeje, C. U., & Iwilade, A. (2012). A farewell to innocence? African youth and violence in the twenty-first century. *International Journal of Conflict and Violence, 6*, 339–351.

Uwazuruike, A. (2022). #EndSARS: The movement against police brutality in Nigeria. *Harvard Human Right Journal, 35.* Retrieved February 18, 2020 from https://harvardhrj.com/2020/11/endsars-the-movement-against-police-brutality-in-nigeria?

World Development Report. (2007). *Youth, poverty reduction, and growth.* Retrieved June 17, 2022 from https://doi.org/10.1596/978-0-8213-6541-0_ch1

Olayinka Akanle, Ph.D. is a Lecturer in the Department of Sociology, Faculty of the Social Sciences, University of Ibadan, Nigeria, and a Senior Research Associate of the Department of Sociology, Faculty of Humanities, University of Johannesburg (UJ), South Africa. He was a Postdoctoral Fellow at the South African Research Chair Initiative (SARChI) in Social Policy, College of Graduate Studies, University of South Africa (UNISA), South Africa. He has won other scholarly awards like being a World Social Science Fellow (WSSF) of the International Social Science Council (ISSC), Paris, France, Laureate of the Council for the Development of Social Science Research in Africa (CODESRIA), Dakar, Senegal, and the University of Ibadan, Nigeria postgraduate school prize for scholarly publication awardee. He is a recipient of Folke Bernadotte Academy, a Swedish government agency for peace, security and development's Certificate of Achievement. He is a scholar and expert on international development, migration and diaspora studies, social policy, gender, and child and youth studies. He has published extensively in reputable journals, books, and encyclopedias, among others. He is the co-editor of *The Development of Africa: Issues, Diagnosis and Prognosis* (Springer, 2018) and *Corruption and Development in Nigeria* (Routledge, 2022).

Goodluck Uzieyi, B.A. holds a degree in Sociology from the Department of Sociology, Faculty of the Social Sciences, University of Ibadan, Nigeria. He is a Writer, an Entrepreneur, and a Transformational Leader. Aside from being a scholar and researcher, he has transformative leadership skills to empower youth in all-round capacity building. He has a great research interest that revolves around interrogative academic works, social lifestyles, youth studies, gender, business, and leadership.

Index

K. Naidoo et al. (eds.), *Young People, Violence and Strategic Interventions in Sub-Saharan Africa*, Clinical Sociology: Research and Practice,
https://doi.org/10.1007/978-3-031-20679-5

CPSIA information can be obtained
at www.ICGtesting.com
Printed in the USA
LVHW021001260323
742629LV00002B/283